Mystery Movie Ser
of 1940s Hollywood

Mystery Movie Series of 1940s Hollywood

RON BACKER

McFarland & Company, Inc., Publishers
Jefferson, North Carolina, and London

LIBRARY OF CONGRESS CATALOGUING-IN-PUBLICATION DATA

Backer, Ron, 1951–
Mystery movie series of 1940s Hollywood / Ron Backer.
p. cm.
Includes bibliographical references and index.

ISBN 978-0-7864-4864-7
softcover : 50# alkaline paper ∞

1. Detective and mystery films— History and criticism. 2. Motion
pictures— United States— History— 20th century. I. Title.
PN1995.9.D4B33 2010 791.43'6556 — dc22 2010015586

British Library cataloguing data are available

Front cover: *Pillow of Death* poster, 1945 (Universal Pictures/Photofest)

Manufactured in the United States of America

*McFarland & Company, Inc., Publishers
Box 611, Jefferson, North Carolina 28640
www.mcfarlandpub.com*

To my mother, who gave me my first mystery to read

Table of Contents

Introduction

While there were many detective and mystery movies produced during the silent era, such as the numerous films about Sherlock Holmes, Boston Blackie and the Lone Wolf, the Hollywood mystery movie, and thus the Hollywood mystery movie series, came into its own only after sound became a staple of the cinema. Almost with the beginning of the sound era, Hollywood recognized the profitability of a series with a continuing detective. Thus, the Philo Vance series commenced in 1929 with *The Canary Murder Case* and continued in one form or another until 1947. The Charlie Chan series began in 1931 with *Charlie Chan Carries On* and ended in 1949 after 44 films were produced.

The Hollywood mystery series that commenced in the first decade of the sound era were some of the best ever, and it was difficult for the series produced primarily in the 1940s to compete, since the latter films were generally low-budget creations, intended as second features only. Nevertheless, despite their lack of high aspirations and sometimes cookie-cutter approach to writing and production, as a group the 1940s films are well worth a view, and on an individual basis, there is some crime-drama gold hidden among the brass of these mystery programmers.

While the 1940s mystery movies may not have employed many stars who were still in their prime, the films did provide a last home for actors who were stars in prior decades of the cinema but were now in the final years of their film careers, among them Chester Morris (Boston Blackie), Warner Baxter (Crime Doctor), Warren William (Lone Wolf) and even Basil Rathbone (Sherlock Holmes). This innovative casting added to the class of the productions. Of interest today, there were a number of up-and-coming actors who made early screen appearances in these films, such as Walter Pidgeon (who starred in the Nick Carter series), Lloyd Bridges, Dorothy Malone and Ida Lupino.

The 1940s mystery series were also a training ground for future directors like Edward Dmytryk (*Secrets of the Lone Wolf* [1941]), Jacques Tourneur (*Nick Carter, Master Detective* [1939]) and William Castle (*The Whistler* [1944]). Sometimes these young directors brought their own brand of style and innovation to these second features, elevating the films above the quality expected from this type of film. And while these mystery movies were usually low-budget, many times the productions were a lesson in turning out a first-class product at a low cost. For example, the Basil Rathbone Sherlock Holmes movies seemed like big-budget releases, because of the detail of the direction and the magnificence of the sets. The Dick Tracy and Whistler movies illustrated that a little bit of style in the direction and inspiration in the cinematography could turn a low-budget movie into a high-quality product.

Of course, acting, directing and cinematography are essentials to creating a good movie, but for a mystery movie, the writing is often the key. Some of the best mystery

1

movies of the 1940s relied heavily on their source material for the plot, resulting in classic movie mysteries such as *The Hound of the Baskervilles* (1939) and *The Saint in New York* (1938). Other screenplays were created by writers who had an independent success with the mystery novel, such as Jonathan Latimer, Stuart Palmer and Craig Rice. Still others were written by excellent plotters who are known today primarily for their work in Hollywood, such as Paul Yawitz, Frank Gruber, Brenda Weisberg, Lynn Root and Frank Fenton. From time to time this group of talented writers, even writing within the restrictions of the genre, turned out surprisingly inventive mystery stories.

The result was that, in addition to excellent mystery series of the 1940s such as the Saint, Sherlock Holmes, Dick Tracy and Whistler series, there were often surprisingly good films hidden in otherwise inconsistent series. What a joy to discover *Boston Blackie Booked on Suspicion* (1945), *The Falcon in Mexico* (1944), *The Lone Wolf Takes a Chance* (1941), *Crime Doctor* (1943) and many others. Even when a film might ultimately be disappointing, such as the Inner Sanctum series' *Weird Woman* (1944) or *The Lone Wolf Spy Hunt* (1941), there was often some element of mystery or intrigue that made the movie worth a view.

What follows is a discussion of each of the films, the lead characters, the contributors and the source material for all of the films in the Hollywood mystery series of the 1940s. Whether the viewer desires a traditional or hardboiled mystery or even a spy story, a detective who is a professional or one who is an amateur or even a reformed thief, there is something for every mystery fan in these Hollywood crime movies.

There are 146 films addressed in this book. Each is from a Hollywood mystery series whose movies were primarily released during the 1940s. While there were many Charlie Chan movies and several Philo Vance films released during the 1940s, those movies are not covered in this book because each of those film series began near the beginning of the sound era and reached their peak during the 1930s. They are therefore properly the subject of a book about Hollywood crime series of the 1930s, should one ever be written. The same would also apply to the Thin Man series, the Bulldog Drummond series, and the Mr. Wong series.

Similarly, although the Saint series, the Basil Rathbone Sherlock Holmes series, the Lone Wolf series and some others began in the 1930s, they are better known for their output during the 1940s. All of the films in those series are considered herein, even the ones released during the 1930s.

By definition, a mystery series contains at least three movies. Therefore, I have not addressed those situations where there was only one sequel made to the original film. Consistent with the title of the book, I have not addressed crime series that were primarily produced in England or other foreign countries, except to complete the discussion of the movies in the Saint series.

For each film discussed that was based on a written work, I have tried to find the work, read it and then compare and contrast it with the film. In some cases, it was not easy to find the written works, as many have been out-of-print for some time. However, after scouring libraries, used book stores and the internet, I was able to find almost all of the written works for which I was searching. In all, I read or re-read twenty-nine novels, one novelette, sixteen short stories and two plays; in addition, based upon secondary sources, references are made to two additional novels and one play in the two instances in which I was unable to locate the original work.

One phenomenon of the 1940s mystery movie series was their reliance on radio programs as the source material. Unfortunately, as many fans of old time radio will wistfully state, a substantial portion of the original radio broadcasts are lost forever. Thus, while I was able to listen to shows in most of the radio mystery series that were turned into film series, I was unable to listen to the particular episode that provided the source for a particular movie (although that was an unusual circumstance in any event). Thus, much of the discussion of the radio programs in this book is based upon secondary sources.

Although there are no detailed synopses of the plots of each of the movies covered, as that would be excruciatingly boring, this book does contain short synopses and a detailed analysis of the plots, usually addressing the issues of whether the mystery makes sense, is fair to the viewer and the like. In order to do the subject justice, many of the plot twists, surprise endings and identities of the murderers must also be discussed. This obviously results in many spoilers. However, to preface each spoiler with a warning, such as "Spoiler Alert," would disrupt the flow of the chapters and make them hard to read. Therefore, if you do not want to read a spoiler, carefully skim over the discussions of those parts of those movies that you have not already seen and then come back to those discussions later, once you have viewed the film.

1

The Saint
The Robin Hood of Modern Crime

It is the most famous drawing in all of detective fiction. As described by Inspector Fernack in the novel *The Saint in New York*, the picture is like the figure of a man that kids might draw when they get hold of a pencil for the first time. There is just a circle for the head, a straight line for the body, four more lines for the arms and legs, and above the head, a circle that is supposed to be a halo. Fernack could have easily added that the back arm rests on the rear of the figure and the front arm points ahead, as if the figure were mocking the reader or perhaps mocking the police. Of course, the figure is that of Simon Templar, better known as the Saint.

The character of the Saint was created by Leslie Charteris in 1928, and novels, novelettes and short stories about the Saint followed for many years thereafter. In 1938, RKO started a film series about the Saint's exploits, which series was described, in *The RKO Story* by Richard B. Jewell, as the most important series produced by RKO since the Astaire–Rogers pictures. In all, there were nine films in the Saint series, most of which were released by RKO.

Background

THE BOOKS

Leslie Charteris was born Leslie Charles Bowyer Yin, in Singapore (then a British colony) on May 12, 1907, to Dr. S.C. Yin and Lydia Florence Bowyer. His father was a Chinese surgeon and his mother was of English descent. Because he was born outside of England, Charteris learned Chinese and Malay from the family's native servants before he could speak English. Charteris' formal education, however, occurred in England, first at a prep school and then at a public school, with Charteris finally receiving a law degree in 1926. In that same year, he changed his name to Leslie Charteris and began to pursue his interest in writing. Charteris' first book was published in 1927, with his first novel about the Saint, titled *Meet the Tiger*, coming out the following year.

Meet the Tiger established many of the features of the Saint character for years to come. As the novel opens, Simon Templar is already a soldier of fortune, working on commission, trying to recover gold stolen from a Chicago bank. During the course of the novel, Templar meets Patricia Holm, who would become his on-again off-again love interest for many years to come. Just as in later works, Templar is not above committing criminal acts for a greater purpose. Templar tends to address all issues, even those of life and death, with jocularity. He jousts with but assists a Scotland Yard inspector in investigating the crime (although the policeman is not named Inspector Teal in this early story).

Over the years, the Saint became known for his calling card, which had his signature stick figure described above. He was also prone to the use of a knife he concealed in his coat sleeve; he never shied away from a good fight. Templar made a career of stealing from thieves, killing murderers and helping damsels in distress.

The character and the stories did evolve over the years. Templar's world travels often echoed those of Charteris, as the Saint moved from London to New York to Florida and eventually to the West Coast of the United States. In some books, he became more of a vigilante than an investigator. During World War II, he fought against the Nazis. Over the years, he became involved in everything from whodunits to gangster stories to science-fiction adventures. Patricia Holm and some of the other regular characters disappeared from the stories after World War II.

Leslie Charteris wrote stories about the Saint from 1928 through 1963 and thereafter, collaborated with other writers on more Saint stories. In all, Charteris produced about 50 books about the Robin Hood of Modern Crime, consisting of full-length novels, novelettes and numerous short stories.

THE FILM SERIES

Leslie Charteris' stories about the Saint seemed a natural for adaptation to the big screen, as they were generally not whodunits (which could be boring on the screen) and they had more action in them than the more traditional Philo Vance or Charlie Chan books, which, by the early 1930s, already were the subject of very successful movie series. RKO purchased the rights to the Saint stories from Charteris and tested the waters with *The Saint in New York*, released in 1938. In that film, the Saint was played by Louis Hayward.

Hayward was born in 1909 in South Africa but was educated in England and Europe, giving him the credentials to play the British detective, Simon Templar. Hayward is best known today for significant roles in period pieces such as *Anthony Adverse* (1936), *The Man in the Iron Mask* (1939) and *The Black Arrow* (1948). For mystery fans, he played the male lead and prime suspect Philip Lombard in the most famous film version of Agatha Christie's *And Then There Were None*, released in 1945.

After the success of the first Saint film, RKO turned to George Sanders to carry the lead in what RKO expected to be a long-running series. Sanders played the role of Simon Templar through the next five films, concluding with *The Saint in Palm Springs* (1941). Although Sanders was born in Russia in 1906, his parents were English and he was educated in England. He moved to Hollywood in the late 1930s where, in addition to starring in the Saint and the Falcon mystery series, he had a number of good supporting parts in major films. For mystery fans, he was unforgettable as Jack Favell in Alfred Hitchcock's *Rebecca* (1940).

Charteris was apparently never happy with the casting of either Hayward or Sanders as the Saint. Charteris had hoped for bigger stars such as Ronald Colman, Cary Grant or Douglas Fairbanks, Jr., for the lead. Why Charteris felt any of them would participate in a B-movie series is unknown.

After *The Saint in Palm Springs*, RKO decided to move the series to England to make use of RKO funds which were frozen in England. The new production, *The Saint's Vacation* (1941), produced by RKO Radio British Productions, had an all–English cast. Sanders was therefore dropped from the series and was replaced by Hugh Sinclair. Sinclair was born in 1903 in London, England, and essentially spent his entire film career in English films. Sinclair is surely the forgotten Saint actor, appearing in just two films, *The Saint's Vacation* and *The Saint Meets the Tiger*. Sinclair was the first actor to play the Saint with a moustache. Both of his films were produced in 1941 but the latter was not released in the United States until 1943. The film was not a success and the series ended.

Over ten years later, one final film, *The Saint's Girl Friday*, was produced. It was first released in England in 1953 under the name *The Saint Returns* and then the following year in the United States under its American title. It was produced in England by Hammer Films; RKO was the American distributor. It marked the return of Louis Hayward to the title role, meaning he appeared in the first and last of the RKO Saint movies.

The Saint of the written works was somewhat of a loner, so there were few continuing characters to be used in the movie series. However, when the film Templar was in England, he generally interacted with Inspector Teal, played by Gavin McLeod. Teal was an important character in the novels, usually as an adversary of Templar, with Templar often infuriating Teal with his exploits just within or just outside the law. When the film Saint was in America, he generally interacted with Inspector Fernack of the New York Police Department. Fernack was played by Jonathan Hale and although he was a character from the Saint stories, Fernack carried much more importance in the movie series than in the Charteris stories. As noted above, in the books, Templar did have a love interest from time to time in the person of Patricia Holm, but that character was only carried over into the film series for *The Saint Meets the Tiger* (1943).

The Hollywood Films

THE SAINT IN NEW YORK (1938)

Based on the book by Leslie Charteris of the same name, *The Saint in New York* is an excellent beginning to this famous detective series about Simon Templar. Much of the credit must go to Louis Hayward's skill in playing the title character. Hayward glides through the film with his hat tipped slightly on his head, as if to signify the lack of seriousness of his character. He delivers some of the funny lines with an expression that suggests he knows the lines are funny and that we are all in on the joke. Hayward has a rakish smirk on his face that is quite endearing to the audience and even to one of the mobsters' henchmen. Hayward's performance is actually closer to those given by Roger Moore in the later television series than the more stodgy performances of George Sanders in the next several movies in the series. Hayward set the light tone for the movie, without the necessity of using specific characters for comic relief, thus avoiding a problem that other mystery movie series of the 1940s often experienced.

The Saint in New York starts out with an unusual premise: there is a crime wave in New York City. In an attempt to assist the police, several prominent citizens have formed the Citizens' Committee for Crime Prevention. At a meeting in the Commissioner's office, the Committee is introduced to Inspector Fernack, a veteran police officer, who complains that the problem is caused by a handful of mobsters (six in number) who, even though they are sometimes arrested, are never convicted.

One member of the Committee, William Valcross, convinces the Committee to hire Simon Templar, the famous Saint, to fight the mobsters who are threatening the City. The Committee agrees and in a fun series of vignettes, Valcross travels the world to locate Templar, who has fomented a revolution in at least one of the countries he has just visited. Valcross finally finds the Saint in Costa Grande and convinces him to return to New York to help out. Templar has just one condition: that no one questions his techniques.

By the use of witness tampering, one of the six mobsters, Jake Erboll, has just been acquitted of the murder of a policeman. Soon thereafter, as Jake is about to attain his revenge on Inspector Fernack for arresting him by shooting the policeman in the back, Templar, disguised as a nun, shoots and kills Erboll. One down, five to go.

As the story progresses, Templar dispatches more of the mobsters. He also rescues a young girl who has been kidnapped by the gang. Along the way he meets Fay Edwards, a beautiful moll in the Big Fellow's gang, who saves Templar's life on at least two occasions. The Big Fellow is the unknown leader of the mobsters, and although Fay is unwilling to disclose the name of the Big Fellow to anyone (based on a promise she made to the Big Fellow), she does reveal to Templar that the gang leaders had agreed to run the rackets for

In *The Saint in New York* (1938), Simon Templar (Louis Hayward, far right) turns the tables on two of the Big Fellow's henchmen by grabbing Hymie Fanro (Paul Guilfoyle) as Red Jenks (Jack Carson) begins to pull out his gun.

three years, deposit the proceeds in one bank account, and then divide all of the profits among themselves. The three year period is just about to come to an end.

Fay falls in love with the Saint and although she will still not reveal the name of the Big Fellow to Templar, she offers to point out the Big Fellow the next time they have a meeting. One is set up near a bank on a New York street and at that point, Fay surprises the Saint by fingering Valcross as the Big Fellow. In the ensuing gun battle Fay is shot, the Big Fellow is captured and the Saint has saved the day. However, the achievement is bittersweet, as the Saint had also fallen in love with Fay Edwards. Just before she dies, the Saint and Fay wistfully understand that their dreams will never be fulfilled and they will never visit Vermont together.

The outing of the Big Fellow is clever and comes as a surprise to the viewer. It is never really explained why, if Valcross is the Big Fellow, he was so intent at the beginning of the film on hiring Templar to end mobster influence in New York. However, one can assume that he secretly hoped Templar would kill all of the other leaders of his gang, so that Valcross could retain all of the profits in the gang bank account for himself. It is not clear why this explanation was not included in the film.

The one aspect of *The Saint in New York* that does not work well is the romance between Fay and the Saint. There is really not enough time in the film for them to fall in love, Fay seems a cold figure at best, and there are no sparks between Fay and Templar. The ending dialogue between the two, as Fay is about to die, falls flat. Actually, there is more electricity between Inspector Fernack and Templar, as Fernack does not know Templar's real mission in New York, suspecting that Templar may be a criminal. Nonetheless, Fernack develops a grudging admiration for the Saint. There is even a suggestive scene between the two where Fernack has to tie Templar's tie for him, after Templar has been injured.

In addition to the Saint's clever way with words, there is true humor in the serial provided by Hymie Fanro (Paul Guilfoyle), a henchman who is impressed by the Saint's clever use of language and his ability to adapt to the most difficult of situations. Even though Hymie is a ruthless killer, when Hymie is finally dispatched by the Saint, the audience feels a loss. Hymie is a unique character in the panoply of supporting characters in the 1940s crime series.

This is a particularly violent film. While there is no graphic violence, a number of people meet their death during the film, most of whom are killed by the Saint. Indeed, *The Saint in New York* is more gangster film than mystery story, also giving it a different feel than other 1940s crime series movies. It is probably the best Saint film and was an excellent way to debut a new mystery series.

Note on the Source Material: The novel, *The Saint in New York*, was originally published in 1935. Just about every major incident in the film comes from the book, making this one of the most faithful adaptations of a mystery novel ever filmed in Hollywood. Thus, in the book, the Saint is hired by Valcross to clean up the New York crime scene, although in the books the ostensible reason for Valcross' decision to bring Templar on board as a sort of vigilante is the death of Valcross' son many years before at the hand of the criminals, and Valcross' desire for revenge.

The Saint, disguised as a nun, kills Jake Erboll in the book, although it is a cold-blooded killing, not to protect Inspector Fernack as in the movie. The Saint then goes on a killing spree, dispatching many additional mobsters, making the Saint more of a vigilante in the book than in the movie, if that were at all possible. Along the way he rescues young Viola Inselheim from a kidnapping (making the same joke about her name in both media), meets Hymie, the hired gun (although he has a different last name in the movie and his character is developed better in the movie) and becomes infatuated with Fay Edwards, before even exchanging any dialogue with her. However, there is none of the movie schmaltz about visiting Vermont together and the relationship of Simon and Fay in the book is more realistic than the one portrayed in the movie.

Once again, Valcross is the surprise villain, finally revealed to be the Big Fellow. That raises the question, both in the movie and the book, as to why Valcross would hire the Saint in the first place. The reasoning, though, is explained in the book: Templar was hired by Valcross to kill the other mobsters, so that Valcross could retain all the mob money for himself. Also, Valcross initially asked Fay to assist the Saint whenever possible, because he did not want the Saint killed before his dirty work was completed. Thus, there is also an explanation in the book for Fay's actions in saving Templar's life on two occasions, before they even knew each other. The explanations make complete sense and there is no reason why they were not also provided in the movie.

The movie would have been more effective if those plot elements were explained, instead of requiring the viewer to make educated guesses about the motives of the characters. Nevertheless, the movie is an excellent adaptation of a very good novel and both the movie and the novel are recommended.

THE SAINT STRIKES BACK (1939)

For the second film in the Saint series, Louis Hayward was dropped from the title role and George Sanders was given the part. This was not a good decision. Although Sanders was only three years older than Hayward in real life, he appears much older in the film. The jaunty, devil-may-care attitude of Hayward is replaced by the serious, sophisticated style of Sanders. Also, Sanders wears his hat straight on his head, instead of with the cocky tilt of Hayward. Thus, while Sanders is speaking lines in *The Saint Strikes Back* that are probably as clever as those spoken by Hayward in the previous film, they simply do not turn out as funny when spoken in the Sanders style.

Another problem with *The Saint Strikes Back* is with the character of Inspector Fernack, once again well-played by Jonathan Hale. In the original film, Fernack was an experienced and competent policeman, determined to end racketeering in New York City. In *The Saint Strikes Back*, Fernack has become more of a figure of comic relief. The Saint tricks Fernack into getting off an intercontinental plane in his pajamas and then strands him in Texas on his way to San Francisco. Later, in order to remove Fernack from the action, the Saint tricks Fernack into eating a large dinner, causing him stomach problems, which leads into an embarrassing dream sequence. Why did the writers of these 1940s crime films believe that a bumbling policeman was a requisite element of a successful mystery? The interesting character of Fernack from the first movie has become the standard comic relief of the second film.

The story opens on New Year's Eve in the Colony Club in San Francisco. A woman, Val Travers (Wendy Barrie) and two men are sitting at a table in the club and it is one minute to midnight. One of the men, Tommy Voss, gets up, walks behind a potted plant and takes aim with a gun. There is a glimpse of the Saint dancing with a young lady. Suddenly, there is a shot and Voss is killed. Val Lawson and her other friend exit the club quickly.

While this is an excellent opening scene, with fluid camerawork and a surprise killing, the story then degenerates into a complicated plot that is hard to follow. The Saint accosts Val Lawson outside the club and engages in some banter with her. The viewer then learns some of the back story of the film, which is that Val's father was a police inspector who was discharged from the force when he was accused of being a part of the notorious Waldeman gang. Her father then committed suicide. The viewer later learns that Val has organized her own group of low-class criminals to commit some crimes, with the intent of finding Waldeman and exonerating her father. The logic of her approach is never explained in the film and it surely defies all reason.

The Saint learns that Val suspects Martin Eastman, a wealthy philanthropist, of being involved with Waldeman. The Saint goes to Eastman's house, interrupts a burglary of Eastman's safe by Zipper Dyson, an agent of Val, and then uses that man to steal the money in Eastman's safe. This leads to a series of events in which Eastman is killed, a policeman named Cullis confesses to framing Val Lawson's father, and the least likely suspect of all, Allen Breck, a friend of Val's father and her potential suitor, is unmasked as Waldeman. At the end of the story, the San Francisco police commissioner announces that Templar was working with the police from the beginning, thus explaining some of Templar's unusual actions during the course of the film.

The plot makes little sense. Why did Val suspect Eastman? Why did her little gang of crooks go along with her schemes? Other plot points are never explained. For example, at one point, the Saint discovers poison in his milk, but there is never any resolution in the movie as to who tried to kill him. Indeed, there is never any resolution in the film as to who killed Tommy Voss, the event that started the movie. If, in fact, the Saint was the person who shot Tommy Voss, why was Voss trying to kill the Saint?

Allen Breck, as the choice for the true identity of Waldeman, makes little sense, other than as an unexpected plot twist. Seasoned viewers, however, will probably guess that Breck is the mastermind, solely on the basis that the least likely suspect would undoubtedly be the actual culprit, even though there are no clues to Breck's guilt. Breck's identity as the villain is revealed when he is shot by Fernack in a darkened room, in a scene in which Breck's face is never shown. Thus, the filmmakers missed an opportunity to surprise the viewer by suddenly revealing Breck's face. Then there is never a verbal confrontation by either Templar or Val with Breck. Thus, the filmmakers once again miss the dramatic opportunities that any such scene might have brought.

The Saint Strikes Back is characterized by an unconvincing plot, poor comedy relief and missed opportunities. It is a disappointing film, particularly since it came right after the quality start of the Saint series in *The Saint in New York*.

Note on the Source Material: This film was based on a Charteris' novel identified in the credits as *Angels of Doom*, which was the title of the book when it was published in the United States. The novel was originally published in England in 1931 under the name *She Was a Lady*, and in later editions, sometimes under the title *The Saint Meets His Match*. It is the story of Jill Trelawny, whose father was fired from the London police force for criminal activity and died shortly thereafter from the disgrace. Jill then formed the Angels of Doom, an underworld organization established to embarrass the police, as a part of her quest to find Waldstein, the leader of the gang of criminals she believes framed her father.

While that plot seems similar to the one from the movie, there is really little similarity after the first third of the book. It is true there are some instances in the book that were used in the movie, such as the poisoning of the milk that the Saint was about to drink and a minor scene showing the Saint's byplay with a street singer outside Jill's apartment, but those are the exceptions rather than the rule. The Saint of the novel eventually saves Jill's life and the two then join forces to clear her father's name and bring the criminals to justice. Thus, most of the book bears little resemblance to the movie.

The novel is set in London, not San Francisco, and Inspector Fernack does not make an appearance. Indeed, the Saint had yet to meet Fernack in the books as Templar's first trip to New York occurrs several years later in the novels. There is no Allen Breck as the least likely suspect. While there is a policeman named Cullis in the story who turns out to be the man who framed Jill's father, his capture is handled in a substantially different manner than in the movie (although in both media he unknowingly confesses when a recording is being made). The book is quite exciting, with the Saint trapped in a number of serious predicaments, always somehow managing to escape without serious injury. The film undoubtedly would have turned out better if it had relied more on the Charteris plot rather than creating a story especially for the movie, feeling the obligation to include the character of Inspector Fernack, comedy bits and an attempt at a surprise ending.

The Saint in London (1939)

The Saint film series got back on track with this interesting tale set in Simon Templar's home turf of London, England. The story itself is much less complicated than the two previous outings, and the comedy touches come more from the clever dialogue than comic relief or comic situations uncomfortably squeezed into the mystery plot, as was common in other 1940s mysteries. There is no attempt to surprise the audience at the end with a least likely suspect turning out to be the true villain, thus avoiding another pitfall from the prior film. George Sanders' performance seems more in keeping with the tone of the movie than in the previous installment, as Templar moves from dealing with gangsters in America to thwarting spies and international counterfeiters in England.

The movie commences outside a restaurant where Templar runs into a pickpocket named Dugan. Templar and Dugan pick each other's pocket, leading to an offer of a job for Dugan, an ex-con, as Templar's assistant. The tone of the story then moves into serious territory as Templar is given an assignment by Blake of the Secret Service. Although the audience is not made privy to the discussion, it leads to Templar meeting Bruno Lang, a wealthy Englishman of some ill repute. Templar leaves him one of the signature Saint notes with the stick figure as a sort of challenge to Lang. Templar also meets an attractive young Englishwoman named Penelope Parker, who tags along with him throughout the movie, sometimes helping him escape from dangerous situations and sometimes getting herself caught by the villains, and then being used as bait to trap Templar.

The Saint burgles some important documents from Lang's safe. During the escape, Templar rescues an unknown man who is running down the street in his bare feet. The man is very ill, having been tortured by his captors. Templar brings the man to a small hotel run by a Mrs. Buckley. While there, Templar learns the injured man's story. The ill man is Count Stephen Duni (from an unnamed foreign country) who was kidnapped and forced to print a million dollars of counterfeit currency. His captors were Lang and a countryman of Duni's named Kusella.

Later, Duni is murdered. Based on a phone call that Duni had made before his death, the Saint traces the murder to a man named Stengler, who works at Duni's embassy. In the meantime, Dugan captures most of the gang at Lang's house. However, by the time the Saint and Penelope return to Lang's house, the tables have turned and Dugan is a prisoner of the counterfeiters. Lang gives the Saint one hour to return the documents he has stolen from his safe or Penelope will be killed. The Saint then manages to elude Lang by use of his hidden knife, which was seen in the prior two films and is also an element from the books. Kusella is accidentally shot by his chauffeur and the rest of the gang is rounded up. It is then revealed that from the time of his meeting with Blake early in the film, the Saint has been working for the British government in its attempt to capture Lang.

Given that the Saint films had B-movie budgets, it is surprising that RKO sprung for a trip to England for the filming of this movie on location. No other mystery movie series of the 1940s filmed on location in Europe. (The actual reason was to meet British quotas as described below.) The decision was fortuitous as the film is helped by its authentic British locations and primarily British cast. The Saint is an Englishman, so a London venue is appropriate for a Saint movie. George Sanders fits into the setting nicely as he was of English descent. Henry Oscar is excellent as Bruno Lang, who at one point advises Templar that there will come a time when even a smart person such as the Saint will meet someone smarter and that will be the end of him. In one of the last scenes of the film, of course, Lang admits that it is he who has met the smarter person, not the Saint.

Inspector Teal, a regular from the Charteris' novels, is played by Gordon McLeod in the stiff British tradition, although he does seem to be harassed by a number of telephone calls from his wife. Sally Gray is pretty and vivacious as Penelope Parker. The one American in the cast, David Burns, stands out playing Dugan, an alumnus of San Quentin prison where he cooked meals for over a thousand inmates a day without complaint. The dialogue is clever, including a moment where one villain comments that Templar does not appear to have a halo over his head. All in all, this is one of the best of the Saint films.

Note on the Source Material: This film was based in part on the novelette, "The Million Pound Day," which was first published in *The Saint vs. Scotland Yard* (1932). In England, the book was titled *The Holy Terror*. Charteris chose the story for inclusion in *The First Saint Omnibus*, which was published in 1939.

The novelette starts with the Saint resting by the roadside in his car, when a man comes running down the street and faints in the Saint's arms. The man has been severely tortured and is near death. The Saint takes brutal care of the huge man who was chasing the beaten man and then hides the sick man incognito at the Berkeley Apartments under the name of Inspector Teal. There the Saint learns that the injured man is the Duke of Fortezza, the acting president of the Bank of Italy. He had brought plates for the production of a new Italian currency to England and then a criminal gang led by Kuzela (as the name is spelled in the book) tortured him into producing another million of Italian currency, which the gang intended to distribute as counterfeit money. The Saint goes after Kuzela to obtain the fake money, with the Saint severely injuring a number of people along the way and then deliberately killing Kuzela with poison. This is a particularly brutal book.

Obviously, the movie takes its core plot from the Charteris story but the differences between the two works are greater than their similarities. Fortezza survives in the novelette. The film is nowhere near as violent as the story. The woman in the story is Templar's sometimes girlfriend from the books, Patricia Holm, and not Penelope Parker as in the movie. Dugan and Lang are new characters created especially for the film and the movie does benefit from the introduction of those interesting personalities. Indeed, both works are best suited to the form in which they were released and both works are quite enjoyable.

Note on the Production: The film was produced by RKO Radio Pictures Limited, a British subsidiary of RKO, specially set up by RKO to meet the film quota laws of the United Kingdom. In the late 1920s, the United Kingdom was trying to boost its national film industry. The Cinematograph Films Act of 1927 mandated that a certain percentage of films shown in England had to be made domestically (the mandated number started at 5 percent and rose to 20 percent by the end of the 1930s). The Act also imposed quotas on the number of British citizens who must be employed on a production. Thus, it was not unusual for American companies to establish British subsidiaries to meet the quotas and also to allow their other American-made films to be shown in Britain.

THE SAINT'S DOUBLE TROUBLE (1940)

This is another engaging entry in the Saint series, enlivened by Georges Sanders in a double role and the unusual casting of horror star Bela Lugosi as one of the criminals. There is also the welcome return of Jonathan Hale as Inspector Fernack and an interesting plot concerning smuggled diamonds.

The story opens with the Partner (Bela Lugosi) shipping an Egyptian mummy to Professor Horatio Bitts in Philadelphia, although the package lists the sender's name as Simon Templar. The film then cuts to Professor Bitts' home in America where Bitts receives the sarcophagus. Later that evening, Simon Templar, an old student of the professor, arrives at the Bitts' home and checks on the mummy. He also renews his acquaintance with Bitts' daughter, Anne, who had a crush on him many years before. At the same time, the Saint's old friend from New York, Inspector Fernack, is visiting Philadelphia and happens to be in Detective Bohlen's office when a call comes in concerning a murder just outside Bitts' house. The two policemen investigate and Fernack finds a card on the body that indicates the Saint did the killing. As the story progresses, the real Simon Templar learns that he has an exact double in criminal Boss Duke Bates, who has been impersonating Templar and throwing suspicion on the Saint for various crimes.

Throughout the film, there are scenes back and forth with each side being confused with whom they are speaking, whether it is Templar or Boss Duke. Finally, with the unknown assistance of the Saint, Duke and his gang are captured, although the police believe they have Templar in jail. The real Templar then dresses as a woman in a veil, visits Duke in jail, allows Duke to knock him out and escape in the female disguise, only to be shot and killed by the police, as set up by Templar. This is a rare case in the film series (although not in the books) of seeing a particularly vicious streak in Templar, as he essentially caused the murder of Boss Duke Bates. Perhaps it was in exchange for the vicious and unnecessary killing by Duke of Professor Bitts earlier in the movie.

This is an interesting mystery, particularly in the early part of the film before the viewer learns that the Saint has a double. If the viewer can then suspend disbelief as to a person having an exact double with the exact same voice, the story moves logically to its interesting conclusion. There is little comedy in the movie and even less romance so that the mystery is always in the forefront of the plot.

It is always interesting to see Bela Lugosi in a non–horror role, particularly when he is in good health and enthusiastic in playing the part. It is nice to see Lugosi with a meaningful role and not just playing a red herring as he often did in non–horror movies. Lugosi is off-beat casting for this series and is a decided plus for the movie.

Prolific serial star Walter Miller has a bit part as a crooked bar keeper in *The Saint's*

Simon Templar (George Sanders)—or is it Boss Duke Bates—and Anne Bitts (Helene Whitney) examine the mummy case just delivered to Professor Bitts in *The Saint's Double Trouble* (1940).

Double Trouble, which is fitting because the film has two traditional serial cliffhanger moments. One involves Anne Bitts, knocked out in a car, which is speeding without a driver toward the wharf and to a high drop into the sea. Templar, who is riding on the back bumper of the car, rescues Anne just before the dangerous fall. Then at the end of the film, Templar is bound and gagged in the bottom of a boat when one of the crooks tries to escape. The crook is shot and killed by Inspector Fernack, who in the process also shoots holes in the frame of the boat, not knowing Templar is aboard. The craft starts sinking, with Templar tied up inside. Templar barely manages to untie himself and swim to safety before the boat sinks.

These two action sequences are somewhat unusual for the Saint series, which tends to rely on dialogue and stationary scenes for suspense and mystery. The novelty of these incidents simply adds to the interest of a fine entry in this quality mystery series.

Note on the Source Material: This movie and *The Saint in Palm Springs* give credit to the story by Leslie Charteris. However, the two films were not based on any published work by Charteris. Charteris had no input into *Double Trouble* and while he did write a screenplay for *Palm Springs*, RKO did not use any of the script he wrote, even though the studio paid Charteris $10,000 for his scenario.

THE SAINT TAKES OVER (1940)

RKO Pictures must have had a little extra money in the budget for *The Saint Takes Over*, so this film starts with a cartoon of the stick-figured Saint walking toward the audience before the credits begin. The movie also marks the return of two familiar performers, as Wendy Barrie appears in her second role in the series (the first was in *The Saint Strikes Back*) and Paul Guilfoyle also returns to the series for a second time (his first appearance was in *The Saint in New York*, as the memorable Hymie). The movie begins in a strong manner, with an interesting mystery, but bogs down significantly in the second half.

As the film opens Simon Templar is on board an ocean liner, returning to New York to help his good friend, Inspector Henry Fernack, who has been removed from the police force because he was unable to explain the $50,000 bundle that was found in the safe in his home. At the time, Fernack was hot on the trail of a gang of racetrack gamblers and was about to make an arrest.

On board ship, Templar meets a woman, Ruth, who will only give Templar her first name. When Simon tries to kiss her, she is more than upset, and thereafter Templar buys her a corsage of roses in an attempt to win her over. Once in New York, Templar proceeds to the home of Ben Egan, the head of the syndicate, where Templar finds Fernack standing over Egan's body. Two more members of the mob are then rapidly killed, and each time, Fernack is found near the body. While the mystery is enticing, discerning viewers will easily pick up the fact that Templar found a rose petal at Egan's place, indicating that Ruth was involved in the killing of Egan and probably the other mobsters as well.

In fact, Templar soon learns that Ruth is really Ruth Summers, the sister of Johnny Summers, whom Fernack had installed as a mole in the criminal organization. Johnny was then discovered and killed by the mobsters. Now Ruth is rapidly killing off members of the mob to avenge her brother's death. It is at this point that the story falls apart, as Ruth is unconvincing as a cold-blooded killer and the fact that she managed to kill three experienced mobsters without being caught strains credulity. All that is left is for Templar to somehow obtain a confession from a gang member for the killing of Summers and the framing of Fernack, which Templar manages to do. Ruth, however, is killed in a shootout with one of the mob just before the conclusion of the film.

This movie has more true humor than any of the previous films in the series. The Saint is constantly needling Fernack, pretending that Fernack has indeed taken the $50,000 bribe and also murdered three people. For example, the Saint advises Fernack that he will get a confession, clearing Fernack's good name, and then says to Fernack, "And if I can squeeze a confession out of him, will you split those 50,000 smackers with me?" Jonathan Hale is excellent as the fuming Fernack having to listen to the Saint's patter, which to him probably seemed unending.

Paul Guilfoyle as Pearly Gates, with his hang-dog look, necessity of drinking milk to relieve his stomach anxiety and interest in the Dick Tracy comic strip, is excellent, as he was in the previous film in which he appeared. When Pearly joins with the Saint in doubting Fernack's honesty and believing that the policeman committed three murders, it seems as if Fernack may literally blow his top. Guilfoyle and Jonathan Hale steal the film.

The end of the film is very disappointing. The trick with the incredibly large recording device hidden in a gang member's filing cabinet, the confession by Reese and Bremer for no reason, and the broadcasting of the same over the police radio are unconvincing. The writers simply had no other way to resolve the mystery except by a confession. Similarly, the killing of Ruth by Bremer at the end of the movie, which does come as a small surprise, nonetheless was preordained by the plot as Ruth had already killed three people, albeit criminals, in cold blood. It would have been unsatisfactory for her to be arrested at the end of the movie; she could not go free in accordance with Hollywood standards of the time. The only choice was to have her die. Given that she was an merciless killer, it is frankly hard to have much sympathy for her, and her death in Templar's arms at the end of the film lacks any emotion.

Simply put, while the acting in the film is uniformly excellent, the story line is not. The good comedy moments are unable to completely compensate for the shoddy plotting. Therefore, despite many engaging aspects to the feature, the movie is fair at best.

THE SAINT IN PALM SPRINGS (1941)

For his fifth and final performance as the Saint, George Sanders is reunited with three actors who had previously made multiple appearances in the series. Jonathan Hale is back as Inspector Fernack of the New York City police department. Hale was always a welcome addition to any movie in the Saint series; once again, he is a delight in this film, even though he only appears near the beginning of the feature.

Paul Guilfoyle repeats his role as Pearly Gates from the previous film, *The Saint Takes Over*, although Pearly now wants to be known as Clarence Gates. While Guilfoyle was always excellent in the series, his performance as Gates begins to wear thin in this movie, as the role is not written quite as well as it was in the prior feature. Guilfoyle's best performance in the series was probably as Hymie Fanro, a professional killer, in *The Saint in New York*, the first film in the series.

Wendy Barrie is also back for her third role in the series, although unlike the other two actors she plays a different part in each film. Her other roles in the series were somewhat challenging, as she played women of conflicting characters and motives. By contrast, in *The Saint in Palm Springs*, Barrie has the much blander role of an all-around good girl and possible female interest for Templar. The part is far from demanding and Barrie only gives an adequate performance.

The film starts out with Inspector Fernack asking Simon Templar to guard Peter Johnson, the brother of an old friend of Fernack. Johnson is carrying three stamps worth $200,000, the family fortune smuggled out of Europe, which he desires to deliver to his niece, Elna Johnson, in Palm Springs. Templar agrees to the bodyguard duties but when he goes to Johnson's apartment, Johnson is immediately killed by an intruder who is after the stamps. After chasing the intruder away, Templar decides to take the valuable stamps to Palm Springs on his own.

On the train he meets Margaret Forbes, who immediately searches the Saint's compartment while the Saint is waiting for her in another car. Once the Saint gets to Palm Springs, he meets his old friend Pearly Gates, who is the house detective, Elna Johnson, the young woman who is entitled to the stamps, and a number of interesting hotel guests who could be after the stamps. After two surprise deaths and several attacks on Templar and Johnson, there is a rendezvous in the desert, where the Saint captures the entire gang that has been after the stamps, and which by that time has committed three murders along the way.

The Saint in Palm Springs has quite an interesting plot, with several surprising twists. Although the killing of Peter Johnson in New York is hardly unforeseen, once Templar sets off for Palm Springs, there are many unexpected developments. The death of the policeman outside a room full of suspects comes as a shock to the viewer. Margaret Forbes' murder after supposedly stealing the stamps from Elna Johnson is surely a surprise. Near the end of the film, the scope of the conspiracy arrayed against Templar in pursuit of the stamps is also unexpected, as it turns out that there has been a large gang working against Templar, and this surprise gives a sharp jolt to the story just when it is needed.

The film does succumb to the usual 1940s plot device of trying to trick the murderer into exposing himself or herself, but interestingly, the first two times Templar tries this ploy, he fails miserably. Indeed, each of the first two traps results in the death of a character, with no important information elicited by Templar. In this case, though, the third time is indeed a charm and at the end of the film the true villains are tricked into confession and capture. Since it is such a trite story device, however, the final scenes engender little suspense or surprise, and the ending of the movie is anticlimactic.

Other problems with *The Saint in Palm Springs* are its cost-cutting production techniques. For example, when Templar, Forbes and Elna are riding side by side on horseback out in the desert, the scene is shot indoors in front of an unconvincing rear-projection screen with the actual horses on which they are riding never shown in close-up and the background moving at a steady pace. This is followed by the worst rear-screen projection shots in the film, as Templar and Gates ride bicycles side by side down a road as they talk. The scene is so unconvincing that the viewer might think Templar and Gates are on exercise bikes in the health club at the hotel and there is a movie projected on the wall to give them a sense of movement.

As bad as these scenes are, though, there are just as poorly produced scenes in two Alfred Hitchcock films, namely *Spellbound*, with its scenes of Gregory Peck skiing in front of a rear projection screen, and *Marnie*, with Tippi Hedren riding a horse in front of a similar screen; so perhaps the criticism of this aspect of *The Saint in Palm Springs* is unfair. But how expensive would it have been to shoot those action scenes of *The Saint in Palm Springs* outside in a natural setting?

All of this is nitpicking to some degree, as overall the film is quite interesting. In particular, Margaret Forbes is an enigmatic character throughout the movie as it is never quite clear what her true motives may be, even though it is clear that she is up to no good. The Forbes character is another example of the film having just enough surprises along the way to keep the viewer totally involved in the complex story. *The Saint in Palm Springs* is therefore recommended.

Note on the Ending: The feature ends with a wistful moment, at least in retrospect. After Elna Johnson tells Templar that she would like to make a date to give him more tennis lessons, Templar says, "So would I, but a few more lessons and I'm liable to forget that singles has always been my game." The film then ends as the Saint mounts his horse and rides off into the distance as the screen fades to dark. Of course, Sanders was also riding out of the Saint series forever, as he never played the role again.

The Later British Films

THE SAINT'S VACATION (1941)

This film marked the debut of Hugh Sinclair in the title role of the famous detective. Indeed, Simon Templar is so famous at the beginning of this film that hordes of reporters are waiting in England, trying to determine what his next adventure will be. They do not believe Templar is simply going on vacation to Switzerland by boat with his good friend, Monty Hayward, and that no criminal investigations are contemplated. Interest is so high in the Saint's personal exploits that one reporter, Mary Landon, even sneaks on board the ship and joins up with the Saint to determine what is really going on. She is soon disappointed, as not much happens during the first ten minutes of the film.

This is, however, a Saint movie, and intrigue is just around the corner. When Templar witnesses a man being assaulted in the woods, he cannot help but get involved, rescuing the injured man and bringing him to his hotel suite. He then finds a locked container in the man's possession, which Templar is unable to open. When he leaves the injured man for just a few minutes, the man is stabbed to death. When Templar returns to the room, one of Templar's old foes, Rudolph Hauser, suddenly arrives to forcibly take the box back from Templar. Thereafter, the chase is on to obtain the contents of the dead man's container, which is apparently just a music box, even though Templar believes it may have some special importance. Eventually, Templar recovers the device for good, and learns that it contains the plans for a circuit for a sound detection device, useful to the War Office of the British government.

The beginning of the film, with the back and forth over the box, is quite confusing, but once the various parties and their interests come into focus, the film becomes quite

Simon Templar (Hugh Sinclair, center) attempts to prevent Rudolph Hauser (Cecil Parker) from recovering a mysterious box as Mary Langdon (Sally Gray) looks on in *The Saint's Vacation* (1941).

entertaining. Highlights of the feature include the various tricks Templar uses to conceal the contents of the box from Hauser and the suspenseful scenes on the train toward the end of the film. Unfortunately, *The Saint's Vacation* has a weak conclusion. The film seems to build to a big climax but then fizzles out at the end.

Hugh Sinclair, the forgotten Saint, is quite good in the role. One reason is that the part is written slightly differently than it was for Louis Hayward and George Sanders. Gone are the clever language, sarcastic retorts and sardonic observations of Simon Templar. Here, the Saint is simply a dashing soldier of fortune, handsome and brave, fighting the forces of evil. Sinclair fits that role remarkably well, and his athleticism is also a plus for the movie. While Sinclair may not have been satisfactory as the title character in the prior movies in the series, he does a fine job in this film.

Veteran British actor Cecil Parker plays villain Rudolph Hauser and it is the performance of the film. Although later in his career Parker specialized in British comedies, at this point he was still playing upper-class Englishman with that smug disdain for others. Parker had a similar (although not villain's) role in *The Lady Vanishes* (1938). In *The Saint's Vacation* there is a reference to a prior history of skirmishes between Templar and Hauser, but they are not fully explained in the film. Clearly the two have respect for each other, as they tussle in a civil manner over the mysterious music box. The exchanges between the two are well-written and well-performed by the antagonists. This is a Sherlock Holmes/Professor Moriarty relationship and it is well developed in the film. It is a shame the character of Hauser was not brought back in subsequent films.

At the end, Gavin McLeod makes a short appearance as Inspector Teal, the Saint's adversary from the books. McLeod had appeared in that role in *The Saint in London* and would reprise that role in the next film in the series. McLeod was always an interesting performer and he was well-cast in that role, which unfortunately is not much more than a cameo in *The Saint's Vacation*.

Although the cartoon opening of the Saint stick figure is reprised from a previous film, during this film Templar never leaves a note with the Saint figure on it, does not whistle the familiar Saint tune, and wears a mustache for the first time. As noted above, the character of the Saint is slightly different from the one portrayed in the prior films. For those reasons, *The Saint's Vacation* sometimes seems like a film from a different mystery series. Nevertheless, whatever the context of the feature, it is an entertaining film and is highly recommended.

Note on the Source Material: *The Saint's Vacation* was based on *Getaway*, Leslie Charteris' 1932 novel about Simon Templar. Indeed, most of the events in the movie come from incidents in the first two-thirds of the book, such as Templar and Monty rescuing a man in the woods who is being attacked, the man having a locked box in his possession, the man being killed with a knife while lying in Templar's room, the box being taken by an archenemy of Templar (in this case Prince Rudolph), Templar trailing Rudolph by hiding on his car, and Templar then recovering the contents of the box right under Rudolph's nose. In one incident, Monty rescues the Saint by pretending to be a policeman, an incident that is also carried over into the film, as is a suspenseful train ride in which the contents of the box are in a mail bag.

Despite the similarities in plot, the movie is far superior to the book. The movie has surprise after surprise as Templar constantly tricks Rudolph/Hauser concerning the location of the contents of the box. These novelties are generally missing from the book. In the novel, the contents of the box are stolen jewels; in the movie the contents are drawings for a secret military device. The difference in the MacGuffins gives the movie more focus and therefore the plot makes more sense. Indeed, in the novel the Saint appears to be continuing the fight for possession of the jewels so that he can recover them for himself. Templar is much more saintly in the film as his battle for the contents of the box appears to be for all the right reasons.

Also, the last third of the book drifts off into a tiresome chase scene with the Saint after the jewels while the villains and the police are after the Saint and his friends. The ending of the book concerns an assault on a police station by Templar to rescue his girlfriend, Patricia Holm. It is an unconvincing moment. Charteris' wordy writing style is also a detriment to the effectiveness of the novel.

Note on the Production: In the early 1940s, England passed the Films Act, which required 50 percent of all revenues from American films shown in England be frozen in England and not taken out of the country. In order to utilize those frozen funds, RKO decided to produce films in England, with a British production company (RKO Radio British Productions) and British actors. Thus George Sanders was out of his role playing the Saint. Of course that was little problem for Sanders, as he simply moved into the starring role in the Falcon series, also produced by RKO.

THE SAINT MEETS THE TIGER (1943)

In *The Saint Meets the Tiger*, Hugh Sinclair returns for his second and last appearance as Simon Templar, and Gavin McLeod returns as Inspector Teal, a role he played in two of the previous films. Two characters from the original Leslie Charteris novels, Patricia Holm, the Saint's girl friend, and Horace, the Saint's butler (Orace in the books), are introduced. The movie was filmed in England and has an all–British cast. The plot is based on a novel by Charteris. Yet for all of these promising characteristics, *The Saint Meets the Tiger* is a very disappointing film.

As the movie opens, Simon Templar receives a phone call from a complete stranger (later identified as Joe Gallo) who asks Templar if he would be interested in a million pounds. Templar invites Gallo to his house but just as the man knocks on his door, Gallo is stabbed to death by a mysterious assailant who runs off into the dark. Just before Gallo dies in the Saint's arms, he whispers, "Tiger, Baycombe, the gold." So off Templar and his butler Horace go to the village of Baycombe to locate the gold, which is presumably the same gold that was stolen in a recent bank robbery. There the Saint meets a number of suspicious characters who may be part of the gang of robbers, including banker Lionel Bentley, who has a checkered past of which Templar is aware, and Bentley's business associate, Bittle, who seems to have an interest in killing Templar. The Saint also meets a pretty young woman, Patricia Holm, and the two quickly become attracted to each other.

Templar soon determines that the gang is led by a mysterious figure known only as the Tiger, and that the villains intend to smuggle the stolen gold bars out of England on Bentley's yacht. Templar, Horace and Patricia, with the help of Inspector Teal, prevent the boat from leaving, capture the criminals and retrieve the gold. They are helped in their success by a falling out among the thieves.

The best parts of the film are the winning performers. Most people prefer George Sanders in the role of the Saint, but Hugh Sinclair is quite good in the part. One criticism, though, is that he never seems to get very excited about anything that happens in the story. Gordon McLeod, with his thick accent and exasperation with Templar while always respecting him, is engaging as Inspector Teal. The true find, though, is Jean Gillie as Patricia Holm. She is perky and energetic, and as a native Englishwoman, completely authentic in the role. Also, she is quite a looker. If the series had continued after this film, she would have made a great regular for the features, as the character of Patricia Holm was a regular in the Saint novels for many years. It is a shame that Gillie died at the age of 33, just a few years after this film was released.

One of the problems with *The Saint Meets the Tiger* is that there is just not much mystery to the story. The unveiling at the end of the film of the true identity of the master villain, the Tiger, could have been intriguing, except that the Tiger's identity had already been revealed to the viewer shortly after Templar reached Baycombe. Why have a mysterious name like the Tiger when your identity is not kept a secret? Indeed, the only mystery in the film is why Gallo called the Saint in the first place. No explanation is given in the movie and the incident makes little sense other than as a vehicle to get the story moving.

There are lots of missed opportunities in the filming. Despite the feature being shot in England, most of the footage is created indoors, making little use of authentic English settings. There is substantially more talk than action and no one seems to get very excited while they are talking, even if the conversation is about life-and-death issues. The plot is simple but can still be hard to follow because there are so many characters, most of whom are given little motivation for the actions they take.

All of these matters contribute to the main problem with the film, which is that it plays very flat, with no excitement generated at any time, even during the climax on Bentley's yacht. Unknown to Templar, Patricia and Horace have boarded the yacht and are disposing of most of the villains on their own, without Templar's help. What excitement can be generated by a group of villains who can be disposed of by a young lady and a butler? Not only is the climax of the film lifeless, so is the rest of the feature. It is not surprising that *The Saint Meets the Tiger* put an end to the production of Saint movies, at least for about a decade.

Note on the Source Material: The film was based on the novel, *Meet the Tiger*, which was the first work by Leslie Charteris concerning his most famous character. The book was initially published in England in 1928. Patricia Holm, who was the Saint's love interest for many years in the Saint stories, was also introduced in the novel, as the Saint and Patricia meet for the first time in the tiny village of Baycombe, where the Saint is trying to locate a large amount of gold stolen from a bank in Chicago. If the Saint locates the gold, the bank has agreed to pay him 20 percent of its value. Also in the village is a Dr. Carn, who the Saint quickly deduces is Inspector Carn of Scotland Yard, operating incognito to recover the gold and arrest the bank robbers' leader, the Tiger. The Tiger's henchmen are known as the Tiger Cubs.

The film is surprisingly faithful to the novel, including scenes where Bittle tries to have Templar arrested for burglarizing his home, the Saint escaping from the Tiger's men and arriving home just before the time that Patricia has been instructed to advise Carn to rescue Templar, the attack on the Tiger Shark's ship by Patricia and Orace alone, and the falling out between the Tiger and the Tiger Cubs. While not every scene is carried over from the novel to the film, most scenes in the film come from the novel.

There are a few significant changes. Templar first learns about the stolen gold from a man named Fernando and that event is told in retrospect, since it occurs before the beginning of the novel. The character of Patricia's Aunt Agatha is a much more important character in the novel than the film. The most important difference between the two works is how the identity of the Tiger is handled. It is a different character in the film than in the novel, but more importantly, the Tiger's identity is kept secret until the end of the novel, where it is, at least, a minor surprise. *Meet the Tiger* is a surprisingly good reading experience for a first novel, especially for a reader whose first introduction to the story is through the movie.

Note on the Production: This was the second of two Saint films produced in England in the 1940s. RKO was so unhappy with the production that it was released in the United States by the independent Republic studio. This also explains the delay in its release in the United States, as the film was completed in 1941 but not released in the United States until 1943.

The Saint's Girl Friday (1954)

Eleven years after *The Saint Meets the Tiger*, another Saint movie finally reached the silver screen. Sixteen years after the release of *The Saint in New York*, Louis Hayward finally returned to the role he had originated in the late 1930s. Time, however, was not necessarily good for the Saint franchise, and *The Saint's Girl Friday* did little for the popularity of Leslie Charteris' Robin Hood of Modern Crime, which was clearly on the downswing in 1954.

As the film opens, Judy Fenton is being pursued by two thugs in a fast car chase, which ends in Fenton's car crashing through a railing and ending in a river. The police believe Fenton's death was an accident but Simon Templar is not so sure. He had received a cable from Judy asking for his help, but he arrived too late to prevent her death. Templar sets out to discover the true facts behind the car crash, which leads him to an illegal gambling den on a river barge. Unfortunately, the operators of the casino immediately recognize the famous Saint and decide to put him out of action on a permanent basis.

Templar is not so easily stymied and he continues his investigation, meeting a number of interesting people along the way. One is socialite Carol Denby, who has been forced to work for the villains to pay off a gambling debt. When Carol starts to help the Saint, Templar dubs her his "Girl Friday," thus explaining the film's title. Another person Templar encounters in his investigation is Keith Merton, son of Lord Merton, who is heavily in debt at the casino. When Keith decides to assist the Saint, his life is immediately put into danger. Another is Irish Cassidy, a counterfeiter who provides the Saint with fake currency to use at the gambling den and other help during the course of the movie. Templar eventually exposes the entire gang, including the Chief, its unknown leader, thereby obtaining his revenge for Judy's death.

Louis Hayward was excellent in *The Saint in New York* and once again in this last movie in the series gives another fine performance. Hayward has aged very well and if his Saint is not quite the jaunty, devil-may-care person of the original film, well, times have changed and so has the Saint. A character from the Charteris' novels, Hoppy Uniatz, makes his first and only film appearance here, reconstituted as Templar's burly valet Hoppy, who has a knack for pickpocketing when the need arises. This new character adds a smidgen of originality for this last film in the series.

The Saint's Girl Friday was produced by English film studios and released in America by RKO. The entire film was shot in England and the settings and primarily British cast give this film an authenticity that some of the earlier films may have lacked. One ongoing theme of the film is Inspector Teal's suspicions of Templar, with Teal often interrupting the action, but these incidents do contribute some amusing moments. There is one gratuitous scene with buxom blond actress Diana Dors, which has some obvious interest, even though the scene has little to do with the plot.

The difficulty with the film stems partly from its story line, which does not hold together very well. There are too many coincidences, such as Templar escaping from the villains in one room of a hotel right into another room with a party going on, which many of the characters happen to be attending. There are two surprises near the end, as seemingly honest characters turn out to be villains, but the surprises are too pat and not very convincing. It is as if the writers believed a detective story must end with a surprise, so they just chose these two, with no foundation laid in the prior events in the film.

Black-and-white detective movies from the 1950s had a different look than those from the 1940s. It is difficult to identify the exact difference, except that the 1950s films, such as this one, often have the look of a long television program. Indeed, this film has the style of the early black-and-white *The Avengers* television show from England or even the early *The Saint* programs starring Roger Moore. Clearly, by 1954, the movie series had long ago lost its momentum, and it was the Roger Moore television series that would soon bring the Saint character back into the public eye.

Since Roger Moore's interpretation of the Saint was much closer to that of Louis Hayward than George Sanders, perhaps *The Saint's Girl Friday* is best viewed as a transition film between the movie series and the television series. It is surely closer in style to the English television series than the Hollywood films of the 1940s.

After the Saint

Leslie Charteris continued to write Saint novels and short stories into 1963. Thereafter, all of the works were either written by Charteris in collaboration with others, were adaptations of television scripts, or were written solely by other writers. Leslie Charteris passed away in Windsor, England, on April 15, 1993.

George Sanders moved to the Falcon series once his career playing the Saint ended, but he left The Falcon series after only four films. Sanders was never thrilled with the role of the Falcon or the role of the Saint and he always desired to appear in more significant films. His wish was fulfilled in 1950, when he received the role of Addison DeWitt in *All About Eve*, for which he received the Oscar for Best Actor in a Supporting Role. Sanders committed suicide in 1972.

Louis Hayward kept busy between his two appearances in the Saint series, which were approximately 16 years apart. Of interest to mystery fans is that he played the Lone Wolf on television for 39 episodes during the 1954–1955 television season. Hayward died in 1985. Hugh Sinclair continued working in films and television until his death in 1962.

There were two Saint movies released in France in the 1960s. In addition to two series on British radio, the Saint came to American radio in 1945. During its different runs on radio, the program was broadcast on several different networks. The most famous radio Saint was Vincent Price, who played the role for several seasons starting in the late 1940s.

The most famous incarnation of the Saint was not in the RKO movies but rather in the English television program made by ABC, an independent British production company, between 1962 and 1969. The program starred Roger Moore as Simon Templar. The only other regular was Ivor Dean, playing Inspector Teal. In all, 118 hour-long episodes were produced. The show was an international success, appearing in the United States, first in syndication and then on NBC from 1967 to 1969. The shows made a star out of Roger Moore, eventually leading to his playing James Bond after Sean Connery left that series for good. The Saint of the novels, and even of the 1940s film series, can be seen as a precursor to James Bond, so Roger Moore was easily adaptable to both parts.

There were other forgettable revivals or attempted revivals of the Saint character over the years. The last significant one was a major motion picture released in 1997, starring Val Kilmer as Simon Templar. The story involved the Russian Mafia and the theft of a formula for cold fusion energy. It was obviously not based on any Charteris story and was an updating of the character. Despite the fact that the film is of recent vintage, it is already long forgotten.

2

The Lone Wolf
The Retired Cracksman

The term "cracksman," which is a fancy word for burglar, is seldom used today, and indeed, in America, it may never have gained widespread use. The similar term in America would be "safecracker." In the early years of crime fiction, cracksmen were the subject of many mystery novels and stories. There was Arsène Lupin, created by Maurice LeBlanc, who was once France's greatest criminal but eventually moved to the side of law and order. The Lupin stories were published from 1907 through 1925. There was also A.J. Raffles, an Englishman, who was considered the greatest cracksman in all of crime literature. His exploits, written by E.W. Hornung, were published from 1899 through 1909, with the first book entitled *The Amateur Cracksman*.

Over the years, there were a number of other criminals who were the lead characters in a series of crime stories. For example, there was Godahl the Infallible, created by Frederick Irving Anderson, and Boston Blackie, created by Jack Boyle. While the two characters were surely criminals, they were never called cracksmen, perhaps because they were both Americans. However, the burglar or cracksman who achieved the greatest success in the cinema, at least based upon the number of movies about the character, was the Lone Wolf, created by Louis Joseph Vance.

Background

THE NOVELS

Louis Joseph Vance was born in 1879. He wrote hundreds of short stories, several adventure novels and a few best-selling mystery novels, most of which are now forgotten. His fame today comes from the eight novels he wrote about cracksman Michael Lanyard, who was often known as the Lone Wolf.

The first novel, published in 1914, was titled *The Lone Wolf* and was about an orphan living at the Troyon Hotel in Paris where he became, on his own, a fairly accomplished amateur thief. His life changed forever when he attempted to rob a professional thief named Bourke, who caught him in the act. Rather than report the young man to the police, Bourke took the orphan under his wing, not only teaching him the skills necessary to become an accomplished thief, but also educating him in the arts and the social graces. Bourke provided the young man, who adopted the name Michael Lanyard, with the rules for being a successful cracksman, the most important of which was to be friendless.

Upon Bourke's death, Lanyard took all of these teachings to heart and became a respected, sophisticated gentleman by day and a daring and successful thief at night. He always remained friendless, and thus the sobriquet "the Lone Wolf," was an apt name for him. In the first novel, a ruthless band of underworld villains in Paris known as the Pack attempt to blackmail Lanyard into joining their criminal gang. He refuses and instead decides to give up his criminal activities and his lone wolf status and spend the remainder of his life with the beautiful but mysterious Lucy Shannon. Much of the novel involves Lanyard's attempts to escape with Lucy from France to England, where they eventually decide to be married.

By the beginning of the second novel, *The False Faces, The Further Adventures of the Lone Wolf*, Lanyard's baby son and Lucy have been killed by Eckstrom, Lanyard's archenemy from the first novel. Lanyard is a lone wolf once again. In the third novel, *Red Masquerade* (1921), readers learn of the Lone Wolf's daughter, a character who was carried over into several Lone Wolf films. The last Vance novel about the Lone Wolf was titled *The Lone Wolf's Last Prowl* and was published in 1934. Vance passed away the year before the novel's publication.

THE EARLY MOVIES

The Lone Wolf first appeared on the screen in *The Lone Wolf* (1917), starring Bert Lytell, who also played another famous thief, Boston Blackie, on the silent screen. This film was substantially based upon the original Vance novel. Henry B. Walthall then played the famous cracksman in *The False Faces* (1919), based on the second Lone Wolf novel. Vance worked on the script for the next feature based on his character, titled *The Lone Wolf's Daughter* (1919), starring Bertram Grassby, and then incorporated the plot of the film into his novel *Red Masquerade* (1921), which had the subtitle "Being the Story of the Lone Wolf's Daughter." Jack Holt played Michael Lanyard in *The Lone Wolf* (1924), which drew on plot elements from the original novel, such as the theft of plans for an innovative airplane and Lanyard falling in love with a woman he believes is a crook but instead turns out to be a secret service agent.

Bert Lytell returned to the role for four more films for Columbia, the last one being the first all-talking film about the Lone Wolf, titled *Last of the Lone Wolf* (1930). In 1932, Fox produced a film starring Thomas Meighan as the Lone Wolf, titled *Cheaters at Play*. Michael Lanyard was then absent from the screen for four years, until Columbia started to release Lone Wolf films in earnest, beginning with *The Lone Wolf Returns* (1935).

THE FILM SERIES

Melvyn Douglas starred as Michael Lanyard in *The Lone Wolf Returns*, which was based loosely on the original Lone Wolf novel by Louis Joseph Vance. This was Melvyn Douglas' only appearance in a Lone Wolf film, and he added a touch of class and status to the movie. Douglas appeared in many prestigious films over the years, including *Ninotchka* (1939) and *I Never Sang for My Father* (1970); he won Oscars for roles in *Hud* (1963) and *Being There* (1979). For mystery fans, he portrayed another famous cracksman in the title role in *Arsène Lupin Returns* (1938).

In *The Lone Wolf in Paris* (1938), Michael Lanyard returned to his roots, at least from the Vance novels, as Lanyard was born in Paris and started his criminal career there. The Lone Wolf was portrayed in the film by Francis Lederer, a Czechoslovakian-born actor, who began appearing in American films in 1934. He appeared in lead roles in a number of films at different studios before receiving his starring role as the Lone Wolf. Thereafter, he had some feature roles in 1940s films and appeared numerous times as a guest star on television.

The true Lone Wolf series began in 1939, with the release of *The Lone Wolf Spy Hunt*, which starred Warren William in the title role. William, who was born in 1894 in Minnesota, began appearing in films on a regular basis in 1931. He is well-known to fans of mystery movies, having previously appeared as Philo Vance in *The Dragon Murder Case* (1934) and *The Gracie Allen Murder Case* (1939), and as Perry Mason in four films, beginning with *The Case of the Howling Dog* (1934). William appeared in a total of nine Lone Wolf films as the reformed cracksman, the most of any actor.

The character of Jamison, Lanyard's loyal but sometimes light-fingered valet, was usually played by British character actor Eric Blore. Blore was born in London, England, in the late 1880s and began making films during the silent era, where he refined his portrayal of an upper-class British valet or waiter or similar service provider. In addition to the Lone Wolf series, Blore is best known today for his appearances in the Fred Astaire–Ginger Rogers movies at RKO, usually playing a role similar in character to Jamison. He also played Philo Vance's valet, Currie, in *The Casino Murder Case* (1935).

During the 1940s series with Warren William, there were two other continuing characters who appeared in many of the films. One was Inspector Crane, Lanyard's archnemesis from the New York police department. The character, who first appeared in *The Lone Wolf Returns* (1936), was played by Thurston Hall. Hall generally played character parts in films and is probably best known today for his continuing role as Mr. Schuyler on the *Topper* television series in the early 1950s. Crane's inept assistant Dickens was played by Fred Kelsey, a character actor in Hollywood who often played policemen.

In 1946, Gerald Mohr replaced William as the Lone Wolf, starring in three films in the series, the first being *The Notorious Lone Wolf*. Mohr was born in New York City in 1914. During his acting career, Mohr became a familiar voice on the radio and a familiar face on the silver screen. Mohr appeared in over 500 radio programs, most notably for mystery fans as Philip Marlowe from 1948 to 1951, in *The Adventures of Philip Marlowe*. His first important film role was the lead villain in the 1941 serial *Jungle Girl*. Thereafter, he appeared in many films but his most significant role was as Michael Lanyard in three films in the Columbia series.

Ron Randell took over the part of Michael Lanyard in the last film, *The Lone Wolf and His Lady* (1949). The Australian-born actor began appearing in films in Hollywood in 1947, playing Bulldog Drummond before he played the Lone Wolf. Randell had a sporadic career in films, and he is better known today for performing on television and Broadway than acting in the cinema.

The Early Films

THE LONE WOLF RETURNS (1935)

For those who are expecting a traditional 1940s mystery movie with a detective who is a reformed thief, *The Lone Wolf Returns* will be a surprise. The film was made in 1935 and reflects the movies of that era, being in the tradition of *Raffles* (1930) and *Arsène Lupin*

(1932) rather than in the tradition of the 1940s Lone Wolf and Boston Blackie movie series. Here, as the film opens, the Lone Wolf is still the consummate jewel thief, and whether or not he will reform is one of the intriguing questions that is addressed throughout the film.

The Lone Wolf Returns begins with an interesting scene in which the Lone Wolf is in the process of stealing a valuable string of pearls from a large mansion when he realizes that the house is surrounded by the police. Lanyard escapes his entrapment by disguising himself as the owner of the house, and then to further his getaway, he sneaks into the adjacent residence. There, where a costume ball is in progress, Lanyard spots two other jewel thieves unsuccessfully attempting to steal the valuable pendant hanging around the neck of the lovely Marcia Stewart. When Marcia returns the pendant to the supposed security of her wall safe, Lanyard, the consummate cracksman, opens the safe and lifts the same.

Lanyard is also the consummate sophisticate, unwilling to pass up a fancy party, and so he proceeds to attend the ball, meets Marcia, and the two instantly become infatuated with each other. As a result, Lanyard returns the pendant to Marcia's safe but steals her picture instead. The Lone Wolf then decides to give up his life of crime; but another gang of jewel thieves does not want that to happen, as they want to use Lanyard's skills in several criminal enterprises. When Lanyard refuses to join with them in stealing Marcia's jewel, they steal the pendant anyway and frame Lanyard for the crime. Lanyard is arrested but he is able to escape from police custody. With only has a few hours to prove his innocence, Lanyard captures the crooks and recovers the pendant. At the end of the film, it is apparent that nuptials are about to occur.

From the opening scene in which Lanyard is trapped in the mansion with the jewels he has just stolen, it is never easy to predict the twists and turns of the plot. The motivations of the characters are not always clear and the leader of the villains, played by Douglas Dumbrille, always seems to be one step ahead of Lanyard, whether outing him as an international jewel thief in front of Marcia or framing him for the burglary of Marcia's pendant. Lanyard steals Marcia's pendant, then returns Marcia's pendant, acquires it once more from the thieves and then returns it once again. This is not a formula type of movie as the later films in the series could be. Despite its age, *The Lone Wolf Returns* always seems fresh.

The performances are universally excellent. Melvyn Douglas is suave and debonair in the lead role. Gail Patrick is quite attractive as Marcia Stewart. Douglas Dumbrille is menacing as always as the lead villain. Raymond Walburn is quite amusing as Lanyard's valet Jenkins and his performance compares well with the more famous ones by Eric Blore in the later films in the series. Thurston Hall gives a surprisingly good performance as Crane, the police detective who is called out of retirement to locate the Lone Wolf. Hall plays the same role in some of the later Warren William films in the series, but here it is a well-written, nuanced part excellently performed by Hall.

The true Lone Wolf series did not begin until Warren William took over the part in 1939, by which time the Lone Wolf had completely reformed. Presumably it would have been difficult to create a long series of mysteries with the hero actually being a thief. However, it is the fact that Lanyard is the consummate cracksman and has larceny in his heart that gives *The Lone Wolf Returns* a unique flavor as contrasted with the later films. It is well worth a view.

Note on the Source Material: Although the screenplay is not based upon any particular work by Louis Joseph Vance, *The Lone Wolf Returns* is one of the few films in the Columbia series that evokes the original conception of the Lone Wolf character as written by the author.

Indeed, just as in this film, in the novel titled *The Lone Wolf* Michael Lanyard is a true jewel thief, stealing valuable pieces of jewelry from the wealthy Madame Omber and cleverly evading the police. Also, just as in this film, once Lanyard falls in love he decides to forsake his life of crime, returns a valuable item that he has stolen to the safe of the rightful owner, and also turns down an offer and then a threat to join a larger criminal syndicate. *The Lone Wolf Returns* was clearly inspired by the original Vance novel, although the basic plot is original to the screenplay.

Some sources state that this movie is based on the 1923 novel by Louis Joseph Vance entitled *The Lone Wolf Returns*. However, while the titles are the same, the two works have little in common. As that novel opens, Michael Lanyard is completely reformed. A nefarious group of criminals does try to ensnare Lanyard into a criminal enterprise, and while that is similar to the movie, the circumstances in each medium are completely different. Two parallels, though, are that the novel also takes place primarily in New York City and Inspector Crane is an important character.

Note on the Production: This is a remake of the 1926 silent film of the same name, which starred Bert Lytell as Michael Lanyard. The Lone Wolf's valet is named "Jenkins" in this film. The name was changed to "Jamison" or "Jameson" for the Warren William films. The part was usually played by Eric Blore. In this 1935 film, Thurston Hall plays Inspector Crane, a retired police detective who is called back on the job because of his intimate knowledge of the Lone Wolf's activities. Hall was to reprise that role in many of the Warren William films, although he was no longer a retired policeman but rather was an important detective on the police force. Director Roy William Neill went on to produce and direct most of the Universal Sherlock Holmes films. Star Gail Patrick became the executive producer of the *Perry Mason* television series under her married name, Gail Patrick Jackson.

The Lone Wolf in Paris (1938)

Unlike the subsequent Warren William films in the series, *The Lone Wolf in Paris* is more of an adventure film than a mystery movie, as Michael Lanyard steals his way across Europe (for a good cause) in this interesting story of international intrigue. With its innovative plot and excellent acting and writing, the film is both unique for the series and is quite entertaining.

By this time in his movie career, Lanyard is completely reformed, having been on the straight and narrow for five years. But that does not prevent Lanyard from returning to his criminal ways for a good cause. He has the chance to do so in this film, when Princess Thania of the small country of Arvonne seeks Lanyard's help in recovering three crown jewels in time for the new king's coronation. The jewels are now in the hands of Grand Duke Gregor, Baroness Gambrell and Marquis Albert de Meyervon, who obtained them when the finances of Arvonne were poor and the Queen received loans from the three with the crown jewels used as collateral. Now the three villains refuse to return the valuable pieces, even though the Queen is willing to pay five times the loan amount to reacquire the crown jewels for her country. The villains' motive in retaining the jewels, despite the huge payout to them if the jewels are returned, is devious. They believe that once the people of Arvonne learn that the jewels are missing, it is likely to lead to a revolution, with Gregor becoming the new king.

The first part of the film involves Lanyard's purloining of each jewel from each of the three villains, in three separate clever incidents. While Lanyard may no longer be dishonest, he is still a gifted thief. In the next part of the feature, Lanyard and the Princess, who now have the jewels, ride in a plane back to Arvonne, but the plane is diverted by the villains who eventually take the jewels back from Lanyard. In the final part of the film, Lanyard recovers the jewels just in time for the new king's coronation by convincing the palace guard that he was in a plot with Gregor to steal the jewels, thus framing Gregor for the crime.

The fun in viewing *The Lone Wolf in Paris* comes, in the first part of the movie, from attempting to anticipate the method by which Lanyard will recover each of the jewels, and then being surprised by the clever method he actually uses. It is quite enjoyable to watch each of the "crimes" that the Lone Wolf commits, with many of the scenes being quite suspenseful. The middle third of the movie is totally different, and is highlighted by Lanyard trying to prevent Gregor from taking back the jewels, with Lanyard, at one point, becoming the target in a knife-throwing act. Once again, many of the scenes are very suspenseful, a characteristic which was generally missing from the later films in the series. The concluding third of the film is also quite interesting, with Lanyard using a clever ruse to finally recover the valuable jewels for good.

The Lone Wolf (Francis Lederer, in the light robe) explains to the hotel manager (Maurice Cass, far left) and the house detective (Vernon Dent) that he was not involved in the theft of gems from the Marquis' room, in *The Lone Wolf in Paris* (1938). The real thief, Princess Thania (Frances Drake), is hiding behind the Lone Wolf.

The performances in the feature are uniformly excellent, in large parts and small. Because of his accent, it takes time to get used to Francis Lederer as the Lone Wolf, but once he becomes a familiar presence in the movie, his performance is quite engaging. Frances Drake is beautiful as Princess Thania and she gives a good performance also. Walter Kingsford is marvelous as the villainous Gregor. The scenes between Lanyard and Gregor where they talk to each other with fake impeccable upper-class manners are particularly entertaining. Indeed, the dialogue throughout the entire film is exceptionally witty.

The Lone Wolf in Paris is never formulaic and never boring. It is never interrupted by those long and tedious comedy sequences that were a trademark of the 1940s mystery movies, including those in the Lone Wolf series. It is a fun film to watch and is essentially the end of a 20-year era of Lone Wolf films, set in a world of sophistication, with the plots being inspired by the Lone Wolf of the Louis Joseph Vance novels rather than being written in the style of many 1940s Hollywood mystery movies.

None of the Warren William films were based on any works by Louis Joseph Vance, and in those films the character of the reformed cracksman never seems quite as sophisticated or as classy as the Lone Wolf was portrayed in the earlier movies. In many ways, the quality of *The Lone Wolf Returns* and *The Lone Wolf in Paris* was never matched by the later films in the series.

The Warren William Films

THE LONE WOLF SPY HUNT

This film marks the true start of the Columbia film series about the Lone Wolf, as Warren William now plays the role of the famous cracksman who is completely reformed. Unfortunately, *The Lone Wolf Spy Hunt* also marks a serious drop in the quality of the Columbia Lone Wolf films from the previous two entries. Melvyn Douglas and Francis Lederer played urbane and classy Michael Lanyards, very much in keeping with the Lone Wolf of the Louis Joseph Vance novels. Warren William, on the other hand, is saddled with a script that puts significant emphasis on the antics of his girlfriend, Val Carson, and his daughter, Patricia. The result is to knock a few rungs off the sophistication level of the Lone Wolf, undercutting the attribute of the lead character that gave the Vance stories and the prior films their unique flavor.

The main story commences in the rain, when Michael Lanyard is captured by several hoods and taken to the house of a strange man who does not show his face. The man, later identified as Spiro Gregory, offers to pay Lanyard $10,000 if he will steal the secret plans of a new anti-aircraft gun from the safe of the United States War Department. Lanyard refuses, and he is surprised that, despite his unwillingness to cooperate with the villains, they simply let him go. The viewer quickly learns that the reason for the kidnapping and the quick release of Lanyard is that the villains never expected Lanyard to cooperate with them. They abducted Lanyard only so that Gregory could obtain some of Lanyard's special brand of cigarettes from Lanyard's cigarette case. Gregory is scheming to plant one of Lanyard's cigarettes at the War Department's safe when his thugs steal the plans on their own, thus framing the Lone Wolf for the crime.

The dastardly deed is done and the police immediately suspect Lanyard of the crime. However, it turns out that several pages of the plans were missing from the safe when Gregory's men stole the documents. The villains therefore kidnap Lanyard one more time to force him to steal the remaining plans from the safe of the inventor and also so that Lanyard can be incriminated in another theft. The rest of the film is a cat-and-mouse game between Gregory and Lanyard, with plans stolen, regained and then lost again. In the end, Lanyard saves the plans for the country and also rescues his daughter who is trapped by the villains.

There is much that is right with this film. The back-and-forth with the safe cracking and the plan stealing is always interesting and often quite clever. It is difficult for the viewer to anticipate the tricks Lanyard pulls on the villains, or, for that matter, to anticipate the counter-moves by Gregory. Ralph Morgan, who plays Gregory, was always great in films playing the villain, and he does not disappoint in this film. Morgan is able to convey villainy despite being soft-spoken and never becoming angry. He states his threats to Lanyard and others in a civil tone, making his wickedness seem all the greater for it. Rita Hayworth, billed third in the credits but in a relatively small role, is stunningly beautiful as Gregory's henchwoman. Hayworth was only a year away from becoming a major star in Hollywood and with her appearance in *The Lone Wolf Spy Hunt*, it is easy to see why.

All of that said, this is a very disappointing film. Most of *Spy Hunt's* potential is frittered away in a side story about Val Carson, a senator's daughter, who is romantically involved with Lanyard. As the movie progresses, Val becomes frustrated when Lanyard stands her up for dates or becomes jealous when Lanyard spends time with other women. Her scenes, of which there are many, are not funny at all. The part of Val Carson is poorly written and then poorly performed by Ida Lupino. Lupino could be an excellent actress in dramatic films such as *The Adventures of Sherlock Holmes* (1939) and *High Sierra* (1941), but comedy was clearly not her forte. She is more irritating than funny, becoming an interruption to the plot rather than a participant in it. When Ida Lupino is more irritating and less humorous than Tom Dugan playing a bumbling policeman, there is clearly something amiss in the film.

Perhaps the problem with the movie (which also occurs in later films in the series) is the filmmakers' attitude toward the Lone Wolf character, as epitomized by the fact that most of the characters refer to Michael Lanyard as "Mike," rather than as "Michael" or "Mr. Lanyard." Even his young daughter calls him "Mike." The characters do not treat the Lone Wolf in the sophisticated manner he deserves, so how can the viewer? Michael Lanyard is no longer an urbane cracksman; he has become just another participant in comedy sketches with Val Carson. Thus, the script, the dialogue and the style of the film have turned the Lone Wolf into just another movie detective, to the serious detriment of this film.

Note on the Source Material: The daughter of Michael Lanyard made her first appearance in the 1919 silent film, *The Lone Wolf's Daughter*. Louis Joseph Vance worked on the screenplay and then adapted the script into his 1921 novel, *Red Masquerade*, with its subtitle, *Being the Story of the Lone Wolf's Daughter*. In the "Apology" at the beginning of the book, Vance wrote that the "tale quite brazenly derives" from the motion picture but that Vance has taken "as many high-handed liberties" from the movie as the director had taken from his script.

The novel is divided into two parts. The first section is a flashback to the younger days of Michael Lanyard, to the time when he was at an auction where a bidding war broke out between the beautiful Princess Sofia and her estranged husband, Prince Victor, over a painting by the artist Corot that the auctioneer could not guarantee was legitimate. Nevertheless, the bidding between Sofia and Victor was vociferous, and when Sofia ran out of money, Lanyard impetuously bid on his own, receiving the painting for a large amount of money.

When Lanyard brought the painting back to his apartment, he checked under the canvas and discovered love letters written to Sofia from a member of a royal family, which would have created a serious scandal. The hidden letters were the reason both Sofia and Victor wanted the painting. When Victor tried to recover the letters from Lanyard, Lanyard humiliated the man, forcing him to pay for the painting without receiving a return of the letters. Lanyard then returned the letters to Sofia, resulting in Lanyard staying the night with Sofia.

The second half of the book involves the Lone Wolf's daughter, also named Sofia, who has been raised as an orphan. Prince Victor pretends he is Sofia's father and brings her to his home to use as a wedge against Lanyard, who is investigating Victor's criminal activities, which include spreading poisonous gas in London so that Victor can take over as ruler of England and turn it into a Bolshevik state. Lanyard, who has been posing as a servant of Victor, thwarts the criminal's plans, rescues his daughter, and kills Victor in the process.

The plots of the 1919 film and the novel have a substantial similarity. The 1929 silent remake, *The Lone Wolf's Daughter*, does not appear to have any similarity to the earlier work. The 1939 film, *The Lone Wolf Spy Hunt*, also has no similarity to the original novel. The melodramatic nature of the core of the book had little relevance in World War II America, although the beginning of the book about the love letters hidden in the painting was consistent with the tone of the earlier 1930s Lone Wolf films.

In *The Lone Wolf Spy Hunt*, Lanyard's daughter is named Patricia and she is much younger than the Sofia of the book. There is no explanation given in the film as to why Lanyard has a daughter living with him or where the mother is. There is no other mention of Lanyard's daughter in any of the remaining films in the series.

THE LONE WOLF STRIKES (1940)

This film commences with an interesting set of scenes, as the lovely Binnie Weldon prepares to attend a party with Phillip Jordan, a much older gentleman. Binnie asks to see the priceless pearl necklace that Jordan is holding in his safe. Jordan allows Binnie to try the necklace on; she likes it so much that Jordan permits her to wear it to the party. When the two return to Jordan's house after the party, the viewer expects that a robbery will occur, but no: Binnie returns the necklace to Jordan and all seems well. Shortly thereafter, however, the viewer learns that Binnie has pawned a fake necklace onto Jordan and kept the valuable necklace for herself and her partner, Jim Ryder.

Jordan learns about the switch the next day and calls Binnie, advising her that he is coming over to claim the pearls. Jordan never gets there, being killed in an auto accident along the way, probably engineered by Ryder, although it is unclear how he could have accomplished the task in such a short time. Jordan's partner, Stanley Young, comes to the Lone Wolf to request his aid in recovering the necklace and finding out who killed Jordan. At the same time, a completely separate gang of thugs is after the necklace, aided by the villainy of one Ralph Bolton, who pretends to be interested in Jordan's daughter, Delia, so that he can obtain information about the pearls. Eventually, of course, the real necklace is recovered by the Lone Wolf and the crooks are caught.

There is much to like in the feature. While the filler material about the Lone Wolf's aquarium in his house is unfunny, little screen time is devoted to that issue, so the scenes are not too distracting from the main story. Eric Blore, assuming the role of Lanyard's butler, Jamison, is outstanding as always with his strange voice and expressive face. Joan Perry is quite lovely as Delia Jordan. Montagu Love does a fabulous turn as the foreign fence Emil Gorlick. His scenes with Warren William are the highlight of the film.

There is nothing really wrong with this movie; it just seems a little flat. As usual, there are twists and turns in the plot, but in this film, the twists are not unexpected, and even though not unexpected, they make little sense. For example, why would Delia Jordan go to Gorlick's hotel room after a talk with Lanyard, a move which resulted in Gorlick escaping from his confinement by the Lone Wolf, thus almost preventing the recovery of the necklace? Also, the plot device of Delia and Stanley Young confiding important information about the necklace to Ralph Bolton, at just the wrong time, undercuts the believability of the story.

At the end, there are two car chases simultaneously. In one the villains are pursuing Lanyard, while in the other the police are chasing Jamison in the hopes he will lead them to Lanyard. Since Lanyard and Jamison are trying to arrive at a ferry at exactly the same time the police and the villains are supposed to arrive, Lanyard and Jamison both take their time getting to the ferry, each even stopping once along the way. Who knew that the slow-speed car chase was invented in this film?

Unfortunately, the term "slow speed" epitomizes the problems with *The Lone Wolf Strikes*. Even though there are two sets of crooks chasing the same necklace and the Lone Wolf has to fend off both groups, which on its face should have led to an exciting story, the movie moves at a very slow speed. There is more talk than action and often uninteresting talk, at that. The two murders take place off-screen, removing that element of suspense and excitement from the film. When the police capture both sets of villains, they put up no fight, also removing a potential element of excitement from the movie.

A little more action and suspense could have gone a long way in improving this film. Despite its potential, *The Lone Wolf Strikes* is a mediocre entry in the series.

The Lone Wolf Meets a Lady (1940)

This third film in the Lone Wolf series starring Warren William uses the same plot pattern as the prior film. The first ten minutes or so of *The Lone Wolf Meets a Lady* are used to set up the mystery, with the Lone Wolf nowhere in sight. Michael Lanyard then becomes involved in the action in a quest to assist a female in distress and recover some stolen jewels.

The one important change to the series from the prior two films is the return of Thurston Hall as Inspector Crane, last seen in *The Lone Wolf Returns* (1935). He is a welcome addition to the series, as Inspector Crane is one of the best-written policeman roles in the 1940s mystery series (at least in his early appearances). Thurston Hall performs the part wonderfully, as he parries with the Lone Wolf, is always suspicious of him and is seldom fooled by the former cracksman's devious schemes. Crane is much like Inspector Farraday from *The Boston Blackie* series, but he is a much less comic figure, his only eccentricity being his interest in flowers, a characteristic first evident in the 1935 film. Unfortunately, Crane's interest in flowers drops out in the later films in the series, and Crane eventually becomes the standard semi-dumb policeman of the 1940s mystery movies with no unique attributes. However, that was not the case in *The Lone Wolf Meets a Lady*, to the film's credit.

The movie opens with Joan Bradley at the home of her fiancé, Bob Penyon, who takes a valuable necklace out of the vault so that Joan can wear it that night. Unfortunately, when

Joan returns to her apartment with the necklace, her husband, Pete Rennick, who everyone believed was dead, suddenly appears in the apartment and demands the necklace. Pete is working for well-known criminal Clay Beaudine, who knew Joan had the necklace as a result of a phone call from his mole at the Penyon residence. However, before Rennick can leave with the necklace, he is shot and killed by a person or persons unknown.

Joan panics, rushes into the streets and is almost killed by a car driven by Jamison. Lanyard, a passenger in the car, then becomes involved in Joan's plight, and he sets off to prove Joan innocent of the crime and to recover the necklace. With valuable jewels being stolen, the Lone Wolf is an obvious suspect for the crimes, and thus Lanyard must also prove his own innocence in addition to that of Joan. The mystery is aided by the fact that there are several potential suspects for the crime.

There are a number of surprise elements to the film. Lanyard concocts a story for Joan to use when she calls the police to report the murder in her apartment, but her plausible story is tripped up by the discovery of her apartment key in Rennick's pocket. In an attempt to locate the necklace, Lanyard goes to Nick, a jeweler he knows, who has contacts in the underworld. Nick reports back that the necklace had actually been sold the year before. Does that mean the jewels in the necklace are fake? At the end of the film Lanyard creates an elaborate trap for the murderer, knowing that he or she will be forced to appear on a dock at the river to see if Lanyard can recover the necklace, which was thrown into the river from Joan's apartment. Unfortunately for Lanyard three of the suspects show up, so it looks like the trap will be a failure.

The mystery itself is quite interesting although the revelation of the killer is hardly surprising, since little attention is paid in the film to the various suspects and by the end it was hard to remember exactly who is who. Much like *The Lone Wolf Strikes*, the pace of the film is very slow, with little action among the incessant talking. William gives a lazy performance in the title role, showing little enthusiasm for his actions and little interest in the events that occur in the film.

The Lone Wolf Meets a Lady is a better-than-average movie and is worth a view. However, the Warren William films had yet to hit their stride, still not reaching the quality of the Melvyn Douglas and Francis Lederer films of the 1930s.

THE LONE WOLF KEEPS A DATE (1941)

While this is the best of the Warren William Lone Wolf movies to date, at this point the series still has yet to meet its full potential. Here, Michael Lanyard is no longer the former cracksman, stealing to help the downtrodden as he was in *The Lone Wolf in Paris* and *The Lone Wolf Strikes*. Rather Lanyard is more like Boston Blackie, helping a damsel in distress but not displaying sophistication or cracksman skills. Indeed, there is more action than cleverness in the script, making *The Lone Wolf Keeps a Date* a fun movie to watch even though it seems to lack that certain something that made the earlier Lone Wolf movies so entertaining.

The story starts out in Havana, with Lanyard and his valet on their way to the airport. Lanyard had gone to Cuba to obtain an important stamp for his stamp collection. Jamison spent his time on the island running a crooked dice game, and so, with his victims in hot pursuit, he is interested in departing the country as soon as possible. On the way to the airport they meet pretty Patricia Lawrence, and when they land in Florida, Lanyard sees her being abducted by two men in a car.

Lanyard breaks up the kidnapping, but in the process loses his stamp collection. Patricia finally admits she had gone to Havana to obtain an envelope, which she intended to give to a Portuguese man who had information which would help release her fiancé, Scotty, from jail. Scotty has been arrested for murder. Lanyard convinces Patricia to open the envelope, and to the surprise of both of them it contains $100,000 in cash. When Lanyard then learns about the kidnapping of wealthy Cyrus Colby, it is clear that the $100,000 is the missing ransom money.

The plot is somewhat complicated for a 1940s film in a mystery series. Casino owner Big Joe Brady is involved in the kidnapping. The ransom money went missing when one of Brady's gang double-crossed him and mailed the money to himself in Havana. Brady then killed the traitor and Patricia's fiancé Scotty was unfortunately accused of the crime. The Lone Wolf has to solve the murder, save Cyrus Colby's life, protect the ransom money and clear Scotty's name. It is a big task for a crime dilettante such as Michael Lanyard, but not surprisingly, he is successful in the end.

The plot itself is fairly interesting, with the complex story line being doled out in bits and pieces to the viewer. Along the way there are a number of action scenes, such as the killing of the Portuguese, Lanyard's attempted escape from Brady's gang, a boat chase and the eventual capture of the Brady gang. These action sequences are a decided plus; the lack of the same in the prior two movies substantially reduced the enjoyment of those films.

There are, of course, the too-frequent comedy moments, although at least some of them are funny, with Lanyard pretending to be crazy over his stamp collection, a loud local policeman and his strange police force, and Dickens setting off a police siren to the chagrin of Inspector Crane. Dickens, as played by Fred Kelsey, is the requisite inept policeman of many of the Hollywood mystery series, but in this film even Inspector Crane seems a little on the dumb side, which is different than how he was portrayed in the prior films in the series. Kelsey is irritating, but perhaps a little less so than in the prior Lone Wolf films.

Eric Blore is wonderful as always as Jamison, still wishing that he and the Lone Wolf were flirting with a life of crime instead of staying on the right side of the law. Warren William puts a little more gusto into the film than in his previous endeavor, and that also contributes to the effectiveness of the film. While the Lone Wolf never keeps a date in the film, he does solve an interesting mystery, making this a good entry in the Lone Wolf series.

THE LONE WOLF TAKES A CHANCE (1941)

Building on the momentum from the prior two films in the Lone Wolf series, *The Lone Wolf Takes a Chance* is an excellent mystery movie. It is surely the most suspenseful film in the series and its effectiveness is aided greatly by its brief moments of humor, seamlessly melded into the plot of the feature.

The story concerns Johnny Baker, the inventor of a burglar-proof railroad car. Once the car is locked, it cannot be opened except through the combination lock, the combination of which is known only by Johnny. If anyone tries to open the car in any other manner, poison gas will flood the car and the surrounding area outside, killing anyone around. Perhaps this is a dangerous device to install on a mail car on a passenger train, but the federal government has enthusiastically endorsed its use.

At the Hotel Bradshaw, Johnny meets private detective Wallace and shows him a telegram from Gloria Foster, Johnny's movie star girlfriend, asking Johnny to meet her in Room 909 of the hotel. Johnny is suspicious of the telegram and has asked Wallace to accompany him to the room. Sure enough, when Johnny enters the room he is abducted

Inspector Crane (Thurston Hall, left) finally gets the handcuffs on Michael Lanyard (Warren William) in *The Lone Wolf Takes a Chance* (1941). Also shown is actress Gloria Foster, played by June Storey.

by several thugs, and when Wallace tries to rescue Johnny, Wallace is shot on the high ledge near the outside of the room and falls to his death. Unfortunately the detective was just outside Michael Lanyard's window when the shooting occurred, and when Wallace fell he grabbed the cord from the blinds from Lanyard's room. The police immediately suspect Lanyard of the murder, and Lanyard is therefore on the hunt to locate Johnny to clear his own name. Along the way Lanyard recovers the engraving plates that the crooks stole from the mail car, captures the gang and saves Johnny's life.

The movie opens with a delightful scene, where a valuable string of pearls is dropped in a jewelry store, landing on a neck of a black cat that proceeds to exit the store and walk down the street. As the owner is calling the police, Lanyard and Jamison spot the cat and start to follow it and the valuable necklace. The cat jumps up and sneaks into a bank window and when Lanyard and Jamison get close to the bank door to see where the cat had gone, an alarm goes off and a set of bars come down, trapping the Lone Wolf and his valet. When Inspector Crane arrives, Lanyard is very sheepish as he tries to explain what happened to the police.

That leads to a bet between Crane and Lanyard, with Crane betting two months' salary that the Lone Wolf cannot stay out of trouble for 24 hours. Since this is the beginning of a new Lone Wolf film, it is easy to forecast who will win that bet. This is a charming opening scene, laced with light humor that is quite engaging.

After Johnny's kidnapping, the action moves to a long story arc on a train, where Johnny is being held as a supposed patient of a supposed doctor so that he will provide the combination of the lock to the villains. Lanyard tries to essay Johnny's escape but he is thwarted by the clever moves of the villains, including one who masquerades as a doctor to the chagrin of Lanyard. The train scene has moves and countermoves by both sides and is aided by many of the attributes of a train melodrama — the tight corridors, the small state-rooms and the rhythms of the train substituting for mood music. It is the best scene in the film.

The action then moves to an apparently deserted house, which gives the film the feel of an old dark house mystery. It is an interesting setting for the film, particularly the scenes just outside the house in the heavy winds. Again, it is time for moves and countermoves, but this time with the police becoming involved in the action. Lanyard learns that Johnny is locked within his special mail car on the train, which is speeding to Indiana, and when it gets there the government intends to open the car by breaking in, which will cause the poison gas to be emitted, killing Johnny.

In the film's most suspenseful sequence, Lanyard learns the combination of the mail car lock from a newsreel of Johnny opening the lock, takes a plane to overtake the train and then boards the train to try to open the safe before the train reaches Gary, Indiana, where the government is ready to proceed. With the sound of the train once again substituting for a music soundtrack, and with the wind in his face, Lanyard tries the combination on the lock and fails twice. After disposing of an interfering conductor, Lanyard finally opens the lock just after the train stops and rescues Johnny just as the gas starts to spew from the railroad car. It is a quality ending to an already suspenseful film.

The moments of humor in the feature are small but delightful, such as Lanyard accidentally grabbing a man's toupee as he tries to escape from the train, a defective door in the old house falling on Dickens, a local policeman making fun of Crane for his sloppy police methods, and Jamison paying off their bets with the police with counterfeit money. Less is often more when it comes to humor and this film has many more laughs than the Lone Wolf films with longer comedy bits in them. With an energetic performance by Warren William, this is an excellent film in the series.

SECRETS OF THE LONE WOLF (1941)

The credits to this film seem promising. The story and screenplay are by Stuart Palmer, creator of the Hildegard Withers mystery novels and a contributor to the screenplays of many mystery movie series, including films in The Falcon and Bulldog Drummond series. The director is Edward Dmytryk, who directed films in the Falcon and Boston Blackie series but is most famous today for his work on major films such as *Crossfire* (1947) and *The Caine Mutiny* (1954). In the mystery field, Dmytryk is best known for directing *Murder, My Sweet* (1944), an adaptation of Raymond Chandler's novel *Farewell, My Lovely*.

The opening of the film also seems promising. After an amusing vignette of the Lone Wolf addressing a women's group on the subject of crime not paying, Sergeant Dickens handcuffs Lanyard and forcibly brings him to meet Inspector Crane at a ship which is docked in the harbor. The boat contains a valuable shipment of gems, known as the Napoleon jewels. The precious stones have been brought to America by a group of French refugees who want to sell them to obtain funds to fight the Germans in Europe. Crane is guarding the jewels and he asks Lanyard's advice as to how some thieves might attempt to steal them, despite the elaborate security precautions in place. Lanyard gives some suggestions, such as hiding his tools on a wire over the side of the boat, sneaking on board ship as a customs officer, stealing the jewels by use of his tools, and then escaping in the confusion caused by shorting the electric system and starting a fire to create a diversion. Lanyard then leaves.

In the meantime, a pretty young girl has delivered a note for the Lone Wolf, saying that she is in desperate trouble and asking him to meet her that night at 9:00 P.M. in room 417 of the Burton Hotel. When Lanyard is busy with Inspector Crane, Jamison attends the meeting, and is then surprised to find himself in a den of thieves, led by Dapper Dan Streever. The crooks mistake Jamison for the Lone Wolf and expect him to help the gang steal the Napoleon jewels from the ship. This puts Jamison in an uncomfortable position, but he tricks the gang into allowing him to go back to his hotel room to collect his tools. There, in the most amusing scene in the film, Jamison poses as the Lone Wolf and the Lone Wolf poses as Jamison. Shortly thereafter, the two manage to extract themselves from the clutches of the gang.

Up to this point the movie has been quite entertaining, as Lanyard has had the opportunity to pontificate on gem-stealing techniques and Jamison has had the task of trying to talk himself out of his problems with the Streever gang. Also, the international intrigue related to the potential stealing of the jewels on the boat somewhat invokes the spirit of the original Louis Joseph Vance novels.

At this point, however, the story falls apart. The Streever gang steals the jewels on its own and in a manner that is similar to Lanyard's original ideas expressed to Inspector Crane. Since Lanyard is onboard when the crime occurs, he is immediately suspected of the theft. What follows is a tiresome back-and-forth between the police and Lanyard, seen many times before in the series, with Lanyard being captured and then escaping several times, eventually discovering the identity of the true thief. The only feature that is even slightly surprising about the film is the ending, when it turns out the real thief is Dapper Dan Streever, the most likely suspect.

The plot makes little sense. If the Streever gang already had a good plan in place to steal the jewels, why capture Lanyard to help them? If Michael Lanyard was so famous to the gang, how could they mistake Jamison for him? Also the film is cheaply made, being filmed on a limited number of indoor sets, with almost no outdoor scenes. The scenes on the boat, in particular, are usually shot in the dark, probably to conceal the threadbare nature of the sets and to disguise the fact that the scenes on the boat were not filmed on a boat at all. This is a film of promise unfulfilled and is surely a disappointment after the high quality of the previous film in the series, *The Lone Wolf Takes a Chance.*

COUNTER—ESPIONAGE (1942)

This entertaining entry in the Lone Wolf series, set in London during the German blitz of World War II, begins with some puzzling incidents. As Harvey Leeds, secretary to Sir Stafford Hart, is about to leave the Hart residence to meet his fiancée Pamela, who is Sir

Opposite: **Four of the principal actors in *Secrets of the Lone Wolf* (1941) are shown across the top of this lobby card. Pictured from left to right are Fred Kelsey, as dumb policeman Dickens, Thurston Hall, as the much smarter Inspector Crane, Ruth Ford as the enigmatic model Helene De Loeon, and of course Warren William as the Lone Wolf, Michael Lanyard.**

Henry's daughter, Leeds stops to look through the briefcase of Kent Wells, Stafford's assistant. Wells, who is spying on Hart, takes no action. Outside the house, Leeds is knocked out by phony air raid warden, Anton Schugg, and is then driven off in a car. Wells witnesses the incident through a window of the Stafford home, and despite the abduction of a fellow employee, takes no action.

Suddenly, Wells hears a noise in Stafford's library and alerts Stafford. The viewer then sees that there is a burglar in the library, and that the cracksman is in fact Michael Lanyard, the Lone Wolf. Has our hero finally returned to the life of crime he had forsaken so many years before? Lanyard escapes with the government's secret beam detector plans, which, if they find their way into the hands of the enemy, could leave England defenseless against German air attacks. Once Stafford looks around, he discovers a cuff link with an engraved "L" on it lying on the floor. If Lanyard has returned to a life of crime, have his skills deteriorated so much? The old Lone Wolf would never have left such an obvious clue to his identity at the scene of a crime.

The remainder of the film concerns Lanyard's efforts to trap a gang of Germans in London who are trying to steal the beam detector plans and essentially fax them back to Germany by radio transmission. Lanyard, who was working clandestinely for Stafford in the scheme, must also clear his own name because Stafford is unexpectedly killed in a German air raid and therefore no one knows that Lanyard is secretly working on behalf of England. Everyone believes that the Lone Wolf is acting as a spy for Germany.

The espionage aspects of the film hearken back to some of the original novels about the Lone Wolf by Louis Joseph Vance and therefore give this film an added interest. The change in locale to London and the primarily British cast also bring freshness to the series. Hillary Brooke plays Pamela Stafford and although Brooke was an American, her naturally cultured voice makes her seem British upon occasion, even when not appearing in a film set in England. Brooke, who is a blond in many of her screen appearances, is quite attractive in this movie, in a rare appearance as a brunette. Kurt Katch, a Polish actor, does an excellent turn as the evil Nazi Gustave Sossel, somewhat unconcerned when he accidentally kills his assistant Wells, exultant when he believes he has successfully transmitted the beam detector plans back to Germany, and then panicking when he realizes his scheme has failed.

One of the most interesting scenes in the film occurs when Lanyard tries to retrace his steps to Stossel's hideout, where he was taken the night before while blindfolded. Lanyard had counted steps and turns on his original journey and remembers several unusual sounds that he heard on the walk. The next day, Jamison once again walks the Lone Wolf down the street blindfolded, and Lanyard uses those remembered sounds as guides to the German's hideout. The two discover that the remembered sound of a high whistle came from a peanut vendor's equipment, the sound of tapping came from the cane of a blind man walking down the street, and the sound of a high squeak came from the sign on a bar which was swinging in the wind. This interesting sequence, which does make the film seem like a true detective story, particularly one from the early 1900s, leads to the suspenseful conclusion of the story in a restaurant full of Nazi spies and in the basement of the restaurant where Lanyard and the others have been captured.

The one irritation in the film involves the appearance of Inspector Crane and Dickens, who happen to be in England when this is all going on and happen to be assisting Scotland Yard in its investigation. There was no need to shoehorn these two New York policemen into a spy story in England just because they were regular members of the cast. Even though

Dickens' part is blessedly small and he is not as annoying as he usually is in the series, Crane and Dickens are still a distraction from the main story line.

For a movie shot in Hollywood, this feature provides an excellent feel of London during the German blitz, with blackouts, air raid wardens, bomb shelters and German air attacks. There is particularly effective usage of stock footage from a raid on London used near the end of the movie. With an interesting tale of spies in England effortlessly weaved among scenes of wartime London, *Counter-Espionage* is one of the best films in the Lone Wolf series.

ONE DANGEROUS NIGHT (1943)

Although it starts with an intriguing premise, *One Dangerous Night* is by far the weakest of the Lone Wolf movies to date. As the film opens, blackmailer Harry Cooper has invited three attractive young women to his house to continue extorting them over the gambling debts they have run up. The women are Eve Andrews, who is about to be married to the wealthy Johnnie Sheldon; Sonia Beaudine, who is married to a wealthy physician; and Jane Merrick, a successful Broadway actress. Cooper demands that each of them turn over a valuable piece of jewelry to him. When Cooper leaves the room for a minute, the three decide to band together and defy his blackmail demands. The lights suddenly go out and when they come back on, Cooper has been shot to death.

Also, Cooper has instructed his valet, Arthur, to make the arrangements so that Cooper can flee the country that night by airplane in the company of an unknown woman. Unbeknownst to Cooper, Arthur is planning a double-cross by having his two partners rob Cooper of the jewelry he is supposed to take from his blackmail victims that night.

The difficulty in devising a plot this complex was in squeezing the Lone Wolf into the story. This was accomplished by having Eve suffer a flat tire on the way to Cooper's house, Lanyard and Jamison giving her a ride to Cooper's house, and Jamison stealing Eve's purse for no reason other than to get the story line going. Since Lanyard has forsaken his former life of crime, he insists that he and Jamison go back to Cooper's house and return Eve's bag. When they arrive, the three women have left and the Lanyard and Jamison discover Cooper's body. Rather than simply calling the police, Lanyard fools around too long, leading to his and Jamison's arrest for the crime. In a novel plot idea, but only if one has never seen a Lone Wolf or Boston Blackie movie, the Lone Wolf must escape the police and then attempt to clear his name by finding the real murderer.

Thereafter, the plot meanders aimlessly, fuelled by coincidence after coincidence. The Lone Wolf goes to Eve's engagement party, where he runs into gossip columnist Sidney Shannon, who tags along on Lanyard's investigations. It does not take long for even the less than astute mystery fan to realize that Shannon must be the killer, or why was he ever included in the story and allowed to accompany the Lone Wolf on his murder investigation? Of course Shannon has no motive that is readily apparent to the viewer and there are no clues to his guilt, but there is still no doubt that he is the murderer.

Later in the movie, the Lone Wolf is back at Cooper's apartment when he happens to take a call from Arthur, Cooper's valet, who mistakenly believes he is talking to Cooper. What a coincidence! Arthur tells the Lone Wolf that the woman will be at the airport on time. That chance phone call gives Lanyard his only opportunity to solve the crime. Lanyard proceeds to the airport where he meets the woman who was supposed to leave the country with Cooper. He follows the woman to her apartment where he takes one of her calling cards. Lanyard thereby learns that the woman is the wife of Shannon, leading him to the conclusion that Shannon shot Cooper out of jealousy. But the Lone Wolf has unfairly withheld the important clue of the calling card from the viewer, eliminating any element of fair play to the story. In addition, since most of the movie has been about either Cooper's blackmailing activities or the stealing of the jewelry, it is also unfair to the viewer to have the motive for the murder unrelated to the blackmailing of Cooper.

In addition to having a mystery plot that makes little sense, is based on coincidences, and does not play fair with the viewer, *One Dangerous Night* is also deadly dull. Frankly, not much happens during the film. For once even Jamison, as played by Eric Blore, is more irritating than entertaining, with his actions making absolutely no sense. His trick of thrusting out his lower lip when he is upset is particularly annoying in this movie. Inspector Crane has become less competent with each film and here has become more comic relief than good detective. What happened to the well-written and well-performed role of Inspector Crane from *The Lone Wolf Returns*?

Some of the actresses are attractive, such as Marguerite Chapman as Eve Andrews and Margaret Hayes as Patricia Shannon. The role of Dickens is mercifully small. Other than that, it is hard to find many positives with the film, which is a true disaster.

Note on the Cast: Harry Cooper is played by Gerald Mohr, who would replace Warren William as the Lone Wolf in three later films in the series. Eric Blore would play Jamison in all of Mohr's Lone Wolf films.

PASSPORT TO SUEZ (1943)

This was the ninth and last film in which Warren William appeared in his most famous role as the Lone Wolf. The films about the Lone Wolf starring William were inconsistent at best, and with the exception of *The Lone Wolf Takes a Chance*, never equaled the quality of the Melvyn Douglas and Francis Lederer films of the 1930s. However, the series ended on a high note, as *Passport to Suez* is an engaging if unremarkable film.

The action has moved to Egypt, where Lanyard has gone on a secret mission for the British government. That is immediate good news for the viewer, as that means Inspector Crane and his inept assistant Dickens cannot be shoehorned into the plot. Lanyard and Jamison are staying at a hotel owned by Johnny Booth, a good friend of Lanyard's from America. Johnny's nightclub has the feel of Rick's Café American from *Casablanca*, as it is filled with an international mixture of locals, tourists, and most importantly spies. For that reason, it is difficult to get a handle on the various characters and whether they are on the side of right or wrong, which adds to the intrigue of the story.

Johnny Booth is played by Sheldon Leonard, who often played low-grade criminals in the movies, and perhaps for that reason it is hard to be convinced that he is on Lanyard's side, even though he is supposed to be a good friend of Lanyard's. Booth smokes a cigarette with an extender, surely making him a particularly suspicious character. There are three spies, Cezanne, Rembrandt and Whistler, who flit in and out of the story, and each of their motives is hard to discern. Two of them suffer particularly brutal deaths during the course of the film. Jamison's son Donald, a lieutenant in the Navy, makes his first and only appearance in the series, and he brings along a fiancée, Valerie King, a war correspondent. At first Valerie seems okay but Booth is suspicious of her, especially after she is discovered with a fake passport.

The main plot involves a German plan to steal the charts of mine fields in the Suez Canal. They cleverly use Lanyard as a diversion, forcing him to commit one theft while they steal the plans they truly want. At the same time they incriminate the Lone Wolf in the espionage. It is a clever trick, once again highlighting the unexpectedness of the story. Also, once the plans are stolen, there is dissension among the ranks of the spies. This leads to an exciting conclusion, with Lanyard shooting at the spies from an airplane, in a sense executing the two of them. It is a rare Lone Wolf film that has an action-packed climax and it is a decided plus for the film.

One scene in *Passport to Suez* is quite striking, with spy Rembrandt shooting spy Cezanne on a public street. As Cezanne starts to run away from Rembrandt, there is a view down the street from behind Rembrandt's back as Rembrandt raises and shoots his gun. Cezanne is hit before he can throw his knife at Rembrandt, stumbles off again, and then without a cut, Rembrandt hits Cezanne with a second shot. There are then some close-ups before the third and fatal shot hits Cezanne, who collapses on the sidewalk. The scene is shot with a sudden burst of style in a film with an otherwise unexceptional directorial effort, making the killing of Cezanne the highlight of the film.

The comedy in *Passport to Suez* is kept to a minimum, essentially limited to Jamison complaining about being constantly abducted and tied up. By the time of this film, Warren William and Eric Blore had achieved a comfort level with their characters and each other, providing just the level of performance that the viewer expects. While the only things remarkable about the film may be the discovery that Jamison's first name is Llewellyn (although in *The Lone Wolf in London* [1947], his first name is Claudius) and that Jamison has a son, nevertheless, because of its always surprising plot and action-filled climax, *Passport to Suez* is a worthy ending to the Warren William Lone Wolf films.

The Later Films

THE NOTORIOUS LONE WOLF (1946)

After a three-year absence, the Lone Wolf finally returns to the silver screen, with Gerald Mohr replacing Warren William as the ex-cracksman, William Davidson taking over the role of Inspector Crane, and happily Crane's assistant Dickens nowhere to be found. The one carryover from the Warren William films is Eric Blore, who still plays the part of Jamison, Lanyard's trusty and sometimes light-fingered valet.

One would think that with such a long break in the production of Lone Wolf movies, the filmmakers would have an abundance of clever new plot ideas ready to engage the Lone Wolf. Unfortunately that is not the case. Indeed, *The Notorious Lone Wolf* has almost no plot at all, and as for clever and new, well, there is none of that either.

The film opens with about 20 minutes or so of irrelevant shtick by the Lone Wolf and his companions, although during this period mention is made of the theft of a valuable sapphire from an Indian prince. The real story begins when Lanyard goes to the Marquis Club to try to convince one Dick Hale to give up Lili, a dancer at the Club, and return to his wife. Since none of the previous Lone Wolf films in the Columbia series were soap operas, it is reasonable to expect that the stolen sapphire will somehow coincidentally show up at the Club and that the sole reason for the plot point of the marital difficulties between Hale and his wife is to get Lanyard into the Marquis Club at just the appropriate time.

Of course that is exactly what happens. Apparently Stonely, the owner of the Club, stole the sapphire and hid it in the headwear of Lili, who performs a provocative dance at the Club just after Lanyard arrives. Also in the Club are the Prince of Rapur and his assistant, who are there to attempt to reclaim the sapphire from whoever stole it. Lanyard, watching Lili's dance while sitting at a front table, immediately recognizes the valuable jewel in Lili's costume. After Lili's dance is over, Dick Hale and Lanyard proceed to the dancer's dressing room, but before they get there, they hear a shot. They then find that Lili has been killed and the sapphire is missing. Despite the fact that Lanyard has a perfect alibi, because he was in the hallway with Hale when the shot was fired, Lanyard is accused of the crime. Of course, perhaps he should not have picked up the gun after Lili was shot, but then the movie needed a plot and after all this time it finally got one. Lanyard is off to recover the jewel, find the murderer and clear his own name. Does that scenario sound familiar?

It is somewhat disconcerting to see Gerald Mohr in the title role in *The Notorious Lone Wolf,* as Warren William was so closely identified with the part by this time. More significantly, Mohr is not very good. He plays the role for comedy rather than mystery, delivering most of his lines in a flippant manner, as if he knows he is in the film solely to generate laughs. William often had material just as bad as Mohr does in this film, but while William often tried to get laughs, there was an underlying seriousness to his performance that is lacking in that of Mohr. Note that Mohr's accent disappears from time to time when he is impersonating the Prince's assistant, making this a particularly sloppy performance. Eric Blore is fine as usual as Jamison, except that Blore seems to have aged considerably since his last appearance and the part now seems to have become only that of a comic sidekick and not much else.

The film is full of vaudeville comedy, such as trying to hide a dead body in a bed that pulls down from a closet, Jamison impersonating the deaf prince and pretending he cannot hear Lanyard, a mouse appearing out of nowhere and running up Jamison's pants, and the oft-repeated shtick of Lanyard and his girlfriend trying to be alone but always being interrupted by third parties. From a critical perspective, none of it is funny. This book, however, is not about comedies; it is about mysteries. As to analyzing the mystery aspects of the film, that cannot be done because there is little if any mystery to the story.

This film is awful.

THE LONE WOLF IN MEXICO (1947)

Although it takes a long time getting to it, *The Lone Wolf in Mexico* has a particularly puzzling mystery to tell, involving real jewels, fake jewels, a crooked gambling casino, safe cracking and two sudden murders. While the explanation at the end for all that has gone on before lacks credibility, the film is still an enjoyable experience, at least for a while.

Michael Lanyard and his valet Jamison are vacationing in Mexico when Lanyard encounters Liliane Dumont, a fellow thief and former love interest. Liliane invites Lanyard and Jamison to dinner at the El Paseo club, along with her wealthy friend Mrs. Van Weir, who likes to gamble at the El Paseo club's private casino. Mrs. Van Weir has been losing substantial sums and so has Sharon Montgomery, the wife of jewel merchant Charles Montgomery. Sharon has been financing her gambling habit by giving her personal jewelry to the casino's owner, Mr. Henderson, as collateral for the casino's loans to her, which Sharon promptly loses at his casino, putting her even more into debt. The situation is further complicated by Liliane's husband Leon, a croupier at the casino and another former thief whom

Lanyard knows. Leon meets with Lanyard in the casino's garden and offers him a partnership in some criminal enterprise. Before Lanyard can learn the details, Leon is shot to death.

After framing Jamison for the theft of one of her pieces of jewelry, Sharon blackmails Lanyard into stealing her jewels back from the casino safe. Lanyard reluctantly does so but once he examines the baubles, he is surprised to learn that the jewels are fakes. When Lanyard enlightens Sharon as to his discovery, she still takes back the jewels and gives them to her husband for safe keeping. After Charles Montgomery puts the fake jewels into his safe, Lanyard steals them back and returns them to the casino safe. Montgomery reports the theft of his jewels to the police and the next day, Henderson is mystified as to how he has the jewels in his safe after they were also stolen from Mr. Montgomery. It is a perplexing matter, especially after Sharon's murdered body suddenly turns up in the casino garden.

While the mystery of the real jewels and the fake jewels is clearly bewildering to the viewer, it must have also perplexed the writers since they were unable to provide a reasonable explanation for the strange chain of events. How did the fake jewelry get into the casino safe in the first place? If Liliane provided them as part of a double-cross on Henderson, how did Sharon still have one piece of fake jewelry on her person? If Sharon knew the jewels were fakes, why did she want the Lone Wolf to steal them back? Why did George Montgomery, a jewelry expert, not realize that the jewels his wife had given him for safe keeping were fakes?

The explanation for the two murders also strains credulity. For example, if Leon was killed for disclosing information to Lanyard, what criminal proposal was Leon intending to make to Lanyard at the beginning of the film? There was nothing that Lanyard could plausibly add to the jewel smuggling operation that was then proceeding with great success. This film typifies Raymond Chandler's criticism of poorly plotted whodunits—the murders are committed solely for the purpose of providing corpses and for no other reason.

Mysteries can survive plot deficiencies if there is some style and panache in the direction and writing of the film. A famous case in point is Alfred Hitchcock's 1935 classic, *The 39 Steps*. At one point, Richard Hannay is arrested by the police in a small town. Rather than even bother to detail how Hannay escapes from the police station, Hitchcock simply pulls his camera back from the outside of the station to the other side of the street. Suddenly, Hannay bursts out of the station window and the chase is on. No explanation is given for Hannay's escape from the police and the audience never demands one, as the romp has been so enjoyable up to that point and Hannay's escape is just one more exciting bit of business in the classic film.

Similarly, late in *The Lone Wolf in Mexico*, Lanyard is arrested and placed in jail. Later that night, there is an outside shot of the jail building, with the bars to Lanyard's cell cut and bent. Lanyard has escaped, but no explanation is given for how he was able to cut and bend the metal bars of the window. Since the plot of the movie was already starting to unravel at this point, there needed to be some explanation for Lanyard's escape. None was forthcoming. This scene is just another example of the poor plotting at the end of the film, which eventually drives the whole production down.

Director D. Ross Lederman is no Alfred Hitchcock and this film is not *The 39 Steps*. Indeed, it is not even *The Falcon in Mexico*, a much better film set in the same locale. *The Lone Wolf in Mexico* is perhaps half of a good mystery, and therefore may be worth a view for the setup of the mystery, but surely not for the denouement.

THE LONE WOLF IN LONDON (1947)

This is the last of the Gerald Mohr Lone Wolf films and it is the best of the three. Leslie Goodwins, directing his only film in the series, imparts a little bit of style to the production, something sorely missing from the previous two films. Gerald Mohr gives his best performance in the role of Michael Lanyard, seldom back sliding into delivering his lines as if he believes he is performing in a comedy rather than a mystery, something Mohr often did in the prior two films. The return to a London setting after a five-year absence (*Counter-Espionage* [1942]) is a welcome change for the series, imparting some of the cosmopolitan settings of the original Louis Joseph Vance novels, aided by utilizing a substantially English cast.

Reformed cracksman Michael Lanyard is in England to work on a book he is writing about famous jewels, a seemingly innocent venture. However, when the priceless Eyes of the Nile diamonds are stolen, Scotland Yard immediately suspects Lanyard of the theft, not believing he has truly reformed. After Lanyard's encounter with the police, he and Jamison receive an invitation from Sir John Kelmscott to visit his country estate. There Sir John admits to Lanyard that he is experiencing financial difficulties and needs to obtain a large loan on some of his valuable jewels. Because of Lanyard's connections in the jewelry business, Sir John wants Lanyard to arrange the loan. Lanyard is unsure as to whether he should agree to the task, because given his reputation with the police, he is afraid he may be unjustly accused of stealing the jewels.

In need of funds, Lanyard finally agrees and Sir John dispatches his butler, Robards, to bring the jewels to Lanyard at a gem dealer's store. Along the way, Robards is killed and the jewels stolen. There are a number of shady characters involved in the matter, any of whom could be a thief and a killer, such as beautiful Iris Chatham, a stage performer, Monty Beresford, the man who discovered Iris and has recently come into a large fortune, and David Woolerton, soon to be the son-in-law of Sir John, and who is very suspicious of Lanyard. In the end, Lanyard identifies the true villain and recovers all of the jewels, including the Eyes of the Nile diamonds.

The revelation in this film is the performance of Evelyn Ankers in the role of the flirtatious and evil Iris Chatham. Ankers is best known today as the queen of the 1940s horror films at Universal, from her roles in *The Wolf Man* (1941) through *Jungle Woman* (1944) as well as for her appearances in the Universal Sherlock Holmes and Inner Sanctum mystery series. Ankers seldom played the part of a villain, and she makes the most of her opportunity in *The Lone Wolf in London*, attempting to keep three men on the string at the same time she is purloining valuable diamonds right under their noses. Ankers is gorgeous when she first appears in the film in her tight-fitting gown, and even shows a little bit of leg late in the film when she finishes a stage performance and returns to her dressing room. This may be Ankers' best performance in films. She never looked more beautiful. It is a shame that she retired from the screen just a few years after this film was released.

The Lone Wolf in London also marked Eric Blore's last appearance as Jamison, the Lone Wolf's trusty sidekick. Blore seemed to have aged substantially in the prior films and that detracted from the effectiveness of his performances. Here Blore seems to have gained a substantial amount of weight, looks much better and gives an energetic performance, much like the ones he gave at the beginning of the series.

While all of the acting is quite good, it is the plot that contributes most to the effectiveness of the film. Even before the opening credits, there is a long shot of an apparent

In *The Lone Wolf in London* (1947) Inspector Garvey (Denis Green, center) shows Sir John Kelmscott (Vernon Steele, seated on the left) the jewels he has recovered from the Lone Wolf (Gerald Mohr, seated at right). The Lone Wolf does not seem all that upset that he is being accused of the theft of the jewels. Also shown are Sir John's daughter, Ann Kelmscott (Nancy Saunders, standing at left) and her fiancé, David Woolerton (Richard Fraser, standing at right).

burglary, shot from above, giving this film a fast start to the movie, atypical for the series. Thereafter, it takes some time for the plot to get going, but matters pick up once Sir John makes his proposal to Lanyard. The surprise murder of the butler, Robards, is perplexing to say the least, with a number of potential suspects for the crime. The double- and triple-crosses at the end of the film are surprising, and it can be difficult for the viewer to keep up with all the plot developments, something one expects in a good mystery.

It is disconcerting to see Lanyard short of funds and trying to hold down his expenses until he can make some money. That is not the independently wealthy, tuxedo-wearing, world-traveling Michael Lanyard that viewers had come to know and admire. But this is somewhat nitpicking. For a film so late in a long mystery series, *The Lone Wolf in London* is a pleasant surprise.

THE LONE WOLF AND HIS LADY (1949)

After a two year absence from the screen, the Lone Wolf is back, with Ron Randall playing Michael Lanyard and Alan Mowbray playing Jamison. Randall is actually quite good as the ex-cracksman, and he is substantially better in the role than Gerald Mohr was. Mohr always seemed to be playing the part for laughs, while there is an earnestness about Randall that makes his performance much more convincing. Mowbray is good as Jamison, as were all of the other actors who played the part (Raymond Walburn in *The Lone Wolf Returns* [1935] and Leonard Carey in *The Lone Wolf Spy Hunt* [1939]), but Eric Blore had made the role his own over 11 features and he is sorely missed in this film. William Frawley was brought in to play the part of Inspector Crane and while Frawley is also quite good, as he usually was in these types of supporting roles, he cannot match the work of Thurston Hall as Inspector Crane, especially in the earlier films when the part of Crane was well-written, as it often was not in the later features. Here Crane is just another of the traditional less-than-bright police inspectors who seem to inhabit these types of films.

However, while the acting is good, the rest of the film is not. By this late date in the series, the screenwriters must have been phoning in their scripts, since the storyline shows little originality or cleverness. The early part of the film seems like a part of the Big Town series, as it is about a newspaper, *The Daily Register*, trying to reinvent itself to increase circulation. Lanyard accidentally meets the new crime beat reporter, who decides to interview him for a series of front-page stories about his career. Then someone gets the bright idea to have Lanyard cover the unveiling of the valuable Tahara diamond at the Tanner Gallery as a special reporter for *The Daily Register*. That is both good news and bad news for the storyline. Finally, after about 20 minutes of film, there is some hope of a mystery actually appearing in this mystery film. On the other hand, are there any regular viewers of the Lone Wolf films who do not expect the Tahara diamond to be stolen and the Lone Wolf accused of the crime?

Even with that hackneyed framework of a traditional Lone Wolf story, the writers still could not devise a cogent or interesting script. The rest of the story is full of coincidences, undercutting any credibility the script may have had. For example, Jamison is on the roof of the building when the theft occurs and he happens to spot some suspicious characters in the next building over, who happen to be the true thieves. Then, Lanyard escapes from the building where the theft occurred by jumping onto the terrace of that other building, next to the window where the thieves are trying to have the diamond cut, also coincidentally solving the crime. That is not all. When Jamison throws the valuable stone out the window, it lands many floors below, right on the street where newspaper reporter and Lanyard's ally Grace Duffy can recover the same. Were the writers really trying? There is also a strange re-writing of the part of Jamison, with Jamison concerned that Lanyard may return to his life of crime with the temptation of the Tahara diamond, while in the prior films, Jamison seemed to be encouraging the Lone Wolf to return to his past criminal life.

There is one surprise, late in *The Lone Wolf and His Lady*, involving the lapidary who cut the Tahara diamond. There is much humor in the film, some of which is actually quite funny. Collette Lyons delivers an amusing performance as Martha Frisbie, an attractive blonde who has an interest in Jamison. However, there is little else to recommend in the film. Columbia Pictures simply made one Lone Wolf movie too many. At least the studio had the sense not to continue the series beyond this film.

After The Lone Wolf

The Lone Wolf character was slow to come to radio but it finally happened in 1948, when the film series had just about reached its conclusion. The show, which was on the

Mutual Radio Network, starred Gerald Mohr, who was then playing Michael Lanyard in the movies. Mohr was eventually replaced in the lead role by Walter Coy. In this version of the character, the Lone Wolf was now an American private eye, although one the police still did not trust. Jamison was also a character.

After the end of the movie series in 1949, there were no more Lone Wolf films. There was, however, a television series about the Lone Wolf that played in syndication for one season starting in 1954. The show sometimes went under the title *Streets of Danger*. There were only 39 episodes produced. Michael Lanyard was played by British actor Louis Hayward, who originated the role of the movie Saint in *The Saint in New York* (1938).

After Eric Blore's last appearance in the series in 1947, he made only a few other appearances in film or television. He died in 1959. Similarly, Warren William only made a few appearances in films after he left the series in 1943. He died from cancer in 1948, at the age of 53. After his movie and radio career wound down, Gerald Mohr guest-starred in numerous television shows from the late 1940s into the 1960s. Mohr died in 1968.

3

Sherlock Holmes
The World's Greatest Detective

While few would dispute the designation, the title of "The World's Greatest Detective" comes from a plaque erected at the Reichenbach Falls in Switzerland in 1947, commemorating the spot where Sherlock Holmes and Professor Moriarty apparently fell to their deaths at the end of the Holmes short story, "The Final Problem." According to the plaque, the date of the fictional fall was May 4, 1891.

If Sherlock Holmes is not the greatest detective of all time, he is surely the most famous. In addition to the novels and short stories by Sir Arthur Conan Doyle, there have been numerous written works by other authors and, of course there have been numerous radio shows, television programs, stage plays and feature films that starred the great detective. Without a doubt, the most famous Sherlock Holmes movies of them all were the 14 movies made by Basil Rathbone and Nigel Bruce in Hollywood from 1939 to 1946.

Background

THE CANON

Even those who have not read any of the Sherlock Holmes stories are likely to recognize the name of the author, Sir Arthur Conan Doyle. Conan Doyle was born in Edinburgh, Scotland, on May 22, 1859. He entered medical school at Edinburgh University in 1876 and received his degree in 1881. While in school, Conan Doyle began writing short stories, publishing his first one in 1879.

After becoming a doctor, Conan Doyle divided his time between establishing a medical practice and becoming a successful author. In March 1886, he started writing the novel which was published in 1887 under the title *A Study in Scarlet*. This was the work that introduced Sherlock Holmes to Dr. Watson and the two of them to both English and American audiences. Conan Doyle followed that work with a second Holmes novel, *The Sign of the Four*, but it was not until Conan Doyle conceived the idea of writing a series of short stories about Holmes that the Holmes character achieved popularity and immortality. The first short story about Holmes was "A Scandal in Bohemia." It was published in the *Strand Magazine* in England in 1891 and then in America later the same year.

In all, Conan Doyle wrote four novels and 56 short stories about the great detective. To Holmes aficionados, these works are known as the "Canon" or the "Sacred Writings." In 1902, Doyle was knighted by King Edward VII for his services to England as a writer during the Boer War. Thus, all the credits to the Hollywood Holmes movies refer to the author as "Sir Arthur Conan Doyle." Conan Doyle passed away in 1930.

PRIOR FILMS

There were numerous films made about Sherlock Holmes, starting long before the Basil Rathbone series was produced. Because of the number of films, any detailed discussion of those works is beyond the scope of this book. Suffice it to say, Holmes appeared in a short silent film as early as 1903, with the interesting title *Sherlock Holmes Baffled*. In 1916 there was a silent movie version of William Gillette's famous stage play about Holmes, in which Gillette starred. In all, it is estimated that there were over 125 silent films about Sherlock Holmes, many of which were shorts.

In 1929, Clive Brook played the great detective in *The Return of Sherlock Holmes*, the first sound movie about Sherlock Holmes. The film involved a murder around the time of the wedding of Dr. Watson's daughter, with her fiancé accused of the crime. Over the next decade there were numerous sound interpretations of the character on the screen, culminating in the decision by Twentieth Century–Fox to produce its own version of Conan Doyle's most famous Sherlock Holmes novel, *The Hound of the Baskervilles*, in 1939.

THE FILM SERIES

As one version of the story goes, the head of Twentieth Century–Fox, Darryl F. Zanuck, was at a cocktail party when he suddenly turned to British actor Basil Rathbone and stated that Rathbone would be the perfect Sherlock Holmes. Plans were immediately made for a lavish production of *The Hound of the Baskervilles*, Conan Doyle's most famous work about the great detective. The movie was set in Victorian times, making this the first Holmes movie to be deliberately set in the time period of Conan Doyle's stories. Nigel Bruce was cast as Dr. Watson. The film was released in March of 1939.

The movie was very successful and Fox followed it with a sequel, released just five months later in August, 1939, also starring Rathbone and Bruce. The film was *The Adventures of Sherlock Holmes*, purportedly another adaptation of the famous William Gillette stage play. The film was not as successful as the first film and Fox let the idea of a Sherlock Holmes film series lapse.

In 1942, Universal decided to resurrect the idea of a series of movies about the great detective and his assistant. According to *Hollywood Reporter*, as quoted at the *Turner Classic Movies* website, Universal paid $300,000 for a seven-year lease on the film rights to 21 Sherlock Holmes stories controlled by the Arthur Conan Doyle estate. Because of that large investment, Universal did not want to make the same mistake that Fox made in *The Hound of the Baskervilles*, where Rathbone was billed below Richard Greene, who played the young heir to the Baskerville fortune in the film, thus downplaying the importance of the lead characters. Each of the Universal movies therefore started with a shot of Basil Rathbone and Nigel Bruce before the credits, with their names and the characters they portrayed, emphasizing that each movie was part of a long series of mystery films about the world's greatest detective.

In all, there were twelve Holmes films released by Universal, with the last one being *Dressed to Kill* (1946). Each was set during the 1940s, unlike the first two films from Twentieth Century–Fox which were set in the original time period of the Conan Doyle stories.

Basil Rathbone played Sherlock Holmes in all of the movies. Rathbone was born in South Africa in 1892. He began working in silent films, first in England and then sporadically in America, but reached his greatest success during the 1930s, playing villains in adaptations of famous works of literature, such as *David Copperfield* (1935) and *Anna Karenina* (1935), and dueling with Errol Flynn in *Captain Blood* (1935) and *The Adventures of Robin Hood* (1938). For mystery and horror fans, other than his most famous role as Sherlock Holmes, Rathbone is best-remembered for playing Philo Vance in *The Bishop Murder Case* (1930) and Baron Wolf von Frankenstein in *Son of Frankenstein* (1939).

Nigel Bruce was born in 1895 and became a stage actor in 1920. He began appearing in American films in the 1930s, with good roles in films such as *Treasure Island* (1934) and *Becky Sharp* (1935). Of interest to mystery fans is that he appeared in two Alfred Hitchcock movies, *Rebecca* (1940) and *Suspicion* (1941).

Other regulars in the series were Mary Gordon as Mrs. Hudson, the landlady for Holmes and Watson, and Dennis Hoey as Inspector Lestrade of Scotland Yard. While Sherlock Holmes fans often criticize how Dr. Watson is portrayed as a bumbler in a number of these films, as contrasted with a more respectful characterization in the Conan Doyle works, one of the minor delights of the Universal films are the scenes in which Watson subtly insults Lestrade's alleged detective acumen.

Beginning with *Sherlock Holmes and the Secret Weapon* (1942), all of the films in the series were directed by Roy William Neill. Neill was born in Ireland in 1887 and began directing films in Hollywood during the silent era. During the course of his career, he specialized in directing mystery and horror films, such as *The Lone Wolf Returns* (1935) and *Frankenstein Meets the Wolf Man* (1943).

The film series could have continued after 1946 but Rathbone was so typecast in the role of Holmes he felt that if the series were not curtailed, he would never be able to find other film work. After 14 films with Rathbone and Bruce playing the sleuthing pair it would have been impossible to replace Rathbone with another actor, and so Universal canceled the series.

The Twentieth Century–Fox Films

THE HOUND OF THE BASKERVILLES (1939)

After the death of Sir Charles Baskerville under suspicious circumstances, Dr. Mortimer, concerned about the safety of Sir Henry Baskerville, the heir to the Baskerville estate, consults Sherlock Holmes. Mortimer relates a Baskerville legend about a vicious hound that stalks the heirs to the family fortune. Was Sir Charles a victim of the hound and is Sir Henry next?

Holmes pretends he is not concerned but nevertheless asks Dr. Watson to accompany Sir Henry back to the ancestral home while Holmes is off on other business. Back in Dartmoor, Watson discovers that an escaped convict is haunting the moors, and then to the surprise of everyone (except Sherlock Holmes, of course) there is indeed a vicious hound on the moors. However, it is being used by a distant relative of the Baskervilles to kill off the main family line so that he can inherit the Baskerville fortune. In an exciting scene at the end of the movie, Holmes saves Sir Henry's life from the vicious animal attack and reveals the identity of the villain.

The Hound of the Baskervilles sometimes plays more like a horror movie than a mystery film, as highlighted by the attack and rescue scene near the end, which is the focal point of the film. Sir Henry decides to walk back from the Stapletons' house across the moors to Baskerville Hall, believing that all threats to him have been eliminated. That gives John Stapleton the opportunity he wants to release the vicious hound onto the trail of Sir Henry. At the same time, Holmes and Watson are rushing back to the moors in order to save Sir Henry's life. The moors are partially enshrouded in fog.

The sequence is shot without mood music and from the time Sir Henry starts his walk across the moors until Holmes rescues him, there is almost no dialogue. The primary sounds are footsteps, the rustling of tree branches, the opening of the vault where the hound is hidden, and the growling and howling of the hound. The lack of music heightens the suspense and the sense of foreboding, as the hound is stalking Sir Henry across the landscape. Also, the cuts between various parties involved in the action are not the quick cuts or montage that are usually employed in this type of scene, but rather are slow cuts between Sir Henry, the hound, Holmes and Watson and even Beryl Stapleton back at her house. When the attack finally comes, it is first shown in a long shot, so that just the silhouettes of Sir Henry and the beast are visible.

The entire sequence seems to be shot in a counter-intuitive manner (no music, dialogue or quick cuts), but the director is not trying to create a sense of excitement in the scene. He is trying to create a feeling of apprehension and horror and the technique used is quite successful. To cap the sequence off, at the climax the director uses close-ups of the dog attacking Sir Henry, turning the anticipated horror into a real horror. At that point, the hound is everything the mythical legend of the Baskervilles said it would be and more. It is this sequence in the film, superbly directed by Sidney Lanfield, that makes the movie.

The acting in *The Hound of the Baskervilles*, as would be the case throughout the entire film series, is excellent. Lionel Atwill plays Dr. Mortimer, a rare non-villainous role for Atwill at this point in his career. Atwill brings his usual brand of sophistication and intensity to the part, and of course, he would go on to play Professor Moriarty later in the series. Atwill was often associated with horror films, and so was John Carradine, who plays the butler, Barryman. Carradine imbues that part with a hint of evil in a way that only Carradine could, making the butler a prime suspect in the case. Wendy Barrie, who is better known for appearing in The Saint and The Falcon mystery series from RKO, appears here as Beryl Stapleton. Barrie also gives an excellent performance and she probably looks lovelier here than in any of the other films in which she appeared. Barlowe Borland does an amusing turn as Franklin, the irascible neighbor of the Stapletons, starting a tradition in the series of great performances in very small roles.

Although Basil Rathbone does not receive top billing, the core performance in any Sherlock Holmes film is that of the great detective, and Rathbone brings an energy and enthusiasm to the role that was sometimes missing in his later screen portrayals of the great detective. When Holmes appears disguised as an itinerant peddler on the moors, even the sophisticated viewer cannot tell it is Basil Rathbone under the beard. Nigel Bruce is good as Dr. Watson although he has not yet grown into the role that he would later make his own. Here the part is written close to the characterization of Dr. Watson in the Conan Doyle stories and Watson has yet to become a figure of comic relief as he did in some of the later films from Universal. In *The Hound of the Baskervilles*, Watson is a competent assistant to Holmes, and indeed carries the middle portion of the story while Holmes is off investigating on his own.

The sets are terrific, particularly the large and foreboding Baskerville Hall, with its denuded landscaping on the outside and its shadowed rooms on the inside. The craggy, treeless moors where much of the action takes place seem realistic, intimidating even by sunlight and a place of horror when the fog enshrouds the terrain. Indeed, the enduring appeal of both the book and this movie are their aspects of horror, such as the legend of the strange beast, the howling during the night and finally the spotting of the large beast on the moors. Some of the style of this film was later adopted by Universal for its horror films of the 1940s.

Surprisingly, though, the movie seems flat in spots, with protracted periods of dialogue in which little action occurs. For example, after the death of Charles Baskerville at the beginning of the film, the movie has a long scene at the inquest, and then Dr. Mortimer reads about the legend of the hound to Holmes with an irrelevant flashback scene. Later, at Dartmoor, there is a scene with a séance that ends abruptly before the it starts and also a long dinner sequence at the Stapletons, all of which considerably slow down the pace of the film. Interspersed among the slow points, though, are some compelling moments such as a beautifully shot sequence of an attempted killing of Henry Baskerville while walking down a street in London, Watson investigating a mysterious light on the moors, and the sudden appearances of the escaped convict. These scenes do keep the story moving somewhat until the core sequence late in the movie involving the hound's attack on Henry.

The viewer is treated to a number of moments in the film that are homage to the original Conan Doyle stories or earlier incarnations of Holmes on the stage. There is the deerstalker cap that Holmes wears, the playing of the violin to allow Holmes to think, the investigation of Dr. Mortimer's cane to determine facts about its owner, the appearance of Holmes' landlady, Mrs. Hudson (played by Mary Gordon, a role she would reprise in later films) and the setting of the story in its true time period in 1889. There are the singular clues, such as the disappearance of a new boot of Sir Henry's, its sudden return, and then the disappearance of an old boot of Sir Henry's. At the end of the movie, with the crime solved, Holmes asks for his needle, a reference that would not be lost on even cursory readers of the Conan Doyle stories.

The Hound of the Baskervilles recreates the milieu of the original Holmes stories as no other movie in the series would. Even though the film does not quite live up to the great reputation it has acquired over time, this is clearly one of the best screen adaptations of the enduring Conan Doyle novel. It is worth seeing over and over again for many reasons, but particularly for the attack and rescue of Sir Henry on the moors.

Note on the Source Material: The novel, *The Hound of the Baskervilles*, was one of only four novels written by Sir Arthur Conan Doyle about Sherlock Holmes and it is far and away the best of the four novels. It was originally serialized in the *Strand Magazine* from August, 1901 to April, 1902, and then published in book form in 1902. It was published after Holmes' apparent death in "The Final Problem" and before his resurrection in "The Adventure of the Empty House," and so it is a remembrance of an adventure of Sherlock Holmes from several years before.

The movie is substantially based upon the book, in both important and minor matters. Thus, the book and the movie relate the same significant events of the story, such as the death of Sir Charles Baskerville by fright, the shadowing of Sir Henry Baskerville in London, Watson accompanying Sir Henry back to Baskerville Hall while Holmes is supposedly busy on other matters, an escaped convict on the moors, and the killing of the hound as it is attacking Sir Henry. The villain and the motive are also the same. The movie also takes small matters from the book, such as Holmes deducing certain characteristics of

Dr. Mortimer from the cane he left behind in Holmes' apartment, the London cabbie saying that the man who was shadowing Sir Henry gave his name as Sherlock Holmes, and the neighbor Franklin who enjoys suing people.

There are, however, a few significant differences between the two works. There is a character named Laura Lyons in the novel, who was in love with Stapleton and unknowingly drew Sir Charles outside his home on the night of his death. That character is missing from the movie. There is a scene in the movie after the killing of the hound where Stapleton tries to poison Sir Henry and Holmes unmasks Stapleton as the killer, a sequence which is original to the film. The scenes with the aborted séance and the dinner at the Stapletons are also original to the film.

The main difference between the two works is that in the novel Beryl Stapleton is secretly married to John Stapleton and is under his power. Sir Henry falls in love with Beryl, not knowing she is married. Beryl is somewhat aware of the schemes of her brother and it is Beryl who sends the warning note to Sir Henry in London, knowing that if he comes to Baskerville Hall, he will surely be killed.

The movie, on the other hand, provides a more traditional Hollywood ending, with Sir Henry and Beryl (who is Stapleton's sister and unaware of his crimes) truly falling in love and presumably marrying and living happily thereafter once John Stapleton's dastardly deeds are discovered. While that change works cinematically, there is never an explanation in the film as to who sent the warning note in London to Sir Henry. It could not have been Beryl, who knew nothing of her brother's crimes, nor could it have been anyone else. It is an anomaly best left unaddressed in any detailed analysis of the movie version.

The Adventures of Sherlock Holmes (1939)

Professor Moriarty makes it to the screen for the first of three appearances in the Basil Rathbone-Nigel Bruce Sherlock Holmes films, with the Napoleon of Crime played in this case by well-known character actor and movie villain George Zucco. In later films in the series, the part would be played by both Lionel Atwill and Henry Daniell, two excellent actors who gave wonderful performances in the role of the master criminal. Arguably, though, George Zucco's portrayal is the best-written and best-performed of the trio, as he personally challenges Sherlock Holmes to try to prevent the crime of the century, jousts with his valet while his valet is shaving Moriarty with a sharp razor, and mourns the death of a flower while plotting the killing of two innocent human beings. Zucco is quite believable as Moriarty, sometimes approaching his crimes from the detached perspective of a criminal tactician and other times reveling in the expected humiliation of his archrival, Sherlock Holmes.

Moriarty is after the Crown Jewels of England, which are under heavy guard at the Tower of London. He sends a letter to Sir Ronald Ramsgate, the guardian of the jewels, proclaiming that the valuable Star of Delhi emerald, now on its way to London from outside the country, will never reach the safety of the Tower. Moriarty's scheme is quite clever. He knows that Ramsgate will take the note to Holmes, who will have little interest in its contents as a result of a diversion Moriarty is about to create, and therefore once the Crown Jewels are stolen, Holmes will be humiliated in the eyes of the public.

The diversion Moriarty creates involves a note he sends to Lloyd Brandon, which has a picture of an albatross with a knife piercing Lloyd's body. Lloyds's sister, Ann, brings the note to Holmes because her father had received a similar note many years ago just before he was murdered. This is a puzzle in which Holmes has a great interest, and Moriarty stokes that interest by pretending to be an acquaintance of Ann's fiancé Jerrold Hunter, having Lloyd killed by a strange method that involves both strangling and beating, providing a clue that the killer has a club foot, and sending a note with the same drawing to Ann, suggesting that she may be killed on the day the Star of Delhi is to arrive in England. Holmes

Sherlock Holmes (Basil Rathbone, right) is pointing out some footprints in the ground to Dr. Watson (Nigel Bruce), in *The Adventures of Sherlock Holmes* (1939). Holmes deduces that the prints were made by a club-footed man, about five feet, eleven inches in height.

decides to concentrate on Ann's situation and leave the problems at the Tower of London to Dr. Watson, not a good idea when Professor Moriarty is around.

There is a strong difference of opinion among mystery fans as to which is the better film, *The Hound of the Baskervilles* or *The Adventures of Sherlock Holmes*. Not surprisingly, since the films came from the same studio in the same year, each has similar positives and negatives. The acting is superb in each with Nigel Bruce perhaps giving a more engaging performance in the second film, with just a little more humor associated with the part of Dr. Watson, presaging the development of the character in the later Universal films. The settings and attention to detail in recreating Victorian England are excellent in both movies, and while *The Hound of the Baskervilles* clearly employs more fog to create suspenseful situations, the latter film has more than enough fog when the story requires it. Both have an excellent beginning, sag in the middle and then reach suspenseful climaxes, here with Sherlock Holmes just preventing the murder of Ann Brandon and then rushing to the Tower of London to prevent the further misdeeds of Professor Moriarty. In *The Adventures of Sherlock Holmes*, the direction comes alive in those scenes at the end of the film, with effective use of shadows, close-ups and montage to create a feeling of suspense, foreboding and mystery.

For this viewer, however, *The Adventures of Sherlock Holmes* is a slight letdown from the prior film. Since *The Hound of the Baskervilles* is a fairly faithful adaptation of the Conan Doyle work, the film recreates the true feel of a Sherlock Holmes tale, a component which is lacking in the second film. Indeed, *The Adventures of Sherlock Holmes* is quite gimmicky. Professor Moriarty creates this complex plot concerning the Brandon family, commits one murder and attempts to commit another, just to throw Holmes off the scent of the robbery at the Tower of London. But why get Holmes involved in the first place? Just steal the jewels and write Holmes a letter later, humiliating him about the crime that was committed in his home city of London. It just seems unlikely that Conan Doyle's Napoleon of Crime would have intentionally involved The World's Greatest Detective in the Crime of the Century, substantially lessening its chances of success. Conan Doyle's Moriarty would have stolen the jewels, without bothering to play cat-and-mouse with Holmes. The plot of *The Adventures of Sherlock Holmes* therefore seems somewhat contrived.

Nevertheless, *The Adventures of Sherlock Holmes*, only the second Holmes film to be set in its true time period of Victorian England, is an excellent production. The story is cleverly written, excellently acted and skillfully directed. If it is not quite the equal of the first film in the series, it is surely far better than many of the Holmes films that came after, all the way up to the present day.

Note on the Source Material: According to the credits, *The Adventures of Sherlock Holmes* was based on the play *Sherlock Holmes* by William Gillette and Arthur Conan Doyle. The play was first performed in Buffalo, New York, on October 23, 1899, and then it moved to New York City, where it opened two weeks later at the Garrick Theatre. *Sherlock Holmes* played to capacity audiences at almost every performance for the next seven months. In addition to writing the play, William Gillette starred as the great detective. After a successful tour of the United States, the play opened in London at the Lyceum Theater on September 9, 1901, where it also played to capacity crowds. *Sherlock Holmes* then toured the English provinces, with the play sometimes performed as far north as Edinburgh, Conan Doyle's city of birth.

After 1902, William Gillette made a career of playing Holmes in the play he wrote.

The play was revived numerous times in America and England. Gillette even played the part of Sherlock Holmes in a 1916 silent movie adaptation of the play. It is said that Gillette performed the stage role about 1,300 times over his long career. He played the role for the last time in Princeton, New Jersey, on May 12, 1932. Gillette died five years later, on April 29, 1937, at the age of 83. The play has been revived a number of times since Gillette's death, including a successful run on Broadway starting in 1974.

It was William Gillette's genius to take the character of Professor Moriarty, who was well-known in 1899 from the last new Holmes' story that had been published to that date, "The Final Problem" (even though that short story was first published back in 1893), and bring him to the forefront of his play. It is probably because of Gillette's play that Professor Moriarty has become the lead villain in many Sherlock Holmes movies, even though the character essentially appeared in only one Conan Doyle story.

The Adventures of Sherlock Holmes carries over from the play the emphasis on Professor Moriarty as a master villain, but takes nothing else from the written work. There is no attempt in the play to steal the Crown Jewels of England or to terrorize the Brandon family. Rather, the MacGuffin in the play is the recovery of love letters that would embarrass a member of European royalty, a concept taken from "A Scandal in Bohemia." The second half of the play focuses on the struggle between Moriarty and Holmes, in a sense inspiring the movie. Nevertheless, it is not clear why the William Gillette play is cited in the credits as the source for *The Adventures of Sherlock Holmes*.

The Universal Films

SHERLOCK HOLMES AND THE VOICE OF TERROR (1942)

With Universal Pictures' release of *Sherlock Holmes and the Voice of Terror* in 1942, the Basil Rathbone/Nigel Bruce Sherlock Holmes series started in earnest. The time period of the Universal features was accelerated from the Victorian England of the Twentieth Century–Fox films and the Conan Doyle works to the contemporary period of the 1940s, giving the 12 Universal films a different feel and style than the two films from Fox. Instead of Holmes investigating mythical beasts on the moors of Dartmoor or the theft of valuable jewels, Holmes was immediately thrown into the fight against Nazi Germany during the Second World War.

Sherlock Holmes and the Voice of Terror begins in a compelling manner, with a montage of a string of successful sabotage efforts by Nazi Germany against both military and public targets in Britain. Each is announced over the radio by the sarcastic "Voice of Terror," a German propaganda instrument that taunts the British folk with news of the successful terrorist attacks by the Axis powers. The British Intelligence Inner Council appears helpless in its attempts to stop the Voice of Terror, and so one member, Sir Evan Barham, wants to call in Sherlock Holmes for assistance. Other members of the Council disagree, believing that while Holmes is a great detective, he is ill-equipped to handle espionage, sabotage and wartime activities. The fair-minded viewer would probably agree with the protesters on Council, but this is a Sherlock Holmes movie, so the great detective is hired for the job.

It turns out the employment of Holmes to thwart the espionage activities of the Axis powers is an excellent idea, as Holmes eventually prevents a Nazi invasion of England and unmasks the mole in the Inner Council. Unfortunately there is no clear explanation of how Holmes manages to solve the case. Most of Holmes' information is obtained off-screen, so the viewer has no chance of solving the crimes along with Holmes. As a result, despite the feature's strong beginning, the quality of the film starts to deteriorate almost immediately.

Holmes' first step on the case is apparently to ask an operative, Gavin, to investigate something, but since this event occurs off-screen, the viewer is unaware of it. Suddenly Gavin falls into Holmes' apartment with a knife in his back. Before dying, he utters one word, "Christopher," and so Holmes and Watson are off to the Limehouse district of London to try to learn the significance of the word. With the assistance of Kitty, Gavin's widow, Holmes and Watson proceed to the Christopher Docks where they meet the local Nazi head, Meade, whom Holmes first captures and then lets escape. Holmes then sends Kitty to Meade's house to act as Holmes' mole, hoping to discover the Nazis' plans for additional sabotage. However, if Holmes already knew where Meade lived, and presumably everything about him, what was the point of the trip to the docks?

While there are two prime suspects for the mole in the Inner Circle — Anthony Lloyd, who was never happy with Holmes' involvement in the matter in the first place, and Sir Evan Barham, who first employed Holmes and for that reason alone cannot be the mole — in fact it turns out that Barham is the mole. Holmes had found out that Barham was really a German national living in England (named Heinrich Von Bork), who substituted for the real Evan Barham many years before. How Holmes learned that information is never revealed to the viewer, a typical problem with this film. The explanation as to why Barham talked the Inner Council into employing Holmes is unconvincing. The last thing Barham would have wanted was for the greatest detective in the world to be hot in his pursuit.

The acting in the film is impeccable. Henry Daniell (later to play Professor Moriarty in the series) as Anthony Lloyd and Reginald Denny as Evan Barham provide a nice British touch to the characters. Evelyn Ankers, Universal's contract player extraordinaire of the 1940s, has one of her best roles ever as Kitty Gavin and she is up to the task. Thomas Gomez, who often played villains but not usually of German descent, is quite good as Meade. Also there is an exciting climax, with the capture of the Nazis, the killing of Meade, the surprise death of one other person and the prevention of a Nazi invasion of England.

This film illustrates the principle that when the script is weak, great acting and excellent production values are not enough to carry a movie. The Sherlock Holmes stories were about great deductions, not great guesswork. They were also about real crime, not wartime espionage. This was a disappointing start to the Universal film series, calling into question the wisdom of the decision to move the Holmes stories to contemporary times.

Notes on the Source Material: The credits state that the film, *Sherlock Holmes and the Voice of Terror*, was based on the story "His Last Bow" by Sir Arthur Conan Doyle. The short story was first published in September 1917 in the *Strand Magazine* and was later collected in the short story collection of the Holmes works, entitled *His Last Bow*. Although "His Last Bow" was not the last story that Conan Doyle wrote and published about Holmes, the time period of the story was chronologically the last event in the life of Holmes that Conan Doyle chronicled. As an aside, the last published Conan Doyle work about Holmes was the short story "The Adventure of Shoscombe Old Place," from 1927.

"His Last Bow" tells the story of a German spy in England named Von Bork who, on August 2, 1914, is fleeing England after four years of stealing her military secrets. Von Bork has one last meeting with his British source, American-born Altamont, to collect an important final piece of secret intelligence. In a surprise move, Altamont turns on Von Bork and knocks him out with a chloroformed sponge. It turns out that Altamont is really Sherlock Holmes and he has been giving Von Bork incorrect information about British readiness for about two years. In order to capture the German, Holmes enlisted the aid of Dr. Watson, whom he has not seen for many years.

"His Last Bow" is a pretty flimsy story and was a poor way to end the career of Sherlock Holmes in print. The movie, *Sherlock Holmes and the Voice of Terror*, is an original work and takes nothing from the story, except the concept of Holmes defeating a German spy in England. Universal undoubtedly cited "His Last Bow" in the credits to give some credence to filming a story about Holmes fighting German spies in England during wartime and could fairly argue that the film was inspired by the story, even though none of the plot was used (although the name of the main villain, Von Bork, is used in both works).

At the end of the story, Holmes says to Watson, "There's an east wind coming, Watson." Watson replies, "I think not, Holmes. It is very warm." Holmes goes on to talk about the east wind, clearly analogizing it to the difficult time ahead with Germany. At the end of the movie, almost the exact same dialogue from the story is spoken by Holmes, even with the interruption by Watson. It is interesting how prescient and relevant Conan Doyle's language is to events in England in 1942, even though the dialogue was first written in 1917.

Notes on the Production: In order to justify the move of Sherlock Holmes from the Victorian Era to the time of World War II, the film started with the following written preface: "Sherlock Holmes, the immortal character of fiction created by Sir Arthur Conan Doyle, is ageless, invincible and unchanging. In solving significant problems of the present day he remains—as ever—the supreme master of deductive reasoning." That explanation was apparently enough for most viewers, as the Universal Sherlock Holmes series ran to a total of 12 films.

SHERLOCK HOLMES AND THE SECRET WEAPON (1942)

Having successfully defeated the Voice of Terror, Sherlock Holmes appears to have become a regular in the espionage forces of England during World War II. As this film opens, Holmes is engaged in engineering the escape of Dr. Franz Tobel and his innovative bombsight out of Switzerland and into England, right under the noses of two Nazi agents. The escape involves two characters substituting for Holmes and Tobel to draw the Nazis in the wrong direction, hiding parts of the bombsight in the hollowed-out insides of large books, and riding back to Britain in an RAF plane which was hidden in a secret location. John Le Carré would have been proud of the great detective, although he would probably have wondered why the British secret service could not have accomplished the same task without the assistance of a talented amateur.

Once in England Tobel disappears, but not before distributing four parts of the bombsight to four esteemed scientists so that no one can steal his secret. The only clue to the locations of the sections is contained in a cipher of dancing men, which Tobel left with his wife Charlotte in a sealed envelope, to give to Holmes if there were ever a problem. However, when Charlotte finally gives the envelope to Holmes the cipher is missing, having been replaced with a note that says, "We meet again, Mr. Holmes." Sherlock quickly deduces that Professor Moriarty, long thought dead, is back in the picture. In fact Moriarty is trying to collect all four pieces of the bombsight to sell to the Nazis.

What follows thereafter is a cat-and-mouse game between Holmes and Moriarty, with Moriarty attempting to kill Holmes on more than one occasion. There is a race between the two to solve the cipher of the dancing men, with Moriarty winning the battle to find the names of the first three scientists who have the bombsight parts, but Holmes first in solving the cipher as to the fourth scientist, allowing Holmes to substitute for that man when he is kidnapped by Moriarty. This leads to an exciting conclusion where Holmes is almost killed by Moriarty, but instead it is Holmes who dispatches Moriarty by way of Moriarty's own death trap.

This film works better than *Voice of Terror* because there is no pretense of Holmes using his deductive skills to solve a crime. This is a pure wartime espionage movie and it works quite well within that framework. The film is shot in stark blacks and whites, with much of the action taking place at night or in dark areas. That adds to the suspense and gives this movie a style often missing in other mystery movies of the 1940s.

The highlight of the film is Lionel Atwill playing Professor Moriarty. Atwill was one of the best movie villains of all time, having been memorable in *The Mystery of the Wax Museum* (1933) playing a mad sculptor, and continuing into the 1940s in such roles as

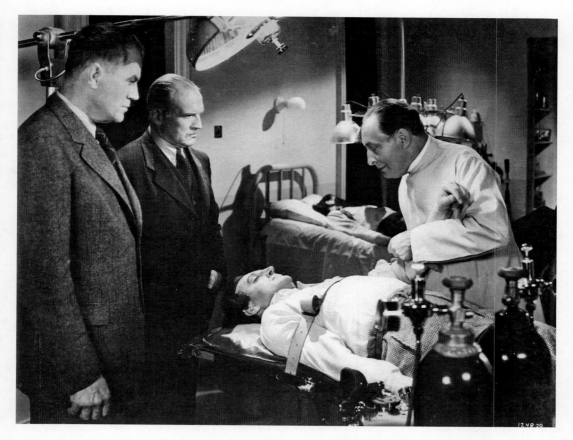

Dr. Moriarty (Lionel Atwill, far right) has captured the prone Sherlock Holmes (Basil Rathbone) and is attempting to kill Holmes by drawing the blood from his body, drop by drop, in *Sherlock Holmes and the Secret Weapon* (1942). Looking on are two Nazi agents to whom Moriarty plans to sell a secret bombsight. They are played, from left to right, by Paul Fix and George Burr Macannan.

the evil mad scientist Dr. Rigas in *Man Made Monster* (1941) and the evil Dr. Maldor in the serial *Captain America* (1944). Atwill is the consummate Professor Moriarty, whether brutally killing three of the scientists torturing Dr. Tobel for the location of the fourth bombsight, or deciding to kill Sherlock Holmes by draining all of the blood from the great detective's body. Throughout Moriarty's encounters with Holmes, the two trade witticisms with each other, displaying grudging respect for each others' acumen and resolve. In either guise, whether as brutal killer or gentleman criminal, Atwill is always convincing.

There are touches of the Sherlock Holmes of Sir Arthur Conan Doyle in this film, as in the other Universals set in modern times, as Holmes makes startling personal deductions about characters from little evidence, lives in the cluttered but comfortable abode at 221-B Baker Street, and has an interesting relationship with Inspector Lestrade of Scotland Yard. Nevertheless, this film does not recreate the true milieu of the Holmes stories from the printed page, primarily because of the film's emphasis on wartime espionage. However, the introduction of Moriarty to the series is a start in the right direction.

Notes on the Source Material: The credits state that *Sherlock Holmes and the Secret Weapon* was based on the story "The Dancing Men" by Sir Arthur Conan Doyle. The actual name of the story is "The Adventures of the Dancing Men," first published in December, 1903 in the *Strand Magazine*. It is collected in the volume of Sherlock Holmes stories entitled *The Return of Sherlock Holmes*.

Actually the movie has an original screenplay, as the Holmes created by Conan Doyle was never quite the spy as portrayed in the Universal film series. The Doyle short story involves one Hilton Cubitt who comes to Sherlock Holmes with an interesting puzzle. His wife of one year, Elsie, is being terrorized by drawings of dancing men, which have been drawn on a window sill in their house and included in a letter Elsie received. Cubitt does not understand the significance of the strange figures but he implores Holmes to solve the matter, for Elsie's well-being.

Holmes agrees, but when he arrives in the countryside, it turns out that he is too late. Hilton is dead from a bullet wound and Elsie is seriously injured with a head wound. Holmes does, however, unravel the puzzle of the dancing men, determining that it was a substitution cipher, with each dancing figure representing a different letter of the alphabet. Holmes successfully causes the arrest of the party who is guilty of Hilton's killing.

The only element of the story taken by the film is the cipher of the dancing men. Interestingly, the movie Watson tries to solve the cryptogram in the same manner used in the story, by substituting the letters most commonly used in the English alphabet for the figures used most often in the ciphers. That does not work for Watson in the film. The code of the dancing men as created by Dr. Tobel is much more complicated than the one from the story, and in order to correctly deduce the location of the missing bombsight parts, some figures in the cryptogram had to be skipped and some figures analyzed in reverse order.

At the end of the film, Holmes gives his traditional patriotic speech. Responding to Watson's comments that things are looking up and that this island (England) is still on the map, Holmes comments, "Yes, this fortress built by Nature for herself. This blessed plot, this Earth, this realm, this England." Those words were originally written by William Shakespeare and spoken by John of Gaunt near the beginning of Act II, Scene 1 of *Richard II*.

SHERLOCK HOLMES IN WASHINGTON (1943)

This was the last in the trilogy of World War II espionage movies produced by Universal for the Sherlock Holmes and Dr. Watson characters. Fans of the Sherlock Holmes stories surely breathed a sigh of relief when this one was in the can and no more spy movies were planned for the British detective. It was not that the three films were bad. In fact, they were all first-class productions and all three films could be quite entertaining at times. It was just that the films were not true to the spirit of Sherlock Holmes as envisioned by Sir Arthur Conan Doyle.

In *Sherlock Holmes in Washington*, the great detective is called in once again by the British government to assist with an espionage case. As shown in the opening segment of the film, British Secret Service agent Alfred Pettibone, masquerading as lawyer John Grayson, is carrying secret documents from London to New York on the transcontinental plane and then from New York to Washington by train. Also on the flight and the train are a group of German spies led by William Easter. When the spies finally determine that Grayson is the person who is carrying the important documents they seek, the spies abduct him right off the train. However, they are unable to locate the documents because, just before his abduction, Grayson was sharp enough to leave a matchbook folder containing microfilm of the documents in the purse of Nancy Partridge, another passenger on the train.

Before coming to America, Holmes starts his involvement in the case by investigating the background of Alfred Pettibone. With some excellent deductions from the evidence at Pettibone's house, Holmes concludes that Pettibone photographed the large secret documents onto microfilm and then secreted the microfilm in the inside of a matchbook cover.

Upon arriving in Washington, the dead body of Pettigrew is delivered to Holmes' hotel room in a trunk. It is wrapped in blanket, which could provide a clue to the location of the matchbook cover. At this point, there is an incongruous moment in the film that illustrates the problem with moving the Sherlock Holmes character into the contemporary world. Holmes asks Detective Grogan of the Washington police department to have his police laboratory go over the blanket and trunk in a microscopic examination, leaving nothing uninspected. Grayson is perturbed, responding that the United States has the best police laboratories in the world. Holmes then apologizes for his unintentional rebuke of American police methods, replying, "I am so accustomed to working quite alone in my lodgings at Baker Street that I sometimes forget the more modern scientific methods so particularly effective here in America."

The Holmes in the Conan Doyle stories was the first modern detective, with his monographs on many subjects (such as the distinction between the ashes of various tobaccos or the influence of a trade on the shape of a worker's hand), his encyclopedic knowledge of information and patterns that help in the investigation of crime, and his own microscopic inspection of physical evidence to find that one little detail that can lead to the solution of the crime. By the 1940s, police departments had in many ways adopted Holmes' methods and, indeed, because of their sophisticated equipment and large staffs, were far better at it than Holmes could ever have been. Holmes seems like a true anachronism at this point in the film.

Later, to make matters worse, the police lab misses an obvious clue in the blanket which Holmes is able to find, leading Holmes to an antique shop, the missing matchbook and the kidnapped Nancy Partridge; but not before Holmes and Watson canvas all of the antique stores in Washington, without asking for the help of the local police, even though the Britishers are unfamiliar with the city of Washington. That leads to an exciting conclusion, with the villains caught or killed and the secret document recovered.

The highlights of the film include those scenes wherein the matchbook cover transfers from person to person in the story, none recognizing its true importance. It ends up in the pocket of the main villain, Henreich Hinkle, an international spy, but he also does not know what he has on his person. Hinkle is played by George Zucco and villain William Easter is played by Henry Daniell, both of whom played Moriarty at some time during the film series. The two are fun to watch.

Even though *Sherlock Holmes in Washington* has a plot that makes little sense, it is still worth a view because of the excellent acting and some interesting moments sprinkled throughout. If one can deal with the fact that this is not Conan Doyle's Sherlock Holmes but rather Hollywood's, the movie can be enjoyed as a good example of a World War II espionage film.

SHERLOCK HOLMES FACES DEATH (1943)

While this film is clearly set in contemporary times, with soldiers seen in the first scene in the movie, modern cars shown in an establishing shot in England, and a few references to World War II inserted in the dialogue, the feature has the feel of the time period of the early Conan Doyle stories, as much of the action takes place at Musgrave Manor, an English old dark house, held for centuries in the same family. There are no modern police techniques used. and thankfully Holmes is investigating a murder mystery rather than being engaged as a spy on behalf of Mother England. Surely the setting and atmosphere of the film is a decided plus.

As the story opens, there are two different sets of occupants at Musgrave Manor. One set contains the remaining Musgrave heirs, namely two brothers, Geoffrey and Phillip, their sister Sally, and the Musgrave servants, a butler and a housekeeper. The brothers are upset that Sally is very interested in an American flyer, Captain Vickery, who is convalescing at the home. Vickery is a member of the other group of occupants of the Manor, veterans recovering from war-related injuries. Dr. Watson has volunteered his time to help the soldiers, as has a Dr. Sexton.

The opening scenes of this film are particularly effective, creating the atmosphere of a horror film a (Universal specialty) rather than a mystery story. At The Rat and Raven Pub, a patron cuts his hand on some glass and a real raven flies through the bar. The raven comes from Musgrave Manor and the owner hints that it is a dangerous place to go, as there are strange goings on there. The scene raises memories of the opening moments of *Dracula* (1931).

Director Roy William Neill's camera then cuts to the outside gates of Musgrave Manor, fluidly moving down the driveway and around the house, with strong winds rustling the trees and leaves blowing about. The dark house itself is shot in shades of black and white, with a long hallway of shadows; this is not the black and white of noir, but rather that of the horror film.

A door opens and Dr. Sexton falls into the library. He relates a strange tale of being attacked in the dark by a figure dressed all in black. The clock in the tower then strikes thirteen, an omen of impending death. Through this point in the film, the story is an excellent example of a horror/mystery tale.

Watson calls Sherlock Holmes for help, but when they return to the Manor they discover Geoffrey Musgrave's murdered body. Family tradition requires the next surviving heir plus one to recite the Musgrave Ritual, a strange set of words handed down from generation to generation. Sally is therefore called upon to recite the ritual on the day after the murder. She is surprisingly interrupted by the butler, Brunton, who corrects some of the words she uses. In short order, Phillip Musgrave's murdered body is found in the rumble seat of Sally's car and then the butler disappears and is presumed dead.

At this point, the story falls apart. Holmes discovers the secret of the Musgrave Ritual, which is an elaborate clue to a fortune due the Musgrave family. The actual murderer, Dr. Sexton, is fairly obvious. Even though there are a number of strange war veterans in the house who serve as red herrings, there is only one true potential suspect, and it is clear to any experienced viewer that Holmes' action in pretending there is a clue to Brunton's murderer on the floor of the basement is intended to trap the murderer into a confession. When Dr. Sexton grabs Holmes' gun in the basement, the viewer knows for sure that the whole event is a set-up, and indeed after confessing for everyone to hear, Dr. Sexton shoots Holmes, only to discover that the gun contains blanks. It is a mundane and trite ending to the interesting story that had gone before.

The purported motive of Dr. Sexton, which is that he expected to marry Sally and obtain the Musgrave fortune for himself, makes little sense since Sally was in love with another man and showed no interest in Dr. Sexton. At least there are some clues to the murderer which are shown to the viewer, such as Dr. Sexton being involved in the only attack that does not succeed and his making clumsy attempts to prevent Holmes from discovering the secret of the Musgrave Ritual. However, the solution to the Ritual itself is very short, as contrasted with the longer one from the original short story, also contributing to the weakness of the second half of the film. Indeed, the film's greatest strengths are the comfortable familiarity of Rathbone and Bruce in their most famous roles, and the sure hand of Neill in creating the atmosphere of horror and mystery that pervades the old dark house of the Musgraves.

Note on the Source Material: While the credits do not cite any specific story in the Canon as its source, *Sherlock Holmes Faces Death* is clearly based on "The Musgrave Ritual," first published in *Strand Magazine* in May 1893 and collected in *The Memoirs of Sherlock Holmes*. While the main stories of the convalescent home and the killing of two of the Musgrave heirs by Dr. Sexton are original to the movie, the core stories in both film and short story concerning the Musgrave Ritual are surprisingly similar.

This is a rare story in the Canon wherein Holmes narrates most of the events, recalling to Watson one of his earliest crime investigations. A schoolmate of Holmes', Reginald Musgrave, approaches Holmes with a strange tale from his family home, Hurlstone. Musgrave had recently discovered his butler Brunton in the library, reading a copy of an old family observance, the Musgrave Ritual. Musgrave fired the butler on the spot. Brunton later convinced Musgrave to allow him to stay for one more week, but on the third day Brunton disappeared completely. When his former girlfriend, Rachel Howells, a maid at Hurlstone who had been ailing after Brunton had thrown her over, heard about the disappearance of Brunton, she started shrieking hysterically. On the third day after Brunton's disappearance, she disappeared also. The only item found when they dragged the lake for Rachel's body was a linen bag that contained a mass of rusted metal and some dull-colored pieces of pebble or glass.

Holmes goes with Musgrave immediately to Hurlstone, believing the Musgrave Ritual is the key to the two disappearances. He correctly deduces that the Ritual is a guide to a hidden place, and much like in the movie, it brings him to a locked basement on the grounds of the manor. However, the Musgrave Ritual of the story is more complicated and interesting than the one in the movie, relying in part on geometry to locate a direction and distance, making the story a useful tool over many decades for high school math teachers who have to explain the usefulness of this difficult part of mathematics to doubting students.

Under a floor slab in the basement, Holmes discovers the body of Brunton. Holmes deduces that Brunton had also figured out the meaning of the Musgrave Ritual, and had secured Rachel Howell's help in moving the large slab blocking the entrance to the lower floor with the treasure. Then, once he was down below, she accidentally or purposely let the slab fall back, trapping Brunton below, where he suffocated. The treasure in the bag turns out to be the ancient crown of the Kings of England, which Brunton had handed up to Howells from below before the floor slab fell. Later Howells made her escape.

In addition to similarities in the core plot, the beginning of "The Musgrave Ritual" is narrated by Dr. Watson, who complains about Holmes' untidiness in their apartment, including his habit when he is in one of his queer humors of using his hair-trigger pistol to adorn the wall of the apartment with a patriotic V.R. (for Victoria Regina) in bullet marks. In the movie, when Watson first comes to visit Holmes, he has just been shooting bullet holes in the apartment wall, allegedly as part of a crime investigation.

THE SPIDER WOMAN (1944)

For those mystery fans who do not believe Sherlock Holmes was the world's greatest detective, observe what happens at the beginning of this movie when all of England believes Holmes is dead. A crime wave immediately breaks out in Britain. One newspaper headline declares, "Lawlessness Rampant." Would the same have happened in America if Philip Marlowe, Philo Vance or Michael Shayne passed away? Probably not.

Holmes fakes his death to go undercover to solve the puzzling pajama suicides. It seems that a number of prominent men have mysteriously committed suicide for unknown reasons, although none left a suicide note. Holmes suspects they were driven to suicide and observes that all of the victims had an interest in gaming. Holmes goes undercover as Raghni Singh, an Indian officer and compulsive gambler, and proceeds to the Urban Casino where he meets a mysterious woman named Adrea Spedding. Singh loses in the casino and then pretends he is out of funds and about to kill himself. Spedding convinces the disguised Holmes to assign his life insurance policy to a friend of Spedding for a loan. Once that is done, the death of Singh, just like all of the other victims, is next on the agenda, so that Spedding can eventually collect on the life insurance policy.

The following night, when the two meet again, Spedding realizes that she is dealing with Sherlock Holmes and that reports of his death were greatly exaggerated. Spedding sets Holmes up for another assisted suicide, by sending a deadly spider through the air duct into his hotel room. The venom of the spider will cause so much pain that Holmes will commit suicide, just like the other pajama victims. Holmes, however, is too clever to put himself at such risk. He kills the spider and the chase is on to obtain sufficient evidence to prove Spedding drove the pajama suicides to their deaths. Holmes is eventually successful, although he is almost killed in a shooting gallery at a carnival.

If not much attention is paid to the logic of the plot of this film, the story is quite interesting at times. Holmes refers to the Spider Woman as a "female Moriarty," and that is clearly the truth. The best scenes in the film are those in which Holmes verbally spars with Spedding, much as he did with Moriarty in other films. Gale Sondegaard is particularly effective in these scenes with her quiet malevolence, holding her own against Rathbone, making the Spider Woman one of the most memorable female villains of the 1940s mystery series.

A number of bits in the movie are well-written and well-acted. Adrea's strange mute nephew Larry, played by child actor Teddy Infuhr, arrives at Holmes' apartment with Adrea, alternately catching flies, irritating Dr. Watson and then throwing a poisonous candy wrapper into the fire, filling the apartment with dangerous fumes. A fake specialist in insects named Ordway seems authentic at first, with his eccentric and crusty manner, but he turns out to be a fake, discovered by Holmes and the viewer at the same time. The small part is marvelously performed by Scottish character actor Alec Craig. Unfortunately, Holmes' fake death at the beginning of the film can easily be deduced by the viewer and Holmes' surprising return in disguise is a surprise to Dr. Watson and to no one else.

The conclusion to the film is one of the best in the series, as Holmes is tied to the rear side of a Hitler figure in a carnival shooting gallery, with Dr. Watson the unaware party doing the shooting. It is truly a fiendish device for the elimination of Holmes, surely worthy of Professor Moriarty and illustrating why Holmes dubbed the Spider Woman the "female Moriarty." The film is well worth a view.

Note on the Source Material: Although *The Spider Woman's* credits state that the film is based on a story by Sir Arthur Conan Doyle, that is not the case. The film is an original screenplay, although it does borrow ideas or snippets of plots from a few of Conan Doyle's works about the great detective. The opening of the film, where Holmes apparently drowns in Scotland although his body is not recovered, draws somewhat from "The Final Problem," where Holmes apparently falls to his death over the Reichenbach Falls in Switzerland. "The Final Problem" was first published in the *Strand Magazine* in December 1893 and was collected in *The Memoirs of Sherlock Holmes.*

Also, when Holmes later reveals to Watson that he is indeed alive, Holmes enters 221-B Baker Street disguised as a uniformed messenger. In "The Adventure of the Empty House," first published in the *Strand Magazine* in October 1903 and collected in *The Return of Sherlock Holmes*, when Holmes first advises Watson that he never went over the Reichenbach Falls, Holmes arrives at Watson's abode dressed as an old book collector. In both cases, Holmes surprises Watson with the startling news, and in both cases Holmes seems somewhat inconsiderate of Watson's feelings in springing the news on him in such an unexpected manner.

The idea of the spider being introduced into the victim's room through an air duct has some similarity to the method of murder in "The Adventure of the Speckled Band," where the killer introduces a deadly snake into the victim's room through an air ventilator. "The Speckled Band" was first published in *Strand Magazine* in February 1892 and collected in *The Adventures of Sherlock Holmes.*

The concept of a pygmy being involved in bringing the spider through the air duct is inspired by a part of the novel, *The Sign of the Four*, published in 1890. In that mystery, Holmes deduces that an aborigine of the Andaman Islands, with a height of less than four feet, managed to sneak into a room through a small opening.

Some sources state that *The Spider Woman* is based on "The Adventure of the Dying

Detective" (*Strand Magazine*, December 1913, included in *His Last Bow*). In fact, the story and the film do not have any plot elements or scenes in common.

Note on the "Sequel": Two years after *The Spider Woman* was produced, Universal released a picture titled *The Spider Woman Strikes Back*. It also stars Gale Sondegaard, although she portrays a different character in that movie. The only similarity between the two movies is the involvement of spiders in the plot.

THE SCARLET CLAW (1944)

The Scarlet Claw has the reputation of being the best film in the Universal Sherlock Holmes series, and it lives up to that reputation. With an always interesting script, sure-handed direction, excellent production values and wonderful performances in both the major and minor roles, this is one of the best mystery movies of the 1940s.

In Sherlock Holmes' second movie trip to the New World, most of this story takes place in the small town of La Morte Rouge near Quebec, Canada. The town received that morbid name (translated into English as "The Red Death") because about 100 years ago, a strange apparition appeared in the village. The following morning, three people were found dead with their throats cut out. Recently, several of the most prominent citizens of the village have once again seen an apparition on the marshes, and the next morning sheep have been found with their throats torn out. Has the vicious ghost of the marshes returned?

The film starts with a beautifully atmospheric scene with a church bell hauntingly ringing at night in a fog-enshrouded area. As the local postman, Potts, comes into a pub, the bell can still be heard ringing in the background. Potts and the patrons tell stories of the strange apparitions on the marshes, and the local priest, deprecating the claims of the supernatural, decides to investigate. Tension in this scene is elevated by extreme close-ups of some of the speakers, shots from below the faces of the characters, and internal lighting of the scene from the flickering of the fireplace of the pub.

Potts takes the priest out to the church in his horse-drawn buggy. There is an interesting long shot of the vehicle, framed by the leafless and odd-shaped tree branches and the imposing edifice of the church on the left side. The priest enters the church by himself, in an interesting shot framed by the church door and a small arch. Inside, the priest finds the dead body of Lady Lillian Penrose clutching the bell rope. She had crawled into the church after being attacked and had been pulling on the bell in a last attempt to summon help.

The scene shifts to a meeting of The Royal Canadian Occult Society, where Holmes learns about the history of La Morte Rouge and has a disagreement with Lord William Penrose, who believes in the occult while Holmes expresses his belief in facts and logical deductions. While the argument goes on, Penrose is advised of the death of his wife. Over the objections of Lord Penrose, Holmes and Watson come to the village of La Morte Rouge to investigate Lady Penrose's death. There, Holmes is able to tie the death to an escaped convict and former actor, Alastair Ramson, who is disguised as one of the villagers. Holmes is unable to prevent two more deaths in the small community, but he is eventually able to determine that the postman Potts is the real killer.

This movie, much like *Sherlock Holmes Faces Death*, is part horror film and part mystery, and is therefore well within the expertise of the Universal production team. Shots in the marshes and in fog enshrouded areas bring back memories of similar scenes in *The Wolf*

Dr. Watson (Nigel Bruce, left) and Sherlock Holmes (Basil Rathbone) visit Penrose Manor in the search for clues in the death of Lady Penrose in *The Scarlet Claw* (1944).

Man (1941) and its sequels. Much of the success of this film must be attributed to the directorial touches of Roy William Neill, himself an alumnus of a horror-film favorite, *Frankenstein Meets the Wolf Man* (1943), which has some similarities in atmosphere to this film, particularly in the former's opening grave yard scene.

Under Neill's sure directorial hand, the viewer is caught off-balance because there are almost no typical movie shots in this film. As an example, when the postman leaves the church and goes to Penrose Manor to deliver a letter, the first shot in which Potts is talking to the butler is shot from a balcony of a large living room, with the performers small figures on the left side of the screen and most of the shot showing the large room. The next view of the two talking is shot from a lower and somewhat closer angle, but instead of a normal two-shot, there is a large lamp in the left side of the frame, turning the scene into an interesting composition of three objects. The two characters then walk farther away from the camera as they converse, surely an uncommon film technique.

These examples are typical of the shot composition of the film, with a third object almost always included in a scene with two performers. There are many unexpected angles for close-ups, long shots where close shots are usually employed, shots of actors' backs while they are talking, and tracking shots of actors walking where a tree or other object suddenly blocks the view of the performer. The effect is to put the viewer on edge, never quite comfortable with what the next shot may bring. This only adds to the uneasy effect of the story, which could be about a supernatural event or could be just a simple case of murder, but in any event is about violence and death.

The story itself has its own twists and turns, with suspicion reasonably alternating from character to character, with the viewer always one step behind the next twist in the tale. The performances are superb, including Gerald Hamer masquerading in multiple roles as the murderer, Paul Cavanaugh as Lord Penrose, Miles Mander as Judge Brisson, and Arthur Hohl as Emile Journet, each a potential suspect and each a potential victim. One of the joys of many of the entries in the Holmes series is the performances in the smaller parts, in this case George Kirby as the priest, who does not reappear after the opening events, David Clyde as Sergeant Thompson, the local policeman, and Ian Wolfe as Lord Penrose's butler.

This is a film with excellent acting, confident direction and innovative plotting, causing it to rise above the usual B-mystery of the 1940s, wherein the plotting and direction were often suspect. This is a highly recommended film.

Note on the Source Material: The screenplay of this film is based on an original story written by Paul Gangelin and Brenda Weisberg. The film is not based on any story in the Canon but rather is based on characters created by Sir Arthur Conan Doyle, according to the credits. Nevertheless, the broad concept of *The Scarlet Claw* is inspired by the *Hound of the Baskervilles*, with a strange apparition supposedly committing several killings in the Canadian marshes substituted for a large beast committing several killings on the Scottish moors. Indeed, early on in the film, Dr. Watson mentions both "The Hound of the Baskervilles" and "The Adventure of the Sussex Vampire" to members of the Royal Canadian Occult Society, two of the crime duo's adventures with supernatural overtones.

When Dr. Watson is in the pub pontificating to the patrons about detective work, he makes reference to one of the most famous short detective stories in all of mystery literature, "The Invisible Man" by G.K. Chesterton. The story, published in the collection *The Innocence of Father Brown* (1911), involves Chesterton's famous detective, Father Brown. The mystery concerns a murder that is committed in a house, which is surrounded by people watching it. Once the body is discovered, everyone states that no one entered or left the house. Father Brown correctly deduces that the murderer was a postman and nobody mentioned seeing him because no one ever seems to notice the postman. He tends to fit into the background.

While the plot device from "The Invisible Man" was not used in *The Scarlet Claw*, it is interesting that the villain was the postman in each case. Thus, Dr. Watson foretold the identity of the murderer in his case by mentioning the famous story by G.K. Chesterton.

The Pearl of Death (1944)

Although this is a generally interesting film with a good reputation among mystery aficionados, there is really little new in the feature. At the beginning of the movie, Holmes is in disguise as a priest in order to recover a purloined pearl. This is not the first time, however, that Holmes disguised himself in the series, and this acting stunt was starting to become repetitive. Holmes does battle with another master criminal, in this case Giles Conover, who seems to be the equal of Holmes. Once again, this concept was becoming repetitive. In addition, Dr. Watson seems particularly obtuse in several scenes and Inspector Lestrade seems especially dimwitted in his deductive capabilities. At the end, Holmes disguises himself as one of the potential victims in order to trap Conover, which is supposed to be a surprise to the audience but will hardly be a surprise to experienced viewers of this mystery series. Holmes pulled the same trick at the end of *Sherlock Holmes and the Secret Weapon*. Also, by this time in the series, instead of ending the film with a Holmes' soliloquy about war or patriotism, the films now end with Holmes' observations about good and evil, which frankly make little sense.

For fans of the original Conan Doyle stories who decry the characterization of Dr. Watson in these films as an ineffectual bumbler, this film will sorely test their patience. In one scene, Watson attempts to paste a newspaper article into a book, it accidentally sticks to the elbow of his coat, and then he cannot locate it. Has another great Universal star, Lou Costello, suddenly appeared in a Sherlock Holmes movie? Later, Watson attempts to replicate Holmes' great deductive abilities and make educated guesses about a visitor to 221-B Baker Street. Watson is wrong in every one of his conclusions. Watson seems more of a figure of comic relief in this film than in any other feature that preceded it in the series and that hardly contributes to the effectiveness of the movie.

The one early innovation in the story is that Holmes is complicit in the theft of the valuable Borgia pearl. Holmes, in attempting to demonstrate to the curator of the Royal Regent Museum that the museum's elaborate theft prevention system is defective, is so conceited that he disconnects the wires to the museum alarm system, allowing Giles Conover to abscond with the jewel. It is actually quite satisfying for one and all when Holmes receives a rare comeuppance in the series and Inspector Lestrade is hard-pressed to conceal his secret glee at the rare event.

The story picks up considerably in the second half, when three people are murdered by having their backs broken and substantial amounts of bric-a-brac are scattered on the floor next to the bodies. Here is a puzzle worthy of the talents of the great Sherlock Holmes. There appears to be no relationship between the victims, but Holmes believes the secret to the mystery is contained in the scattered pieces on the floor. Holmes finally determines that the stolen Borgia pearl was hidden in one of six figurines of Napoleon, and Conover, through his hulking brute killer the Creeper, is murdering all of the purchasers of the figurines in order to locate the pearl. In order to disguise his breaking of the Napoleon statues to locate the pearl, the Creeper has broken the other bric-a-brac and scattered it next to the bodies of the victims.

Miles Mander plays Giles Conover. Mander was usually effective in films, mostly playing supporting roles, often as a suspect or a victim in other 1940s mysteries such as *The Scarlet Claw* (1944) and *Crime Doctor's Warning* (1945). In this film, though, Mander's quiet performance, sophisticated British accent and meek appearance do not quite fit the role of master criminal Giles Conover. The part was written in the style of Professor Moriarty but performed in the style of an average crook. Mander's performance could have used a bit more spice and flamboyance.

Roy William Neill's direction is not as individualistic as it was in *The Scarlet Claw*, although he does employ some long tracking shots when characters converse while they are walking, although that technique does not necessarily contribute to the effectiveness of the feature. Neill handles the scenes with the Creeper the best, always showing him in shadow until the very end, when the Creeper finally turns toward the camera and shows his face for the first time. It is reminiscent of the scene in *Frankenstein* (1931) when the monster's face is first revealed. Here actor Rondo Hatton, with his hulking body, lumbering gait and frightening face that was distorted from a real-life disease, seems much like the Frankenstein monster as he advances on Holmes to kill him. It is an exciting and indeed horrifying end to the film, topping off a good but fairly typical entry in the Universal series.

Note on the Source Material: The film cites as its source "The Six Napoleons" by Sir Arthur Conan Doyle. The actual name of the story is "The Adventure of the Six Napoleons." It was first published in *Strand Magazine* in May 1904 and is collected in *The Return of Sherlock Holmes*.

The story begins with Inspector Lestrade telling Sherlock Holmes about a curious case he is investigating, which he believes is only a minor matter, but nevertheless might interest the great detective. Three plaster casts of the famous head of Napoleon by the French sculptor Devine are involved. One was shattered in the art store of Morse Hudson and two were stolen from the house and offices of a Dr. Barnicott and then shattered. Lestrade believes it may be the work of a madman. Holmes disagrees but there is not much he can do at that point, since there has been no real crime committed.

The next day Lestrade calls concerning another burglary and shattering of a Napoleon statue, but in addition, there has been a murder connected with the incident. This puts Sherlock Holmes on the case. He eventually deduces that a desperate thief, who was the subject of a hot pursuit by the police, placed a valuable object in one of six Napoleon casts sitting on a work bench just before he was arrested. Released from prison after serving a one year prison sentence, the thief went on a mission to locate the figurines and recover the stolen item. At the end of the story, Holmes breaks the last figurine and recovers the purloined Borgia pearl.

This is another example of a screenplay where the writers concocted an original story concerning master thief Giles Conover and his killing machine, the Creeper, and then seamlessly inserted a puzzle from one of the Conan Doyle stories into the storyline. The writers even added a layer to the mystery of the smashed figurines by having the Creeper shatter bric-a-brac in the room, hiding the broken Napoleons. The best part of the film is the mystery of the six Napoleons, as adapted from the Conan Doyle short story, providing a jolt to the second half of the movie.

There is an interesting line of dialogue in the film as Holmes is about to smash the last figurine, predicting that the Borgia pearl will be located inside. Holmes says, "If it isn't, I will retire to Sussex and keep bees." In fact, in the Conan Doyle stories, that is exactly what Holmes did when he retired from the consulting detective racket. Holmes' retirement hobby is mentioned in "His Last Bow" and "The Adventure of the Second Stain."

Notes on the "Sequels": The Creeper, as played by Rondo Hatton, was such a striking creature that Universal decided to use the character in two B-horror films. One is *House of Horrors* (1945) and the other is *Brute Man* (1946). Neither film has a relationship with *The Pearl of Death*, although in all three films the Creeper is a vicious killer. Hatton died in 1946 from the disease that caused his deformity.

THE HOUSE OF FEAR (1945)

This film is a real stunner. While it does not have the reputation of *The Scarlet Claw*, it is every bit as good. In addition, this feature contains the best puzzle in all the Sherlock Holmes stories, including the first two produced at Twentieth Century–Fox, raising this film into the pantheon of 1940s mystery movies.

The picture starts out with an intriguing story arc, with an unknown narrator introducing the viewers to Drearcliff House, which true to its name is located on a high dreary cliff next to the sea on the west coast of Scotland. There, seven members of the Good Comrades, dressed in formal wear, are gathered for dinner when the melancholy housekeeper, Mrs. Monteith, interrupts the affair and brings an envelope on a silver dish to one of the members, Ralph King, a retired barrister. King opens the envelope and finds seven orange pips inside. The members have a good laugh about the contents, but on the following night, King's car goes over a cliff and King perishes in the fiery crash. A few nights later, as the Good Comrades gather to drink a final toast to King, Mrs. Monteith arrives with another envelope addressed to Stanley Rayburn, once a distinguished actor. His envelope contains only six orange, pips but sure enough, several days later his battered body is discovered after a boating mishap.

This entire opening segment is silent except for the narration, which the viewer soon learns is told to Sherlock Holmes and Dr. Watson by an insurance agent, Mr. Chalmers. Chalmers asks Holmes to investigate the multiple deaths because each of the Good Comrades changed his life insurance policy to have the proceeds paid to the remaining mem-

In *The House of Fear* (1945), Sherlock Holmes (Basil Rathbone) and Dr. Watson (Nigel Bruce), from left to right in overcoats, visit Drearcliff House to investigate the deaths of three of the Good Comrades. The remaining Good Comrades are present, and they are, from left to right, Dr. Merrivale (Paul Cavanagh), Bruce Alastair (Aubrey Mather), Captain Simpson (Harry Cording) and Alan Cosgrave (Holmes Herbert). (The officer is unidentified.)

bers of the club, and the insurance company is tired of paying out such large sums of money in such mysterious circumstances.

Holmes and Watson proceed to Drearcliff House to investigate, but they are unable to stop murder after murder, each committed after a Good Comrade receives an envelope containing a steadily declining number of orange pips, until only one Comrade, Bruce Alastair, is left. Inspector Lestrade immediately arrests him for the crimes. Holmes, however, follows the clues and discovers that all of the other members are still alive, intending to flee the country with the insurance proceeds. They substituted corpses of recently deceased villagers for their own bodies and then mutilated the same beyond recognition to escape detection.

The House of Fear plays out as a true suspense film, with each of the suspects being killed, one after the other, reducing the number of potential murderers with each death. The film is intriguing as it is never clear which Good Comrade will receive the next orange pips and how he will be murdered, especially with the police surrounding the house to prevent any future homicides. The solution to the mystery is nearly impossible to predict. Also, the story does not end with the common 1940s cop-out, with the perpetrator being tricked into confessing even though there is no proof of his guilt. Here, there are real clues—the disappearance of John Simpson's strange tobacco indicating he may be alive, Dr. McGre-

Dr. Watson (Nigel Bruce, left) and Sherlock Holmes (Basil Rathbone) are back at 221B Baker Street after solving the murders of the Good Comrades in *The House of Fear* (1945).

gor claiming he was always in his room even though it had just been empty when Dr. Watson looked in, and most importantly, a villager, Alex MacGregor, sending a note to the police indicating he knows something about the murders. Before he is killed, MacGregor mentions that he does not believe in ghosts, convincing Holmes that at least one of the victims must be alive.

Roy William Neill's sure direction is similar to that from *The Scarlet Claw*, as once again he employs unusual camera angles, shots of speakers with an extra object in the frame to create a more interesting and unsettling view, and the use of darkness and shadows to increase the sense of dread. The true innovation of this film, however, is to make Drearcliff House one of the most important characters in the story. Most of the action takes place inside or just outside the large structure. The set is huge, with high ceilings, long stairs, and rooms full of interesting objects, such as the library which contains a suit of armor, a bookshelf full of mystery stories, large candle holders, a huge globe and some test tubes and beakers. The face of the house is the quiet Mrs. Monteith, who exudes evil as she delivers the notes of death to the wary recipients. Monteith seems to be the personification of the malevolence that lurks in Drearcliff House, aptly referred to in the film's title as the House of Fear.

The film works as an old house mystery and as a whodunit. It works as a thriller and as a suspense film. Best of all, it works as an excellent homage to the spirit of the Sherlock Holmes of the Conan Doyle stories, with Holmes presented with a perplexing and singular problem, which he solves by doggedly following the clues and using his powers of deductive reasoning. Dr. Watson and the viewer are hard-pressed to keep up with Holmes' detective acumen. This film is highly recommended.

Notes on the Source Material: The credits to the film cite as its source "The Adventure of the Five Orange Pips" by Sir Arthur Conan Doyle. The story was first published in *Strand Magazine* in November 1891 and collected in the first Sherlock Holmes anthology, *The Adventures of Sherlock Holmes*. Actually, the story and the film have nothing in common, except for the orange pips being a portent of upcoming death.

In the short story, John Openshaw consults Holmes about a troubling problem. It seems that his uncle, Elias Openshaw, who used to live in the Southern United States, received a letter one day marked "KKK" and containing five orange pips, which upset Elias very much. It turned out that Elias was rattled with good reason. A short time later he was found dead in a garden pond. Elias' fortune was willed to John's dad, Joseph, who some years later received a letter marked "KKK," containing five orange pips and a directive to place the papers on a sundial. Since Elias had burned almost all of his papers before his death, there was nothing to leave on the sundial. Joseph was later found dead in a chalk pit.

John inherited the family fortune and things were going well until he received a letter similar to the one Joseph received, along with five orange pips. That prompted John, rightfully fearful for his own life, to consult with Holmes. After hearing the story, the great detective suggests that John put some remnants of Elias' papers on the sundial, but John is killed on his way home before he can do so.

Holmes determines that KKK stands for Klu Klux Klan, a somewhat unfamiliar name in London during the time of Holmes' life. Whoever committed the murders was after documents that could implicate some KKK members in crime activities in America. Holmes tries to wreak his revenge on the murderers by sending them a message with five orange pips to the ship on which they are crewing, but the ship is lost in a storm and the murders avenged in that manner.

The short story is quite interesting but the movie is far better. Indeed, the film owes more to Agatha Christie's *And Then There Were None* and *Murder on the Orient Express* than it does to the Conan Doyle story, and perhaps that is why *House of Fear* contains the best puzzle in the entire film series.

THE WOMAN IN GREEN (1945)

While the Universal Sherlock Holmes series may not have been quite A-productions, they were never less than B-plus films, at least in terms of the quality of the product that appeared on the screen. This is shown once again in *The Woman in Green*, the ninth entry in the series. As with many of the prior films, director Roy William Neill was given the time and budget to employ unusual camera angles, dark lighting and tracking shots to tell the tale of mystery and horror. Also, and was often the case in the prior films, the sets were lavish, enhancing the authenticity of the locations and adding to the interest of the story.

For example, in an early scene Holmes and Inspector Grayson go to a restaurant and bar called Pembroke House to discuss the problem of the finger murders, a series of homicides wherein a seemingly unrelated group of young women are murdered and one of their fingers cut off. The plot purpose for the trip to Pembroke House is so that Holmes can spot Sir George Fenwick, a slight acquaintance of his, in the company of a beautiful young woman, later identified as Lydia Marlowe. For purposes of the story, a small restaurant would have sufficed. Instead, Pembroke House is a huge restaurant with a small orchestra, a dance floor, a bar with a large mirror, columns in the main dining room and large chandeliers on the ceilings.

When the movie moves to Marlowe's apartment, it is surprisingly large and lavish. George Fenwick's house, barely used in the film, is huge and stately. This is clearly not a low-budget mystery produced at Monogram; indeed, the sets utilized in this film alone could have broken the budgets of the Crime Doctor and Boston Blackie series together. These Sherlock Holmes films from Universal were always first-rate productions.

Unfortunately the plot does not match the production values, as it turns out that Professor Moriarty is blackmailing hypnotized and wealthy Londoners into believing that each is the finger murderer. Thus, the real killer is cutting off a victim's finger and then planting it in the pocket of the blackmail victim to convince the victim that he is the murderer. Does that make any sense? Why not just hypnotize them into handing over all of their cash to Moriarty?

Once Holmes focuses on Lydia Marlowe as the hypnotist, the story becomes mundane, with each plot twist easily predicted by the savvy viewer. Does anyone who watches this movie truly believe that Holmes was hypnotized by Marlowe or that Moriarty would convince Holmes to fall off a high ledge?

The film is not without its pleasures. In addition to the production values, two performers are a joy to watch. Hillary Brooke as the evil Lydia Marlowe has one of her best roles in her career. She had previously appeared in other films in this series and other mystery movies of the 1940s, but here she excels as the beautiful but deadly hypnotist, first seducing and then hypnotizing her victims. She is a true Spider Woman. Henry Daniell plays Professor Moriarty, succeeding appearances in the same role by George Zucco and Lionel Atwill. (Moriarty is back from the dead from *Sherlock Holmes and the Secret Weapon*, although his prior demise from that film is never mentioned.) Daniell has heady competition for the best performance as Moriarty in the entire series, and Daniell, always an excellent actor, rises to the challenge. He is superb in the role, with his sophisticated tone of voice and steady gaze. He brings a less flamboyant approach to the evil that is Moriarty but he is just as effective as Zucco and Atwill as he exudes understated wickedness in his dealings with George Fenwick and Sherlock Holmes.

While there is much to appreciate in this film, a mystery story often rises and falls on the coherency of its plot and the surprise and logic to its plot twists. In those attributes, *The Woman in Green* falls short, with an incoherent plot and few surprises in the mystery. *The Woman in Green* is therefore only a mediocre entry in the Universal film series.

Note on the Source Material: Sherlock Holmes supposedly died at the Reichenbach Falls at the end of "The Final Problem," a story first published in the *Strand Magazine* in December 1893 and collected in *The Memoirs of Sherlock Holmes*. That story described the most famous encounter between the World's Greatest Detective and the Napoleon of Crime, at least as related in the original works by Conan Doyle.

At one point in "The Final Problem," Moriarty visits Holmes to try to convince him to give up his pursuit:

MORIARTY: "All that I have to say has already crossed your mind."
HOLMES: "Then possibly my answer has crossed yours."
MORIARTY: "You stand fast?"
HOLMES: "Absolutely."

In *The Woman in Green*, Moriarty also visits Holmes to try to convince him to give up the case of the finger murders. In the intense scene between the two, dialogue substantially similar to that quoted from the short story is used in the screenplay.

Just before the end of "The Final Problem," Moriarty tricks Watson into setting off on a bogus medical emergency, leaving Moriarty and Holmes alone for their titanic struggle above the Reichenbach Falls. Similarly, in the movie Watson is called off on a bogus medical emergency a few minutes before the verbal encounter between Holmes and Moriarty, so that Moriarty can speak to Holmes directly and set up Holmes' murder.

"The Adventure of the Empty House," first published in the *Strand Magazine* in October 1903 and collected in *The Return of Sherlock Holmes*, is often cited as the source for some of the subject matter of *The Woman in Green*. "The Empty House" was the story in which the public first learned that Holmes had survived his encounter with Professor Moriarty at the Reichenbach Falls.

In fact (and as was always the case in the Rathbone/Bruce series at Universal), the screenplay of *The Woman in Green* was original, but it incorporated a significant incident from a Conan Doyle story, in this case one from "The Adventure of the Empty House." In the story, Holmes devises a plan to capture Colonel Sebastian Moran, the second-most dangerous man in London (after Professor Moriarty). Knowing that Moran is determined to kill him, Holmes places a wax bust of his face in the window of 221-B Baker Street and then hides in the dark of the empty house across the street. Moran arrives, shoots a bullet through the replica of Holmes' head with an air gun, and then is immediately captured by Holmes.

In the movie Holmes, recognizing that Moriarty intends to kill him, uses a bust of Caesar already in his apartment as the decoy. He places it near the window making it appear that Holmes is reading a book. Corporal Williams, a sniper from the British Army who has been hypnotized by Marlowe to kill Holmes, attempts to do so, instead shooting a bullet through the bust of the head in the window. Williams is immediately captured by Holmes and Watson.

The scene in the film is a near replication of the events in the story of "The Empty House." However, that is the only portion of the plot of "The Empty House" incorporated into the screenplay.

Pursuit to Algiers (1945)

It is amazing that this late into the mystery series the quality of the Universal Sherlock Holmes movies had not declined. *Pursuit to Algiers* is a clever mixture of the Sherlock Holmes of Victorian England, a modern day spy story, and an old-fashioned Conan Doyle mystery, cleverly packaged in an always suspenseful tale set primarily on a steam ship on its way from London to Algiers.

The first scenes evoke the Victorian England of the original Conan Doyle stories, as Holmes and Watson walk down a London street, enter a restaurant and later enter a mysterious house, following clues that are artfully given to them by various unexpected individuals. These scenes are highlighted by the effective direction of Roy William Neill, with tracking shots and unusual camera angles and shot compositions. These scenes could have been the introduction to another *Hound of the Baskervilles* or *House of Fear*.

Instead, Holmes is employed by representatives of the small country of Rovina, located near the Mediterranean, to escort Prince Nikolas, who has been educated in England from a young age, back to his country to assume the leadership thereof, since the king has been recently assassinated. The plot is really a throwback to the first three Universal Sherlock Holmes movies, since this is more spy story than mystery, although given the year of the film's release, the Nazis are no longer involved. After pretending he is going to take the Prince by plane, Holmes actually brings him by boat, with Dr. Watson along for the trip.

In the early scenes on the boat, there is a fear that some of the passengers or crew may be out to assassinate young Nikolas. Suspicious characters abound, including Sheila Woodbury, an American singer with something to hide, a steward who acts suspiciously on board ship, two suspicious gentlemen who make several puzzling comments that Watson overhears, and Agatha Dunham, a wealthy passenger who likes to take long walks before meals and carries a gun in her handbag. However, just outside Lisbon three new passengers board the ship, and there is no doubt they are the assassins who will attempt to kill Prince Nikolas.

The movie is actually quite suspenseful before the assassins arrive, but once they are aboard the tension never lets up. Holmes deftly turns aside an attempt to knife Nikolas, explode a bomb in his lap and even kidnap him just as the journey is about to end. Indeed, the clever Holmes has tricked his opponents throughout the entire journey, as Nikolas may not actually be the person he appears to be.

Along the way, Holmes solves the mystery of singer Joan Woodbury and her tendency to hold onto her briefcase of sheet music, avoiding Holmes at all costs. Although the screenplay is original, this vignette involving Woodbury could easily have come from a Holmes short story, with Holmes making correct deductions on scant evidence.

The acting is wonderful in this feature, as it always seemed to be in the Sherlock Holmes series. There are wonderful performances in large and small parts, such as relative unknown Marjorie Riordan as singer Sheila Woodbury, the always villainous Martin Kosleck as the knife-throwing assassin, Rex Evans as the hefty leader of the assassins and Rosalind Ivan as the irritating Agatha Dunham. Acting honors, however, go to Nigel Bruce as Dr. Watson. This film gives him one of his largest roles in the series, as he probably enjoys more screen time than Basil Rathbone. Bruce is up to the task in his portrayal of a fussy upper-class Englishman, dismissive of fish and chips and American coffee but supporting the effectiveness of the British public schools. He always respects the niceties of English society with his impeccable manners, even though he often makes clever comments under his breath, this time directed toward Agatha Dunham rather than Inspector Lestrade (who is not in the film). Bruce even gets to sing a song for the audience, leading to loud applause from the other passengers. Bruce's contributions to this film series should not be underestimated.

This film has everything the audience could desire from a Holmes film: mystery, suspense, clever repartee between Holmes and one of the villains, and a dash of humor. If this is not quite the Sherlock Holmes that Conan Doyle envisioned in his writings, it is the next best thing. *Pursuit to Algiers* upholds the lofty standards of the prior films in the series.

Note on the Source Material: *Pursuit to Algiers* is an original work but there are interesting references to the Conan Doyle short stories contained therein. At a party on board ship, Dr. Watson is enticed into recalling the details of one of Holmes' great adventures. Watson chooses the case of the giant rat of Sumatra. Although there is no work in the Canon with that title, the case is mentioned in "The Adventure of the Sussex Vampire" (*Strand Magazine*, January 1924; *The Case-Book of Sherlock Holmes*), with Holmes describing it as "a story for which the world is not yet prepared."

At the beginning of "The Adventure of the Norwood Builder" (*Strand Magazine*, November 1903; *The Return of Sherlock Holmes*), Dr. Watson makes a passing reference "to the shocking affair of the Dutch steamship, *Friesland*, which so nearly cost us both our lives." In *Pursuit to Algiers*, the action takes place on the *S.S. Friesland*, a Swedish ship, where the lives of Holmes and Watson are clearly in danger. Perhaps, then, the writer of *Pursuit to Algiers* was trying to provide his version of this adventure of the World's Greatest Detective, which Dr. Watson never had the time to immortalize in print.

TERROR BY NIGHT (1946)

Terror by Night is the penultimate film in the Universal Sherlock Holmes movie series, and once again it is amazing how good this film is, given how late in the series it comes. Unlike many of the other mystery movie series of the 1940s, the Universal Holmes films maintained their quality throughout their entire run. One reason was the consistent casting of Basil Rathbone and Nigel Bruce in the lead roles. They were consummate actors and their chemistry together grew over the course of the series. Another important factor was Roy William Neill, the producer of many of the movies and the director all of them except the first one. Neill ensured a consistency of production values and top-notch direction for the entire series. Even *Terror by Night*, filmed almost entirely on a limited number of indoor sets, has an A-production look even though it probably had only a minimal budget.

In the end, though, it was the writing that made the difference in the Sherlock Holmes series. In the first several films, the writers adapted elements of the Conan Doyle short stories into original screenplays, creating unique plot ideas. Later, when the original Holmes stories became less important to the screenplays, the writers still created intriguing plots rather than merely rehashing ideas from earlier film scripts, as often happened in other mystery series. In the case of *Terror by Night*, the idea of setting the entire story on a train ride from England to Scotland was ingenious, making this movie different from any other film in the series, and indeed from just about any other mystery movie of the 1940s.

Holmes is hired by Ronald Carstairs, over the objections of his mother, Lady Margaret Carstairs, to guard the valuable Star of Rhodesia diamond on its return from London to Edinburgh by way of the overnight Scotch Express train. Almost immediately, Ronald Carstairs is murdered and the valuable jewel stolen, so Lady Margaret may have been correct in her evaluation of Holmes' abilities.

It is clear that a passenger in the railroad car in which Carstairs was traveling is the guilty party, and Holmes believes the villain is Colonel Sebastian Moran, an associate of Moriarty, who must be masquerading as one of those passengers or working in concert with one of them. Unfortunately there are many suspects for the arch-villain or his ally, including Major Duncan-Bleek (whom Watson knew from many years ago, both belonging to the same club), beautiful Vivian Vedder (who is in mourning, bringing her mother's body back to Scotland in a coffin located in the baggage car), Professor Kilbane (a mathematics instructor who is particularly upset by Dr. Watson's questioning), and an elderly couple named Mr. and Mrs. Shallcross (who surely act guilty about some activity in their past).

Holmes then discovers that the Vedder's coffin has a hidden section below the body, which allows a small man to board the train in secret and then commit the murder of Carstairs and the theft of the jewel. Duncan-Bleek turns out to be Moran, who appears to cleverly escape near the end of the film when a phony Scottish policeman boards the train and tries to take him away. But, Holmes is too smart, keeping Moran on the train when the fake police leave and also holding onto the Star of Rhodesia jewel, finally returning the gem to its rightful owner.

This film is part of a sub-category of mystery and spy story that can be dubbed "train melodrama." It has attributes of other train melodramas such as the earlier *The Lady Vanishes* (1938) and the later *Murder on the Orient Express* (1974). Director Roy William Neill makes the most of the close quarters on the train, such as the tight corridors, sliding doors into compartments, and small seating areas, creating a claustrophobic feel to the story and adding to the suspense. Rather than employing the more atmospheric style of the previous films in the series, Neill has modified his technique by using quicker cuts and the sound of the train's rattling and sharp whistles to create the mood of the film. There is even an exciting scene where Holmes has to hang onto the outside of a train car as another train, coming in the opposite direction, passes close by.

As always, the acting is superb, particularly from Alan Mowbray (who previously played Lestrade in *A Study in Scarlet* [1933]) who is convincing both when posing as the upper-class Englishman Duncan-Bleek and when his character turns out to be the evil yet brilliant Sebastian Moran, and from Frederic Worlock as Professor Kilbane, always humorous as he tries to make Dr. Watson's life miserable on the train. A trademark of the Universal Holmes films was the perfect casting and acting in the small roles, such as the always interesting Skelton Knaggs as the killer who hides in the coffin, Boyd Davis as the fake Scottish police inspector who almost gets Moran off the train without anyone realizing it, and Tom Pilkington as the suspicious-looking baggage car attendant who may or may not be in on the crimes.

There are some who believe this is the best film in the Universal Sherlock Holmes series. While that may not be the case, it is surely one of the best train melodramas of them all, with more time spent on the moving train or in a train station than any other film in the sub-genre. *Terror by Night* is highly recommended, either as an enjoyable mystery or as an exciting train melodrama.

Notes on the Source Material: While the credits state that this film was based on a short story by Sir Arthur Conan Doyle, that is not accurate, as there is no story in the Sacred Writings in which Holmes is hired to protect a valuable jewel onboard a train. There are, however, some interesting references to the Conan Doyle stories. The character of Lady Margaret Carstairs may have been named after the title character in "The Disappearance of Lady Frances Carfax" (*Strand Magazine*, December 1911; *His Last Bow*). In both that story and the film, an unusual coffin provides an important plot point. The main criminal in the film, Colonel Sebastian Moran, made an appearance in "The Adventure of the Empty House" (*Strand Magazine*, October 1903; *The Return of Sherlock Holmes*). "The Adventure of the Blue Carbunkle" (*Strand Magazine*, January 1892; *The Adventures of Sherlock Holmes*) also involved a precious stone, although the story line is completely different from that of *Terror by Night*.

DRESSED TO KILL (1946)

This last film in the Universal Sherlock Holmes series brings back memories of previous films. The MacGuffins of the tale are three music boxes that contain a coded message concerning the location of stolen engraving plates from the Bank of England, which can be used to print five-pound notes. The music boxes are sent out of Dartmoor Prison and then sold to three different purchasers at an auction. The villains are out to steal the music boxes at whatever cost, including murder. There was a similar idea in *The Pearl of Death,* where one of six figurines of the bust of Napoleon contained a valuable jewel, and the villains were after the several innocent people who had unknowingly purchased the statuettes.

Holmes' adversary in this case is Hilda Courtney, a very beautiful but also evil and clever woman. This brings back memories of the title character in *The Spider Woman*, played by Gale Sondergaard, another deadly woman who was almost the equal of Holmes. The Holmes films often turned on the quality of his adversary, and in this case Courtney is more than enough of a challenge for the great detective.

Dressed to Kill opens with a short scene in Dartmoor Prison and then a very interesting scene at the auction, where the three music boxes are sold for very low sums. Just after the sale, Colonel Cavanaugh convinces the auctioneer to disclose information about the purchasers, and then he, along with Mrs. Courtney, are in the hunt to locate and acquire the same. One of the purchasers is "Stinky" Emery, an old friend of Dr. Watson's. A little bit later, Stinky coincidentally visits 221-B Baker Street and relates a story that Holmes finds interesting. Stinky, who is a collector of music boxes, some of which are very valuable, was recently knocked unconscious and a music box stolen from his home. However, the thief stole an inexpensive box and left the valuable ones alone.

This is just the type of puzzle that intrigues Holmes, and off he goes to Stinky's home to investigate. This is also just the type of puzzle that Conan Doyle used in his stories, where a seemingly insignificant incident could become the start of a significant investigation. After Holmes and Watson leave Stinky's abode, Stinky is killed by Mrs. Courtney's chauffeur and Courtney thereby acquires one of the three music boxes. The chase is then on for the other two music boxes and the coded message disclosing the location of the Bank of England plates.

Once again, it is hard to overestimate the effectiveness of the acting in this film, particularly in the small parts. Edmond Breon is wonderful as Stinky, an older upper-class Englishman with an eye for the women. Other performances of note in the smaller roles are given by Holmes Herbert as the auctioneer, Delos Jewkes as a small-time hood who can identify any song and Sally Shepherd as the proprietor of a tobacco shop.

The performances in the lead roles are also superb. Basil Rathbone gives an energetic performance as the great detective, with his enthusiasm for the hunt overwhelming the viewer. Others have speculated that Rathbone gave such a vigorous performance in this film because he knew the series was about to end and that he could move on to better things, but whatever the reason, it is one of Rathbone's best performances in the series. The beautiful Patricia Morison is excellent as Mrs. Courtney, almost besting Holmes by tricking him into following the clue of a cigarette butt directly into a trap. This part is better written than that of the Spider Woman, and the combination of great writing and acting makes Courtney one of the most memorable of all of the Holmes adversaries.

All of that said, this film is not up to the standards of the most recent films in the series. The story often has a slow pace and can be slightly boring at times. There is little of the mood of suspense or the atmosphere of foreboding that were the hallmarks of the prior films. The underlying quest for the music boxes makes little sense. Surely it would have been substantially easier to send a coded letter from Dartmoor Prison about the location of the bank plates, rather than going through the convoluted process of using music boxes to convey the secret message.

As noted above, however, the film has much to commend it and it is quite good for the last film in a long movie series. Since the Universal Sherlock Holmes films are justifiably regarded by many mystery connoisseurs as the best mystery movie series of the 1940s, even a lesser entry in the series is worth a view.

Notes on the Source Material: The screenplay is an original work but there are interesting references to stories from the Canon. Early on, Watson is reading the latest edition of the *Strand Magazine*, which has just published Watson's story about Holmes entitled "A Scandal in Bohemia." (Actually, the story was first published in the *Strand Magazine* in the July 1891 issue and collected in *The Adventures of Sherlock Holmes*.) In that story, Holmes is employed by the King of Bohemia to recover a photograph showing the King in the company of the beautiful Irene Adler. Holmes finds the secret location of the photograph in Adler's abode by starting a fake fire therein, knowing that Adler will grab the valuable item before exiting the building. In *Dressed to Kill*, Hilda Courtney pulls the same stunt on Dr. Watson in order to locate the third music box that is in Watson's possession. As Holmes then points out to Watson, Mrs. Courtney must have conceived the deceit after reading the recently published "A Scandal in Bohemia."

Watson also makes reference to "The Adventure of the Solitary Cyclist" (*Strand Magazine*, January 1904, collected in *The Return of Sherlock Holmes*), but he does not tie the story into any particular element of the movie. Mrs. Courtney mentions Holmes' monograph on the ashes of 140 different varieties of tobacco. That particular scientific work by Sherlock Holmes is referred to in *The Sign of the Four*.

Afterwards

With the release of *Dressed to Kill*, Rathbone ended his association with the Universal series, believing he was fatally typecast. That turned out to be true, as Rathbone's career subsequent to the end of the series never reached the heights it had before 1939. Although he had a few good roles in films, such as the villainous Andre Trochard in *We're No Angels* (1955) and as banker Norman Cass in *The Last Hurrah* (1958), most of Rathbone's subsequent work was in television, including playing Sherlock Holmes on one occasion, in 1953, and once on Broadway, in that same year. Rathbone died in 1967. After the end of the Sherlock Holmes series, Nigel Bruce made few appearances on the screen or on television. He passed away in 1953. Producer-director Roy William Neill passed away only five months after the 1946 release of *Dressed to Kill*.

Rathbone and Bruce played Holmes and Watson in a long-running radio program during the course of the film series. The series began in 1939, right after the success of their first two films, and continued until 1946, when Rathbone bowed out of the series. Bruce continued in the series until 1947, with Tom Conway, alumnus of the Falcon movie series, playing Sherlock Holmes. The stories were always told in retrospect, by Dr. Watson to a visitor to his home. There were also a number of other radio series about the great detective, both before and after the Rathbone-Bruce series ended.

There have been numerous television adaptations of the Holmes character, beginning in the 1950s and continuing to the present day. Also, movies about Sherlock Holmes continue to be made. Interestingly, however, the Rathbone-Bruce films were so popular that it was over ten years before any other studio dared to release a Holmes film without Rathbone and Bruce in the leads. That film, *The Hound of the Baskervilles* (1959), was another version of Conan Doyle's most famous work. Made by Hammer Films in England, it starred Peter Cushing as Sherlock Holmes.

4

The Shadow
The Caped Avenger

There were several masked and caped vigilante crime fighters in 1930s popular culture. There was the Spider, who made his debut in the first issue of *Spider Magazine,* which was published in October 1933. The Spider wore a black hat and black cape (and in the pulp magazine stories was also hunchbacked and had fangs) as he fought against crime, keeping his true identity as Richard Wentworth, a wealthy socialite and amateur detective, secret even from Commissioner Kirkpatrick. There was also Batman, who first appeared in *Detective Comics* #27, dated May 1939. Batman kept his true identity as wealthy playboy Bruce Wayne hidden under a cowl, costume and cape as he fought evil-doing in Gotham City, assisting Commissioner Gordon.

Another was the Shadow, who donned a slouch hat and cape to fight crime, without the world knowing his true identity, which was Kent Allard in the pulps and Lamont Cranston on the radio. Commissioner Weston was his foe and ally on the police force. All three of these masked avengers were the subject of 15 chapter serials from Columbia during the 1930s and 1940s but only the Shadow was the subject of feature films during those same decades.

Background

RADIO AND THE PULPS

The Shadow first came to the public's attention in 1930 on the radio, as the narrator of *The Detective Story Hour,* a mystery anthology whose tales came from a pulp magazine of the era, *Detective Story Magazine.* The publication was from Street & Smith and the intent was to have the radio show promote the magazine. Instead, listeners were more interested in the announcer with the deep and eerie voice, and they flocked to newsstands seeking issues of *The Shadow Magazine,* which did not exist. Street & Smith was smart enough to respond to the demand, and it quickly started a new magazine about the character, which was called, appropriately enough, *The Shadow Magazine.* It debuted with the April 1931 issue.

Walter B. Gibson, at the time a freelance writer, was called in by Street & Smith to develop the character and launch the new publication. Gibson came up with the idea of a suicidal man, Henry Vincent, who was convinced not to jump off a bridge by the Shadow. In return, Vincent would work for him as an agent in the fight against crime. The Shadow eventually had other agents helping him, such as socialite Margo Lane and taxi driver Moe Shrenitz. In the pulps, the Shadow was always an elusive crime fighter who disguised himself under a slouch hat and black cape. Contrary to popular belief, the Shadow was not Lamont Cranston in the pulps. He merely pretended to be the millionaire when Cranston was out of town. Eventually, it was revealed that the true identity of the Shadow was Kent Allard, a World War I flying ace.

The pulp magazine was a huge success. Gibson wrote almost all of the more than 300 Shadow stories issued over the next twenty years, using the pen name of Maxwell Grant. The success of the magazine led to a change in the radio program. By 1932, the radio show was renamed *The Shadow*, but the Shadow was still the narrator of mystery stories. These shows aired on CBS and on NBC's Blue Network. By the end of that run, however, the Shadow started participating in the stories. The first radio show featuring the Shadow as an adventure character debuted on the Mutual Radio Network on September 26, 1937. The catchphrase of the new radio show, which has become a part of American culture, was a deep, sepulchral voice intoning, "Who knows what evil lurks in the hearts of men? The Shadow knows!" followed by eerie laughter.

The radio program contradicted the pulps, for there the Shadow's real identity was millionaire Lamont Cranston. The Shadow had learned to cloud men's minds in the Orient. Eventually, some of the wilder elements of the stories were downplayed in the radio show, making the character more like the detective of the magazines.

For the new series, the Shadow was initially played by Orson Welles. Agnes Moorhead played Margo and Ray Collins played Commissioner Weston. Welles left the show in 1938. Many other actors played the Shadow over the next 18 years.

FILM SERIES

The Shadow got off to a slow start in feature films. In the late 1930s, independent film company Grand National produced two films about Lamont Cranston, *The Shadow Strikes* (1937) and *International Crime* (1938). Apparently, Grand National could not decide how to handle the character. In the first film, Cranston does appear to be a crime fighter of some variety and he does dress in the slouch hat and cape upon occasion. However, none of the regular characters from either the pulp stories or the radio appear with him.

In *International Crime* (1938), Cranston has now become a newspaper columnist, radio reporter, criminologist and amateur detective. Several characters from the stories and radio are part of the film: Commissioner Weston, Margo Lane (although she is called Phoebe) and taxi driver Moe Shrenitz. However, Cranston never wears the black hat and cape which are the symbols of the Shadow, and although he identifies himself as the Shadow in his media appearances, he displays none of the attributes of the mythical character.

Rod La Rocque played Lamont Cranston in both films. Born in Chicago, Illinois, in the late 1890s, La Rocque started acting in films around 1915. He was soon a regular performer in silent films, with his first big break being a role in *The Ten Commandments* (1923). Thereafter, La Rocque had starring roles in a number of silent films. With the advent of sound, however, La Rocque's career faltered, and thereafter he either starred in B-movies or had small parts in A-films.

In 1946, B-movie studio Monogram Pictures released three Shadow movies in a short-lived new series. Although the films did not recreate the atmosphere of the pulp magazine stories, the adaptations were closer to the original than the two La Rocque movies from the

1930s. In each film, the Shadow assisted the police in investigating crimes, whether murders, thefts or blackmail.

Kane Richmond played Lamont Cranston, a.k.a. the Shadow. Richmond, whose real name was Fred Bowditch, was born in Minneapolis, Minnesota, in 1906. He moved to Hollywood in the 1920s in an attempt to break into films. He generally received only bit parts in the early sound era, although at one point he was a contract player at MGM. His breakthrough in the movies was the starring roles he obtained in two serials from 1935, which then led to starring roles in four serials in the 1940s. Richmond also had small roles in three Charlie Chan movies.

Other characters were also carried over from the pulp magazine and radio stories. Commissioner Weston was played by Pierre Watkin, a well-known character actor who appeared in over 300 films in his career, usually playing district attorneys, newspaper editors, lead villains and the like. Watkin, who appeared in a number of movies in the 1940s mystery series, is probably best known for playing Perry White in two Superman serials. Cranston's fiancée, Margo Lane, was played by Barbara Reed in all three films. Reed appeared in about 20 films in her short career. Cab driver Shrevvy was played by Tom Dugan and then Andy Clyde, and Inspector Cardona was played by Joseph Creehan and then James Flavin.

The Rod La Rocque Films

THE SHADOW STRIKES (1937)

The Shadow Strikes is an uneasy mixture of a private eye/vigilante story, on the one hand, and a classic drawing room whodunit on the other hand. While that may have seemed like an innovative and effective story idea when it was first conceived, the combination does not, in fact, work very well. The plots are hard enough to follow on their own, and with the two intertwined in the film, the storylines are quite confusing. Since the intrinsically charismatic Shadow of the pulps is generally missing from the movie, there is little reason to recommend this feature.

The vigilante aspects of the story commence early in the film, with the Shadow preventing the burglary of an attorney's safe, capturing the two burglars and holding them for the police. It is not quite clear what the two thieves were after in the safe and how and why the Shadow became involved, but it has something to do with the notorious gambler and racketeer, Brossett. Periodically during the film, the Shadow tangles with Brossett and eventually causes Brossett's death. However, the relationship between the Shadow and Brossett is murky, at best.

The Agatha Christie-style murder mystery commences with the killing of Caleb Delthern, just as he is asking the Shadow, in the Shadow's guise as attorney Chester Randall, to change Caleb's will to eliminate Caleb's niece Marcia as an heir. Later, there is the shotgun death of another heir, and the Shadow believes that the deaths are tied to the will of Caleb Delthern. The killer is unmasked at the end of the movie, but since the motive for the murders comes out of the blue, without any groundwork laid for it earlier in the film, and with no clues to the identity of the murderer, the ending of *The Shadow Strikes* is truly unsatisfactory.

There is much that is sloppy about the movie. The Shadow's real name is revealed at the end of the film and it is Lamont Granston, not Lamont Cranston. How could that mistake have been made? In the opening of the film, the Shadow mentions trying to discover the identity of his father's killer, but that plot point is never mentioned again. In fact, that idea for a storyline seems far more interesting than the one that was actually filmed. The Shadow is assisted by a man named Henry Hendricks who is neither capable enough to be a strong and helpful ally to the Shadow, nor bumbling or funny enough to be the comic relief, as Goldie was to the Falcon and the Runt was to Boston Blackie. It is not clear why the part was written in the manner that it was.

Rod La Rocque is quite good as the Shadow; he is probably the best thing in the movie. Most of the rest of the cast, however, is disappointing. Their acting reflects the style of the early sound era rather than the more modern style of 1937. There are long pauses when the characters speak, slowing down the pace of an already slow movie even further.

There is very little of the Shadow character of the pulps and the radio series in *The Shadow Strikes*. With the exception of the appearance of the shadowy figure at the beginning of the film, which is quite effective, he hardly ever reappears again. In any event, the character of the Shadow does not fit well with a traditional drawing room mystery story. None of the Shadow's regular cast of characters from other media appear in the movie, as it would have been difficult to fit them into the story. With a difficult plot and

This is a publicity photo for *The Shadow Strikes* (1937) with star Rod La Rocque attempting to recreate some of the eeriness of the original Shadow stories from the pulps.

none of the trappings of the true Shadow in the feature, there is scant reason to view this film.

Note on the Source Material: *The Shadow Strikes*, is, according to its credits, based on the Street & Smith *Shadow Magazine* story by Maxwell Grant titled "The Ghost in the Manor." That novel was originally published in the June 15, 1933 issue of *The Shadow Magazine*. The story involves the will of the newly deceased Caleb Delthern, which provides that his considerable estate will be divided among his five heirs who attend a conference thirty days after the reading of the will. The oldest heir present at the meeting will receive one-half of the estate and the remaining heirs will divide the remaining one-half of the estate on an equal basis.

Surely Delthern must have realized that his bequests created a considerable incentive for the heirs of his estate to murder each other, increasing their own share of the estate so long as they were not themselves murdered. Not surprisingly, since this is a Shadow mystery, that is exactly what happens. After several deaths, the Shadow discovers the real murderer and prevents the death of another heir.

While there is a superficial similarity between the story from the pulps and the portion of the film about the heirs of Caleb Delthern, the two stories develop in totally different manners and the actual villain is not the same in each version. The plot about the gambler Brossett is new to the film.

INTERNATIONAL CRIME (1938)

This film raises an interesting question. If the Shadow never wears a slouch hat and a cape, is he still the Shadow? The lead character in *International Crime* is named Lamont Cranston. Using the pseudonym of The Shadow, Cranston has a newspaper column in *The Star* and a crime-oriented radio show, wherein he relates the hottest crime stories of the day to his readers and listeners. Cranston is assisted by a Jewish taxi driver, Moe, and by a society girl, Phoebe (not Margo) Lane. He supports and battles the police as personified by Commissioner Weston. Yet, without the slouch hat and cape, Cranston does not truly seem to be the mysterious crime fighter known only as The Shadow. Rather, Cranston just seems to be your average run-of-the-mill amateur detective.

One night, *The Star's* young reporter, Phoebe Lane, bursts into a Shadow radio program with news about an imminent robbery at the downtown Metropolitan Theatre. Cranston broadcasts the news and after he gives them more information, the police converge on the supposed crime scene. The tip turns out to be a ruse, as simultaneously with the diversion of the police to the downtown area, there is an explosion in another part of town at the home of financier Gerald Morton. Morton is killed in the blast. To the police, it looks like the explosion was used to open the safe and Morton was accidentally killed during the robbery. Cranston, a criminologist in addition to being a radio personality and newspaper columnist, believes that the killing of Morton was a deliberate murder.

Cranston then attempts to solve the crime, employing an unusual investigative technique. The man who gave the original tip about the robbery to Phoebe was Viennese. On the theory that foreigners often go out to restaurants at night, Cranston and Margo go bar-hopping to see if Phoebe can recognize the tipster at one of the establishments. This approach defies all logic. If this were done every night for an entire year, Phoebe would probably have a one-percent chance of finding the man. Surprisingly, after canvassing just a few restaurants, Phoebe spots the culprit on the very first night. That leads Cranston to his quarry, and after some interplay between Cranston and the villains, he is able to prevent the killing of another financier and capture the bad guys. The crimes have something to do with enemy agents in America.

Rod La Rocque returns in his second and last appearance as Lamont Cranston, although in the prior film his name was erroneously spelled as Lamont Granston. Once again, La Rocque is the best thing in the film. He imbues the part of Cranston with just the right mixture of cynicism and toughness. Another good performance is given by Thomas Jackson as Commissioner Weston, not all that happy about the criticism Cranston directs at the police in both his newspaper column and radio show. On the other hand, Astrid Allwyn is merely irritating as Phoebe Lane. It is probably not her fault; the part is written in an irritating manner. Lew Hearn is embarrassing in his ethnic overacting in the part of Cranston's Jewish assistant, cab driver Moe.

Not much happens in the film. There is little mystery, except for the question of why Cranston has a drawing of a profile of the traditional Shadow, black hat and cape, on the wall of the radio studio, when he never dresses in that disguise. The best moment in the film, small though it may be, is when Cranston admits to Phoebe that he does not know what to do next. When Phoebe expresses surprise, Cranston says, "That's right. The Shadow doesn't know."

For a better example of a film version of the Shadow from this era, the 1940 serial from Columbia, titled *The Shadow*, is a far better choice. Victor Jory plays Lamont Cranston and the Shadow in the chapter play, and Jory always wears the slouch hat and cape when he becomes the mysterious crime fighter. The serial is thus more in keeping with the tone of the original pulp stories than the two Rod La Rocque features, which surprisingly downplay the importance of the Shadow character.

Note on the Source Material: There is nothing in the credits of *International Crime* to indicate that it was based on a written work. Nevertheless, many sources state that the film was based on *Foxhound* by Theodore Tinsley, writing under the name Maxwell Grant, published in the January 15, 1937 issue of *The Shadow Magazine*. However, a comparison of the plot summary at "The Shadow in Review" website indicates that there are no similarities between the story lines in the pulp magazine and the film.

The Kane Richmond Films

THE SHADOW RETURNS (1946)

The Shadow returns to the cinema after an absence of eight years, bringing along his cape, mask, dark hat and a number of the regulars from the pulps and the radio. There is also a new star in the lead, with Kane Richmond appearing in the title role. Nevertheless, instead of attempting to recreate the mysterious nature of The Shadow, with his vigilantism and exotic sudden appearances and disappearances, the character is shoehorned into a traditional and fairly boring whodunit, with Lamont Cranston taking the lead in the story over his alter ego, to the detriment of the film.

The MacGuffin in *The Shadow Returns* is a pouch of valuable jewels, unearthed from a coffin at the beginning of the story. The police accompany a man named Yomans and the jewels to the house of Michael Hasden, the apparent owner of the jewels. Yomans disappears upon entering the house, and later Hasden apparently commits suicide by jumping off a high balcony of the house. Lamont Cranston suspects the death was murder, although he cannot figure out how the killing was committed. Cranston decides to investigate the murder, along with the disappearance of Yomans.

The investigation focuses on several suspects who were at the Hasden house at the time of the killing. They are part of a syndicate that was formed to buy the jewels, and they include Charles Frobay, an importer-exporter, William Monk, an ex-racketeer, Lenore Jessup, an attractive showgirl, and Breck, of whom little is known. During the film there are two more murders, and a dead body unexpectedly appears in Cranston's taxicab. There are several side trips to a dark warehouse owned by Frobay, and it is there that Cranston discovers the secret of the diamonds, which allows him to unmask the real killer of Hasden and the others back at the mansion. Also, Cranston discovers the reason for the disappearance of Yomans at the beginning of the film.

Cranston does appear from time to time in his Shadow garb, either to extract information from a suspect or provide a clue to the police. Unfortunately, there is little suspense or menace in the Shadow's appearances, undercutting the effectiveness of the scenes.

In *The Shadow Returns* (1946), Margo Lane (Barbara Reed) watches as Lamont Cranston (Kane Richmond) dissolves plastic diamonds in order to locate a piece of microfilm hidden inside containing a secret formula.

(Still, this is an improvement over the Rod La Rocque Shadow films, where the caped vigilante was usually nowhere to be seen.) The unmasking of the killer at the end of the film occurs in a deadly dull set of scenes, and since there has been little differentiation in the suspects throughout the film, the killer's identity is simply uninteresting. The scenes in the warehouse are confusing and also engender little suspense. The film is quite disappointing.

The very handsome Kane Richmond is good as Lamont Cranston/The Shadow, although even at age 40 he still seems young for the part. Perhaps it is because in this version of the character Cranston is the nephew of police commissioner Weston, making Cranston seem younger than he is usually portrayed. The police are treated with respect in this film, which is a marked improvement over other 1940s mysteries, and Pierre Watkin and Joseph Creehan are good in their investigative roles. Tom Dugan plays cab driver Shrevvy, a big improvement over the overly Semitic portrayal of the character in the prior Rod La Rocque film. Dugan made a career out of not being funny in comedy relief parts, from serials in the early 1930s through mystery movies in the 1940s. At least in this film Dugan is not all that irritating. Cranston's fiancée Margo Lane accompanies him on most of his investigations, but she adds little to the movie.

The one interesting aspect of the film is the method of murder. It appears that three people committed suicide by jumping off high ledges, falling to their deaths. While the audience assumes they were all murdered (or why have a mystery movie at all), there was no one else around when the deaths occurred and it does appear that the victims jumped. At the end of the film, Cranston discovers the clever means of murder, although there are no clues to allow the viewer to work it out on his own. Nevertheless, it is the one nice touch in the film, but is not enough to raise *The Shadow Returns* above the mundane.

BEHIND THE MASK (1946)

At the beginning of *Behind the Mask*, it appears that a new screen genre may have been invented: the film noir comedy. In terms of plot, character, setting and direction, the movie opens with a legitimate film noir section. The opening scenes then segue into a pre-wedding party for Lamont Cranston and Margo Lane, which is generally played for amiable laughs. However, the film never returns to its noir beginnings and continues with its almost nonstop comedy vignettes, making *Behind the Mask* just another one of the many films in that typical 1940s genre: a dismal comedy with scant mystery interruptions.

The movie concerns the murder of Jeff Mann, the gossip columnist for *The Daily Bulletin*, who has been blackmailing a number of less-than-desirables in town, such as Marty Greane, who runs his own blackmail racket at the Paradise Club, and Mae Bishop, who runs a bookie operation at the Winter Garden nightclub. Mann is killed in his office at the newspaper, and through the glass door the other employees can see the shadow of a masked man with a cape committing the killing. Everyone jumps to the conclusion that the Shadow has perpetrated the murder.

Lamont Cranston has to forgo his wedding plans to clear the name of his masked alterego. The investigation is complicated by the fact that the coroner has determined Mann's death, and that of a policeman who was found dead at the same time, were caused by heart failure and not by murder. Mann's assistant, Edie Merrill, is then found dead in an elevator, and the cause of that death is also determined to be heart failure. Cranston, on the other hand, believes that the heart failures of all of the victims were caused by the injection of air into their bloodstreams. At the end of the feature, all of the suspects are gathered at the newspaper office and the surprise killer is unmasked.

The true plot must fill about 20 minutes of the 65-minute running time of this feature. The rest of the film is filled with increasingly tiresome and unfunny comedy bits, which seldom move the plot forward. The writers must have felt that the character of Shrevvy, who was the comic relief in the last film in the series, was not enough to carry the comedy elements of *Behind the Mask*, so this time an unfunny girlfriend of his was added. The police chief and the district attorney were also apparently not enough, so Ed Gargan was called in to perform his patented role of a bumbling policeman.

The acting is generally poor throughout and is always over the top. Barbara Reed, who was quite good in the last film in the series, is shrill and irritating as Margo Lane, who is now more comedy relief than love interest to Lamont Cranston. At one point she masquerades as the Shadow and the real killer knocks her out with a punch to the face. When she recovers, the real Shadow mistakenly knocks her out again with another punch to the face. Which clever writer thought that violence to women would create great laughs?

The plot makes little sense. How could the coroner determine that the deaths resulted from natural causes when Cranston was able to determine that they were murders? Why is it that ... but what's the point? There is so little plot among the comedy elements that there is little point in criticizing the storyline.

The opening is terrific, with Mann visiting several of his blackmail victims, announcing that he is raising his cash demands. The scenes occur in the rain, with contemporary music in the background. There is the noir contrast of light and dark, Mann shown in a reflection in a puddle of water in the street, and a mysterious dark figure following Mann. These scenes are beautifully composed and directed by Phil Karlson, who subsequently directed many gritty crime films such as *99 River Street* (1953) and *The Phenix City Story* (1955). Karlson apparently fell ill during production and William Beaudine substituted for him for much of the film. Perhaps that is why all of the directorial style is gone from the latter parts of the movie.

Nevertheless, the change in directors is somewhat irrelevant to the final product on the screen. With such a tiny plot hidden among the vast comedy elements, no director could have made a difference in the effectiveness of this film. *Behind the Mask* is really bad.

THE MISSING LADY (1946)

Although it is faint praise, *The Missing Lady* is the best of the Shadow movies, even including the 1930s features starring Rod La Rocque. This positive evaluation is not because the film eschewed the long comedy bits which hurt the prior two films. In fact, there are plenty of unfunny comedy moments here, generally involving Margo Lane and Jennie, two characters who are superfluous to the storyline. A running joke relates to the phrase "the missing lady," which refers to a missing jade statue worth $250,000. When numerous characters express their belief that "the missing lady" refers to a kidnapped woman, Lamont Cranston never takes the time to correct their misunderstanding, in the vain hope of creating some humor. Most of the comedy of the feature, such as that running joke, falls flat.

Nor is *The Missing Lady* the best Shadow film because of its plot, which is murky at best. Much of the plot is quite illogical. The film opens with the killing of collector James Douglas and the stealing of the jade lady. It will turn out that thug Ox Welsh killed Douglas for the statue but was then himself knocked out and the statue stolen from him. A month later, everyone is after the missing lady, no one seems to know where it is, and each person suspects every other person of having the statue. In addition to the murder of Douglas, two other characters are killed and those murders are related, in some way, to the missing lady.

Nor is *The Missing Lady* the best Shadow film because of its clever mystery and surprise denouement, since the film is missing both. Cranston gathers all of the suspects together and in the last scene explains exactly what had gone before, including identifying the killer of the last two victims, who is not only the least likely suspect, but also the only person left for Cranston to finger. Cranston's entire explanation amounts to total guesswork. The ending is completely unconvincing.

Despite these shortcomings, *The Missing Lady* has many positive attributes, not the least of which are its attractive female performers. Jo Carroll Dennison plays one of the suspects, Gilda Marsh, an artist's model. She is a knockout wearing a short tennis outfit when being painted by suspect Jon Field, and she is quite sultry when trying to seduce Cranston before knocking him unconscious with a blow to the head. Also quite attractive are Frances Robinson as suspect Anne Walsh and Barbara Reed as Margo Lane, once she ditches the strange hats that she wears throughout the film.

More importantly, the character of The Shadow is handled very well in the feature, at least during the first half of the film. The masked avenger is never shown as a full figure; he is either a shadow on the wall or a silhouette seen through a window. This adds to the spookiness and mysteriousness of the caped crime fighter, evoking the feel of the pulp stories. But why did the character disappear during the last half of the film, when he was so successfully utilized during the first half of the movie?

What makes this film most special is its directorial style and film noir attributes. Much like *Behind the Mask*, this film's opening scenes are firmly rooted in film noir. There is a shot from above of two characters talking about the stolen statue with a bright streetlight illuminating the scene from the upper right corner, indoor and outdoor scenes lit by a passing elevated train, scenes in a bar with jazz or boogie-woogie music playing in the background, and then the street lit by a blinking hotel sign. The shadowy figure of The Shadow adds to the noir effect. Later in the feature, the tough-talking, devious ladies and even tougher talking and violent thugs add to the noir atmosphere.

Director Phil Karlson imbues the film with interesting direction, epitomized by the scene in which Cranston is being questioned by the police. It is shot with only one cut, lit by a single light, Cardonna standing behind Cranston and asking questions, and each of the other policemen leaning into the light to ask Cranston a question. The scene is shot in a manner which turns a boring and cliché movie moment into a very interesting one. In essence, Karlson has turned a trite scene into a fascinating moment for the viewer.

Unfortunately, excellent direction and beautifully composed scenes do not, on their own, make a good mystery film. *The Missing Lady* still has many of the faults of the prior films in the series, but the excellent direction by Phil Karlson does lift this film a notch above the prior Shadow features.

After The Shadow

After his two performances as Lamont Cranston/The Shadow, Rod La Rocque made only a few more screen appearances. His last part was a supporting role in *Meet John Doe*

(1941). Rod La Rocque passed away in 1969. Kane Richmond only made a handful of films after his work as The Shadow. His last film role was in *Stage Struck* (1948). Richmond died in 1973.

The Shadow Magazine published stories about The Shadow for 18 years, ending in 1949. In all, 325 Shadow novels were published in the magazine. The franchise was revived a few times in later years. The radio Shadow was on the air for 21 seasons, with its last broadcast on December 26, 1954. A pilot was produced for a television series about The Shadow in 1954 but it did not result in a television series.

The character did return to the cinema on two more occasions. In 1958, Republic released *Bourbon Street Shadows*, which is also known as *Invisible Avenger*. Richard Derr played Lamont Cranston, who had the power to become invisible. This was originally intended to be the start of a new television series. In 1994, Universal released a big-budget version of the story, titled *The Shadow*, with Alec Baldwin as the mysterious masked figure. The film was not a success.

5

Nick Carter
The Master Detective

"If I'm wrong, I'll apologize."

Those words are the catchphrase of Nick Carter, the master detective, who appeared in three films released by MGM in 1939 and 1940. It was the last true detective series introduced by MGM, which had been a serious participant in the mystery series business in the 1930s with the Philo Vance and Thin Man movies, among others. It is somewhat surprising that the Nick Carter movie series did not catch on, as Nick Carter was a very popular figure in dime novels and pulp magazines for over half a century.

Background

THE STORIES

Nick Carter first appeared in Smith and Street's *New York Weekly*, on September 18, 1886, in a story called "The Old Detective's Pupil" by John R. Coryell. The old detective was Sim Carter, Nick's father, who taught him everything he knew. In the first serialized story, Nick solved the murder of his father and met and proposed to Ethel Livingston, who would later become his wife. After two more stories by Coryell, 37 different writers produced stories about the master detective during the dime novel era. One was Frederick Van Renssaelear Dey, who wrote Nick Carter stories for over 17 years, often writing a 25,000 word story each week. In all, Dey purportedly wrote over 1,000 stories about the master detective, although the true figure might be half that amount.

New York Weekly was a dime novel, and Nick Carter was America's top dime novel detective. The dime novel era continued until 1915, and upon its demise, the Nick Carter stories moved to the pulp magazines, being occasionally published in the twice monthly pulp *Street & Smith's Detective Story Magazine*. In these stories, Carter fought the New York underworld or evil criminal geniuses. Reprints of the Nick Carter stories were still being published as late as 1934.

THE FILM SERIES

Nick Carter began appearing in silent films in four serials released by a French company starting as early as 1908, and then there were two series of short films about the master detective released in the early 1920s. However, the best known Nick Carter mystery films were the three released by MGM starting in 1939.

In these films, Nick Carter appears to be a private detective, hired to prevent the theft of secret airplane designs, to prevent insurance fraud related to the destruction of merchant vessels, and to prevent foreign infiltrators from succeeding in their propaganda efforts in America. In the first and last films, Carter's exploits are related to Fifth Columnists in the United States, giving the movies the flavor of a spy story in addition to a mystery movie.

Walter Pidgeon starred as the master detective, as Carter was sometimes known in the written works about the character. Pidgeon was born in 1897 in New Brunswick, Canada. He moved to Hollywood during the silent era, and when talkies arrived he began appearing somewhat regularly in films, but always in supporting roles. In 1937 Pidgeon was put under contract by MGM, but once again he never received top billing, although he did appear in more important films such as *Saratoga* (1937) with Clark Gable and Jean Harlow. Indeed, the Nick Carter series was one of the earliest opportunities for Pidgeon to display his acting skills in a leading role.

The only other continuing role in the series was Bartholomew, the bee man, a character that was created especially for the movie series. Bartholomew sometimes appears to be an interloper in the mysteries and sometimes seems to be Carter's assistant. The role was played by Donald Meek, the diminutive Scottish actor who was born in 1878. Meek was a familiar face in films, playing character parts throughout the 1930s in movies as diverse as *Captain Blood* (1935) starring Errol Flynn and *Stagecoach* (1939) with John Wayne. In the latter film, Meek played one of the passengers on the fated stagecoach. Meek also starred in a number of short mystery films in the early 1930s, playing Dr. Crabtree.

The Films

NICK CARTER, MASTER DETECTIVE (1939)

This first film in the short-lived mystery series is sparked by good performances by Walter Pidgeon as the master detective and Donald Meek as his interloping assistant, and by some interesting flying sequences at the beginning and the end of the film. However, the movie is dragged down by a mundane plot about Fifth Columnists in the United States just before the beginning of World War II.

The film opens on an airplane with two interesting passengers on board. One is John Keller, the inventor of a new type of plane, and the other is an incognito Nick Carter, who is there to protect Keller and his invention. Once the plane is in the air, the pilot, who is in league with foreign spies, pretends the plane is in trouble and lands the aircraft just in the right location for the spies to attempt to steal Keller's plans. Carter breaks up the rendezvous, kills the pilot, and recovers the plans. The co–pilot/stewardess, Lou Farnsby, manages to get the plane back in the air just before the spies can attack once again. Carter, though, is suspicious. Is Lou actually allied with the spies? She attempted to take Keller's briefcase from him on the plane when he was sleeping, and she was very slow in getting the plane back into the air as the spies were attacking.

At the Radex Airplane Factory, where Keller works, Carter is advised that despite what appears to be the greatest precautions, secret blueprints of important airplane designs have been disappearing from the plant. No one can figure how they are getting out of the facility. Carter eventually discovers that the villain is the plant doctor, who takes pictures of the plans and then hides them on the bodies of allegedly injured workmen, who are then able to leave the plant in the middle of the day without inviting much scrutiny. In an exciting conclusion, Carter takes to the air to prevent the spies from escaping by boat with the secret plans, and incidentally, to rescue Lou who is being held hostage.

The best scenes in the film are at the beginning and the end, with some interesting flying sequences and unexpected twists. Both scenes are quite suspenseful and exciting and are well-handled by director Jacques Tourneur. However, the direction of most of the film is competent at best, very disappointing from a man who was soon to direct *Cat People* (1942) and *I Walked with a Zombie* (1943) for producer Val Lewton at RKO.

As expected, Walter Pidgeon is excellent in the role of the great detective, Nick Carter. While Pidgeon had been in motion pictures for some time, this is one of his first starring roles and he makes the most of it. Character actor Donald Meek is excellent as Bartholomew, but his presence in the series is a matter of taste. He surely can be funny but he can also be quite irritating. In watching these films, it is always puzzling as to why a master detective tolerates such a bumbling associate, or for that matter how Bartholomew even gets involved in some of the stories at all.

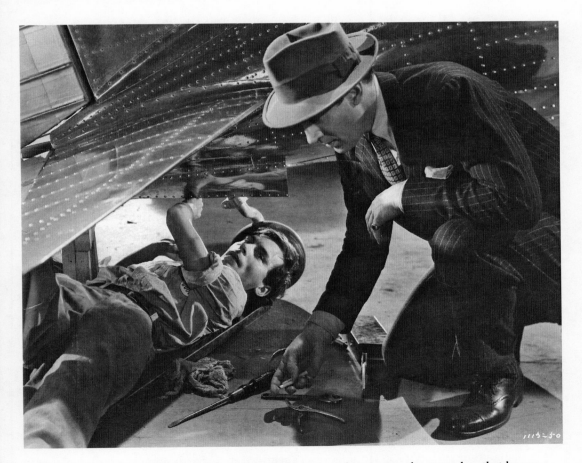

Nick Carter (Walter Pidgeon, right) negligently drops two cigarettes to the ground so that he can check on airline mechanic Otto King (Martin Kosleck), who may be a spy, in *Nick Carter, Master Detective* (1939).

Stanley Ridges is quite effective playing the company doctor, first seeming to be a competent professional and later turning out to be a hardened spy. There are a number of familiar actors in the smaller roles, such as Frank Faylen (Dobie Gillis' television father) as the traitorous pilot, Milburn Stone (Doc Adams on *Gunsmoke*) as one of the workers who conceals the plans and takes them out of the airplane facility, and Addison Richards (a regular in 1940s mystery movies) as the president of the airplane factory. The sight of these familiar faces always adds a layer of interest to any movie in which they appear.

Given the serious nature of the subject matter of this film, particularly on the eve of World War II, the tone throughout the film is surprisingly light, with Carter not seeming to take most matters seriously and Bartholomew inserting his nose into the story at seemingly inopportune times, thus undercutting much of the suspense the film could have engendered. The movie is typical of its era. It is more spy story than mystery movie, unfaithful to the written concept of Master Detective Nick Carter. The film had potential but it turned out to be a disappointing start to a new film series.

Phantom Raiders (1940)

Al Taurez is surely the most villainous of villains from the 1940s mystery series. Living in Panama, he has concocted a scheme to collect huge amounts of insurance money. First, he uses fake bills of lading so that merchant ships that are supposedly carrying valuable sacks of wheat only contain worthless sacks of sand. Then, once the ships are out in international waters, Taurez personally detonates bombs by remote control, and then makes insurance claims on the wheat that was supposed to be on the vessels. In the process, he kills the many crew members on each ship. To add poignancy to one of the incidents, the viewer gets to overhear a little talk among the crew, before they are blown to bits. Taurez does not seem to mind, however, since the insurance payoffs are so great. Professor Moriarty was never quite so cruel on such a large scale.

Nick Carter is hired to investigate the repetitive insurance claims and since he had tangled with Taurez several times before back in the States, he immediately suspects Taurez. However, obtaining proof of Taurez's involvement and discovering his method of destroying the ships is not so easy. Carter finally traps Taurez on one of the boats that is about to be destroyed and is able to wring a confession from him, just as one of his bombs is supposedly about to explode.

This film has a tight script, with a story by Jonathan Latimer, who contributed scripts and stories for other mystery movies in the 1940s. Latimer had previously written the Bill Crane mystery novels in the 1930s, and he later contributed a number of scripts for the *Perry Mason* television show in the 1950s and 1960s, so the quality of his work here is not surprising. Latimer creates a clever surprise near the end of the movie, when Taurez places his lovely assistant, Cora Barnes, and her boyfriend, John Ramsell, Jr., on board one of the ships he intends to destroy. Although it is only suggested in the movie, it appears that Taurez put them in harm's way because he was jealous of the relationship between Cora and John. What a villain!

The acting, as expected in a film from MGM, is excellent. Joseph Schildkraut is fabulous as Al Taurez, the master villain. The Austrian born actor with the light accent is the epitome of sophisticated villainy. Donald Meek as Bartholomew is wonderful as always. The diminutive actor somehow seems menacing while holding a gun on the villains yet humorous when he is trying to convince Carter to continue on the case. Other

Master detective Nick Carter (Walter Pidgeon, center right, holding glass) is standing next to master villain, Al Taurez (Joseph Schildkraut, hand in pocket), in a bar in Panama in *Phantom Raiders* (1940). Also shown are the bartender (Harry Semels), "Mac" MacMillan (Alec Craig), a sailor who works for Taurez, and Dolores (Steffi Duna), Carter's friend who understands very little English.

well-known character actors appear, such as Nat Pendleton as former boxer Gunboat Jacklin, British actor Cecil Kellaway as the owner of the shipping company, and in a brief moment, horror film supporting player Dwight Frye as a hired gun. It is all bound together by the winning performance of Walter Pidgeon, at once a ladies' man, boxer and detective. It is easy to see why Pidgeon went on to better things after completion of the three Nick Carter films.

The highlights of the feature are the opening sequence, where the villainy of Taurez is laid out for the viewer, including his knifing of a Scotland Yard investigator in the back, and the suspenseful scene at the end of the movie where it appears the ship may blow up with Nick Carter and the others on board. While the long segment where Bartholomew pretends to be crazy is far from amusing, the scenes with Carter's friend Dolores are quite funny. Dolores only knows a few phrases in English and she usually says them at inappropriate times. Dolores' antics are true comic relief that does not detract from the main story line of the film.

With a clever method of blowing up the merchant vessels, a falling out among the gang of thieves which results in additional deaths, an exciting and suspenseful conclusion, and a dynamite performance from the lead villain, *Phantom Raiders* is a significant improvement over the first film in the series. It is one of the most violent of the 1940s mystery movies, giving this film a substantially different feel than the other mysteries of its era.

Sky Murder (1940)

It is amazing how quickly MGM ran out of story ideas for Nick Carter. In only the third film in the series, there is so little plot that the movie is filled with comic incidents that crowd out the mystery elements, unfortunately making this film more of a comedy than a mystery. As a result, the semi-intriguing incident of a murder on an airplane in a locked cabin seems to get lost in all of the extraneous material. Where did the potential of the Nick Carter character from the dime novels and the pulps ever go?

Much like the first film in the series, in *Sky Murder* Nick Carter is after Fifth Columnists in the United States. Carter is called to Washington by his good friend, Cortland Grand, to ask him to assist Senator Monrose and his subcommittee in their investigations of subversive activity in wartime America. Carter demurs but later becomes intrigued when he overhears Andrew Henden, an international polo star, threatening to take some action against Pat Evens, a model who is at Grand's house. Henden wants Evens to engage in some espionage activity on behalf her native country, but Evens threatens to kill Henden unless he stops bothering her.

On the plane ride back to New York, Henden is found murdered in his cabin, with Pat Evens' nail file stuck in his throat. Since Pat was the last person in the cabin with him and had once threatened to kill him, she is the obvious suspect. In addition, there does not appear to be any way another person could have committed the homicide in the locked airplane cabin. Thereafter there are several attempts on Pat's life, leading Carter to the conclusion that perhaps Pat is innocent. Carter later rounds up the entire gang of Fifth Columnists and solves the howdunit of the Henden murder in the locked cabin of the airplane.

The opening of the film is quite good, as a truck from Luxor Printing Company, which is distributing propaganda material, crashes and one of the spies injures his leg. In order to ensure that the police, who are on their way with sirens blaring, do not capture the guy, the other spy callously kills him. The last scenes of the film are back on the plane, with Senator Monrose becoming bait as another potential murder victim to figure out the means and method of Henden's killing. It is a clever and suspenseful scene, but unfortunately it is a long time coming after all of the comedy interruptions in the film.

In between these good first and last scenes in the film, it is all filler material. Using the excuse that Carter would not have come to Washington without the promise of beautiful women around, Cortland Grand has six models at his house when Carter arrives. While the women are lovely, they do nothing to move the plot forward. Bartholomew is back, without any justification for his appearance in the story, and despite that fact, probably has more screen time than Nick Carter. It is true that Bartholomew can be funny from time to time, as for example when he beats up two thugs who are substantially bigger than he. Nevertheless, the diminutive detective's screen time generally consists of unjustified intrusions to the story. If one comic relief character is not enough, there is also Chris Cross, a ditzy female private detective, who is consistently not funny. If two comic relief characters are not enough, then there is a country judge, a country policeman, and Cross' nerdy fiancé thrown in for more humor. How about just a little less comedy and a little more mystery?

The identity of the secret head of the spy organization is obvious almost from the beginning of *Sky Murder*. Senator Montrose only tells Cortland Grand that Henden is to be arrested the next day for espionage, and then Henden is suddenly murdered. That makes Grand the obvious suspect, since he wanted to ensure that Henden would never talk in custody. Of course, if Grand is the chief villain, why did he bring Carter into the case in the first place? The explanation in the film is, as it almost always was in these mystery movies, quite feeble.

It is interesting to see Tom Conway, soon to play The Falcon in a series of 1940s mystery movies from RKO, playing the villainous Andrew Henden. Walter Pidgeon may be the handsomest and classiest actor to appear in a 1940s mystery movie while still in his prime. The solution to the locked cabin mystery is interesting. Other than that, there is not much to recommend in this film. It is not surprising that the Nick Carter mystery series ended with this feature.

Aftermath

Nick Carter was a star in many media. In the 1940s, Nick Carter was most famous as the star of his own radio series, *Nick Carter, Master Detective*, which was sometimes known as *The Return of Nick Carter*. It was broadcast on the Mutual Radio Network from 1943 to 1955 in 722 half-hour weekly episodes. In the 1960s and 1970s, Nick Carter became a James Bond-style espionage agent in a series of books written by anonymous authors. Nick Carter also appeared in comic books and then in two films made in France in the 1960s. His only television appearance was in the failed pilot, *The Adventures of Nick Carter* (1972), starring Robert Conrad of *Wild Wild West* fame.

Walter Pidgeon had a very successful career after leaving the Nick Carter movie series. He became a leading man in Hollywood, starring in famous and successful movies such as *How Green Was My Valley* (1941) and *Mrs. Miniver* (1942). He continued appearing in significant films throughout the 1950s and 1960s, although usually in important character parts, such as the Senate Majority Leader in *Advise and Consent* (1962). Of interest to mystery fans, Pidgeon played Bulldog Drummond in the 1951 feature *Calling Bulldog Drummond*. Walter Pidgeon passed away in 1984.

Donald Meek continued to appear regularly in films after the conclusion of the Nick Carter film series, including playing a small part in *The Thin Man Goes Home* (1944). Meek passed away in 1946.

6

Michael Shayne
The Private Detective

Michael Shayne is different than most of the detectives in the 1940s mystery movie series. Unlike Boston Blackie, The Saint, The Falcon, Ellery Queen and The Lone Wolf, Shayne is not a dilettante who becomes involved in crime investigations by accident or because he has a reputation of being outside the law. Rather, Shayne actually earns a living as a shamus. Shayne is one of the classic private eyes as immortalized by Hammet and Chandler, and even though the streets that the movie Shayne walks may not be all that dark and the cities in which he operates may not be all jungles of concrete, Shayne is still the quintessential private eye, operating as a loner with a quick wit and even quicker fists, ready to solve any crime that comes his way.

Background

THE BOOKS

David Dresser was born in 1904 in Chicago, Illinois, but spent most of his childhood in Texas. He joined the army at the age of 14, was discharged at the age of 16, finally finished high school, and eventually graduated from college where he received a degree in civil engineering. Dresser began writing full time in 1927, first producing many different types of pulp magazine stories, and then writing mystery novels under various pseudonyms. Despite his extensive writings, Dresser's main claim to fame today is for the numerous Michael Shayne novels written under the Brett Halliday moniker.

The first Shayne novel was *Dividend on Death*, published in 1939. It introduced the six-foot, one-inch tall redheaded private detective from Miami, Florida, who interfered with crime scene evidence, got into numerous fights, and had a penchant for drinking. Shayne was the typical hardboiled detective of the era, similar to Sam Spade and Philip Marlowe.

Dividend for Death also introduced young Phyllis Brighton as Shayne's client and love interest. Brighton reappeared in the second novel, with the detective marrying her by the third. That was a surprisingly modern approach to crime fiction, presaging the era of the late 20th century when it seemed that all detective novels addressed the private life and loves of the detective in great detail. In the 1940s, however, the focus on the private life of a detective, and one who was now married, was inconsistent with the manner in which detectives were portrayed in Hollywood. Since the Shayne novels were now being adapted for the cinema, Phyllis became expendable. She was killed off between the eighth and ninth books.

A new love interest, Lucy Hamilton, was then introduced into the stories. She became Shayne's secretary, and despite her interest in the great detective, the two were never married. Thus the Hamilton character was a more traditional detective story character, like Velda from the Mike Hammer books by Mickey Spillane, than Phyllis Brighton had been. There were a number of other regular characters in the stories, such as friendly policeman Will Gentry, antagonistic policeman Peter Painter, and newspaper reporter Tim Rourke.

THE FILM SERIES

The Michael Shayne novels were brought to the screen by Twentieth Century–Fox starting in 1941, with the release of *Michael Shayne, Private Detective*. Phyllis Brighton appeared in that movie, as did antagonistic policeman Peter Painter. However, those characters never reappeared in subsequent movies in the series.

The first film was based on a Brett Halliday novel, but thereafter the studio went to other mystery authors for the source material, such as Frederic Nebel and Clayton Rawston. The film *Time to Kill* was the first screen adaptation of *The High Window* by Raymond Chandler. In all there were seven Shayne films produced at Twentieth Century–Fox in the space of only two years, making this one of the quickest output of films in all of the Hollywood mystery series from a major studio.

Lloyd Nolan played private eye Michael Shayne in all seven of these films. Nolan, who was born in 1902 in San Francisco, had been in films since 1935, often playing a policeman or a gangster in films such as *G-Men* (1935) and *King of Gamblers* (1937). In addition to playing Michael Shayne, Nolan is best known in the movie mystery field for his performance as policeman-villain Lt. DeGarmot in *Lady in the Lake* (1947).

The last Shayne film starring Lloyd Nolan was *Time to Kill* (1942). Thereafter, the character was off the screen until 1946, when minor studio PRC started a new series of films about the detective with the release of *Murder Is My Business*. PRC was a particularly low-budget organization and the new series of films was not as slickly produced as the Twentieth Century–Fox films. The PRC films did keep up with one development from the novels, introducing the character of Shayne's secretary, Lucy Hamilton, although she was renamed Phyllis Hamilton for the films. The name appears to be a combination of Phyllis Brighton and Lucy Hamilton.

The new Michael Shayne was Hugh Beaumont, a Hollywood character actor who was born in 1909 in Lawrence, Kansas. Beaumont began appearing in films in 1940, usually in small and often uncredited parts. Never a star, Beaumont's continuing role as Michael Shayne must be considered the highlight of his film career. Of course, Beaumont's greatest success occurred later, in the *Leave It to Beaver* television series. Phyllis Hamilton was played by three different actresses in the five films, with Cheryl Walker performing the role three times. Walker was in films in Hollywood for about ten years, with few significant roles. Her career ended soon after her work in the Shayne series was completed.

The Lloyd Nolan Films

MICHAEL SHAYNE, PRIVATE DETECTIVE (1940)

At the beginning of this film, which is set at a race track, Michael Shayne acts the part of hardboiled private dick. For no apparent reason, Shayne interferes in the attempt by pretty Phyllis Brighton to use a valuable bracelet she owns as collateral for a bet she would like to make on a longshot horse, Banjo Boy. The reason for Shayne's interference may be that he is dubious of the bona fides of Phyllis' suspect acquaintance, Harry Grange. Nevertheless, perhaps Shayne should not have interfered, because Banjo Boy turns out to be a surprise winner and Phyllis has no bet on him. Matters are complicated further by the suspicion of track officials that the only reason Banjo Boy won the race was because he had been drugged by the horse's shady owner, Elliot Thomas. An investigation commences.

The next main scene in the film occurs at a casino, which like a race track is another common setting in a hardboiled detective story, particularly a casino that is apparently as dishonest as this one owned by the unsavory Benny Gordon. Here, Harry Grange is feeding money to Phyllis, fuelling her gambling habit so that Grange can receive a percentage of the take from the casino. There is also a love triangle between Phyllis, Grange and Marsha Gordon, the daughter of Benny Gordon, with Marsha appearing particularly unstable.

Throughout these scenes, Lloyd Nolan plays Michael Shayne as the tough figure of crime literature, with his tough talk, sarcastic remarks and his sudden use of his fists. Thus the settings, writing and acting beautifully set up a classic hardboiled detective story, surely with a murder about to occur.

And then it all ends.

Harry Grange is shot and killed in Phyllis' car, in such manner that the police easily conclude that Shayne is the likely killer. Indeed, Shayne has accidentally set himself up to be the fall guy for the crime. Shayne, Phyllis and Phyllis' Aunt Olivia then team up to try to solve the murder, but they do very little true investigating. Indeed, there is really not much happening in the movie at this point and the tone of the film becomes considerably lighter than it was in the race track and casino scenes. Of course this is a 1940s mystery, so there is the usual parrying of the private detective with the police, and there are also traps concocted by Shayne to snare the killer because there is no real evidence to convict anyone of the crime. Indeed, there are no clues at all to assist the viewer or Shayne in solving the murder, but that does not stop Shayne. He can solve any mystery, even without clues.

The writers continually take their eyes off the ball, often not concentrating on the murder investigation. Shayne sneaks into an apartment and then rips his pants, segueing into a supposedly funny scene when Phyllis wants to talk to Shayne while he is changing his clothes. Aunt Olivia keeps mentioning events she remembers from the detective stories she has read, with the boredom clearly showing on Michael Shayne's face and probably that of the viewer as each is forced to listen to her incessant ranting.

The policemen are as bumbling as they usually are in this type of 1940s mystery series film, but even if they were the best detectives of all time, there is no way they could have solved the crime in this movie. Shayne either takes any evidence he finds with him, so that the police never see it, or actually tampers with evidence, such as exchanging the gun barrels on two potential murder weapons so that the police will be totally confused. No wonder the police are unable to solve the murder of Grange.

At the end of the film, Shayne explains to everyone what has transpired, including who murdered whom and why. It is a quite interesting tale that he tells. The only problem with the explanation is that there is no way Shayne could have ever figured out the various schemes and motives of the parties as he describes them. Most of the events Shayne relates have never been mentioned before in the film. For example, the whole plot was initiated when a faster horse was substituted for the long shot, Banjo Bill, allowing the underdog horse to surprisingly win the race shown at the beginning of the film. However, there is not one scene or fact anywhere in the movie that gives even a hint of that development. Listening to Shayne's final explanatory speech is similar to being read the end of a detective novel, without actually reading the first part of the book. All of the events related to the solutions to the crimes would have been far more interesting and convincing if some of them had been shown in the film instead of just talked about at the end.

The acting is quite good. In addition to the fine performance by Lloyd Nolan in the title role, Marjorie Weaver is attractive and vivacious as Phyllis and Elizabeth Patterson is quite amusing as Aunt Olivia. However, the promise of the film's opening quickly dissipates into a mundane and slightly boring mystery, with Shayne being unimpressive as a private eye, usually trapping himself in his own "clever" schemes. Perhaps that is the reason his office furniture was being repossessed at the beginning of the film.

Note on the Source Material: The credits to *Michael Shayne, Private Detective* state that the film is based on a novel by Brett Halliday, but the credits do not state the name of the novel. A number of sources list *Dividend on Death* (1939), the first Michael Shayne novel, as the source. That is incorrect. The plots of the novel and film have nothing in common. The only similarities between the two are the name of the female protagonist, Phyllis Brighton, and Michael Shayne's early penchant for interfering with crime scene evidence.

The film is actually based on the second Michael Shayne novel, *The Private Practice of Michael Shayne*, released in 1940. There, Shayne continues his romance with Phyllis Brighton, whom he met in the first novel, which romance would eventually lead to their marriage in the books. Near the opening of the story, Phyllis is gambling at John Marco's casino, with the encouragement of playboy Harry Grange. When Shayne becomes involved and tries to protect Phyllis, the detective is framed for the murder of Harry Grange.

Most of the scenes in the film come from the book, such as Marco's daughter being jealous of Phyllis and Grange, Shayne tricking an average citizen into being a witness to Shayne supposedly discovering the weapon that caused Grange's death, and the switching of the barrels on two guns to confuse the police. While the killer is the same in both works and Shayne tricks him into a confession in both novel and film, the trap is different in each case. Also, the comedy elements in the film do not come from the novel. While there are other differences, the movie is substantially based on the original work by Brett Halliday.

SLEEPERS WEST (1941)

Movies, mysteries and trains— what a wonderful combination they are, from *The Lady Vanishes* (1938) to *The Narrow Margin* (1952) to *Murder on the Orient Express* (1974). The 1940s mystery series recognized the potential of a train setting for a crime story, in films such as *Terror by Night* (1946) in the Sherlock Holmes series, *The Lone Wolf Takes a Chance* (1941) and *The Saint's Vacation* (1941). *Sleepers West* is in the tradition of the great train movie melodramas of the past, but unfortunately, after the first half of the movie, much of the suspense of the setting dissipates, resulting in little more than an average feature in the Michael Shayne series.

The film opens as Michael Shayne is about to board *The Comanche* train, which is on its way to San Francisco from Denver. Shayne is guarding Helen Carlson, an important witness in a trial in San Francisco. Shayne, who has guaranteed her safe passage to San Francisco, is concerned that someone will come along and prevent Carlson from reaching the trial. The similarity to *The Narrow Margin* is obvious. Shayne sneaks Carlson on the train as an invalid on a stretcher.

At this point, there are a number of potential suspects for the person who may be interested in dealing with Carlson on a permanent basis. In the train station, Shayne meets old flame Kay Bentley and her fiancé, Tom Linscott, to whom Shayne takes an instant dislike. A railroad detective, George Trautwein, boards the train at the last moment in Denver. At the first stop, a nervous man named Everett Jason boards the train. Later, a porter discovers that Jason has a large wad of money in his suitcase. Just as the train is leaving that station, Carl Izzard rushes from a taxicab and climbs onto the train by the back of the rear car. The stage is now set for an absorbing mystery of who is actually after Callahan and how Shayne can prevent the murder. It is an intriguing setup.

The problems with the film start with a long sequence of comedy relief, with Kay Bentley trying to trick Shayne into revealing the location of Helen Carlson. Shayne knows what Kay is trying to do and therefore leads Kay on a wild goose chase through the passenger car, ending in a slapstick moment when Kay's sleeve is caught in the upper bunk in a passenger berth. These scenes are actually quite amusing, but unfortunately they deflate the suspense that had been engendered by the setting and the mysterious people on the train, thus starting the film on its downward spiral.

Indeed, the production makes little clever use of its train setting, as other successful train melodramas have. The rumbling of the train down the tracks is seldom heard in the scenes shot in the passenger cars, eliminating the background musical quality and excitement those sounds tend to bring to this type of feature. The berths themselves seem particularly large, eliminating the claustrophobic effect they usually provide. Little use is made of the narrow corridors on the train. Indeed, it sometimes seems as if the action of the movie is not even set on a moving train.

In the second half of the film, the character of Michael Shayne disappears for large segments of the story, once again undercutting the mystery elements of the film. There are long scenes between Helen Carlson and Everett Jason as they meet, tell their life stories and seem to fall in love. Once it becomes clear that Jason is no longer a potential villain in the story, these scenes also deflate the suspense in the train melodrama.

Near the end of the feature, the villain, Izzard, is shot and wounded by the train detective, eliminating all of the risk to Helen; but the film continues on for another ten minutes or so, with Helen, Kay and Jason fleeing the train wreck scene in a car, the car breaking down, interaction with the owner of a farm and Shayne arriving on the scene. The segment seems to promise the potential of another villain picking up their trail, leading to an exciting conclusion, but that hoped-for excitement never occurs, making this a particularly flat ending to the movie.

As the United States Supreme Court wrote in its 1941 decision of *Railroad Commission of Texas v. Pullman Co.*, it is well-known that porters on Pullman trains are black and the conductors are white. So it is not surprising that the porters on this train are played by African American actors, such as Ben Carter and Mantan Moreland. Since this is a 1940s movie, it is also not surprising that the roles are written in a slightly demeaning manner. On the other hand, perhaps the film is not that demeaning to the porters, as far and away the dumbest character on the train is the white train detective played by Edward Brophy. At least the porters provide good service to their customers.

In addition to the early part of the movie, there are other positives in *Sleepers West*. There are some good railroad scenes in the film, but these are confined to the moments that occur in the train's engine, where the engineer is pushing the train at top speed so that he can get back on schedule after a late start from the station. Here, the filmmakers succeeded in creating a feeling of speed and movement, aided by shots of the train from the outside rushing down the tracks. This culminates in a spectacular train/oil truck collision and flash fire in the cabin, surely the most exciting scene in the movie.

The acting is excellent, as it always was for this series. In addition to another fine performance by Lloyd Nolan in the lead, Louis Jean Heydt plays Everett Jason, a nervous and slightly perplexed man who is running away from his life of quiet desperation in Avondale and moving to South America. Heydt conveys Jason's mixed up feelings about his life and his future to perfection. It is the performance of the film. Heydt is a familiar actor in the movies, even if his name is not well known. For mystery fans, he is best-remembered for his performance in *The Big Sleep* (1946), playing Joe Brody.

Sleepers West is sometimes diverting but is often disappointing. It is occasionally entertaining but it is just as often infuriating. Once again, the potential in this Michael Shayne mystery is never reached, with the excellent set up in the early scenes in the film squandered in the second half of the feature.

Note on the Source Material: *Sleepers West* was based on the novel *Sleepers East* by Frederick Nebel. Nebel is best known for creating several memorable detective series for the pulps, such as a group of mysteries about Captain Steve McBride, a policeman, and Kennedy, a brash young reporter, who fought crime in Richmond City. Warner Brothers turned the concept into the Torchy Blane mystery series of the 1930s.

Sleepers East is one of the few novels that Nebel wrote. It does not contain any of the series characters created by Nebel. The book was apparently never published in paperback and it has been out of print for many years. It was previously filmed by Fox in 1934 under its original title.

The movie is substantially based on the Nebel novel, with attorney Martin Knox on a train hiding Lena Karelson, an important witness in the Callahan trial that is ongoing back east. Callahan appears to be innocent, having been framed for political reasons. Knox is concerned about the safety of Karelson and for good reason. Linscott, the fiancé of newspaper reporter Ada Robillard, a former love interest of Knox, and Carl Izzard, a private detective, are in on a plot to locate Karelson on the train and, at least from Izzard's perspective, to permanently eliminate her.

Within this story of crime, there are two subplots that are familiar from the movie. Everett Jason, who has decided to leave his wife and his boring job, falls in love with Lena after only meeting her for a few moments on the train. Also, the train is late on its run and the engineer is running the train at top speed, leading to a train crash near the end of the story.

Obviously, some of the character names and the direction of the train were changed for the film. More importantly, the book has a surprise ending, with Lena mistakenly shot by a railroad detective when Everett and Lena flee the train after it crashes. Thus Martin Knox has failed in his mission. For the film series, it would have been difficult to depict Shayne failing in any of his assignments, so the clever ending of *Sleepers East* was replaced by the disappointing ending of *Sleepers West*.

Dressed to Kill (1941)

As the film opens, Michael Shayne, wearing his new suit, is ready to marry singer Joanne La Marr. As the two leave her room at the Hotel Du Nord and proceed to their nuptials, Shayne hears a scream from the floor above. Up the stairs he goes, where he discovers a panicking maid and two dead bodies in very strange costumes. The wedding is on hold until the mystery can be solved. Has someone accidentally inserted a Falcon movie into the DVD player?

The bodies are those of Louis Lathrop, a one-time famous Broadway producer who owns the hotel and the theater attached to it, and Desiree Vance, Lathop's former leading lady. The two are dressed in medieval costumes and Lathrop is also wearing the costume head of a dog. It turns out that the costumes came from one of Lathrop's hit shows which he had produced many years before. Shayne sets out to solve the murders so he can earn some money for his upcoming marriage. As the movie develops, many of the cast members and other contributors to Lathrop's hit show keep appearing on the scene, thus becoming suspects. Shayne is successful in solving the crime but loses his fiancée in the process.

Unlike the two previous films in the series, which started out in a strong manner and then gradually diminished in interest over the course of the film, *Dressed to Kill* commences in a weak manner and never improves. Part of the problem is the stagy treatment of the subject. More than half the "action" takes place in Lathrop's hotel room, and all or most of the rest of the film is shot indoors, with lots of talking and not much happening. It is surprising that this film was based on a mystery novel and not a play.

A more serious problem with the movie is endemic to the entire series so far. The character of Michael Shayne, as envisioned by Brett Halliday, was that of a hardboiled detective in an urban jungle, much like Philip Marlowe and Sam Spade. The films from the 1940s about the latter characters were shot in a serious manner, often in the style of film noir. Although the Marlowe and Spade films were big-budget movies and the Shayne films were mere second features, film noir and its related directorial style often work better in the B-film product than in a major film, so it was surely worth a try in the Shayne movies. However, no attempt was made to recreate the environment of the books or to craft a film noir style for the Shayne features, even though that was a prevailing cinema technique for mysteries of the 1940s.

The tone of all of these films has been light when it should have been dark. The attempted comedy comes from set pieces rather than clever dialogue. The direction is uninspired when it could have been inventive. While these deficits were present in the first two films in the series, they stand out in *Dressed to Kill* with its stage bound, boring investigation into an admittedly strange pair of murders. A good example of the type of problems with *Dressed to Kill* occurs when Shayne attempts to recreate the double killings in Lathrop's apartment, demonstrating how the two murders could have been done simultaneously by one killer. Shayne recruits two African American stage hands from the theater to help him with the demonstration, thus turning what could have been an interesting scene into a humorless and demeaning interruption to the tale.

The overlay story of Shayne's impending marriage adds nothing, except filler material. Henry Daniell, memorable as Professor Moriarty in *The Woman in Green* and a fine actor in many other films, is woefully miscast in *Dressed to Kill* as a semi-comic figure, Julian Davis, one of the suspects. Shayne is back to his unethical and irritating ways of concealing evidence from the police, but here he actually knocks Inspector Pierson unconscious

Michael Shayne (Lloyd Nolan) is reading the apparent suicide note of Emily (Virginia Brissac) in the presence of Julian Davis (Henry Daniell) in *Dressed to Kill* (1941). The body of Emily is lying on the bed.

with a blow to the head, clearly going over the boundaries of conduct for any private detective, even one in the movies.

The prior films in the series were initially interesting but ultimately disappointing; *Dressed to Kill* is disappointing from the very outset. It would be nice for a true private eye story to appear somewhere in the series. However, based upon the story lines and attitudes of the films so far, that hope appears likely to remain unfulfilled.

Note on the Source Material: *Dressed to Kill* is based on the 1941 mystery novel by Richard Burke entitled *The Dead Take No Bows*. The plot of the film and the book are substantially similar, even though the book is obviously not a Michael Shayne mystery. In the novel, former policeman Quinny Hite interrupts his wedding day to investigate the simultaneous murder of producer Louis Lathrop and his former leading lady, Desiree La Ford. As in the film, most of the suspects are related in some way to a hit Broadway play that Lathrop had once produced.

Almost all of the scenes in the film come from the novel, except the embarrassing moments with the African American stage hands. The killer is the same in both formats and so is his motive. Hite even knocks Inspector Pierson unconscious, although it is accidental in the book. One significant change from the movie is at the end of the book, it is made quite clear that Hite's wedding will surely go on. Thus unlike Michael Shayne, Hite solves the crime and gets the girl.

BLUE, WHITE AND PERFECT (1941)

The second Michael Shayne film, *Sleepers West*, was a train melodrama in the tradition of a number of mysteries in which a substantial portion of the film was set on a train. *Blue, White and Perfect* can be dubbed an "ocean liner melodrama," as most of the last half of the film involves events on an ocean liner traveling from California to Hawaii. There are not as many ocean liner film mysteries as there are train mysteries, or perhaps the ocean liner mysteries are not as memorable as the train mysteries. There are a few, however, such as *Pursuit to Algiers* (1945) in the Sherlock Holmes series and *Charlie Chan's Murder Cruise* (1940).

Blue, White and Perfect is a typical Michael Shayne movie until he boards the ocean liner. Shayne has been hired by the Thomas Aircraft factory to investigate sabotage at its plant. On Shayne's first day on the job, $100,000 worth of industrial diamonds is stolen from the plant. Shayne suspects an inside job by Vanderhoefen, an employee of the factory, who was supposedly knocked out during the theft. When Vanderhoefen leaves the factory, Shayne trails him to a dress store, where he meets Hagerman, the apparent head of a gang of Nazis who are smuggling the diamonds out of the country so that they can be shipped back to Germany for military purposes. Shayne is captured by the villains and soon escapes.

While the first half of the film is mildly interesting, it is dragged down by the usual feeble attempts at comedy, including Shayne jousting with his girlfriend, pretending to be a Southern gentlemen so that he can investigate the dress shop, calling his girlfriend on the phone and making noises so that she will believe he is working as a riveter at the aircraft factory, and tricking his girlfriend into giving him $1,000 by concocting a fake real estate purchase. That last incident is particularly mean-spirited and is just the opposite of funny.

However, once Shayne boards the ocean liner, the movie improves substantially. The silliness drops away and while there is still some humor, it comes from clever dialog and interactions between the parties. The boat is filled with mysterious people, including Nazi spy Hagerman who is watching Shayne while avoiding him; Connie Ross, the pseudonym of a former acquaintance of Shayne who seems to be in league with Hagerman; Juan Arturo O'Hara, seemingly just a passenger but who is probably something more; and Nappy, the overly competent ship's steward but who may also be hiding something. Everyone seems to have his or her own agenda and the story constantly keeps the viewer guessing.

The scenes on the ocean liner are punctuated by an attack on Shayne's life with a gunshot fired from a weapon with a silencer, and a suspenseful scene where Shayne and O'Hara are trapped in a hold of the ship which is flooding. There is one final twist on the boat when one of the villains is unexpectedly killed. The movie then ends with a surprise as to who the leader of the Nazi villains is. It is a true shock, yet the revelation still makes some sense.

George Reeves plays O'Hara in a surprisingly natural manner. Reeves was strikingly handsome at this stage of his career and he is excellent in the role. Helene Reynolds plays Connie Ross and she is quite attractive in the part. Reynolds only appeared in a handful of other movies, all in the early 1940s. Curt Bois plays the ship's steward, Nappy, and he is very good. This was a typical role for Bois, who often played head waiters or pompous clerks during his film career. Bois is best-remembered today, though, for playing the pickpocket in *Casablanca* (1942). Mary Beth Hughes, who had appeared in the two previous films in the series, plays Shayne's girlfriend, Merle. While Hughes is competent in the role, it is hard to appreciate her performance in a poorly written part.

Blue, White and Perfect, a phrase which refers to diamonds, is the best film in the Michael Shayne series since the beginning. It is sparked by an interesting plot and by an even more interesting setting on the Hawaiian-bound ocean liner. The film goes to show that when a mystery movie concentrates on the mystery and not on the comedy, a satisfying result can be achieved.

Note on the Source Material: This film was based on a story of the same name by Borden Chase, which was serialized in *Argosy Magazine* from September 18, 1937, to October 23, 1937. The story was published in six consecutive issues of the pulp magazine. It was later published in paperback as a short novel, entitled *Diamonds of Death*.

The story involves U.S. Treasury Agent Smooth Kyle and his girlfriend Gilda Garland, who break up a gang smuggling diamonds between New York and Havana, Cuba. The smuggling is by way of the passenger ship, *The Princess Nola*, and the trips back and forth thereon by the suspicious Sonia Clonet, although no one can quite figure out exactly how the smuggling is actually accomplished. In the end, Kyle exposes the leader of the gang, known as the Boss, and recovers a fortune in diamonds.

Although the second half of *Blue, White and Perfect* has a superficial resemblance to the pulp novel in that both involve the smuggling of diamonds accomplished by a female traveler on board a ship, attempts to kill Shayne on board that ship, and the surprise revelation of the leader of the gang, there are really no incidents in common between the two works of fiction. It seems as if the screenwriters found some inspiration from the Chase novel, but took little else from the work.

Borden Chase is best known today for his Westerns, such as *Guns on the Chisholm Trail*, which became the basis for Chase's screenplay for *Red River* (1948), one of John Wayne's most famous films. Chase also wrote screenplays for other films and for television Westerns.

THE MAN WHO WOULDN'T DIE (1942)

Just about everything is wrong about this film, and that is symptomatic of the problems with the entire Michael Shayne series. An interesting plot is immediately diffused by comic elements, there is no fair play for the viewer, and at the end of the film, Shayne relates a complex tale of the murderer's motive and hidden events of the story, without any explanation of how he discovered the facts or why anyone should believe that what he says is true.

Surprisingly, the film starts off strongly, in the style of Universal's Sherlock Holmes series, with what appears to be an old dark house mystery. There is a large mansion, scenes shot in shadows, a body to be buried in a windswept grave lit only by handheld lanterns, and an unobserved man watching the proceedings. Later, Kay Wolff returns to her family home to announce her marriage to one Roger Blake, and that night she is shot at in her room by a strange figure with blazing eyes. A trip back to the graveyard finds the grave dug out and the body gone, adding to the spookiness of the opening. For ten minutes or so, *The Man Who Wouldn't Die* looks like it will be a terrific film.

Unfortunately, Kay hires Michael Shayne to investigate the attempt on her life, and the mood of the film immediately dissipates, to be replaced by the light-hearted approach that is the norm of the series. As part of his method of investigation, Shayne decides to masquerade as Kay's new husband, probably just so he can act obnoxiously to Kay's father, Dudley Wolff, for whatever humor that may bring to the feature. In the course of his investigation, Shayne meets Dr. Haggard, who is conducting scientific experiments in the basement of the mansion; Alfred Dunning, who is Mr. Wolff's secretary; and Wolff's young and beautiful second wife, Anna Wolfe. Each of the trio acts somewhat suspiciously in Shayne's presence and the viewer already knows that each had some involvement with the burial of the body at the beginning of the film.

Shayne does little or no investigation during the movie, although once Haggard is killed and the intruder enters the house for the third time, Shayne, along with the police detective, chase the killer until his car crashes over the side of a hill, where he apparently dies. Shayne then goes to a friend of his who is a stage magician. There he discovers that the dead villain is Zorah Bay, a magician who was famous for his ability to use a shallow breathing technique that allowed him to be buried alive. Shayne also discovers a picture of the magician's assistant and some facts about Bay, but none of that information is provided to the viewer, who thus has no chance of solving the crime.

In addition to Shayne's patter, which is less than amusing, there are bits inserted into the film for no reason, such as Shayne almost getting electrocuted in one of Dr. Haggard's experimental chairs, Shayne playing two hands of gin by himself, the funny and incompe-

In *The Man Who Wouldn't Die* (1942), Michael Shayne (Lloyd Nolan, center) confronts Dr. Haggard (Henry Wilcoxon) with a box of 32-caliber shells as Catherine Wolff (Marjorie Weaver) looks on. The setting is the basement laboratory of Dr. Haggard.

tent policeman with the funny and incompetent hair, and Shayne pretending to be a newspaper reporter just to embarrass the police about the missing body from the mortuary. On second thought, these vignettes are inserted into the film for their comedy value, which is zero or less.

Then there are those unexplained moments in the film. Was it Shane who turned off the burglar alarm, thus allowing an intruder to enter the house and kill Dr. Haggard? If so, why did Shayne do that? Shayne is clearly the one who later turned the burglar system back on, but why did he do that, if he turned it off in the first place? Did Shayne steal the body of the magician from the mortuary, and if so, where did he hide it before he brought it back to the mansion? How did he get it into the house and up the stairs? By the end of the film, does anyone really care?

Shane learns from an old publicity photograph of Bay that Anna Wolff was his stage assistant at one time. Shayne then uses the body of Zorah Bay to trap Anna Wolff into incriminating herself, but she never really does so. Shayne then relates a complex tale of the relationship between Anna and the magician, his attempt to blackmail Anna, Anna's relationship with Haggard, the three of them concocting a blackmail scheme against Dudley Wolff, and the double-cross by Anna and Haggard of Bay and the scheme to bury Bay alive. It is a hard tale to believe and there is absolutely no evidence to support Shayne's concoction. Anna is smart enough not to confess to the crimes and it may be assumed that if she were ever arrested, she would never be convicted.

It would be nice if at least a part of Shayne's solutions in these films were based on some facts in evidence. Indeed, in a moment of vivid self-understanding by the screenwriters at the end of the film, Kay asks Shayne where he got all of the facts about the crimes that he just related. Shayne has no explanation. The viewer has none either, illustrating the weakness of the plot. Perhaps Shayne just made it all up. Indeed, if it were not for the radiant Helene Reynolds playing Anna Wolff, there would be nothing to recommend in this film.

Note on the Source Material: *The Man Who Wouldn't Die* is based on Clayton Rawson's novel, *No Coffin for the Corpse*, first published in 1942. Rawson, who was born in Elyria, Ohio, in 1906, was a famous magician before he turned to writing, performing under the name of The Great Merlini. Rawson used his knowledge of magic to create his most famous series character, named (not surprisingly) The Great Merlini, a professional magician and amateur detective. Rawson wrote four books about Merlini, all told from the perspective of freelance writer Ross Harte, Merlini's younger friend.

The movie is substantially based on the first and last parts of the book. An intruder known as Smith attempts to blackmail Dudley Wolfe, causing an altercation wherein Dudley punches the man to the floor, killing him. Because Dudley is then the subject of an investigation by a Senate committee, he does not want any publicity; so he, his wife and some others bury the body in a desolate grave. Thereafter, the Dudley mansion is haunted by a ghost that knocks vases down, escapes from rooms where there are no escapes and eventually apparently kills Dudley.

It is finally determined that the ghost is Zareh Bey, a magician who had mastered a shallow breathing technique. Bey and Anna Wolfe had concocted a scheme to blackmail Dudley by convincing him that he had killed Bey. After the burial of Bey, Anna was supposed to save Bey's life by having him dug up. Anna then double-crossed Bey and left him to die. Luckily for Bey, Scotty Douglas, Dudley's boat keeper, dug Bey up, giving him the opportunity to haunt the house as the ghost. Bey is later murdered by Anna Wolfe, who booby-traps his car, causing Bey to crash to his death.

The obvious significant difference between the movie and the book is the main detective. The movie adapted a book about a magician-detective into a film about a private detective, and one who always treats his investigations in a light manner. With this change, the core of the book, about the investigation of the ghost at the Wolfe mansion by The Great Merlini, has been eliminated. A character named The Great Merlini does appear in the movie, but only briefly, and only to provide Shayne with a clue about the movie ghost's identity.

The book develops clues and motives and therefore the revelation that Anna Wolfe is the killer appears logical, rather than just a lucky guess by Shayne as it was in the movie. Indeed, at the end of film, Shayne appears to be quoting the solution to the crimes directly from the book, even though no foundation was laid for them in the film. Thus, in answer to Kay Wolfe's question about how Shayne solved the crime, if he were honest, Shayne would have replied, "I just read *No Coffin for the Corpse*. That's the only way I could have figured it out."

JUST OFF BROADWAY (1942)

It is hard to believe that any attorney would permit Michael Shayne to be seated on a jury, but as *Just Off Broadway* opens, Shayne has been listening to testimony for two weeks in the trial of Lillian Hubbard, who has been accused of killing her fiancé, Harley Forsythe. The first witness shown in the film, singer Rita Darling, testifies that she saw Hubbard at Forsythe's apartment at 9:30 P.M. on the night of the murder, which would have been around the time of the killing. The first defense witness, Henry Randolph, a butler in the apartment next to Lillian's, testifies that Lillian arrived back at her apartment around 7:15 P.M. and therefore could not have committed the murder. As the district attorney starts to cross-examine Randolph, the butler is killed by a knife thrown by a man in the back of the courtroom. The killer escapes.

Never missing a chance to interfere with the scene of the crime and to ensure that the police will never find the knife thrower, Shayne jumps from the jury box and hides the murder weapon under a table. That night, Shayne escapes from the hotel in which the jurors have been sequestered and sets out to find the murderers of Randolph and Forsythe. He is accompanied by newspaper reporter Judy Taylor. The two start out on the trail of the knife thrower, which leads to a killing in a warehouse, a confrontation in a night club, and eventually results in the unveiling of the surprise killer the next day in court.

This film is no masterpiece but it is one of the best of the Michael Shayne movies. It is aided by the short time frame of the film, as Shayne must solve the murders and get back to his hotel room before court starts the next morning. This compressed storyline adds a frenetic pace to the movie that is helpful in keeping the interest ongoing. Although hardly shot in film noir style, there is an interesting atmosphere to the film, since all of the outdoor scenes occur at night. Although a substantial portion of the film is shot in the courtroom, the scenes never seem stagebound, due to interesting camera angles, many shot from above the spectators high in the courtroom. The comedy scenes are kept to a minimum, unlike prior films in the series, and those that remain, such as a photographer trying to snatch a picture of Shayne, or Shayne trying to get back into his hotel room before the sheriff arrives, actually have a little bit of suspense to them. The comedy scenes work well in the context of the film and do not feel like interruptions to the storyline.

There is actually quite an interesting whodunit here. Assuming that the defendant, Lillian Hubbard, is not guilty (and in this type of movie, that is a reasonable assumption), there are several other potential suspects for the crime. There is Rita Darling, whose testimony is most harmful to Lillian and who was also in love with Forsythe; and there is Rita's boyfriend, George Dolphin, who may have been jealous of Forsythe and was surely capable of such a crime. The clue of a dolphin-shaped brooch found on the body of the knife thrower brings two more suspects into the picture.

The end of the film becomes a little silly as Shayne, from the jury box, orchestrates the questioning of witnesses by both the prosecution and the defense. The judge even allows Shayne, a juror, to cross-examine several witnesses, which is surely not a common trial practice, even in New York City. In the end, the killer is the least likely suspect, and even though some of the clues were withheld from the viewer, there are a couple of pointers to the real killer and the ending is surely not much different than the endings of many of the *Perry Mason* television shows. As absurd as the last courtroom scene may be, it is still entertaining.

Even better, Shayne is sentenced to jail at the end of the film, presumably for sneaking out of his hotel room and for hiding evidence. He should have received more jail time. It is quite likely that the police would have been able to trace the murder weapon back to the knife thrower faster than Shayne, if Shayne just stopped interfering with the important crime evidence. So Shayne receives his just desserts and the viewer receives an interesting whodunit, rare for a film in this series.

TIME TO KILL (1943)

Continuing the practice of basing Michael Shayne movies on the works of mystery writers other than Brett Halliday, the source material for *Time to Kill* is the 1942 Philip Marlowe novel by Raymond Chandler entitled *The High Window*. There were two Marlowe novels filmed around this time, the other being *Farewell, My Lovely* in the Falcon series, with that film titled *The Falcon Takes Over* (1942). The Falcon movie was a disappointment, because the filmmakers cut the complex plot of the Chandler novel to fit it into a standard Falcon movie mold, with not just detective Gay Lawrence but also his sidekick Goldy, a newspaper reporter, and a bumbling policeman getting involved in the storyline. The Michael Shayne movie went in the other direction, limiting the comedy antics of Shayne that were a characteristic of the prior films in the series so that more of the Raymond Chandler novel could be filmed. As a result, *Time to Kill* is a far better adaptation of a Philip Marlowe novel than was *The Falcon Takes Over*.

Michael Shayne is called out to the house of wealthy but eccentric Mrs. Murdock, who hires him to locate a valuable coin known as the Brasher Doubloon, which she believes was stolen by her daughter-in-law, Linda Conquest. Mrs. Murdock also requests that while Shayne is looking for the valuable coin, he do all he can to break up her son Leslie's marriage to Conquest. Shayne is off to locate the coin and Conquest, first going to the home of Lois Morney, a friend of Linda's, who is married to nightclub owner Alex Morney. There Shayne also meets Louis Venter, a gigolo who is involved with Lois. Then Shayne accosts George Anson Phillips, a detective who has been following him and who has some unknown involvement with the missing doubloon, and thereafter questions coin dealer Elisha Washburn, who may know the location of the valuable coin. Those leads dry up quickly for Shayne when both Phillips and Washburn turn up murdered shortly after he talks to them.

As Michael Shayne (Lloyd Nolan, right) looks on, Lieutenant Breeze (Richard Lane, left) shows Hench (William Pawley) the gun that may have been used to kill George Anson Phillips in *Time to Kill* (1943). This was the last film in which Nolan played Michael Shayne and one of the many films in which Lane played a policeman.

Then it is on to the Idle Valley Club, which is owned by Morney, where Shayne finally meets singer Linda Conquest, who denies stealing the coin. Venter, Shayne and Alex Morny then have a confrontation, and later Venter's murdered body is also discovered. Shayne keeps pursuing leads, including a counterfeit doubloon, finally solving all of the deaths including that of Venter, who was blackmailing Mrs. Murdock. Shayne even solves the murder of Mrs. Murdock's husband, who fell to his death from a high window many years before. In the process, Shayne helps relieve Merle Davis, Mrs. Murdock's secretary, of some of the guilt she has been carrying for many years over the death of Mr. Murdock.

Time to Kill is one of the best of the Michael Shayne movies, with the strong Raymond Chandler plot carrying the story. The movie's pace is quick, seldom bogged down by the comedy bits of Lloyd Nolan, often a fault of many of the earlier films. The performances in the supporting roles are not as good as they would be in the later version of the story, *The Brasher Doubloon* (1947), but Lloyd Nolan gives a better performance as the lead detective than George Montgomery would give in the latter film.

While its quick pace seems to fuel the story, *Time to Kill* often seems to move too quickly. For those who are familiar with the novel, too many incidents from the book are thrown into the movie, giving the scenes little time to develop. Thus, when Phillips is killed, suspicion is thrown on the occupants of the apartment across the hall, but the viewer barely gets a chance to meet that couple before they are gone, almost never to be mentioned again. The key character in the novel, Merle Davis, is a throwaway character in this film, with almost no development of her past experiences or ongoing mental difficulties. Thus, when the climax of the film revolves around Davis, it is difficult to understand anyone's motivations or the context of anyone's actions.

Indeed, the end of the film is rushed, with Shayne once again explaining everything that happened previously, without any facts to back up his explanation. As usual, Shayne seems to be making it up as he goes along, and for some reason everyone is willing to believe his complex explanation of the crimes. The incident of Mr. Murdock's fall out of the high window comes out of the blue, as if it were from a different film. Indeed, *Time to Kill* would have been a better film if it had skipped that aspect of the novel and only concentrated on the stolen Brasher Doubloon.

The direction of Herbert I. Leeds is poor, often forgoing close-ups when they are truly needed, such as when Merle Davis is trying to explain some of her emotional problems and her problematic history with the Murdocks. Richard Lane from the Boston Blackie series plays a policeman, but if not for his distinctive voice, the viewer would never be aware of his involvement in the film, because Lane never receives a close up. The same applies to Ralph Byrd as Louis Venter.

With all these problems, *Time to Kill* is still a good film for the Michael Shayne series, and many people believe it is better than *The Brasher Doubloon*, a higher budget film. While that is not the case, as the latter film has more style and character development, it goes to show that *Time to Kill* is well worth a view, particularly for those who are fans of the Philip Marlowe stories as well as the Michael Shayne movies.

Note on the Source Material: As noted above, *Time to Kill* was based on Raymond Chandler's third novel, *The High Window*, published in 1942. In 1947, Twentieth Century–Fox remade the film as a Philip Marlowe movie, under the title *The Brasher Doubloon*

It is quite surprising how closely the plot of *Time to Kill* follows the storyline of the book, with the Mrs. Murdock of the novel hiring Marlowe to locate the stolen Brasher Doubloon that she believes was taken by her daughter-in-law Linda Conquest, Marlowe meeting Linda Morney at her house where he also meets lothario Mr. Vannier (Venter in the film), being trailed by private eye George Anson Phillips, meeting coin dealer Elisha Morningstar (Washburn in the film), the subsequent deaths of Phillips and Morningstar, the later death of Venter, and the resolution of the death of Mrs. Murdock's husband from a fall out of a high window.

Although there are obvious changes from one medium to the next, the most significant difference between the book and the movie is that the character of Merle Davis, her emotional problems and her relationship to Mrs. Murdock, are not developed in the movie. This is one of the weakest aspects in the movie, with the central theme of the book almost becoming an afterthought in the film. Although the murder victims are the same and so are the killers, the movie spends little time explaining their true motivations, concocting a story about a conspiracy to produce counterfeit Brasher Doubloons as the key to the tale. While the concept of counterfeit doubloons manufactured from dental gold material does come from the book, it is a minor aspect of that story.

A little more selective use of incidents from the book and better development of the characters would have resulted in a better film. That was the approach taken in the remake, *The Brasher Doubloon*. For that reason the remake is the better of the two films.

The Hugh Beaumont Films

MURDER IS MY BUSINESS (1946)

After a four-year absence, the character of Michael Shayne returns to the silver screen, but instead of the films being produced at Twentieth Century–Fox, Shayne is relegated to very minor studio, PRC, and the title role is handed over to the then-virtually unknown Hugh Beaumont. The budget of the new five-picture series is clearly less than the budget of the Lloyd Nolan films. Yet despite all of these apparent deficiencies, *Murder Is My Business* does a far better job of recreating the milieu and attitude of the Michael Shayne novels than most of the earlier Lloyd Nolan films.

Murder Is My Business starts out slowly, with Shayne in a car with his secretary, Phyllis Hamilton, talking about the office, their relationship, and Shayne's difficulties with Rafferty, a local policeman. The setting then switches to the Tally Ho nightclub, where Shayne and Phyllis have drinks and then dinner. There they see two mysterious characters, Duell Renslow, an ex-convict who seems to recognize Shayne, and lovely Mona Tabor, a hostess at the nightclub. They are talking about another ex-con, Carl Meldrum, who is supposedly trying to get his hooks into the Ramsay girl. While not much actually happens in the nightclub scene, some of the characters in the melodrama to follow are mentioned; perhaps more importantly, the urban and hardboiled nature of the characters, the setting and the story are established.

The main plot picks up when Shayne is hired by Eleanor Ramsey, who wants him to investigate some blackmail letters she has received. Eleanor's husband Arnold Ramsey pulls Shayne aside and asks him for help in an insurance scam. He wants Shayne to find someone to pretend to rob his house of his wife's jewels so that Ramsay can file an insurance claim for the value of the jewels. The supposed burglar can keep the $1000 that will be left in the jewelry box. Shayne says he will think about it, but back at the office, he blurts the story out to Phyllis in front of a down-on-his-luck ex-convict, Joe Darnell. Unknown to Shayne, Joe decides to take up the fake burglary directly with Ramsay.

The next day Shayne is advised that the night before, Joe killed Mrs. Ramsay at the house and Arnold Ramsay killed Joe. Shayne then makes it his business to find the real killer. Along the way there is another murder, which Shayne also makes his business to solve.

The film has a quite complicated plot. Although Arnold Ramsay is the obvious killer of Joe, there are a number of potential suspects for one or both of the crimes, including Arnold's two grown children who hated Mrs. Ramsay, the ex-convict Renslow who is Mrs. Ramsay's brother, a gigolo named Carl Meldrum who had an affair with Mrs. Ramsay and is now dating her step-daughter, and the mysterious Mona from the nightclub. Unlike the films in the Lloyd Nolan series, *Murder Is My Business* never strays from its plot with irrelevant comedy scenes, and the role of Shayne is not written in a flip manner, except in his repartee with the police. The story keeps the viewer guessing and because the most likely suspect is finally tagged with the crimes, the dénouement makes sense.

Beaumont is good as Shayne and his familiarity from his subsequent television work does not mar his effectiveness. Cheryl Walker is also good as Phyllis Hamilton, who eventually becomes involved in the investigation, reminding the viewer of Nikki Porter from the Ellery Queen series. However, *Murder Is My Business* never becomes a story about Phyllis, unlike the Ellery Queen movies, which sometimes seemed to focus more on Nikki than Ellery. Also Phyllis is not a figure of comic relief as Nikki often was. Cheryl Walker is quite attractive in the role of Shayne's loyal secretary and can hold her own in the beauty department against the very lovely Margaret Lindsay.

Some of the other performances in the film are a little disappointing, particularly the actor and actress playing the Ramsay children. There is nothing special about the direction by Sam Newfield, who would go on to direct three more films in the series. However, these are minor flaws. With an emphasis on the crimes that occur in the hardboiled city and with several attractive actresses in key roles, *Murder Is My Business* is a good entry in what is really the first film in a new mystery series.

Notes on the Source Material: Despite the title of this film, *Murder Is My Business* is not based on the Shayne novel of the same name from 1945, but rather is based on the third Shayne novel, *The Uncomplaining Corpses*, published in 1940. The character of Michael Shayne in the novels was more hardboiled and willing to go outside the law than the Michael Shayne of the movies. Thus in the book, Shayne bears some responsibility for Joe Darnell going out to the Thrip (Ramsey) mansion, being deemed a thief and then being shot and killed. Much of the book revolves around Shayne trying to keep his investigator's license and stay out of jail as a result of his involvement with Darnell and the attempted robbery. In the process, Shayne beats up the Thrip son and even two policemen, incidents which do not occur in the film.

The novel is set just after Shayne's honeymoon with Phyllis, so it is Phyllis who goes out on her own to investigate Carl Meldrum, a task assigned to Shayne's secretary in the movie. This leads to Phyllis' arrest in the novel, another event which does not occur in the film.

Despite these differences, the movie is substantially based on the book, with the same murders, the same suspects, many of the same incidents, and eventually the same murderer exposed. For example, much like in the movie, Darnell's girlfriend threatens to shoot Shayne because of his involvement with Darnell's death, although in the book this scene is used to get a gun into the hands of Phyllis, while in the film it seems like a superfluous albeit interesting moment. The novel does a much better job of disguising the identity of the real murderer, who is also the individual who wrote those blackmail notes to Mrs. Thrip (Ramsey). For some reason, the movie drops the puzzle of the blackmail notes early on, even though the identity of the author of those notes is a key issue in the novel. Nevertheless, the movie's reliance on the basic plot and incidents from *The Uncomplaining Corpses* contributes substantially to the effectiveness of *Murder Is My Business*.

LARCENY IN HER HEART (1946)

It is difficult to define the hardboiled detective novel, and by extension the hardboiled detective movie. Perhaps it is easier to define the genre by what attributes it does not have. A hardboiled detective story does not contain a detective who wears a bow tie. A detective who wears a bow tie is simply not tough enough to compete against the villains in the concrete jungle. That is why it is so startling to see Michael Shayne wearing a bow tie during the first half of *Larceny in Her Heart*. Shayne's bow tie is a telling symbol of the problems with this feature, which unfortunately does not have the tough, cynical attitude of the first Hugh Beaumont feature in the series.

Shayne and Phyllis Hamilton are just about to embark on a vacation when the wealthy Burton Stallings arrives at Shayne's office unannounced and tries to convince him to investigate the disappearance of his stepdaughter, Helen Stallings. When Shayne demurs, Stallings leaves a $500 retainer check and a picture of the missing woman. Coincidentally, right after Stallings leaves the office an apparently drunken woman appears, mentions something about Stallings and then collapses. Shayne checks the woman's face against the photo of Helen Stallings and concludes she is the missing woman. Shayne leaves the office to take Phyllis to the train station, and when he comes back he finds the unknown woman strangled, with her body lying on his couch.

There are then a lot of shenanigans with the body. Shayne decides to dispose of the corpse with the help of his friend, Tim Rourke, a newspaper reporter, but when they come back to the office, the body is missing. Later the body reappears, suddenly and without explanation. Shayne then disposes of the body on Burton Stallings' front lawn, but the police discover it the next day in the river. In the meantime, Shayne begins to suspect that Helen may be alive. He goes undercover in a sanitarium, where he locates the real Helen Stallings. It turns out the body in Shayne's office was that of a look-alike who had substituted for Helen to help Burton Stallings defend a fraud claim in court. When the substitute got greedy, Stallings decided to kill her.

There is nothing truly wrong with Shayne wearing a bow tie, but it is symptomatic of the lighter nature of this feature than the first Beaumont film. The beginning of the movie is particularly light, with Shayne and Phyllis talking about their vacation and Shayne not knowing what to do with Stallings' retainer check. Later in the film, Shayne's friend, Tim Rourke, even does a pratfall with the body of an unconscious character. The film does turn more serious once it moves to the sanatorium setting, and those are the best scenes in the film. However, Shayne's explanations of the crimes, which are all guesswork, make no sense.

According to Shayne, Stallings was involved in the criminal activity, but if that is so, why did he hire Shayne to locate the fake Helen Stallings? No explanation is given in the film. The fake Helen, having been slipped a mickey by Stallings, coincidentally took a taxi to Shayne's office, where she then collapsed. But why did she go there? She had no idea who Shayne was. If for some reason she did know Shayne and deliberately went to his office, that also makes no sense since she was involved in criminal activity with Stallings and would not want a detective involved. After Stallings killed the fake Helen, Shayne postulates that Stallings returned to the scene of the crime, as all criminals do, to see if he left any clues. Then, because Tim Rourke was just returning to Shayne's office, Stallings hid the body in a closet. Later, after Rourke left, Stallings returned the body to Shayne's couch. Really? Not only does that not make any sense, but Shayne has no factual basis for his crazy theories. In fact, what was his basis for his belief that Helen Stallings was still alive?

A detective story has to make some sense; this one makes none. The plot has some superficial interest, but since the explanation of all that went on is less than convincing, the story falls of its own weight. This is a disappointing entry in the Michael Shayne series.

BLONDE FOR A DAY (1946)

The Michael Shayne movies starring Hugh Beaumont surely had interesting titles. There was *Murder Is My Business*, which could be the catch phrase for just about every film in this book, and then there were *Larceny in her Heart*, *Three on a Ticket*, and *Too Many Winners*, attention-grabbing titles all. Another is *Blonde for a Day*, which is not only an intriguing title because blondes always seem to be at the heart of most hardboiled detective stories, but also because that title provides just about the only clue to the killer in this film.

The feature involves Michael Shayne's investigation into the shooting of Tim Rourke, a newspaperman and one of Shayne's best friends. Rourke had been investigating the death of three gamblers in Los Angeles, even though his publisher was opposed to any more stories on the subject. Rourke persisted, even sneaking a story that postulated that casino owner Hank Brenner was involved into the paper. Rourke also intimated that he had affidavits in his possession proving his claims against Brenner. Rourke then wired Michael Shayne in San Francisco for help, and Shayne came to Los Angeles with his secretary Phyllis Hamilton (now played by Kathryn Adams, who was Hugh Beaumont's wife at the time). Before the two could reach Rourke, the newspaperman was shot. By the time Shayne arrives in town, Rourke is lying in the hospital, close to death. Shayne starts his investigation, and along the way one of the many blondes in the film is found dead, giving Shayne two violent crimes to solve.

It is difficult to find a good, complete print of this film and the inadequate prints available have a deleterious impact on one's enjoyment. Perhaps it is the incomplete print, but the plot of the film makes little sense. Shayne flits from suspect to suspect in his quest to find the person who tried to murder Rourke, questioning Hank Brenner (who along with his henchmen are trying to locate the missing affidavits), Helen Porter (a neighbor of a

Michael Shayne (Hugh Beaumont) is at center, with prime suspect newspaper publisher Walter Bronson (Frank Ferguson) at left and Shayne's adversary on the police force, Pete Rafferty (Cy Kendall), near the conclusion of *Blonde for a Day* (1946).

murder victim who does not act in the least bit suspiciously, appears in the story seemingly by accident, but is nevertheless a prime suspect just because she is in the film), and Walter Bronson (Rourke's publisher, who is being blackmailed by someone). Brenner's henchmen seem to enjoy beating up Shayne, which they attempt to do on several occasions.

The solution to the crimes makes little sense, and in Lloyd Nolan style, Hugh Beaumont seems to arrive at the solution by mere guesswork. In a way, though, this is the fairest of the fair play detective stories, since the viewer can also guess the identity of the villain by merely choosing the least likely suspect, i.e., a person who is in the story for no apparent reason. The interplay between Shayne and Pete Rafferty, his rival on the police force, is strained and without humor. The direction is pedestrian at best, with the scenes having little pacing, resulting in little or no suspense in the film.

The one interesting concept highlighted throughout the movie is the motif of a mysterious blonde who was seen in the company of the murder victims. That is where the title to the film provides the only real clue to the villain. Other than that, it is the small things that are best about the film, such as Shayne being beaten up or beating up others and Phyllis socking the prime suspect, knocking her out with one punch. These highlights, however, are few and far between. After a fast start with *Murder is my Business*, the quality of the Hugh Beaumont films deteriorated rapidly, and the Lloyd Nolan films look better and better all the time.

THREE ON A TICKET (1947)

It does not take a hardboiled detective to figure out why *Three on a Ticket* is a cut above the previous two Michael Shayne films in the series—the movie is based on a book by Brett Halliday instead of being just another original screenplay. Thus, even though the screenwriters were able to attach some comedy elements to the script, the strong plot from the novel always comes to the forefront, making this one of the best of the Hugh Beaumont films in the series.

Three on a Ticket commences with two startling moments. Just after Phyllis Hamilton tells Michael Shayne that Jim Lacy, a private detective Shayne once knew in New York, called and is on his way to the office, a man (soon to be identified as Lacy) opens the door, grabs his stomach, takes a few steps and falls to the floor, dead. Shayne rushes over and discovers part of a baggage claim check clutched tightly in the grasp of the man's hand. There is also some money in his wallet. Shayne takes both. He then leaves the office to create an alibi as Phyllis calls the police.

Next, beautiful Helen Brimstead calls on Shayne at his office, saying she was referred by Jim Lacy. She relates a tale of being in love with a wealthy man, but being blackmailed by her husband, Mace Morgan, who has just escaped from jail. Helen wants to hire Shayne to bump off her husband, clearing the way for her new marriage. Shayne does not definitively turn the job down, and apparently for his thoughtfulness, he receives a kiss from Helen.

The rest of the film concerns a number of different parties trying to acquire the torn baggage claim ticket from Shayne, including Pearson, an FBI agent, who is on the case because Lacy and Morgan were allegedly involved in stealing secret weapons plans from the government. Throughout, Helen's bona fides come under serious suspicion. Phyllis is eventually kidnapped by one of the thugs, and in an exciting conclusion, Shayne secures the release of Phyllis, obtains the bag from the baggage clerk and captures all of the criminals.

As noted above, the film commences with two startling scenes, either of which could have been the basis for a fine detective film. In addition, there are other good moments, such as Shayne being kidnapped and actually rescued by Phyllis, the surprise shooting of Mace Morgan by Helen in a bar, and Shayne's interactions with his best friend, newspaperman Tim Rourke, who believes Shayne is unpatriotic for refusing to turn the partial ticket over to the government. (For some reason, throughout the film, the federal authorities are always referred to as "the government," instead of "the feds" or "the United States" or something more common.)

Louise Currie is quite beautiful as Helen Brimstead, who is fooling no one with her innocent act when she first meets Shayne, with her true colors coming out in her almost contemporaneous exchanges with Phyllis Hamilton. Louise Currie has never looked better in a film, but despite that beauty, she is unconvincing as a femme fatale. Perhaps it is the large hats she often wears in the film; more likely, it is because she does not deliver her lines that well and the lines themselves are nothing special. Just compare the dialogue she is given with those of Barbara Stanwyck in *Double Indemnity* (1944) or Jane Greer in *Out of the Past* (1947).

The shocking twist at the end of the film, that Pearson is not really a government agent but is one of the gang, will surprise no one. Pearson never seems to act like a real federal agent, is unconvincingly working on his own without any federal backup, and is first seen all alone in Helen Brimstead's apartment, apparently burglarizing it. Pearson seems to have no knowledge of proper police procedures. Add to that the fact Gavin Gordon is unconvincing in the role and the whole surprise simply does not work.

Not all of the acting is not bad, however. Hugh Beaumont as Shayne and Cheryl Walker as Phyllis Hamilton are good as usual, although Hamilton is now being used more as a figure of comic relief rather than a detective's important assistant. There are a slew of supporting actors whose faces are familiar if not their names, who give good performances as the thugs and henchmen. Douglas Fowley as Mace Morgan, Charles Quigley as Curt Leroy and Noel Cravat as Trigger are fun to watch.

Three on a Ticket has more action than most of the late 1940s movies in the Hollywood mystery series, and for that reason the low budget of the film, a product of Producers Releasing Corporation ("PRC"), does not seem so low. Other than the non-surprise with FBI agent Pearson, the rest of the film keeps the viewers' interest all the way through to the exciting conclusion. With a stronger plot than usual and suspense and mystery created by the many different parties seeking the torn check receipt, this is one of the best of the low-budget mystery films released by one of the poverty row studios. While that may not be saying much, the film is still well worth a look.

Note on the Source Material: The film is based on the 1942 Shayne novel *The Corpse Came Calling*. Although the Hugh Beaumont Michael Shayne movies did have interesting titles, the filmmakers missed an opportunity by not using the title of the book, which is quite enticing. Of course the corpse who came calling in the book is Jim Lacy, as the book and the movie start out identically. Indeed, most of the scenes in the movie come from the book, although they are often re-worked into different contexts.

At the time of *The Corpse Came Calling*, Phyllis (Brighton) Shayne is still alive in the novels, and it is she who is kidnapped near the end of the story to force Shayne to turn over the torn baggage receipt. The involvement of Shayne's wife in the story makes Helen Brimstead's attempts to entice Shayne into working on her behalf and falling in love with her all the more interesting. There is more of a sexual element to the novel, as Helen kills Mace Morgan in Shayne's apartment while wearing one of Phyllis's negligees after attempting to use her feminine wiles on Shayne. Also, *The Corpse Came Calling* is a war time story, so Shayne's refusal to cooperate with the FBI concerning stolen weapons plans is much more controversial than in a film released in 1947.

Pearson is more of a minor character in the novel and therefore the surprise that he is a phony works much better in the written work. The entire backstory about is the theft of valuable securities and the many parties involved is much more complex in the novel and so are Helen's machinations. The book is quite good, but even though the film may not be quite up to the standard of the novel, it is a good adaptation of the written work with significant merit of its own.

TOO MANY WINNERS (1947)

Similar to the beginning of *Larceny in her Heart* (1946), at the beginning of *Two Many Winners* Michael Shayne and Phyllis Hamilton intend to embark on a vacation trip when crime intervenes. In this case, Shayne is visited by Gil Madden, who was going to offer Shayne $2000 not to take a case, but withdraws his offer when he learns that Shayne is on his way out of the city. Then Shayne receives a call from Mayme Martin, offering him important information on the case he is working on for the small sum of $1000. At the same time Albert Payson, the owner of the Santa Rosita Racetrack, has been trying to contact Shayne to hire him for an investigation. Shayne is then beaten up by two thugs and dropped in the public dump because he refuses to reveal information about a case of which he knows nothing.

Everyone either wants Shayne in the case or out of the case, but Shayne does not even know what the case is about. It is a unique opening to a crime film, although it is not really very believable. Shayne must be the most popular detective in town, or perhaps the only one.

Shayne meets John Hardeman, the manager of the Santa Rosita Racetrack, and finally learns about the case. It seems someone has been counterfeiting winning pari-mutuel tickets and the track has been paying out more on the winners than it has been taking in. Indeed, the track is close to bankruptcy because it has "too many winners." The police are unable to solve the case and Payson decides to call Shayne in for help. Being the excellent detective he is, once Shayne knows what he is investigating he solves the crime with all deliberate speed. Unfortunately, before he can do so three murders are committed.

There is much to like in this film. The mystery has some complexity, there are multiple murders, and there are even some touching moments, as when Shayne meets the wife and young son of a character who may be a crook. There is limited interference by Phyllis Hamilton, now played by Trudy Marshall, and the comedy scenes do not overwhelm the story. The acting is more than adequate, although none of the parts are written with much flair, hardly giving the performers an opportunity to shine in their parts.

But for all of those attributes, *Too Many Winners* is quite dull. The film has no pace or energy and the direction is sluggish. Most of the story is shot indoors; automobile scenes are shot in front of the ubiquitous rear-projection screen. The fight sequences are poorly staged, with the punches clearly being pulled. The film's ending lacks any excitement, with the last remaining villain simply walking into the police's hands rather than making much of an effort to escape. The initial murder in the case, that of Mayme Martin, is unsatisfactorily explained by Shayne. It is another example of that type of poor plotting where a character is murdered solely for the purpose of supplying a corpse.

As disappointing as this feature may be, the five Hugh Beaumont films as a group are surprisingly good, particularly given their paltry budgets. While most people think of Lloyd Nolan when they think of the Michael Shayne of the cinema, Hugh Beaumont more than held his own in these films, and his two best features, *Murder Is My Business* and *Three on a Ticket* are every bit as good as the best of the Nolan films.

Aftermath

Brett Halliday continued writing Michael Shayne novels long after the film series departed the silver screen. Halliday retired from writing in 1958, but ghostwritten Michael Shayne stories under the Halliday name were published until 1976. Dresser, a founding member of the Mystery Writers of America, passed away in 1977.

There were no more Michael Shayne movies ever produced. However, there were three different radio shows featuring the character, with the detective often dubbed "the reckless, red-headed Irishman." The first was *Michael Shayne, Private Detective,* which aired from 1944 to 1947, originally on the West Coast only and later as a national broadcast. The lead was played by Wally Maher. From 1948 to 1950 there was a syndicated broadcast of *The New Adventures of Michael Shayne,* originally starring Jeff Chandler. Finally, ABC broadcast *Michael Shayne, Private Detective,* originally starring Donald Curtis, from 1952 to 1953.

Michel Shayne came to television in 1960, in a show titled *Michael Shayne.* It ran for one season on NBC, from 1960 to 1961. Shayne was played by Richard Denning. The stories were set in Miami Beach, just as the original novels were. Lucy Hamilton, Tim Rourke and Will Gentry were regular characters.

With the conclusion of his portion of the Michael Shayne film series, Lloyd Nolan continued working regularly in films, often in significant parts in significant films, such as Officer McShane in *A Tree Grows in Brooklyn* (1945), Agent George Briggs in *The House on 92nd Street* (1945) and Lt. DeGarmot in *Lady in the Lake* (1947). In the 1950s, Nolan worked often in television, usually as a guest star but also in his own crime series, appearing as the title character in *Martin Kane, Private Eye* in 1951 and 1952 (although the series was on the air both before and after Nolan was on the show), and *Special Agent 7,* a syndicated crime show which ran for one season in syndication starting in 1959.

Nolan is of course best known for his role in *Julia,* the first network show to star a black woman. In the series Diahann Carroll played Julia, who was a nurse, and Nolan played Dr. Chegley, the head of the hospital where Julia worked. The show played on NBC for three seasons starting in 1968. Lloyd Nolan passed away in 1985.

Hugh Beaumont is also best-known for his television work, playing Ward Cleaver, Beaver's dad, on the *Leave It to Beaver* television show, which ran on ABC for six seasons starting in 1957. Ward Cleaver is one of the most recognizable television roles of all time. For mystery fans, Beaumont had previously played detective Dennis O'Brien in a three movie mystery series that began with *Roaring City* in 1951. Each film was an hour in length and had two separate 30-minute stories, thus allowing the films to be released on television in syndication as six 30-minute television shows. Hugh Beaumont died in 1982.

Ellery Queen
The Amateur Detective

According to Steinbrenner and Penzler's *Encyclopedia of Mystery and Detection*, when the character Ellery Queen first debuted in print, he was dubbed "the logical successor to Sherlock Holmes" because of his mental agility and acute observation of detail. In keeping with that description, the early Queen novels were serious, complex whodunits that adhered very closely to the fair-play standard of the era, i.e., that the reader be given all of the clues available to the detective so that both would have an equal chance to solve the crime.

The Ellery Queen novels were extremely popular at the time, and they seemed to be a natural for a Hollywood mystery series. After a brief attempt at Republic Pictures in the 1930s, Columbia produced a seven-film series about the famous detective, starting in 1940. Yet for some reason the film series dropped the serious, complex and fair characteristics of the novels; instead, the films often seemed more like comedies than mysteries. Indeed, there was often little relationship between the Ellery Queen of the original novels and the Ellery Queen of the film series.

Background

THE NOVELS

As most people know by now, the name "Ellery Queen" as an author of mystery fiction was the pseudonym of two cousins, Frederic Dannay and Manfred B. Lee. They were both born in Brooklyn in 1905. In 1928, they responded to a mystery novel contest by *McClure's* magazine in which the first prize was $7,500. They won the competition with their novel titled *The Roman Hat Mystery*, but just before they received the prize the publisher went bankrupt and the successor awarded the prize to a different author. Nevertheless, another publisher, the Frederick A. Stokes Company, decided to publish the manuscript in book form and the rest, as they say, is publishing history.

In an unusual decision to say the least, author "Ellery Queen" decided to name his detective "Ellery Queen." In the early novels, the character was modeled after a very popular detective of the day, Philo Vance, created by S.S. Van Dine, which name was also a pseudonym. Thus, Ellery Queen lived in New York City, had a close working relationship with the police, and the stories were set largely among the sophisticates, such as theater people, artists and collectors. Ellery was quite conceited, symbolized by his wearing a pince-nez. In the first several Queen novels, late in the story, once all of the facts were out for the reader, the action stopped so that Ellery could challenge the reader to solve the mystery before Ellery did.

When he was not solving mysteries, Ellery was a writer of detective fiction. He lived with his father, Inspector Richard Queen of the New York Police Department, who gave him his entree into solving many of the crimes Ellery investigated. Another regular was Sgt. Velie, the assistant to Inspector Queen.

Starting around 1936, Queen started relaxing the formula of his detective stories. The titles were no longer in the format of *The Spanish Cape Mystery* or *The Chinese Orange Mystery*, but became more diverse in style such as *The Devil to Pay* or *The Door Between*. The challenge to the reader was dropped, and Ellery Queen became more likable and less conceited. Many of the stories broadened their scope by exploring character and setting in the context of a murder mystery instead of adhering to the strict formula of Queen's earlier works and the works of other authors of the time period.

THE RADIO SHOW

The Adventures of Ellery Queen debuted on June 18, 1939, on the CBS Radio Network. It was the first hour-long dramatic show in the history of radio. Hugh Marlowe played Ellery, a role he would repeat on television in the 1950s. Nikki Porter, Ellery's secretary, was a new character created for the radio series to add a feminine element. This character, who was originally played by Marian Shockley, was a professional typist to whom Ellery had been taking his nearly illegible manuscripts, until she decided to become Ellery's full-time secretary so that he could dictate the manuscripts instead of writing them out by hand. Throughout the series, Nikki often became personally involved in the radio mysteries. When Nikki later became a character in a few of the books about Ellery Queen, two other versions of her first meeting with Ellery were given and then a fourth was provided in the Columbia movie series.

In early 1940 the show became a half-hour series. It continued on the radio for nine years, with its last new broadcast in May 1948. By that time, the series had also been on NBC and ABC. Throughout most of the history of the radio show, Dannay and Lee wrote all of the scripts, except toward the very end, when Dannay had other commitments and withdrew. Lee then wrote the remaining scripts with uncredited collaborators, such as Anthony Boucher, himself also well-known to mystery fans.

The radio series is important to an understanding of the film series produced at Columbia in the 1940s. Those films sometimes seemed to be based more on the radio show than Dannay and Lee's original conception of their character, particularly with regard to the disproportionate amount of screen time provided to Nikki Porter.

THE FILM SERIES

Dannay and Lee were always interested in having their sleuth's exploits transferred to the silver screen, and when Republic agreed to do a version of *The Spanish Cape Mystery* in 1935, the cousins were happy to agree, even though Republic was a newly formed conglomeration of several independent studios and Republic's expertise was in serials and Westerns.Nevertheless, the movie version of *The Spanish Cape Mystery* turned out to be one of the best Queen movies ever produced. It starred Donald Cook as Ellery Queen, although Helen Twelvetrees received top billing as one of the suspects.

Republic followed that film with a sequel, *The Mandarin Mystery* (1937), which was based on the novel, *The Chinese Orange Mystery*. Donald Cook was replaced by Eddie Quillan, who, with his short stature and comedy background, was miscast in the role of the great detective. *The Mandarin Mystery* was the last Queen work produced by Republic.

After an absence of several years from the screen, the Ellery Queen stories moved to Columbia for the start of a seven picture series, beginning with the release of *Ellery Queen, Master Detective* (1940). The films were lighter in tone and far less complicated than the Queen novels, more in line with the mystery movie series of the 1940s than those of the 1930s. Unfortunately, because the plots were flimsy, the films' running times were padded with comedy bits and light vignettes. This often detracted from some clever murder mysteries, which were lost in the extraneous matter.

The Columbia films were also based more on the radio series than the books. Ellery is a detective story writer who lives with his father, Inspector Queen of the New York Police Department. Inspector Queen is assisted by Sergeant Velie. In the first film in the series, Ellery meets Nikki Porter, an aspiring mystery author herself. Ellery accidentally involves her in a murder mystery, making her the chief suspect. At the end of the film Ellery proposes to Nikki, but only that she become his secretary. She agrees, apparently suddenly giving up most of her own writing ambitions and killing any feminist attitudes the series might have conveyed with the use of a recurring female character.

Ellery Queen was played by Ralph Bellamy in the first four films. Bellamy, who was born in 1904 in Chicago, Illinois, started his screen career in the early 1930s, sometimes playing second leads in major productions and sometimes playing the lead in B-Movies. He received an Oscar nomination for Best Supporting Actor for *The Awful Truth* (1937), where he competed with Cary Grant for the affections of Irene Dunne. For mystery fans, he had previously starred in a four-movie mystery series of the 1930s, playing Inspector Trent.

The supporting players remained the same throughout the series. Nikki Porter was played by Margaret Lindsay, who was born in Iowa in 1910. Although Lindsay was quite attractive and had some good roles in films in the 1930s, she never became a star. Indeed, she is best known today for her appearances in the Ellery Queen film series. Of interest to mystery fans is her role as the love interest of Dr. Ordway in *Crime Doctor* (1944), the first movie in that series.

Inspector Queen was played by well-known character actor Charley Grapewin. He is best known for playing Grandpa Joad in *The Grapes of Wrath* (1940). James Burke, who played Sgt. Velie, was a very familiar face in the movies, having played policemen and many other small roles in films beginning in the early 1930s.

After four films, Ralph Bellamy left the series. He was replaced by William Gargan, who was born in 1905 in Brooklyn, New York. Gargan was a familiar character actor in Hollywood, beginning his career in the early 1930s. Much like Ralph Bellamy before him, Gargan received an Oscar nomination for Best Supporting Actor, in Gargan's case for his performance in *They Knew What They Wanted* (1940), where he played a ranch foreman who had an affair with Carole Lombard.

The Republic Films

THE SPANISH CAPE MYSTERY (1935)

As the feature commences, the viewer receives a quick introduction to the detecting prowess of young Ellery Queen. Inspector Queen of the New York police has called in his son Ellery for help in solving a baffling case. A jeweler has accused Gardner, a known criminal, of stealing a $75,000 necklace from his store when Gardner was being shown various items of merchandise for possible purchase. The Inspector believes Gardner is guilty but he has no proof on which to hold the man. That is where Ellery comes in handy. Within minutes of meeting the parties, Ellery deduces the manner of the theft and the location of the necklace and Gardner is ready to confess to the crime. Not since the days of Philo Vance has the law enforcement establishment of New York relied so heavily on such a talented amateur.

After this interesting prologue concludes, the main story of the film begins as Ellery sets off for a vacation on the West Coast with his friend, Judge Macklin. Nearby, on Spanish Cape, wealthy Walter Godfrey owns a seaside mansion where he lives with his wife and his daughter Stella. Visiting the Cape are a number of Godfrey's relatives who are meeting there to determine a strategy to challenge the will of a wealthy aunt, so that they can all share in the proceeds of the estate.

Stella's uncle, David Kummer, takes Stella away from the main part of the house to discuss her upcoming marriage to Leslie Cort and her flirting with a guest, John Marco. A thug interrupts them and kidnaps Kummer, believing he is Marco. The thug gags and binds Stella in a small house on the cape and escapes with Kummer in a boat. The next day, Stella is discovered by Queen and Macklin when the two enter their vacation home and are surprised to find the young girl tied to a chair.

The story returns to the mansion, where the body of Marco has just been discovered. He was strangled by a wire around his neck. Despite the fact that he was killed overnight, he is wearing only a bathing suit and is covered by an opera cape. Ellery tries to stay out of the investigation but he is pulled back in when the sheriff keeps accusing the wrong people of the crime. In another similarity to the Philo Vance novels, where many of the suspects were often killed during the course of a book, two of the male suspects are soon found dead, also wearing only bathing suits and strangled by a wire, and then a female suspect is killed by being knocked off a high ledge. Despite the few clues, Ellery is able to determine that Kummer was the killer, having faked his kidnapping so that he would have a chance to swim back to the Cape on a daily basis to kill each of the heirs to the aunt's fortune so that he would receive a larger share of the inheritance.

This film and its sequel were produced at Republic studios, better known for its Westerns and serials. Director Lewis D. Collins is also better known for working in those genres. Perhaps because of those influences, this mystery never falls to the depths of a boring talk-fest, a tendency of other movie whodunits. Indeed, the murders come fast and furious, and the unusual setting of a mansion high on a hill above the sea surely adds to the enjoyment of the viewer. The solution makes some sense, although there are few clues to assist the viewer in solving the crime on his own.

Donald Cook is likable enough as Ellery Queen. The role is written and performed so as to make Queen an engaging figure, surely not as pompous as he was in the books of the era. Harry Stubbs is always interesting as the sheriff, making wrong deduction after wrong deduction, but at one point correctly insulting Queen by calling him "Philo." While he may not be much of a detective himself, at least the sheriff knows his fictional detectives. Helen Twelvetrees, who is billed above the title and even above Donald Cook, is vivacious and lovely as Stella Godfrey, and the budding relationship between Stella and Ellery provides some romantic relief from the serious task of crime-solving.

This story has more substance than most of the films from the Columbia series of the

1940s, probably because this film relies heavily on the plot from the Queen novel on which it is based. For that reason, the movie is well worth a look, especially for the fans of the traditional whodunit.

Note on the Source Material: This film was based on the novel *The Spanish Cape Mystery*, published during the same year in which the movie was released. The novel opens with the scene in which David Kummer takes aside his niece, Rosa Godfrey, to discuss her relationship with several young men. They are interrupted by a one-eyed giant who mistakenly believes that Kummer is John Marco. The thug leaves a bound and gagged Rosa in the Waring house, near the Godfrey mansion, and then escapes by boat with the kidnapped David Kummer. The next day, Ellery Queen and Judge Macklin, on their vacation, discover the tied-up Rosa as they enter the Waring abode. When the three return to the Godfrey mansion, the body of John Marco has just been discovered.

Up to this point, the movie closely follows the novel, but now the stories diverge. In the book there are no more murders, although there is a suicide. The motive for Marco's murder in the book is his blackmail activities and not an attempt to increase the murderer's share of an inheritance. However, the solutions to the crimes, the method of murder and the clues are substantially the same.

There are some interesting modifications in the movie. Marco is found naked in the book but is wearing swimming trunks in the movie, clearly reflecting movie censorship standards of the era. The Godfrey daughter is named Rosa in the book and her mother's name is Stella, while in the movie the daughter is named Stella and the mother's first name is not revealed.

Other changes reflect movie-making of the era. The progression of the movie plot is rearranged to place the emphasis on the character of Stella Godfey, played by the vivacious Helen Twelvetrees. There is a hint of romance between Stella and Ellery in the movie, an element that is missing from the novel. Apparently every movie of the era needed some romance, even if it was a serious murder mystery. The romantic element does help to lighten the character of Ellery in the film, making him much more likable than the stodgy character from the Queen novels. Inspector Moley is made to look like a buffoon in the movie, a common characterization of the police in Hollywood murder mysteries. Moley seems earnest if not that bright in the book.

Probably the most important change between the two versions is the motive of the murderer, allowing for several additional killings during the course of the movie. This prevents the movie from becoming a talk-fest, which is seldom a problem in a mystery novel but is a serious problem for a mystery movie. This is one of those situations where the structure of the story works well as a book, with the modifications to the story for the movie enhancing its impact as a film.

THE MANDARIN MYSTERY (1937)

The Mandarin Mystery is usually panned by most fans of the Ellery Queen novels, and with good reason. Eddie Quillan, with his short stature and lack of gravitas, is especially miscast as the master detective Ellery Queen, particularly at a time in the novels when Ellery was a serious, perhaps stuffy individual, even wearing a pince-nez to give him a snobbish appearance. In the later Columbia series, even though he was often required to perform pratfalls and comedy bits while playing the great detective, Ralph Bellamy still had the size and acting abilities to play a resolute Ellery once the movie turned to the serious subject of solving the murder. Quillan, who was excellent in several film comedy roles over the years, is simply unconvincing in this role.

The feature begins on board ship when Jo Temple arrives in New York carrying a rare Chinese stamp worth $50,000. She then proceeds to the apartment suite of Dr. Alex Kirk, who has promised to buy the stamp from her. While Jo is freshening up in her room, the stamp is stolen by the mystery man who has been following Jo since she left the ship. A short time later, that unidentified man is found shot to death. What makes the crime most puzzling is that his coat is on backward and there are two spears inserted in his clothes, from the trousers up through the back of the coat.

Based on her various suspicious activities, the obvious suspect for the murder is Jo Temple. Ellery, however, has fallen in love with her at first sight and he therefore ignores all of the evidence against her, not necessarily the best trait for a master detective. Ellery eventually discovers the true murderer, after deducing (really just guessing) that the spears through the body were used to enable the murderer to escape from a room through an apparently locked door, by having the falling body cause the bolt of the door to pull into a locked position after the escape.

There are other characters in the film who are suspects, but only because they are in the film. There are Dr. Kirk, his two nieces, the fiancé of one of the nieces, a butler and some peripheral characters. However, there are no true clues to the murderer, particularly since it takes some time to identify the victim. As a result, when the murderer is exposed, the "surprise" brings a so-what attitude from the viewer. Also, there is no true explanation as to how Ellery solves the crime, other than by mere guesswork. Since Ellery as played by Eddie Quillan has been a figure of comedy throughout the film, it is hard to believe any explanation he finally gives for the murder.

While there are some funny moments in the film, such as when the police arrest Ellery and Jo and handcuff them together, much of the comedy falls flat. Without a strong actor in the lead detective role, there is no central element to hold the plot together. The most interesting aspect of the crime, namely the victim's coat on backward and the spears in his clothing (taken from the original novel), are downplayed in the film, undercutting their interest. This is an incredible missed opportunity on the part of the filmmakers.

Sometimes it seems as if the filmmakers are deliberately attempting to create a movie Ellery Queen and mystery story that are the exact opposite of the character and type of story popular in the 1930s, at least in terms of the written works about the amateur detective. *The Mandarin Mystery* is therefore a very disappointing film, particularly since it was based on one of the most famous Ellery Queen novels. It is easy to see why Republic Studios decided to exit the mystery movie series business after this film and concentrate on the serials and Westerns for which it was much more famous.

Note on the Source Material: This film is based on *The Chinese Orange Mystery*, published in 1934. The novel is a classic whodunit, with an intriguing puzzle involving an unknown man found murdered in the waiting room of Donald Kirk's office in the Hotel Chancellor. The victim has his clothes on backwards and two spears through his clothing. The furniture in the room has also been turned around, as have the pictures on the wall. Perhaps most importantly, the victim's necktie is missing. The door leading to Kirk's office from the murder room is bolted on the inside, although there is another door leading from the room to the hotel hallway from which the murderer could have escaped. There are numerous suspects for the crime, such as Donald Kirk, his father, his secretary, his business partner, his fiancée and a woman who appears to be blackmailing him. However, until the murder victim can be identified, it is hard to determine who murdered the unknown man and why.

The main plot of the novel is a classic mystery puzzle, because while the situation may be totally unrealistic (and surely Raymond Chandler would agree), the emphasis in detective stories of the time was on the puzzle. In this case, the puzzle is quite intriguing. Ellery investigates the "backwards" nature of the mystery, including books written in Hebrew that are missing, some "backwards" aspects of Chinese culture and even a suspect who is using an alias that is her correct name spelled backwards. Ellery is finally able to determine who the victim is, and at that point the killer becomes obvious, particularly since the spears in the body were used to facilitate the bolting of the murder room door after the murderer left through that door.

While there are several side plots and multiple suspects in the novel, the "backwards" nature of the puzzle is always stressed. This is an important contrast with the movie, which half-heartedly uses the backward coat and the spears in the victim's clothes from the novel, but then seems to forget those aspects of the crime throughout most of the film. In addition, only the victim's coat is on backwards in the movie, not all of his clothing, and the furniture and pictures in the room are not turned around. This failure to incorporate the other "backwards" elements from the story makes the movie much less interesting than the book. Once the central puzzle is removed from the film and the characterization of Ellery in the film is so different from the characterization of Ellery in the Queen novels of the era, the feature becomes a run-of-the-mill detective story that could have been about a detective named Ellery Queen or which could have been about anyone else.

In developing *The Mandarin Mystery* the way they did, the filmmakers squandered the opportunity to adapt one of the best Queen novels from the early 1930s, instead choosing to write an original screenplay incorporating only one element from the plot of the novel. For that reason, there is very little of Dannay and Lee's conception of their great detective in the movie. It was therefore unlikely that the film would be a success, and indeed it was not.

The Ralph Bellamy Films

ELLERY QUEEN, MASTER DETECTIVE (1940)

The tone of this film, the first in the Columbia series about Ellery Queen, is completely different from the first film from Republic. In *The Spanish Cape Mystery*, the opening story arc highlighted the incredible detective skills of the younger Queen, as within minutes he was able to solve a jewel robbery that had baffled the elder Queen, an experienced policeman. By contrast, in *Ellery Queen, Master Detective*, Ellery's first piece of detective work is to attempt to locate a missing person before his father does. Ellery fails miserably in that regard, mistaking Nikki Porter for Barbara Braun and inadvertently causing Nikki to become a murder suspect.

The main plot of the story, once it gets going, is quite interesting. Millionaire John Braun is advised by three doctors that he has a terminal illness and has one or two painful months to live. One of the doctors is James Rogers, who desires to marry Braun's daughter, Barbara. When the old man objects, Barbara flees the house and moves into Nikki's apartment without telling her parents. Once Barbara's mother learns about her husband's imminent death, she then asks the police to locate her missing daughter.

John Braun then decides to change his will, cutting out all of his business associates and his daughter,leaving his entire estate to his wife. The others are quite upset when they learn about that surprise turn of events, perhaps providing each with a motive for murder, as Braun's body with its slit throat is discovered just a short time thereafter. Nikki Porter is trapped just outside Braun's office when the murder is committed. Since there is no other exit from the room, this is a true locked-room murder mystery and Nikki is the obvious killer.

Locked-room murder mysteries are inherently interesting, but the script does not take advantage of that element of the crime. The details of the crime are little discussed and the various possible solutions to the locked room aspects of the crime are little explored. Instead, suspicion is immediately thrown on Nikki Porter, who then hides in the Queens' apartment with Ellery's assistance but without the knowledge of Inspector Queen. That leads to some slightly amusing scenes, with Nikki receiving little to eat while Ellery goes out for a steak dinner and Nikki posing as the temporary cook, providing a horrible meal to Inspector Queen. At times during the film, the mystery elements seem to have disappeared completely, a chronic problem with the entire Columbia series.

The solution is quite interesting, as Dr. Rogers had provided fake x-rays of Braun's body to the other doctors. Braun was not even seriously ill. However, the threat of an imminent death caused Braun to commit suicide, thereby creating the locked room murder mystery. It turned out that a raven had taken Braun's new will and the murder weapon from the room after Braun's death, thus confusing the situation.

While it is a clever solution (except for the part about the bird being a co-conspirator), crimes that are based on causing someone to commit suicide strain credulity. There is no explanation as to how Rogers stole the body of Braun from the morgue or how he managed to replace it with a large statue of Braun. There is virtually no time spent developing the suspects other than Nikki and no clues are given to the viewer to help in solving the mystery. With his limited detective expertise, as displayed in this film, Ellery has hardly earned the moniker of "Master Detective," although it is not quite clear what that title means in any event. With its flimsy plot and much filler material, *Ellery Queen, Master Detective* is an unpromising start to a new mystery movie series.

Note on the Source Material: On its face, *Ellery Queen, Master Detective* has little in common with *The Door Between,* a 1937 murder novel by Ellery Queen. The novel starts out at an apparently happy time in the life of the MacClure family. Dr. John MacClure, the world-famous cancer specialist, is about to marry Karen Leith, a world-famous author, who had spent most of her formative years in Japan where she had adopted many of the Japanese ways. Dr. MacClure's daughter Eva has just become engaged to an aspiring young physician, Richard Scott.

Unexpectedly (for the characters, but not for the readers since this is a murder mystery), Karen Leith is soon found murdered and Eva is accused of the crime. Ellery Queen comes to her rescue and is able to solve the mystery, but only after realizing that the crime dates back to events that occurred many years earlier in Japan and involves two mysterious deaths, those of a sister held prisoner in an upstairs attic and a Japanese maid who was the protector of Karen Leith and her secrets. Comparing that synopsis to the plot of the film, it is easy to see that the two works have no characters in common among the suspects and the underlying reasons for the death of John Braun and Karen Leith are completely different.

Nevertheless, the film is based in part on the book. While the writers constructed a completely new plot for the movie, they purloined the murder, manner of the murder and solution of the murder right from the book. In the novel, author Karen Leith is found stabbed to death in her bedroom. Eva MacClure was just outside the bedroom when Leith was last seen alive by her maid, and stayed until the time Eva discovered the body. Since there was no other exit out of the bedroom except right past Eva and since Eva admits that she saw no one leave the bedroom for the entire time she was there, Eva is the logical suspect, just as Nikki Porter was in the movie.

The locked-room aspects of the murder are better handled in the book than in the movie, as all of the potential possibilities for the crime are explored in great detail in the written work. However, just as in the movie, Leith actually committed suicide, although she was driven to it by a fake diagnosis of cancer by Dr. MacClure. Also, an exotic bird was an accomplice in the crime, having removed the suicide weapon from the room through an upper window.

While it was not unheard of for a murder mystery to be solved as a suicide (see Dorothy Sayers' *Clouds of Witness* [1926]), it is usually unsatisfying, as it is in this case. Ellery's psychology in solving the crime is unconvincing, and when a crime solution requires the intervention of a bird, the denouement rings hollow.

Thus the movie and the book have the same problem with the "murder" and its solution. The book is still more enjoyable because Nikki Porter and her comedy antics are missing and the underlying plot of the novel involving intrigue from Japan and a sister locked for years in an attic of Karen's room is more interesting than the mean old man of the movie deciding to commit suicide. Nevertheless, what makes a comparison of the two works intriguing is how the screenwriters were able to lift a murder and resolution from one story and seamlessly insert it into a totally different story. It is just a shame the screenwriters did not use more of the plot of the novel in the film, which probably would have made the film a more satisfactory work.

Note on the Novelizations: Under its contract with Dannay and Lee, Columbia had the right to adapt and use any element of the published works of Ellery Queen. Columbia chose to produce a novelization of each of the first three movies in the series. The books were *Ellery Queen, Master Detective* (1941), *The Penthouse Mystery* (1941) and *The Perfect Crime* (1942).

ELLERY QUEEN'S PENTHOUSE MYSTERY (1941)

At first blush, *Ellery Queen's Penthouse Mystery* appears to be a serious crime film, forgoing the multiple, unfunny comedy scenes that adversely affected *Ellery Queen, Master Detective*. This false impression is created by the strong opening to the movie. The story starts out in China, where Gordon Cobb, stage ventriloquist and soldier of fortune, is commissioned by a Chinese man to transport a fortune in jewels to New York where they can be sold to bring needed cash to the Chinese people. The film then follows Cobb's travels by boat to San Francisco and by train to New York, during which journey a mysterious Count and an even more mysterious woman seem to be following him. Once in New York, Cobb registers at the Hotel Hollingsworth, unpacks, and calls his Chinese contact in America, Lois Ling. This segment of the film then ends, but it has been a particularly tantalizing opening segment to the movie, clearly the best opening in the entire series.

Unfortunately, this is still an Ellery Queen movie and therefore the mystery writer/detective has to get involved in the story in some manner. Two days later, Cobb's daughter Sheila arrives at Ellery Queen's office to ask Nikki Porter for help in locating her father, who has disappeared. Sheila is worried because Cobb never called her once he got to the hotel. A trip to the police may have made more sense, but, nevertheless, Ellery is finally convinced to go to Cobb's penthouse suite at the Hollingsworth. There he discovers Cobb's body in a locked trunk. Thereafter, the police and Ellery search for the killer while everyone, including the criminals, is searching for the missing jewels Cobb brought into the country from China. One of the criminals named Ritter is also killed, and Ellery solves that crime in addition to the original murder of Cobb.

The first half of *Ellery Queen's Penthouse Mystery* works well, with the writers content to rest the humor of the movie on the word play between Ellery and Nikki. While their patter is not of the quality of the Thin Man series, it is still amusing and does not detract from the plot. (This shows the potential the series had to flesh out the association between Ellery and Nikki, making it more like a Nick and Nora Charles relationship; but for some reason, the filmmakers never chose to do so.) In the second half, however, the film succumbs to

Ellery Queen (Ralph Bellamy, center) discovers a marked deck of cards, perhaps an important clue for solving *Ellery Queen's Penthouse Mystery* (1941). The amateur detective is surrounded by two professionals, Inspector Queen (Charley Grapewin, on the left) and Sergeant Velie (James Burke, on the right).

the problems that are endemic to the series. The action grinds to a halt at one point when a policeman, played by the unfunny Tom Dugan, explains to Sergeant Velie how he was hit over his head after a fight with an unknown assailant. Dugan exaggerates the story, making this an interminable three-minute segment that is irrelevant to the story and without a bit of humor besides. Later, Mantan Moreland, in the role of the servant of one of the villains, is embarrassing playing a poorly written African American stereotype, which role is demeaning without garnering any laughs.

Probably the worst part of the film is when Ellery bursts into a room, believing Nikki is in trouble. He falls down and his gun goes off. While it was common in 1940s mystery series to make fun of the detective's dim-witted assistant or a bungling policeman, it surely undercuts the concept of a master detective by humiliating Ellery instead.

Between the comedy bits, the story is hard to follow and the unmasking of the killer has little interest. In fact, it appears that the two killings were committed by two different people, with the solution of Ritter's murder being particularly unconvincing. This is another disappointing entry in a disappointing series, although it is interesting to see Anna May Wong in one of her last regular screen appearances, playing the mysterious Lois Ling. She does bring a little bit of class to the tale.

Note on the Source Material: Despite the credit in the film, this movie was not based on any novel or story by Ellery Queen. One source states that it was based on the radio play "The Three Scratches" by Ellery Queen, broadcast on December 17, 1939.

ELLERY QUEEN AND THE PERFECT CRIME (1941)

This is probably the best film in the Columbia Ellery Queen series. That is not saying much, as the series as a whole is a huge disappointment. In this case, though, the story starts out with an interesting premise involving insider stock trading and corporate manipulation, which is actually quite relevant today. The second half of the story involves a true whodunit of a body found in an office in a mansion, stabbed to death, with interesting clues and multiple suspects.

The plot starts out with wealthy businessman, John Matthews, learning that one of his company's dams is about to fail as a result of terrific storms and flooding. He immediately calls his broker and sells his and his son's shares in the company. Ray Jardin, a stockholder in the company, then comes to question Matthews about the flood situation and Matthews assures him that everything is fine. Unfortunately, the dam then fails and all of the stockholders are wiped out, except of course for the Matthews family. That presents complications since John's son Walter is in love with Marian Jardin, the daughter of Ray Jardin.

After some comedy bits, including some shtick at Ellery Queen's office and a lengthy scene at an auction, Walter, who is now estranged from his father over his unscrupulous behavior, goes to visit his father but instead finds the elder Mathews' body in his office. Walter is then knocked out by an unknown assailant. Later, Ray Jardin's pencil is found at the scene of the crime, and since he had a true resentment against Matthews because of the stock deal, Ray is arrested. Ellery eventually discovers the true killer, but his discovery seems to be more the result of luck rather than of deduction.

As was common in this series, the effectiveness of the movie is marred by several comedy scenes, usually involving Nikki Porter. In this film, though, there is also a scene with

Inspector Queen practicing with a fishing pole in his office, so even he becomes part of the comedy troupe for this film. Once again Ellery Queen is made into a bumbler, with Ellery and Nikki knocking each other down at one time and Ellery accidentally shooting off a large gun at the auction. If the filmmakers do not treat the lead detective with respect, why should the audience? Also, any movie with a pet monkey as an important character must be treated with some disdain.

Nevertheless, the whodunit aspect of the story is well-handled, with the victim first suspected of committing suicide, and then once suicide is ruled out, suspicion transferring from one person to another. There are many suspects for the crime as a number of strange people inhabit or always seem to be visiting the Matthews mansion. When Ellery determines that the murder did not take place inside the office, but rather on the outside terrace of the mansion with the body then dragged into the house afterwards, a new set of theories about the murder must be devised. Although the murderer turns out to be a person who is even less likely than the least likely suspect to have committed the crime, the murder mystery is well-handled and is always interesting.

Adding to the effectiveness of the feature, the comedy elements are downplayed in the second half of the movie and the murder mystery is highlighted. If only that approach had been used in other films in the series! If you truly do love a mystery, viewing *Ellery Queen and the Perfect Crime* is not a bad way to spend an hour of your life.

Note on the Source Material: Although not set forth in the credits, this film was based on Ellery Queen's 1938 novel *The Devil to Pay*. That explains why the working titles for the film were *The Devil to Pay* and *The Devil Pays*. The book is quite interesting, coming at a time when Dannay and Lee were loosening the strict Ellery Queen formula and making the lead detective more personable. The story is set in Hollywood, with Ellery in California to write for the movie industry. Inspector Queen and Sgt. Velie are not in the novel.

The movie and the novel have the same basic plot, although some of the names have been changed around. Solly Spaeth, having inside information about the collapse of one of his company's dams, sells out before the catastrophe. Others, however, such as wealthy Rhys Jardin, are bankrupted by the company's failure. Solly's son, Walter, who is engaged to Jardin's daughter Valerie, is upset by his father's actions.

Solly is then found stabbed to death, apparently with a poisoned sword, and Rhys Jardin is arrested for the murder. Rhys does not mind the arrest, however, because he has an alibi for the crime that the police do not know. Rhys believes Walter has committed the murder, and so Jardin does not disclose the alibi in an attempt to protect Spaeth's son. Walter, believing Rhys committed the murder, moved the body from the terrace into the office where it was eventually discovered, hoping to clear Rhys of the crime. In the end, Ellery finds the real murderer, a slightly different person than the killer in the movie.

The book is intriguing and is much better than the movie. The novel is told from the perspective of Valerie Jardin, giving the story a different feel than many of the previous Queen novels. In fact, Ellery Queen does not become an important character in the book until late in the story. Valerie is the key character in the book, hoping to solve the murder on her own. In the movie, by contrast, the Valerie character (named Marian Jardin) is a minor player in the story. The reader actually feels Valerie's conflicting motives, sometimes believing her father committed the murder and sometimes believing Walter is the killer. While Marian's conflicting feelings are addressed in the film, it is only for a short moment. The filmmakers missed an opportunity with regard to the character of Jardin's daughter.

The book has a more complicated plot than the movie and adds spice with the characters of Winnie Moon and her lawyer, Anatole Ruhig, who are involved in hiding a legitimate new will of Solly Spaeth's. While those characters are in the movie, it is not quite clear why. Also, there is too much of Winnie's monkey in the movie, although the animal does appear in the printed work.

The real difference between the same works in different media is epitomized by one scene. In the book, Ellery Queen stands in for Walter Spaeth and buys all of Rhys Jardin's furniture and assets at an auction. Walter then returns all of the items to Rhys. The same scene appears in the movie, but it is played more for comedy, as Nikki Porter is perplexed at Ellery's actions, thinking Ellery has gone crazy. Most importantly, in the book the scene runs for just a few pages; in the movie, the scene runs on for eight minutes. It must be a Hollywood rule of thumb: never let a good whodunit get in the way of an unfunny comedy scene.

Ellery Queen and the Murder Ring (1941)

This was the fourth film in the Columbia series and was another one that was based, at least in part, on a book by Ellery Queen. It was also the last movie in the series to star Ralph Bellamy, perhaps because his part was so small or perhaps because the film was so poor. The movie is defeated by long comedy set pieces, and the mystery itself does not provide fair play to the viewer, a hallmark of the Ellery Queen novels. All of this is quite surprising as the novel on which the movie was based is one of Queen's best works from the early 1930s.

The main plot begins with wealthy Augusta Stack contacting the police because of problems she believes are occurring at her hospital, Stack Memorial. She wants the police to watch the institution and its lead physician, Dr. Janney. She is disturbed by the recent death of her sister at the hospital when Dr. Janney disappeared while he was giving the sister a treatment. The sister's body was then quickly cremated. (Note how this plot point, which on its face seems quite interesting, will almost immediately disappear from the feature.)

Inspector Queen assigns the task to his son Ellery, and the only reason that can be inferred for this unusual action by a police official is that Ellery has his name in the title of the film. Ellery is not a member of the police force; he is supposed to be a mystery writer. In fact, when does he have time to write his mystery novels, since he always seems to be investigating cases on behalf of the New York police? Ellery, at the suggestion of Inspector Queen, decides to check into the hospital with a fake throat problem in order to snoop around. The reason for this idea is obvious. It will give Ellery the chance to participate in "comedy" scenes in the hospital.

Mrs. Stack's car is sideswiped by two henchmen in an attempt to kill her. She is rushed to the hospital, and after a successful operation she suddenly dies by asphyxiation. While the hospital believes the death was an accident, the police determine that she was strangled. Although there are truly no clues to the murderer, Dr. Janney's nurse is eventually determined to be the killer. It was her intent to marry Stack's son and share in his inheritance.

This motive, however, comes completely out of nowhere and is particularly unconvincing. The nurse is supposed to have killed Mrs. Stack for her money, before the nurse even married the son or knew what bequests were made in Mrs. Stack's will. The solution to the crime makes little sense, and once again seems to be solved more by luck than by deduction.

The structure of this story is also out of kilter. The master detective, Ellery Queen, has surprisingly little screen time. The murderer is actually discovered by Nikki Porter, his secretary, which is not much different than Dr. Watson solving a murder before Sherlock Holmes was able to do so. There is so little plot to the film that long segments of the story involve two of the henchmen trying to leave the hospital without the police noticing them, a slapstick scene where Ellery runs into a nurse and knocks over her cart, and patter between Nikki and Ellery when Ellery cannot understand Nikki's recitation of certain events. These scenes are not funny and they add nothing to the story.

Margaret Lindsey is particularly lovely as Nikki Porter in this film. It is nice to see B-movie villains George Zucco and Leon Ames around as suspects. However, it is hard to find anything else positive about the movie. Even the title makes no sense as there is only one murderer and no murder ring.

Note on the Source Material: This film was based on Ellery Queen's third detective novel, *The Dutch Shoe Mystery*, published in 1931. The novel is an excellent example of a whodunit of the era, with an interesting hospital setting, a map of the crime scene, multiple suspects, significant clues and a complex solution to the crime. While the novel was too complex to be filmed in its entirety, there was surely enough good material to create an interesting mystery movie.

The novel starts out with Ellery visiting The Dutch Memorial Hospital on an unrelated matter when the murder of Abigail Doorn is discovered. She was the wealthy but elderly benefactor of the hospital who, while visiting the hospital, had fallen down some stairs, ruptured her gall bladder and lapsed into a coma. She was in need of an operation which was to be performed by Dr. Janney, a famous doctor, author and researcher. However, when Doorn was wheeled into the operating room she was already dead, strangled with a picture wire twisted around her neck.

As the investigation goes forward, it seems clear that Doorn was strangled in the anteroom of the operating theater by someone impersonating Dr. Janney. There are many suspects for the crime, including Doorn's daughter and brother, Dr. Janney himself, Janney's son Swanson, Doorn's female companion, and members of the staff of the hospital. A second murder late in the story gives Ellery all of the information he needs to finally solve the crime.

There is surprisingly little in common between the film and the novel. (Indeed, most of the character names have been changed, except for that of Dr. Janney.) The interesting idea of Abigail Doorn being killed just before the operation right outside the operating room by an individual impersonating Dr. Janney is replaced with Augusta Stack being killed in her room after the operation, surely a less interesting setting for the crime. The suspects are different, the motivations are different and none of the clever clues from the novel are incorporated into the movie.

To replace the complexity of the novel, the filmmakers chose to insert unfunny comedy padding. To replace the painstaking investigation by Ellery and the police in the novel, the filmmakers chose to allow Nikki Porter (a character not found in the novel) to solve the crime by accident. The filmmakers missed every opportunity to make a good film from an excellent novel and their poor decisions show on the screen. The book, *The Dutch Shoe Mystery*, is highly recommended. The movie, *Ellery Queen and the Murder Ring*, is not.

The William Gargan Films

A CLOSE CALL FOR ELLERY QUEEN (1942)

This film marked the only significant cast change for the Columbia series, as William Gargan took over the role of Ellery Queen from Ralph Bellamy. The change was hardly noticeable as the role was written in the exact same manner for Gargan as it had been for Bellamy and the part hardly taxed the acting abilities of either performer. That is possibly why Bellamy left the series as soon as he had the opportunity.

Once again, there is an overemphasis on comedy. Unlike any other Hollywood detective series, for some reason the writers make the lead detective into a buffoon, rather than saving that honor for some bumbling sidekick or policeman. Here, Ellery accidentally fires a loaded gun (how many times has the happened in the series?), and then is unable to start a motorboat. When he finally does, the boat goes off erratically. Ellery even finds himself trapped in a bathtub, first being soaked by the shower spray and then scalded by the hot bathwater. No wonder Ellery only wrote mystery stories in these movies and was not a practicing private detective. His manner and style were unlikely to bring many lucrative cases into the office.

The story starts out with Stewart Cole requesting that Ellery investigate a dangerous situation at the lakeside estate of wealthy Alan Rogers, whom Ellery knew slightly when he and Rogers worked in the same building. Two rough individuals, Bates and Corday, have moved onto the estate and seem to be threatening Rogers. Cole is worried about Rogers' safety.

When Queen arrives at the Rogers estate, he learns of an additional unusual situation. Rogers has advertised around the world for his two long-lost daughters, Marie and Margo, in order that he can become reacquainted with them and also so that he can transfer his vast wealth to them. Margo arrived some time ago and wormed her way into the affections of Rogers. Marie is still missing.

Coincidentally, Nikki Porter runs into Rogers' daughter, Marie Dubois, in Ellery's office building. While Marie is interested in seeing the father she has never known, she is unsure about approaching him because she received a letter from Rogers' attorney, Lester Young, warning her about coming. Young has accused Marie of being an impostor. Nikki Porter decides to impersonate Marie and go out to the Rogers' estate in Marie's place. Why she does that, no one knows.

Alan Rogers eventually pays $50,000 in blackmail money to Bates and Corday, who are then found murdered with the money missing. The real Marie Dubois disappears; Rogers is found poisoned. Ellery determines that the real culprits are Stewart Cole and the fake daughter, Margo, who were trying to obtain the entire Rogers' fortune for themselves. Cole had even attempted to kill Nikki by drowning her in the lake.

When the mystery finally gets going in this one, it is not bad at all. Ellery Queen suddenly becomes serious and competent, deftly analyzing the conflicting evidence and stories. However, his competence and that of his father Inspector Queen are called into question when each of them holds in their bare hands a glass containing the poison that supposedly killed Rogers, obliterating any fingerprints there may have been on the glass.

The Ellery Queen novels of the era were known for their fair play. All of the clues were equally available to the reader and the detective, with the reader having a fair chance to solve the murder on his own. That attitude, unfortunately, was not carried over into the films. There is not one clue in the film that could lead anyone to guess Cole is the criminal mastermind behind the venture, other than the fact that he is the least likely suspect. Indeed, Cole is not even present during most of the film. If he were truly the murderer, why hire Ellery in the first place? The explanation in the film for that action on Cole's part is unconvincing. Also, how was he able to forge the lawyer's signature on the fake letter to Marie? There was no way he could have accomplished that task.

As to the title, was there ever a close call for Ellery Queen in the film? He was supposedly shot at in his first boat trip to the Rogers mansion but that could hardly be called a close call. For that matter, who shot at him and why? That was simply another incident in the mystery story that does not stand up to scrutiny. Nevertheless, if the viewer can look past the less than convincing solution to the crimes and the comedy filler material, this is an okay entry in a very disappointing series.

Note on the Source Material: Some sources state that *A Close Call for Ellery Queen* was based on the novel *The Dragon's Teeth*: *A Problem in Deduction*, published in 1939. That is incorrect. While both stories involve two female heiresses to a large fortune, that is all they have in common. The plots, the crime and the characters in the movie are unrelated to those elements in the mystery novel, although the character of Margo has some similarity in both versions.

A Desperate Chance for Ellery Queen (1942)

A Desperate Chance for Ellery Queen marked a move away from the long comedy set-pieces of the previous films in the series and the over-emphasis on the antics of Nikki Porter at the expense of the detective skills of Ellery Queen. Finally, a film in the Ellery Queen series released by Columbia stressed plot over comedy. However, since the plot makes little sense, there is unfortunately scant improvement over the previous quality of the movies in this substandard mystery series.

Adele Beldon, a beautiful but greedy singer in a stage show, is married to George Beldon, who has embezzled funds from a New York bank and has pinned the crime on a Norman Hadley. Since the funds Beldon has in his possession are hot, Adele and George decide to move to San Francisco, where they hope to be able to use the money without police interference. Of course it may not have been the best idea to pay for their airline tickets with the marked $100 bills.

Coincidentally, Ellery Queen has decided to fly to San Francisco with his secretary Nikki Porter to conduct some research for his new book. Irene Hadley, Norman's wife, comes to Ellery Queen with a problem. She understood that her husband had died several years before in a boating accident, but now a friend believes he recently saw Norman in San Francisco. So, logically, Irene hires a mystery writer who happens to be on his way to San Francisco to try to determine if her husband is still alive. Ellery's strange idea to smoke Hadley out of hiding is to have Nikki impersonate Mrs. Hadley and publicize the fact that she has come to San Francisco to re-marry.

Since this is an Ellery Queen mystery, the idea somehow works and Norman Hadley shows up at Nikki's hotel room. Hadley confesses that he had faked his own death so that his wife would not find out he had been accused of embezzlement and had to spend time in prison. Ellery, for no apparent reason, believes Hadley is innocent of the embezzlement. Ellery later believes, for no apparent reason, that Hadley is innocent of the hammer bludg-

In the center of the photo, left to right, are Captain Daley (Frank Thomas) of the San Francisco police, Ellery Queen (William Gargan) from the ranks of the amateur detectives, and Inspector Queen (Charley Grapewin) of the New York City police (other actors are unidentified). They are investigating the death of George Beldon in *A Desperate Chance for Ellery Queen* (1942).

eoning of Beldon, even though it occurs in Hadley's apartment. The remainder of the film is spent on Ellery and Hadley evading the San Francisco police and finding the real murderer.

Part-way through the movie, it is hard to remember exactly what crime, if any, Ellery is supposed to be investigating. What is definitely clear is that Ellery has forgotten that he came to San Francisco to work on his new book. Ellery then solves the murder of Beldon, but since Ellery has no real clues, he must have simply guessed who the real murderer was. While that approach to crime solution is not unheard of in a Hollywood mystery movie, it is surely inappropriate in an Ellery Queen movie, as the novels were bastions of the concept of fair play for the reader. Ellery then obtains a confession from the murderer while the police are listening in, never a satisfactory plot device when there is no real evidence linking the murderer to the crime.

Lillian Bond as Adele Beldon is particularly lovely in her short stage outfits in the early scenes in the film. Morgan Conway, soon to play Dick Tracy in two films, is convincingly slimy as casino owner Ray Stafford. Unfortunately, those are the only high points in the film. While Bond may be pretty, she is not much of an actress and she is hardly convincing as a criminal mastermind.

This is another disappointing entry in the Ellery Queen series. With so many Ellery Queen novels still remaining unfilmed by the early 1940s, it is a shame that the filmmakers decided to rely on completely original scripts, instead of on the many clever books by Dannay and Lee.

Note on the Source Material: One source states that this film was based on the radio play "A Good Samaritan" by Ellery Queen, broadcast on May 8, 1940.

ENEMY AGENTS MEET ELLERY QUEEN (1942)

It is a good thing that this was the last entry in the Ellery Queen movie series, as with this film the series hit rock bottom. There is no longer any pretense of creating a film based on the original conception of Dannay and Lee of an erudite detective. There is no effort to create a whodunit worthy of the audience's time and attention. There is no attempt to create a story that makes any sense. Indeed, the title of the film alone is an indication that this is going to be a World War II spy drama, and what is Ellery Queen doing in such a concoction?

The story has something to do with jewels being smuggled into the United States by an anti–Nazi group, who hope to use the proceeds of their sale in its resistance efforts against Germany. The Nazis are onto the plot, however, and kill the courier and steal the jewels. At the same time, Ellery and Nikki are trying to solve the disappearance of a suspect who escaped from Sergeant Velie's custody on a train, causing Velie to be suspended from the force. Eventually, Ellery discovers that the Nazis are involved in Velie's case also, locates their hideout and has them all captured. At the end of the film, Velie's police career has been resurrected, although the quality of his work throughout the film series hardly justifies his reinstatement.

Instead of using logic and his deductive abilities, Ellery solves the case by simple guesswork, concluding that since a mummy was stolen and there is a graveyard nearby, the spies probably left the mummy in the cemetery. Huh? Then Ellery is able to find the exact tomb where the mummy is located in the large cemetery, even though it is night time and he has no clues to the exact location.

Frankly, the filmmakers were not even trying with this one. There is the usual overemphasis on the comedic antics of Nikki Porter, although Margaret Lindsay is quite attractive as usual. The subplot concerning the suspension of Velie is uninteresting. The scenes in the cemetery where a body disappears, to the surprise of Velie, are telegraphed so far in advance that an audience member could have been stuck in line at the concession stand buying popcorn for ten minutes and never missed a thread of the story. At the end of the film, American seamen and marines save the day in a ridiculous patriotic fight against the Nazis. Even the presence of Gale Sondergaard in the cast is no help, as her part is miniscule. Sig Ruman does his usual good turn as a bombastic Nazi, although in inimitable Ruman style, the role is played more for comedy than suspense (see *To Be or Not to Be* [1942]), once again undercutting the mystery elements of the movie.

This film is a true disaster and probably explains why the Ellery Queen series was cancelled early in the 1940s, at a time when other Hollywood mystery series were very popular and a series based on the popular Ellery Queen books and radio series would seem to

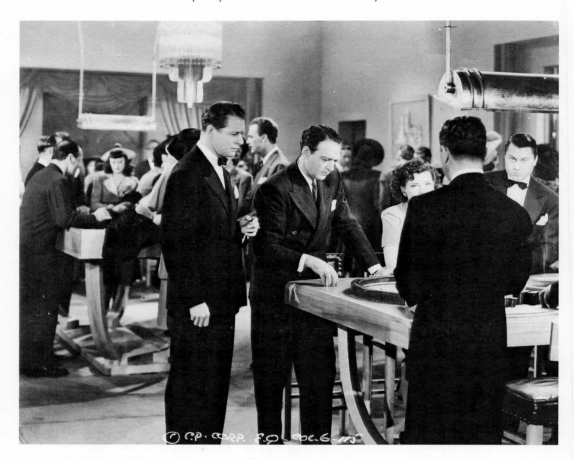

In *A Desperate Chance for Ellery Queen* (1942), Ray Stafford (Morgan Conway, left) shows his upstairs, private gambling casino to Ellery Queen (William Gargan). Conway went on to play Dick Tracy in two films.

have been a money-making proposition. Ralph Bellamy surely looks prescient for leaving the series after only four films.

Afterwards

After leaving the Ellery Queen series, Ralph Bellamy was never out of work, generally playing character parts in films and on television. Having played Inspector Trent and Ellery Queen in movie detective series, he also played private detective Mike Barnett in the television mystery series *Man Against Crime* from 1949 to 1954. Bellamy's most famous performance was as Franklin Delano Roosevelt in *Sunrise at Campobello*, first on Broadway where he won a Tony Award in 1958 and then in the 1960 film. He died in 1991.

Margaret Lindsay's film career was undistinguished after the series ended, as she generally appeared in minor films and television. She died in 1981. Charlie Grapewin made very few film appearances after the end of the series. He died in 1956. James Burke continued to appear regularly in films and then television. He died in 1968. William Gargan also

Mrs. Van Dorn (Gale Sondergaard) has the drop on Ellery Queen (William Gargan) in *Enemy Agents Meet Ellery Queen* (1942). In mystery films, Sondergaard is most famous for playing the title character in *The Spider Woman* (1944), from the Sherlock Holmes series.

continued to appear in films and then television after the end of the Ellery Queen movie series. For mystery fans, he played the title role in the television series *Martin Kane, Private Eye* and in its revival *The New Adventures of Martin Kane*, both in the 1950s. Gargan died in 1979.

Frederic Dannay and Manfred B. Lee continued writing Ellery Queen novels and short stories until Lee's death in 1971. Thereafter, Dannay refused to write more stories about the famous detective, concentrating instead on the *Ellery Queen Mystery Magazine* and mystery anthologies, which he edited. Dannay died in 1982. Prior to that, in 1960, the duo known as Ellery Queen received the Mystery Writers of America Grand Master award.

The Adventures of Ellery Queen continued on the radio until 1948. There were no more films starring Ellery Queen once the movie series ended. However, he was the subject of several television programs, three of which appeared in the 1950s. One was *The Adventures of Ellery Queen*, which ran on the Dumont and ABC networks for 78 episodes from 1950 to 1952. Richard Hart and then Lee Bowman played Ellery Queen. Then there was *The New Adventures of Ellery Queen*, sometimes known as *Murder Is My Business*, which ran in syndication for 32 episodes in 1954. Hugh Marlowe played the great detective. Then there was the appropriately titled *The Further Adventures of Ellery Queen*, which was broadcast for one season (1958–1959) on NBC, originally in live, one-hour episodes. George Nader and then Lee Philips played Ellery Queen.

In 1971, a made-for-television movie starring Peter Lawford as Ellery and Harry Morgan as Inspector Queen was broadcast. It was the pilot for a series that never materialized. In 1975 another television movie was broadcast with Jim Hutton as the younger Queen and David Wayne as his father. That pilot did result in a television series, which lasted for just one season. Those television shows were set in the 1940s and resembled the radio shows in format and tone. The series was created by the famous television writing duo of Richard Levinson and William Link.

8

Boston Blackie
The Reformed Ex-Convict

"Enemy to those who make him an enemy; friend to those who have no friends."

That line was often part of the opening to the Boston Blackie radio program, which was on the air from 1944 to 1950. That expression was not used in any of the movie introductions, since the movies did not come with introductions, but the line was surely applicable to the Boston Blackie character as portrayed in the Columbia film series.

The Boston Blackie of the Columbia film series was always available to those in need, particularly convicts or ex-convicts who needed some assistance in staying on the straight and narrow. As a knight in shining armor, Blackie was not afraid to mix it up with the true criminals and, of course, the police. When Blackie believed in a person's innocence, he was willing to risk it all, usually getting himself into trouble in the process. As portrayed by Chester Morris, Blackie was a common man helping common folk solve a crime problem they were unable to handle by themselves.

Background

JACK BOYLE AND BOSTON BLACKIE

Not much is known for certain about the life of Jack Boyle, the author of the Boston Blackie stories. As related by Edward D. Hoch in the introduction to the Gregg Press reissue of the novel *Boston Blackie* in 1979, Boyle was born sometime prior to 1880 and grew up in Chicago, Illinois. Boyle eventually moved to the west coast, and around 1900 he became a reporter on a newspaper in San Francisco, the city that would later become the locale of many of the Blackie stories. Boyle soon became addicted to opium, which led to a life of crime and his imprisonment for writing bad checks. A subsequent arrest for robbery led to confinement at San Quentin, where his reformation and his writing began.

Boyle's first four tales about Boston Blackie were generally stories told by Blackie to his gang of safecrackers while they relaxed and smoked opium after a successful robbery. The stories were published in *The American Magazine* starting in 1914. In one of the stories, Blackie's nickname is said to have come from his "piercing black eyes and New England birthplace." In 1917, Boyle began publishing his stories about Boston Blackie in *Redbook* magazine. By that time, Blackie had kicked the opium habit and had acquired a wife named Mary.

Two films about Blackie based upon the *Redbook* stories were released in 1918 and 1919.

The films were successful and a small publishing house, H.K. Fly, decided to collect the *Redbook* stories into a book, *Boston Blackie*, which was first published in 1919. Boyle revised the stories slightly so that they could be published in 28 chapters and appear to be a cohesive novel, which was a common publishing practice in those days.

While the Boston Blackie of the novel had certain high ethical standards in that he would never rat out a pal, avoided violence, and stood by those falsely accused of crime, there was no doubt that Blackie was a criminal and not a reformed one, either. In various story arcs, Blackie set out to steal the valuable Wilmerding jewels from a wall safe, decided to steal gold bars from a locked strong room of an ocean liner, and tried to free prisoners from confinement. In the last story in the novel, Blackie himself was imprisoned, but for a crime he did not commit. With a clever plan, Blackie managed to escape from jail, the one motif of the stories that was reused in the Columbia movie series.

Of importance to viewers of the 1940s Boston Blackie series made by Columbia is that none of the regulars from that series come from the Boyle stories. There was no Inspector Farraday or Runt or similar characters ever created by Boyle, and Boyle's most endearing supporting character in the stories, Boston Blackie's Mary, never made it into the film series.

After the publication of the book in 1919, the Boston Blackie stories by Boyle moved to *Cosmopolitan* magazine. No more compilations of the Blackie stories appeared in book form. Boyle died around 1928, after a career that included writing for silent films.

THE EARLY FILMS

Boston Blackie is a familiar name to mystery fans, but it is hardly because of the book by Jack Boyle. Since Boyle only wrote one book and a few other stories about the character, and the book has been out of print for some time, it is clear that Blackie's true fame comes from the movies that were made about him.

Blackie's first screen appearance was in *Boston Blackie's Little Pal* (1918). The movie was based upon the story "The Baby and the Burglar," which comprises the first three chapters of the Boyle book, *Boston Blackie*. The film was followed in 1919 by *Blackie's Redemption*, which was based in part on a story, "Boston Blackie's Mary," which comprised the last six chapters of the Boyle book. In these films, Blackie was played by Bert Lytell, who would later play the Lone Wolf in films.

After the publication of the book, there were other Boston Blackie silent films. *The Face in the Fog* (1922), with Lionel Barrymore playing Blackie, was based on a story Boyle wrote for *Cosmopolitan*. Boyle was also one of the writers of the screenplay, which involved Blackie rescuing a Russian princess and recovering her jewels from the Bolsheviks. *Missing Millions* (1922) involved Blackie robbing a ship's strongbox to gain vengeance against a Wall Street broker who had sent a girl's father to prison unjustly. It was inspired by a similar heist that was chronicled in the middle chapters of the novel.

In *Crooked Alley* (1923), Blackie tried to avenge himself on a judge who refused to pardon a dying convict who was a friend of Blackie. Boyle contributed the story to the film. *Boston Blackie* (1923) involved Blackie exposing a cruel prison warden. The last of the silent films was *The Return of Boston Blackie* (1927), with Blackie helping to reform a pretty blonde jewel thief.

Interestingly, each of these films tended to take something from Jack Boyle or his stories, whether a plot idea or a new contribution from the author. None of these films had the familiar characters from the later Columbia series, such as Inspector Farraday or the Runt.

The Film Series

In the first decade or so of the sound movie era, no further Boston Blackie movies were made. That all changed in 1941, when Columbia commenced the most famous series of films about the ex-convict with the release of *Meet Boston Blackie.* In the Columbia version of the Boston Blackie character, Blackie was a reformed convict who was always available to help those in need. He was assisted by the Runt, his best friend and confidant. Although he had a good relationship with Inspector Farraday, it seemed that no matter what crime Farraday was investigating, Blackie was the prime suspect. Thus, in just about every film in the series, Blackie had to solve the crime to clear his name.

Unlike the Boston Blackie of the novel, the 1940s Boston Blackie, having been paroled from prison many years ago, was scrupulously honest. None of the movies were based on any of the writings by Boyle.

In the title role of the Columbia series was Chester Morris, playing the part for which he is most famous today. Morris was born in 1901 in New York City. He began his film career in the late 1920s (except for some early silent film work as a youngster), receiving an Oscar nomination as best actor for *Alibi* (1929). From that point forward, he never seemed to be out of work in films. One of Morris' notable film roles was in *The Big House* (1930) as Morgan, the convict-forger. That part presaged Morris' role as the most famous ex-con in the movies, Boston Blackie.

George E. Stone played the Runt, Blackie's friend and assistant in 12 of the 14 films in the series. Stone, who was born in 1903, also began appearing in films in the late 1920s. In the 1930s, he specialized in gangster or crime movies, also appearing in prison in *The Last Mile* (1932). Richard Lane, who played Inspector Farraday in all of the movies, was born in Wisconsin in 1899 and began working in films in the middle 1930s, generally playing character parts and uncredited roles. He had small parts in many B-movie mystery series films, such as *Charlie Chan in Honolulu* (1938) and *Mr. Moto in Danger Island* (1939).

Other series regulars included Sergeant Matthews, Farraday's incompetent assistant. The role was played by three different actors, although Frank Sully had the part most often. Arthur Manleder, Blackie's eccentric and wealthy friend, appeared in many of the movies. The part was also played by three different actors, although Lloyd Corrigan is best remembered in the role. From time to time, Blackie obtained important information from pawnshop owner Jumbo Madigan, played by Cy Kendall and later by Joseph Crehan.

Boston Blackie was the most consistent of all the mystery movie series. Chester Morris and Richard Lane appeared in every film and George E. Stone appeared in 12 of the 14 productions. All of the movies were released by Columbia.

The Films

Meet Boston Blackie (1941)

In the first entry in the long film series, the viewers get to meet Boston Blackie, so to speak, along with his assistant, the Runt, and his police nemesis, Inspector Faraday, in an interesting tale that starts as a murder mystery but ends as a spy story. While there were several changes to the series in the second feature, this movie established most of the conventions of the series, with Blackie a reformed safecracker unjustly accused of a crime, the loyal Runt always assisting him as best he can, and Inspector Faraday chasing Blackie, but always in a friendly manner and perhaps deep down not truly believing in Blackie's guilt.

The back story of this film is that Blackie and the Runt left America and traveled to Europe just before Blackie was to be arrested by Faraday for the theft of the Mansfield pearls. As the film commences, Blackie and the Runt are finally returning to this country. On board ship, Blackie sees a young woman, Marilyn Howard, being grabbed by a man, later identified as Martin Vestrick. Blackie saves Howard from the situation, but she shows no interest in him.

Faraday suddenly appears and wants to arrest Blackie, so that he can obtain Blackie's fingerprints to prove that he stole the Mansfield pearls. When Blackie quickly escapes from Faraday's handcuffs, Faraday secures Blackie's promise to voluntarily come to police head-quarters once the ship docks. Blackie, however, is forced to break that promise, because when he returns to his stateroom, he finds Vestrick murdered with Blackie's gun. Blackie is then on a chase to clear his name before the police can capture him.

Blackie first sets out to find Marilyn Howard, his only link to whatever is going on. Blackie finds the mysterious woman at a small amusement park at Coney Island, where the two enter a dark house ride known as the Tunnel of Horror in order to elude two hench-

Outside an amusement park, Boston Blackie (Chester Morris) commandeers the car of Cecilia Bradley (Rochelle Hudson) in order to escape from two killers who are stalking him in *Meet Boston Blackie* (1941).

men who are chasing her. During the ride, Marilyn is killed by a dart thrown into her back by one of the henchmen. Before she dies, she tells Blackie to watch the carnival signs and mentions the mechanical man in a carnival act. The gunmen are then after Blackie, who is able to elude the two by commandeering a car driven by Cecilia Bradley, a beautiful woman previously unknown to Blackie.

As the story progresses, Blackie discovers that the mechanical man and his cronies are actually foreign agents, trying to sneak a stolen bomb sight and its plans to an enemy boat waiting off shore. The spies have been using the carnival as a site to smuggle government secrets out of the country, and Marilyn Howard, a professional spy, was on the case just before she was killed. Blackie, with the help of Faraday, captures the spies and is cleared of any criminal conduct.

Unlike the other entries in the series, this movie is more World War II spy story than mystery, very appropriate for the time period in which it was produced. The mechanical man brings back thoughts of Mr. Memory from *The 39 Steps* (1935), and indeed one of the sideshow attractions, the pinhead, actually appeared in *Freaks* (1932), bringing back memories of that film also. The director of *Meet Boston Blackie* is Robert Florey, famous for his work as a writer and director of some early horror films, who also had substantial experience in directing crime dramas. Florey is always in control of his camera, and the movie never drags, maintaining a quick pace from beginning to end.

Florey's handiwork can be seen in the best scene in the film, the chase and killing in the dark house ride (although there is so much light in the building that the appellation may not truly apply). After Blackie and Marilyn get a push start in their car from the attendant, the two henchmen follow in the next car. As Marilyn starts to tell her story to Blackie, the henchmen leave their car and trail the two on foot through the ride. The story progresses through various shadows, with skeletons and other fright items on the side, and with the henchmen quickly catching up to Marilyn and Blackie. Marilyn is killed by the thrown dart, but the car keeps moving, as Blackie tries to hear her last words. Blackie must then escape or he will almost surely be killed. It is a simply marvelous scene.

Indeed, the carnival setting itself, which returns several times in the movie, gives the story a sense of movement that no other setting could give. Rides are moving, wheels are turning, people are walking fast and others are trailing them, all done either with quick cuts or long tracking sequences alive with movement. Florey's direction clearly adds to the effectiveness and the pacing of the film.

Rochelle Hudson is stunning as Cecilia Bradley. Charles Wagenheim is fine in his only appearance in the series as the Runt. At the heart of the film, though, and indeed at the heart of the entire series, is the byplay between Blackie and Faraday, well-played by Chester Morris and Richard Lane, usually with a smile on their faces, even if the language might be tough. Though the ending of the film comes somewhat abruptly, this was a fine start for a new movie series.

Note on the Character Names: *Meet Boston Blackie* takes place in New York, and with a few exceptions, all of the action in the film series occurs in the Big Apple. None of the films take place in Boston. There is never any explanation given for Boston Blackie's nickname in the movies, just as none was given in the novel, *Boston Blackie*.

In the credits for *Meet Boston Blackie*, Richard Lane's character name is spelled "Faraday." In the other movies in the series, it is spelled "Farraday." In the radio series, the character known in the films as the "Runt" is called "Shorty."

CONFESSIONS OF BOSTON BLACKIE (1941)

In many ways, this film seems more like the first entry in the series than the previous film, *Meet Boston Blackie*. George E. Stone makes his first appearance as the Runt, a role he would play in the remaining films in the series except the last one. Walter Sande, who had a small role as a bumbling uniformed cop at the amusement park in the prior film, now plays Detective Matthews, a bumbling assistant to Inspector Farraday, a role he would play in many films in the series. Lloyd Corrigan appears for the first time as Arthur Manleder, an eccentric and bumbling wealthy friend of Blackie, a role Corrigan would reprise several times during the series. *Confessions of Boston Blackie* is a classic detective story in the nature of the later films in the series, rather than being a spy story. Unfortunately, unlike *Meet Boston Blackie*, there is an overemphasis on comedy, another characteristic of many of the later films in the series, making this short film, which runs only about an hour in length, seem padded in several places.

It seems that Diane Parrish, who needs money to help her sick brother Jimmy, has decided to auction off the one item of value in her family, an original statue of Augustus Caesar. Unfortunately, Diane gave the work to Allison and Buchanan, two crooked art dealers, who have made an exact replica of the statue, intending to auction off the fake and keep the original for themselves, to sell later at a large profit. However, at the auction Diane recognizes the replica as a fake. Buchanan attempts to shoot Diane so that she does not reveal the substitution, and Blackie, who is at the auction with his friend, Arthur Manleder, shoots at Buchanan to try to prevent the killing of Diane. Buchanan still gets off the shot but accidentally kills Allison instead of Diane. Farraday, who is also at the auction, sees the shooting by Blackie and assumes Blackie is the one who has killed Allison.

Manleder buys the fake statue and has it transported to his home, not realizing that the body of Allison has been hidden therein. The other crooks are after the fake statue also, because the combination to the safe that contains the real statue is hidden in Allison's pocket. In the meantime, Blackie is trying to clear his name, while at the same time helping Diane and Jimmy receive the money they deserve from the real statue.

This is a serious letdown from the first film in the series. There is simply not enough story to fill the short running time of one hour. As a result, the filmmakers have inserted a number of set comedy pieces into the film, such as Blackie impersonating an ice cream salesman, Blackie impersonating a doctor, the Runt impersonating an insurance adjustor and Manleder attempting to deal with a particularly difficult set of handcuffs. The filmmakers had to resort to these scenes for humor because the dialogue between Blackie and Farraday is not as clever as it was in the prior film. The amount of attempted humor is depressing rather than entertaining, particularly since some of the unfunny scenes are unrelated to the plot, such as a woman named Mona trying to extort money from Blackie by claiming to be his wife. (And where did she get that hat?)

If the viewer can get through the first hour or so of the film, there is an exciting conclusion in the subterranean workshop of one of the crooks, involving a shootout on an elevator, on some high steps, and amid the statues in the work area. This results in the toppling of the fake statue, revealing the body of Allison. Everyone is then trapped in the basement until Blackie comes up with a clever scheme for escape. If only the rest of the film had been so cleverly written and directed.

For those viewers who grew up watching the *Ozzie and Harriet* television show during the 1950s, it is interesting to see Harriet Hilliard in the role of Diane Parrish. While the part hardly stretched her acting skills, Hilliard is fine in the role. The other performers are also up to the fine acting standards of the series, but without a plot to match the quality of the cast, the film is a disappointment.

ALIAS BOSTON BLACKIE (1942)

During the course of this film, there is some interesting information learned about the background of the characters. In the late 1920s, Boston Blackie was arrested by Farraday and spent four years in jail along with the Runt. Farraday received a promotion as a result of the collar. Inspector Farraday is married and has at least one child, a son. At some time in the past, Blackie saved Farraday's life. None of this information is referred to again in any of the films in the series and not much else is ever learned about the personal lives of the characters in subsequent films.

All of this information is elicited during the course of bus rides to and from the state penitentiary, where Blackie, along with an acting troupe, is putting on a stage show for the inmates on Christmas Eve. Along for the ride is Eve Sands, whose brother Joe is in jail for burglary. Joe has always contended that he is innocent, and that he was framed for the crime by Duke Benton and another man named Steve. Eve is not supposed to come on the trip because she has already visited her brother twice that month, but tearfully convinces

That policeman looks suspiciously like Boston Blackie (Chester Morris). He is with Eve Sanders (Adele Mara), whose brother has been falsely accused of murder in *Alias Boston Blackie* (1942).

Blackie to include her in the troupe. Always suspicious, Inspector Farraday and Matthews decide to join the bus ride en route to the penitentiary, just to keep a wary eye on Blackie.

Once the ensemble is at the jail, Joe senses an opportunity for escape. Joe kidnaps the clown, Roggi McKay, impersonates him in the show, and then escapes with the cast as they ride back to town on the bus. Blackie suspects the substitution but before he can confirm it, Joe disappears. Blackie, knowing that he will be accused of aiding the prison escape and fearful that Joe will make his situation worse by killing the two thugs he claims have framed him, sets out to find Joe. During the search by Blackie, Duke Benton is found shot, but despite indications to the contrary, Blackie does not believe Joe is the killer. A cab driver's hack license found at the scene of the murder provides an important clue for Blackie, who eventually finds the real murderer and clears Joe's and Blackie's names.

This entry fulfills the promise of *Meet Boston Blackie*, as the story has a strong plot and is not sidetracked by set comedy bits. The scenes at the prison have an intrinsic suspense value all of their own, with barred doors opening and closing, the cast members counted by the guards, the prisoners marching into the show and the constant watchful eye of Farraday, Matthews and the prison officials. Once Joe escapes, Blackie works like a true detective, following lead after lead until he finally locates the guilty party. There is still comedy in the story, but it arises from scenes related to the plot, such as a dead body escaping from an ambulance to the chagrin of the drivers.

Adela Mara, probably the most attractive woman to appear in the series (and there were a number of attractive actresses in these films), is beautiful as Eve Sanders, This was one of her first appearances in films and even though she appeared in another 50 movies, she never became well-known. On the other hand, look for a brief appearance by Lloyd Bridges, who plays the bus driver who takes the performers to and from the prison. This was one of his early screen appearances, although he did appear from time to time in other mystery series of the 1940s before becoming a well-known performer later in his career. Larry Parks, later to become famous playing Al Jolson in films, overacts somewhat in the part of Joe Trilby.

The film is energized by the compressed time frame of the story, with all of the action taking place in less than 24 hours. While the story does lose its focus a bit in the second half, it coalesces very well at the end when Blackie finally captures the killer cab driver with the help of Farraday. This is a good entry in the series.

Boston Blackie Goes Hollywood (1942)

The prior movies in the series were mysteries, laced with various amounts of comedy. *Boston Blackie Goes Hollywood* is a comedy interrupted from time to time with a mystery. As a result, since the comedy is not that funny and the mystery is practically nonexistent, this is the weakest film in the series so far.

When the story opens, Blackie receives a phone call from Arthur Manleder, who is in trouble in California. Manleder requests that Blackie collect the $60,000 in cash in Manleder's wall safe and bring it to California so that Manleder can recover the stolen Monterey diamond. Of course Farraday immediately arrests Blackie for the burglary, and of course Blackie immediately escapes. The viewer later learns that Manleder was given the Monterey diamond by its owner, but it mysteriously disappeared when the beautiful Gloria Lane wanted to try it on. Two thugs are with Manleder, telling him that for $60,000, they will be able to recover the gem for him.

Blackie immediately recognizes the scam and Gloria Lane's involvement in it, even though Manleder, a supposed millionaire, cannot. Much of the ensuing action involves the chase for the $60,000 Blackie has brought to California. Blackie tries to protect Manleder's money and recover the stolen diamond, but his plans are upset from time to time by Farraday and Matthews, who have followed Blackie to California for no apparent reason, other than their belief that Blackie was somehow involved in the theft of the diamond. Eventually, good triumphs over evil and Blackie captures the gang, with the grudging assistance of Farraday and Matthews.

It is probably unfair to analyze the plots of these mysteries too closely, but if the owner of the Monterey diamond voluntarily gave it to Manleder and it was then lost, why were the police not aware of that? How dumb is Manleder supposed to be if he could fall for the scam of Gloria Lane and her thugs? Why would Matthews and Farraday follow Blackie and the Runt to California, to investigate a robbery in California? Surely a call to the local police would have been more efficient.

It seems as if the entire movie is filled with set comedy bits, such as Blackie releasing an ant farm into the detectives' hiding place in the baggage compartment of an airplane, causing them to itch; Farraday being arrested by the Hollywood police because they believe he is the famous thief, Boston Blackie; and the Runt dressed in little boy's clothes to elude the police. All of these antics were inserted into the film in an attempt to try to disguise the fact that there was not much plot, surely not one that could fill an hour of running time. Even the change of setting does not help the story, as the Hollywood location does not fit into the plot of the film at all. The entire story might just as well have taken place in New York City.

The best parts of the movie are the opening and closing. At the beginning there is a well-directed scene where a mysterious figure sneaks into Blackie's apartment and starts searching through his belongings. This opening portends an interesting movie to follow. When the figure turns out to be Inspector Farraday, however, it undercuts the suspense that went before. The ending involves a chase up a high fire escape and then down the internal cables of an elevator, both of which are very suspenseful scenes. It is rare for a Boston Blackie movie to end with action sequences so these are decided pluses for the film. But they are too little, too late. Those incidents are not enough to rescue this film from the flimsy, dim-witted plot that went before.

AFTER MIDNIGHT WITH BOSTON BLACKIE (1943)

Mystery movies of the 1940s seldom adequately balanced what seemed to be a requisite combination of crime and comedy, usually leaning more on the side of attempted humor rather than on the side of a clever mystery, to the ultimate detriment of the film. *After Midnight with Boston Blackie* is a rare case where the filmmakers employed just the right mixture of those conflicting elements to produce a satisfying crime film.

Much of the humor arises from the relationship between Blackie and Farraday, with the best dialogue between the two since *Meet Boston Blackie*. It is always amusing to see Blackie playing practical jokes on Farraday, in this case convincing him to drink a strange concoction which will allegedly cure his ulcers. Chester Morris and Richard Lane seem to be enjoying themselves as they perform their parts and their enthusiasm carries over to the viewer. There is also an unrelated storyline which is inserted into the film just for padding and comedy, concerning the Runt's impending marriage to a tall buxom blond named Dixie

Rose Blossom, who is an ex-bubble dancer. This is a rare case, however, where that comedy subplot works, mainly because it truly is funny, as the Runt's great love automatically does a strip tease when she hears her show music, flirts with Arthur Manleder when the Runt is not around, and is finally arrested for bigamy, saving the Runt from making the mistake of a lifetime.

The main story involves Diamond Ed Barnaby, who is released from prison after serving a substantial sentence for stealing some valuable diamonds. Other members of his gang, led by Joe Herschel, the owner of the Flamingo Club, are after Barnaby and the diamonds. Barnaby is cognizant of his perilous situation and apparently hides the jewels in a 30-day safe deposit box at the Arcade Building. When Barnaby subsequently disappears, his daughter Betty contacts Blackie for assistance.

Unknown to Blackie and Betty, Herschel has kidnapped Barnaby to force him to reveal the location of the diamonds. When Barnaby, attempts to call the police, Herschel shoots him in the back. Thereafter, the chase is on for the diamonds and in addition, Blackie must clear his name as Farraday believes Blackie killed Ed Barnaby so that he could steal the diamonds.

This film actually has little mystery to it, except for the location of the diamonds, with confusion resulting from the fact that Blackie has inserted fake diamonds into the mix. Instead, the film has more action than most of the other movies in the series, with Herschel and his henchmen chasing after Blackie, resulting in escapes between two high buildings on a plank stretched between the edifices, a jump into a canvas off a high building and an out-of-control car ride at the end. The direction of Lew Landers is more than adequate, particularly in the action scenes.

Other than the regulars, most of the performers have small roles, although Al Hill is quite good as henchman Sammy Walsh and Jan Buckingham is unforgettable as tall, buxom Dixie Rose Blossom. Cy Kendall plays the chief villain, Herschel, which is interesting because in two of the prior films he played Jumbo Madigan, a pawnbroker who was a source of important information for Blackie. That character returned in the next film in the series, still played by Cy Kendall.

One disappointing aspect of the film is its treatment of African Americans, with its standard portrayal of a dim-witted waiter on a train, and then Blackie wearing blackface in order to sneak into the Flamingo Club. These are minor although irritating deficiencies. On a positive side, the film has historical interest because of its topical references to the war environment in the United States in 1943, including rationing, blackouts and Manleder's servants leaving him for better jobs in the army and in industry. We also learn that Blackie's real name is Horatio Black. However, there is still no explanation as to why his nickname is "Boston."

All in all, this is one of the most entertaining films in the series. It is a shame that in most of the subsequent Boston Blackie movies, the filmmakers were unable to find the right balance between mystery and comedy.

THE CHANCE OF A LIFETIME (1943)

When a mystery movie has very little mystery in it, that can be a problem. When a mystery movie has a very flimsy plot, that can also be a problem. When that same mystery has excessive amounts of comedy padding that are not even slightly funny, there is a disaster in the making. That, unfortunately, is the result in *The Chance of a Lifetime*, the first movie in the series without Boston Blackie's name in the title. Perhaps Blackie was too ashamed to be associated with the film.

The story starts out with Boston Blackie making a pitch to the governor to release certain inmates of relatively good character who can aid in the war effort with the special skills they may have, rather than waste their time in prison. The governor agrees to an experimental project for a small group of inmates, so long as Blackie keeps track of them and so long as they work at Arthur Manleder's tool factory. The parolees are supposed to sleep at Blackie's apartment.

There is an immediate problem with one inmate, Dooley Watson, who was in jail for theft. He is allowed to spend the first night at home with his wife and his son. Unfortunately, instead of just visiting with his family, Dooley sets out to locate the $60,000 that was stolen in the original crime. He finds the loot and just as his wife convinces him to turn the cash over to the police, two of his former accomplices, Red Taggert and Nails Blanton, break into his apartment, demanding their share. A fight breaks out and in the ensuing struggle, Red is shot and killed. As Blackie arrives on the scene, Nails rushes out the door.

Blackie's unorthodox solution to the situation is to confess to Inspector Farraday that he killed Red, all in order to save the prisoner release program. Blackie then escapes from the police and the rest of the film, when not interrupted by comedy bits, concerns Blackie's quest to find Nails and have him confess in order to clear both Dooley and Blackie of the crime.

There is no mystery to the movie because the viewer watched as Dooley accidentally killed Red, so the only interesting moments in the film are Blackie's attempts to locate Dooley. The screenplay is written in a lazy manner, once again relying on the confession from a known criminal for its denouement, a plot device characteristic of uninspired plotting. Indeed, it is hard to believe that the coerced confession in this case would ever stand up in court. The movie is filled with three long comedy set-pieces: Blackie and the Runt escaping from Inspector Farraday, the two posing as carpet installers to obtain entry to a crime scene, and the two robbing the police station by getting two scrub women drunk and then dressing up as the women to replace them. Much like other films in the series, *The Chance of a Lifetime* does not have enough plot to fill the short one hour running time.

Even with director William Castle at the helm, the story has no punch or suspense. Castle made significant contributions to other mystery films of the 1940s, but his one contribution to this film is to shoot a fight scene in the dark, attempting to insert a little bit of style into the movie. Unfortunately, it is not film noir; it is just hard to see.

This was Castle's first directorial effort and his work product improved substantially in later films. That was too late for this film, however, wherein the minutes devoted to the alleged comedy exceed the minutes devoted to the crime, allowing little opportunity for any director to employ style and innovation to raise the quality of the output. Even a great director can do very little with a poor script. *The Chance of a Lifetime* is perhaps the weakest entry in the *Boston Blackie* series.

ONE MYSTERIOUS NIGHT (1944)

This movie marks a number of changes in the Boston Blackie film saga, which are presaged by new theme music heard under the credits. Lyle Lytell takes over the role of Sergeant Matthews, the assistant to Inspector Farraday. With his hat worn way back on his head and his laissez-faire attitude toward his job, Lytell is actually more irritating than Walter Sande in the role. Harrison Greene takes over the role of Blackie's friend Arthur Manleder, but the part is so small in this film that it is hard to evaluate his impact. Even the minor role of pawnshop owner Jumbo Madigan is handed over from Cy Kendall to Joseph Crehan.

More importantly, the question of how Blackie makes ends meet is partially answered in this film, since he and the Runt have apparently obtained full-time employment, having been working in Manleder's tool business for the last year. Another major change is that finally, after Blackie had saved the day over and over again in the prior six films and more than proved his bona fides, Inspector Farraday actually calls Blackie in to help the police solve this movie's mystery, the case of the stolen Blue Star of the Nile diamond.

The film starts out with a clever mystery, with a valuable diamond on public display at a hotel, and a horde of policemen watching the costly jewel. A diversion is created and when the police return to the diamond case, the valuable jewel is missing. It is clear to the audience that one of the criminals is George Daley, a manager at the hotel, and that the other two thieves are two suspicious strangers, later identified as Martens and Healy. The police immediately search everyone in the room where the theft occurred, including George Daley, but the jewel cannot be found. How did the diamond get out of the room? Surely, this is a mystery worthy of investigation by that great former jewel thief, Boston Blackie.

Blackie is called in by Farraday, using the ruse of publicly accusing Blackie of the crime, knowing that Blackie will voluntarily appear at his office to defend his reputation. This appears to be a needless strategy on the part of Farraday because Blackie was working just down the way at the Manleder factory, and a phone call would surely have been sufficient. Blackie agrees to the assignment, disguises himself as elderly Professor Hunter from Hoover University and begins his investigations back at the hotel. This gives Chester Morris the opportunity to overact in the part of the elderly curmudgeon. Blackie quickly discovers that the diamond was left under a table at the hotel in a wad of chewing gum and then retrieved after the police left. When Blackie searches Daley's office and finds chewing gum in his desk drawer, Blackie knows he has discovered one of the thieves.

Blackie and Daley's sister convince Daley to return the diamond to the police and confess to his crimes. Unfortunately, Daley's two accomplices arrive and Daley is shot by them. The chase is then on for the diamond, with Blackie now officially being accused by the police of the theft and also of the murder of George Daley. Once again, Blackie must clear his own name while at the same time finding the rest of the gang that stole the gem.

Pretty Janis Carter plays the role of Dorothy Anderson, a newspaper reporter who inserts herself into Blackie's investigations, accidentally derailing them in many ways. Carter appeared in several 1940s mystery movies and she was always a pleasant addition to the cast. Look for Dorothy Malone in one of her early screen appearances as George Daley's sister, Eileen.

The early part of the film is excellent, with the clever theft of the Blue Star of the Nile diamond and Blackie's skillful investigation of the crime. There are a number of complications to the plot, including the involvement of Daley's sister and the newspaper reporter, which keep the viewer guessing for a time. The surprise killing of Daley by his partners in crime marks the high point of the film.

Thereafter, the story meanders from incident to incident, with the feature focusing on who has the real diamond and who has a fake diamond, if any. Blackie is now officially the object of a police search, for the murder of Daley and the theft of the jewel, with the film now resorting to the same repetitive plot point of Blackie unjustly accused of a crime, instead of focusing on the interesting mystery that has gone before. Once again, there is not enough story to fill the brief one-hour running time. That seems to be a repetitive criticism of the Boston Blackie movies and it will not end with this film.

While there are none of the intrusive set-pieces of comedy which slowed down some of the other films, the story moves very slowly in the second half, and the climax, involving a chase after the two henchmen, ends anticlimactically, with the two simply being captured after escaping down a fire escape, without a shot being fired. A car chase might have been nice, but presumably that would have exploded the film's low budget. There are some funny lines in *One Mysterious Night,* Chester Morris is always entertaining and Janis Carter adds a little spice to the film but in the end, it is a disappointing feature.

BOSTON BLACKIE BOOKED ON SUSPICION (1945)

This is a fast-paced entry in the Boston Blackie series with the ex-con turned detective actually doing some clever investigative work amid a story with some interesting plot twists. Add a touch of light humor, with Blackie impersonating elderly Wilfred Kittredge right under the nose of Inspector Farraday, and the result is one of the best episodes in the long-running series.

The movie starts out with an interesting concept: a fake version of Dickens' *The Pickwick Papers* is to be auctioned off at a store owned by Blackie's friend Arthur Manleder, who knows nothing about the substitution. For the crooks, if successful, the ruse will net a cool $50,000. For the movie audience, it is refreshing to view a unique and clever type of caper, rather than one involving the usual purloined jewels or stolen money. The auction is successful and the fake book is sold for $62,000, with the crooks to receive $50,000 of that sum.

Unfortunately, there is no honor among thieves and when the book forger, Porter Hadley, appears to be double-crossing Gloria Mannard, the book shop assistant and his partner in crime, Gloria shoots Hadley in cold blood. Blackie, who has been on the trail of clues leading to Hadley, arrives at the scene just in time to collect the $50,000 accidentally dropped by Gloria and, of course, also to be accused of the theft and of Hadley's murder. Once again, Blackie must solve the crimes and clear his name before Mannard and her escaped convict husband flee with the money.

This movie is a true mystery, with Blackie following several clues in pursuit of the villains and with an early clever surprise in the story: not so much that the shop assistant, Gloria Mannard, was involved in the crime but that she would so brutally dispose of Porter Hadley. Later, Mannard's husband, a known thief, becomes directly involved in the action, complicating the story and adding to the surprises of the unpredictable plot. There is also an interesting chase up and down an incinerator shaft in an apartment building that is quite exciting, even though it is a direct borrow from a similar scene in a laundry shaft from *One Mysterious Night.* This was hardly a good omen for a mystery series that was already starting to repeat itself.

Once again, there is good rapport between Blackie and Inspector Farraday, with some clever dialogue between them. The auction scene gives Chester Morris the opportunity to impersonate an elderly gentleman, something Morris always appeared to enjoy doing. Frank Sully as Sergeant Matthews is less irritating than Lyle Lytell from the prior entry in the series. Lloyd Corrigan returns as Arthur Manleder, as does the original Blackie theme music. This story has a good pace, always moving forward and seldom being bogged down by comedy

In *Boston Blackie Booked on Suspicion* (1945), Gloria Mannard (Lynn Merrick) accosts her co-conspirator Porter Hadley (George Meader) and demands all of the money raised in their book forgery scheme.

bits. While the movie is not shot in a film noir style, the direction by Arthur Dreifuss always keeps the story going forward, with some out of the ordinary shots such as the cut-out view of the incinerator shaft in which Blackie is trapped.

Lynn Merrick plays Gloria Mannard as a true film noir femme fatale, so devious in character that it takes Blackie some time to realize she is the brains behind the crime. Much like Janis Carter, blonde Lynn Merrick appeared in several movies in the mystery series of the 1940s, although Merrick often played a character of less than scrupulous behavior, most notably in this film and in *A Close Call for Boston Blackie* (1946). The attractive Merrick was always a welcome addition to any mystery movie cast. Steve Cochran makes his film debut as Mannard's husband. Cochran has a larger role in the next Boston Blackie feature.

A comment on the title is necessary. In an unscientific survey, it would appear that Blackie is booked on suspicion in almost every movie in the series. Why then was the title used in this film, when Blackie never even makes it to the police station? Perhaps it was a clever pun on the word "book" since the crime involved a fake book. Leaving the title issue aside, this is clearly one of the best entries in the entire series. *Boston Blackie Booked on Suspicion* illustrates one of the joys in watching these 1940s mystery movie series. Just when all hope seems to be lost for a series, a little gem like this is produced, making all of the effort in watching these movies seem worthwhile.

Boston Blackie's Rendezvous (1945)

With *Boston Blackie's Rendezvous*, the Boston Blackie series reverted to the downward spiral it had been on since *The Chance of a Lifetime* (1943). Plots and incidents seemed to be repeating themselves. It was also getting quite irritating that Inspector Farraday believed that Boston Blackie was responsible for every crime committed in New York City, and particularly in this case, where the crime was the serial strangling of young women and not the theft of a valuable jewel. Farraday knew Blackie far too well by now to truly believe him to be a vicious killer. Thus, the underlying premise of the movie lacks any credibility.

There are some positives to the feature. There is some style to the direction of the opening scenes of the film, creating some early tension in the movie, and later scenes make good use of light and shadow and even sounds, such as the loud buzzer to an apartment door. The core performance in the film is that of Steve Cochran, who is quite good throughout the film as the homicidal maniac, alternately charming and psychotic. However, the poor script undercuts whatever suspense is engendered by the good direction and the performance of Steve Cochran.

The story opens with Arthur Manleder (now played by Harry Hayden) coming to Blackie to request help with a family problem. Manleder's nephew, Jimmy Cook, a homicidal killer, has just escaped from a sanatorium and Manleder wants Blackie to find him. Why Manleder believes Blackie could possibly help is not explained. Why Jimmy, who does not even know Blackie, then shows up in Blackie's apartment, is not explained either.

After Jimmy almost strangles Blackie to death, Jimmy goes to the local dance hall to locate a hostess named Sally Brown, to whom he has been writing love notes for some time. She is not there but Jimmy then becomes involved with another hostess whom he later strangles. As the movie progresses, Jimmy also strangles a hotel chambermaid and almost kills Sally Brown before Blackie and the police intervene. All the while, Blackie is trying to locate the disturbed man and Farraday believes that Blackie is the real killer.

The serial strangling of women is the most serious crime ever covered in a Boston Blackie movie. That did not, however, convince the filmmakers to treat the subject seriously. The entire tone of the movie is light, just as in the prior films. There is a wise-cracking ticket seller at the dance hall, Blackie pretending to be Sally's grandmother on the phone, Farraday insulting Sergeant Matthews, and a deadly and unfunny interlude where Farraday has a police psychiatrist interview Blackie. The Runt's main contribution to the story is to become overly frightened at the concept of a vicious strangler on the loose, and George E. Stone's performance is overwrought, unsubtle and not funny. All of these attempts at humor fall flat, particularly within the context of the serious crime being investigated. The contradiction of vicious killings occurring within the setting of farcical humor simply does not work.

Just when things could not get worse, Blackie and the Runt put on blackface and impersonate two maids in an attempt to avoid a police arrest. In addition to the look, their voices and exaggerated dancing are particularly demeaning to African Americans. What makes this incident worse, if at all possible, is that it is not even original material. Blackie had previously disguised himself in blackface in two other movies, and Blackie and the Runt had previously masqueraded as cleaning women in *The Chance of a Lifetime*.

Sadly, the filmmakers thought this routine was so funny that it was repeated as the last joke in the film, resulting, unfortunately, in the film leaving a very poor last impression on the viewer. *Boston Blackie's Rendezvous* is one of the true disasters of the Boston Blackie series.

A Close Call for Boston Blackie (1946)

This film opens quickly, with Blackie and the Runt in police custody in Farraday's car, apparently to be arrested once again. A serious crime drama appears to be afoot. The situation quickly turns out to be less dramatic, as Farraday and Matthews are just giving their two arch-enemies a courtesy ride home to their apartment. It is a clever trick by the filmmakers, in some ways satirizing some of the plot twists in the prior films and making fun of Farraday always arresting Blackie for a crime he did not commit.

Blackie then spots a woman being attacked and knocked down by some men. Blackie realizes the woman is his former love, Gerry Peyton, who disappointed Blackie a few years ago by marrying John Peyton, who was thereafter jailed for several years for manslaughter. When the three reach Blackie's apartment, they hear the crying of a young baby boy, who turns out to be Gerry and John Peyton's baby. Gerry explains that she never told Peyton about the baby and never visited Peyton in jail because of the way Peyton treated her during their marriage. Peyton has just been paroled and Gerry, afraid of what he might do, came to Blackie for help.

Peyton suddenly appears waving a gun. When Blackie takes it off of him, another man appears at the door of the apartment and shoots Peyton. The assailant disappears. Blackie is then left with a body and a baby, and Farraday on the way.

That was probably the fastest start to any movie in the series. The surprise appearance of Peyton and then his even more surprising killing portend the start of a tantalizing adventure for Boston Blackie. And then the film stops dead in its tracks. For the next 20 minutes or so, there is no mystery at all. Blackie is arrested, escapes, is arrested again and escapes. The Runt takes the baby to his girlfriend's apartment and since she has no milk in the house, the Runt dresses as a maid (how many times has he masqueraded as a woman in this series?) to go out and get some milk. The Runt's girlfriend comes home and is mystified to find a baby in her apartment. The true mystery in the movie is how so many people would be willing to leave a baby by himself for such long periods of time.

Gerry's criminal idea was to pawn the baby off on John Peyton's wealthy father, at a price. The baby was just borrowed from his real father, who later has a few regrets and is himself killed by Gerry's accomplice. It turns out that Gerry got Blackie involved in the plot for, well, for no reason that makes any sense. The crime at the center of this movie also makes absolutely no sense. There are two killings that occur in the movie for no reasons other than to provide corpses. Clearly, the writers of the Boston Blackie series were running out of new ideas for the character. As if to prove that lack of new ideas, near the end of the film, Boston Blackie once again disguises himself as an elderly gentleman, in this case millionaire Cyrus Peyton, an act which should have fooled no one, but in fact fools his ex-girlfriend, Gerry Peyton.

If there are ten minutes of mystery in this 60 minute story, that would be the real surprise in this film. The plot, to the extent there is one, is ridiculous. The best thing about the movie is the baby. He is played by an excellent actor.

The Phantom Thief (1946)

Gradually, and almost imperceptibly during the course of this series, the character of the Runt has changed from friend and able assistant to Boston Blackie to bumbler and comic relief, often doing more harm than good for Blackie's endeavors. George E. Stone, playing the Runt, starts to look and act more like Huntz Hall of Bowery Boys fame than the excellent character actor he used to be in the series. When the Runt becomes more irritating than Sergeant Matthews, cigar and all, it is clear that something has gone awry with the concept of the series.

In *The Phantom Thief*, the Runt involves Blackie in the problems of Eddie Alexander, a man who was released from prison ten years ago, is now a chauffeur to wealthy Anne and Rex Duncan, and has never had a criminal problem since leaving the penitentiary. On this night, Anne has asked Eddie to steal a case for her from the home of a spiritualist named Dr. Nejino. The case is supposed to contain some important documents and nothing else, but when Eddie cannot open the case, he takes it to Blackie, who finds a valuable necklace inside. This first scene is filled with mugging by the Runt and a visit by the police for no apparent reason.

Blackie decides that the three should do the right thing and return the necklace to Dr. Nejino. However, instead of just returning the box, Blackie becomes suspicious of Nejino and decides to attend a séance conducted by Nejino for the benefit of Anne Duncan, with the expectation that Anne's long-dead father might appear to her from the spirit world. During the séance, Anne screams, and when the lights are turned on Eddie is found dead, with a knife in its back. Nejino had previously called the police, so Inspector Farraday arrives just as the murder is discovered. Guess whom he suspects of committing the crime?

Thereafter, there is another murder, two attempted murders, an explosion and another séance. There is an interesting plot twist in the story as Anne's supposedly wealthy husband Rex is involved in the crimes, working with Nejino in attempting to swindle Anne. There is also a very clever howdunit to the murder of Eddie, as Nejino committed Eddie's murder during the séance while apparently strapped to a table in full view of the audience. Thus, there is some mystery to *The Phantom Thief*, making this film better than the ones that came just before it in the series, but the feature is still only fair at best.

Once again, the story is held back by the focus on comedy rather than crime, although there is a funny vignette where Blackie hides in the police station to avoid capture by the police. As noted above, the Runt has become increasingly irritating in these movies and his "comic" antics during the first séance rob that scene of whatever horror and mystery it might have had. Indeed, the film wastes the tantalizing atmosphere of the world of spiritualism, séances and ghosts, and replaces it with the usual banter and slapstick comedy, to the detriment of the film.

By now, the plots of the Boston Blackie movies have scant cohesiveness. In this case, at the end of the movie, when Duncan says that Nejino knifed Eddie to increase his share of the blackmail money from Anne Duncan, the whole plot unravels. So Eddie really was a criminal after all? What possible part could Eddie, a chauffeur, have played in the blackmail scheme? If Eddie really was part of the scheme and working with Nejino, why would Eddie steal anything from Nejino? Why would he bring the locked case to Boston Blackie at the beginning of the film?

In fact, there is no reason for Eddie's murder in the film, other than to start the plot moving and to put Blackie in the position of being falsely accused of another crime by Farraday. So, while there is an interesting mystery at the core of this film, even in a B-murder mystery movie it is important that the solution to the crime makes some sense. In that regard, *The Phantom Thief* does not meet even minimal standards.

Boston Blackie and the Law (1946)

There is little new in this twelfth entry in the Boston Blackie comedy series, except that the Runt is sporting a moustache for the first time. Indeed, the opening of the film is very similar to that of *Alias Boston Blackie* (1942), as in this film Blackie is performing his magic act in a women's prison on Thanksgiving Day, just as he has done for the last five years. On this occasion, however, one inmate, Dinah Moran, volunteers to appear in the act by entering into a "magic box" from which she is supposed to temporarily disappear. However, Dinah disappears for good, right out of the prison.

Boston Blackie is immediately accused of assisting in the prison break, forcing Blackie once again to escape from the police in order to find Dinah Moran and capture her, thus clearing his name. But, is Sergeant Matthews dumb enough to let Blackie escape from police custody once again? If you do not know the answer to that question, then this is your first Boston Blackie movie. The film spends 10 unfunny and unsurprising moments with the trick magic box just to allow Blackie to escape from the police. More time should have been spent on the interesting question raised by the escape — why did Moran want to escape, since she only had six months left in her prison term?

There is actually a relatively interesting mystery in the film, hidden among the comedy bits. It involves a theft of $100,000 several years prior by a magician's assistant, Dinah Moran, who went to jail for the crime. Was the magician also involved in that theft? In any event, the magician has a new assistant who is about to marry him, and the former assistant/former wife, Dinah Moran, escapes from jail for purposes of revenge, finding the stolen money, or both.

Although there were some good directors who worked on the Boston Blackie series, such as Robert Florey, Edward Dmytryk, William Castle and Lew Landers, only Florey brought some style and inventiveness to the mysteries. The other directors, such as D. Ross Lederman in this film, just seemed to be going through the motions, never taking the time to create unusual shots or angles, to shoot in different styles, or to employ interesting cinematography effects. By the time of this movie, the scriptwriters were also on automatic pilot, so once again the true villain is tricked into confessing the crimes, a plot ploy which always strains credulity.

There are some good performances in the film in small parts, such as Eugene Borden playing the proprietor of a magic shop and Eddy Waller as a locksmith. Trudy Marshall, as the magician's fiancée and perhaps villain of the piece, is also quite good. Indeed, Marshall is one of the many beautiful young actresses who graced the Boston Blackie films, an important positive attribute of the series. Chester Morris, an amateur magician himself, seems to be particularly enjoying himself when he is appears on stage in a magic act. But the only true fun left in *Boston Blackie and the Law* is to watch two consummate players, Chester Morris and Richard Lane, give it their best, even with the weakest of scripts.

For those who have never seen a Boston Blackie movie before, this film may be worth a look. For veteran viewers of the series, there is nothing new in this film. Once again, an interesting mystery premise is lost in a sea of comic relief, an unfortunate characteristic of much of the series.

Trapped by Boston Blackie (1948)

In the penultimate feature of the series, there is a much-needed return to the formula that made many of the early Boston Blackie movies so entertaining. Sure, this film has

The principal performers in *Boston Blackie and the Law* (1946) are shown. From left to right, they are Warren Ashe playing John Jani, a magician, Trudy Marshall playing Irene, the magician's assistant, Chester Morris playing Boston Blackie, a reformed thief, and Constance Dowling playing Dinah Moran, an escaped convict.

comedy moments, but they generally come from clever dialogue and not from long set pieces of unfunny comic diversions from the main story line. The Runt is finally back to being a friend and real help to Blackie, not just a caricature of a dumb detective. Sergeant Matthews' screen time is kept to a minimum. Most importantly, there is a real mystery in the theft of a valuable necklace.

The film opens with the death of private detective Joe Kenyon, when his out-of-control automobile runs over a steep hillside. Blackie and the Runt offer to help Mrs. Kenyon keep her husband's detective agency running, and for their first assignment they are employed to attend a masquerade ball at the home of a Mrs. Carter, to guard the expensive necklace she will be wearing that night. Not unexpectedly, the pearls are stolen at the ball, right under the noses of Blackie and the Runt, during a ballet danced by Mrs. Carter and her instructor, Igor Borio. But how was the crime committed in front of so many people? Did Blackie substitute fake pearls for the real ones when they accidentally broke off from Mrs. Carter's neck? Were they stolen by Borio when he retrieved the pearls from Blackie? Or was the crime committed in some other way?

Mrs. Kenyon is arrested by the police for her complicity in allowing Blackie to attend the masquerade ball as a supposed guard. Thus, Blackie must recover the real pearls and identify the true thief, not just to clear his own name, but also to prove Mrs. Kenyon's innocence. For once, there are suspects aplenty and Blackie meets all of them during his investigation. Blackie is particularly suspicious of the ballet instructor and his assistant, Sandra Doray, but this time Blackie turns out to be only half right. It turns out Sandra was working with Mrs. Carter's husband in a series of thefts from wealthy homes, and it was he that stole the real pearls, prior to the ballet dance ever commencing.

For once, the plot is somewhat complicated as Blackie goes from suspect to suspect, trying to identify the real thief or thieves. Suspicion moves from character to character with everyone acting somewhat suspiciously. The identity of the true culprit is mildly surprising, but the solution to how the theft was actually committed is quite clever. The death of Joe Kenyon also ties into the solution of the crimes. George E. Stone, in his last appearance as the Runt, gets to disguise himself once again as a woman, but in this case it is a middle-aged female and Stone is quite convincing in the part. Farraday and Blackie get off their usual share of clever lines. Patricia White plays Joan Howell, another in a long line of beautiful suspects in the Boston Blackie series.

Although there are still many comedy scenes in the film, they never overwhelm the intriguing mystery. Just when the viewer has lost all hope for the series, this entertaining feature manages to turn things around, showing the potential this series always had. Unfortunately, there was only one more film left to go, so *Trapped by Boston Blackie* was another case of too little, too late.

Boston Blackie's Chinese Venture (1949)

The last film in the series comes with two changes. Sid Tomack replaces George E. Stone as the Runt. In addition, the story focuses on a crime and its detection, leaving out the long comedy intervals that had been dragging down the recent movies. As a result, the film actually has more laughs from some clever dialogue and brief comedy moments sprinkled throughout the film than the previous movies, which seemed to have more "comedy" moments than crime detection. Unfortunately, the mystery itself makes little sense, and in the end this is a weak conclusion to the long crime series.

As the film opens, Blackie and the Runt are shown leaving a Chinese laundry owned by Charlie Wu. A few seconds later, Wu's niece, Mei Ling, discovers her murdered uncle's body lying on the floor of the laundry. The police are called but even Inspector Farraday does not have the energy to accuse Blackie of this crime. Mei Ling asks Blackie to investigate the murder and that leads Blackie to a group of thieves who are stealing valuable jewels, having them recut in a secret laboratory in Chinatown, and then removed from Chinatown by the driver of a tour bus. Wu was killed because he accidentally received a box of the jewels in a laundry bag.

There is an interesting trip by the tour company through the back allies of Chinatown, where the tourists can see a Chinese gambling den, a room where slave girls are kept and an attack by a man with a hatchet. Once the tourists leave, the Chinese gamblers renew their bridge game (and one of them uses Yiddish words), the actors in the slave den resume their gossiping, and the hatchet fighters smoke a cigarette together. It is quite an amusing scene. The purpose of the set up is so that Red, a shill for passengers on the bus, can deliver the stolen goods to an immigrant diamond cutter who is locked in the laboratory and then drop the recut goods at a Chinese store, hidden in tea, so that the tour bus driver can collect them at the end of the tour and eventually distribute them.

The problem is: why not simply walk the diamonds to the laboratory and then walk out with the new ones? Why concoct such an elaborate plan when there is no one to fool? Also, early in the film, the secret laboratory in which the diamond cutter is being held is in a room off the secret corridor where the tour party walks. At the end of the film, the same entrance to the laboratory is off a room in a movie theater. How did that occur?

It is somewhat disconcerting to see someone other than George E. Stone playing the Runt, but Sid Tomack is more than adequate in the role. The substitution of actors may have actually helped the movie since Tomack did not have the comedy skills of Stone and therefore the screenwriters were not tempted to focus the script on the Runt, and away from the crime elements of the tale.

Gerard, the owner of the theater, first appears as a ticket taker, but later, he starts appearing so often in the film that it is clear to every viewer he is the mastermind behind the criminal enterprise. Indeed, this movie is full of no surprises for everyone. Even though the comedy elements are downplayed in this last film in the series, a cogent mystery is never developed, and so with this film the Boston Blackie series comes to an unsatisfactory conclusion.

After Boston Blackie

Once the movie series ended, Chester Morris had few other movie roles. He was active in television in the 1950s and 1960s and had his final film role in *The Great White Hope* (1970). Morris died in 1970. George E. Stone continued in small roles in movies and guest appearances on television, although his failing eyesight caused him difficulties in performing. He appeared in many *Perry Mason* television shows as the court bailiff, although he seldom had any lines and he can be hard to spot in any particular program. Stone died in 1967. Richard Lane had sporadic work in movies and television shows after the conclusion of the film series. He is better known during this time period as a local and regional broadcaster in the Los Angeles area, being the announcer for wrestling, midget car racing and roller derby. Lane passed away in 1982.

There were no more Boston Blackie movies ever produced. However, between June and September of 1944, there was a 13-episode radio show about the character with Chester Morris reprising his role as Boston Blackie, once again assisted by Richard Lane as Inspector Farraday. The series was a summer replacement for the popular *Amos and Andy* radio program. The radio shows then aired on a regular basis starting in April 1945 and continuing until 1950, about a year after the film series ended. In these episodes, Richard Kollmar played Blackie and Maurice Tarpin played Farraday.

There was also a television version of the Boston Blackie character in the 1950s. Titled *The Adventures of Boston Blackie*, it starred Kent Taylor as the reformed jewel thief. It ran for 58 episodes in syndication during the 1951–1953 television seasons. Frank Orth played Inspector Farraday and Lois Collier played Blackie's girlfriend Mary, a role that originated in the radio series. The setting was moved from the New York of the film series to Los Angeles, California. Thus the Boston Blackie character had come full circle, as in the original Jack Boyle stories, Blackie had a wife named Mary and the stories took place on the west coast.

9

The Falcon
The Other Robin Hood
of Modern Crime

In 1941, RKO moved the production of the Saint films to England and began using an all–British cast, including Hugh Sinclair in the title role. Because that left George Sanders, the former star of the Saint series, without a mystery series in which to star, RKO announced that it was searching for a new mystery vehicle for the well-liked actor. Surprisingly, the studio chose the character known as the Falcon, the subject of only one short story by Michael Arlen, as the detective in its new crime series for George Sanders.

Arlen was not well-known then, and indeed never became well-known in the mystery field. At the time the Falcon movie series was conceived and the first film released, Arlen's short story had been published just once in an obscure publication few people had read. Why, then, did RKO choose to reduce the number of Saint films and move to such an obscure character for its new mystery movie series?

Background

The Story

Michael Arlen, whose real name was Dikran Kouyoumdjian, was born in 1895 to Armenian parents. The family moved to England when he was about six years old. In 1916, Arlen began his literary career, generally publishing essays under his real name. In 1922, he changed his name to Michael Arlen and became a British citizen. In 1924, *The Green Hat*, a novel about England's fashionable society after the end of World War I, was published. It was far and away Arlen's most successful work, with the author purportedly earning a half-million dollars from the book. Arlen thereafter wrote other novels and short stories, including ghost stories and a few mysteries, but his most famous work today is the short story "Gay Falcon," first published in 1940.

The hero of the story is named Gay Stanhope Falcon, thus the title of the tale. Over the last several years, a number of large insurance companies have paid out significant sums of money as a result of a series of thefts of valuable jewelry. The police have been unable to solve the crimes. Falcon is therefore employed by the heads of those insurance companies to recover the stolen jewelry or the money that has been paid out on the claims or both. During the course of the story, Falcon burglarizes the safe of international beauty Diana Temple, recovers the jewels, and solves two murders.

In his anthology, *To the Queen's Taste*, Ellery Queen commented that the Gay Falcon of the story was a hardboiled, sardonic detective, not like the charming and romantic rogue of the movie series. That is not, however, strictly true. In the story, Gay Falcon seems to romance Diana Temple and he surely gets off his share of witty lines. In any event, with only one story about Gay Falcon in existence, it is difficult to accurately contrast the persona of Falcon as conceived by Michael Arlen with the one portrayed in the long movie series.

In fact, and please do not tell Leslie Charteris, the Gay Falcon of the story most closely resembles the Saint of the Charteris novels and the RKO movie series. Falcon admits to having had many jobs over the years, including being a gambler, secret agent and war correspondent, thus emulating the Saint's worldwide travels. Falcon initially appears to be dishonest, but in this story he actually works on behalf of the insurance companies and the police. Falcon also has a mean streak similar to that of the Saint, and Falcon is not above speaking sarcastically to the police and others. "Gay Falcon" would have fit easily into the line of stories written by Charteris about the Saint and perhaps that is one of the reasons RKO was so interested in the Arlen short story.

THE FILM SERIES

There are several theories for the decision by RKO to reduce the number of Saint movies and put more emphasis on the Falcon films. For one, the studio was becoming tired of Leslie Charteris' interference in the Saint film productions, his criticism of the Saint movies and his requests for additional compensation. RKO was happy to be rid of him. However, the Saint series had been successful and recognizing the profitability of a movie mystery series, the studio wanted to produce something similar. Since the Arlen story was titled "Gay Falcon," that gave RKO the opportunity to give its character a moniker, "The Falcon," that was similar to "The Saint," even though there was never an explanation in the movies as to why Gay Lawrence, and then his brother, were called "The Falcon."

Perhaps more importantly, RKO was paying Charteris the sum of $10,000 for each Saint film; it was able to make a deal with Arlen to pay him much less per movie. Charteris was not happy with RKO's move, claiming that the Falcon films were so much like the Saint films that he was entitled to $10,000 for each of the Falcon movies. Charteris sued RKO and the case settled out of court for, according to Charteris, a large sum of money.

In fact, however, there were substantial differences between the Saint and Falcon characters in each of the movie series. The Saint was more of a world traveler than the Falcon. The movie Saint was also more of a cutthroat than the Falcon, with Simon Templar having no problem permanently dispatching foes with malice aforethought, something the Lawrence brothers never did. The Saint employed wittier repartee than the Falcon, who did not seem to have quite the sarcastic wit that his British counterpart possessed. The Falcon often experienced problems with women, as there were several fiancées around to cause him trouble in a number of his films. The movie Saint, on the other hand, never seemed to get tied down to just one woman. In many of the Falcon movies, and unlike the Saint, the Falcon had a comic sidekick named Goldy or Goldie Locke. The role was played in different films by character actors Allen Jenkins, Edward S. Brophy and Vince Barnett.

The Falcon's real name was changed to Gay Lawrence (or Laurence) for the movie series. When Sanders decided to leave the Falcon series after only four films, the studio decided to give the lead role to Tom Conway, Sander's real-life brother. The transfer of the title role from Sanders to Conway occurred in *The Falcon's Brother* (1942), where the character of Gay Lawrence died a heroic death, but not before his detective franchise could be handed over to his brother, Tom Lawrence. Tom Conway then appeared as the star of the next nine Falcon films released by RKO.

Tom Sanders and his younger brother George Sanders were born in Russia (Tom in 1904), but the family fled to England at the time of the Russian Revolution. The two were then educated in English schools. Tom began appearing in theater and radio in England and brother George persuaded him to come to Hollywood around 1940, where he changed his name to Tom Conway to avoid confusion with his brother. Conway began appearing in films in the early 1940s, and in addition to the Falcon series, he is best known for appearing in three Val Lewton horror films also produced at RKO. In an early screen appearance, he played one of the villains in a Nick Carter mystery, *Sky Murder* (1940).

After the release of a total of 12 Falcon films at RKO, the series lapsed. Two years later, the series then moved to an independent production company, Falcon Productions, Inc., which released three Falcon movies, starting with *Devil's Cargo* (1948). John Calvert assumed the role of the Falcon, but the Falcon's real name in the movie was changed from Lawrence to Michael Waring. Most prints of these three films have the name "Michael Watling" dubbed over the name "Michael Waring" so there may have been some rights problems with the name "Waring," which was then being used in the radio series about the Falcon. In the middle film in the series, the Falcon finally had a regular job, working as an investigator for a major insurance company.

John Calvert appeared in only about a dozen films during his career, the high point being the Falcon films. He is better known for his skills as a professional magician, and he continued appearing on the stage long after his film career was over. The Falcon series ended in 1949.

The George Sanders Films

The Gay Falcon (1941)

The Gay Falcon opens with the Falcon's fiancée, Elinor Benford, entering the new offices of Laurence and Locke, a brokerage firm owned by the Falcon and the Falcon's sidekick, Goldy Locke. At the insistence of Elinor, Gay and Goldy have forsaken a life of crime-fighting for respectable jobs in the financial sector. However, Laurence and his sidekick have no customers, have nothing to do during the day, and they are quite bored with their new profession. After some banter between Elinor and Laurence, work is finally done for the day. When will the mystery ever start?

This opening scene illustrates the problem with this film, and indeed many of the remaining Falcon movies—the overemphasis on comedy. Most crime films start out with a jolt, whether it is the depiction of a crime or the introduction of a puzzling mystery. Here, the filmmakers decided to start the movie with some comedy and defer the crime until more than ten minutes into the film. This overemphasis on comedy was often the downfall of a Falcon movie.

When Laurence arrives home, he discovers Helen Reed in his apartment. She is secretary to wealthy Maxine Wood. Helen asks Laurence to attend a charity ball that night to help protect a huge diamond that a Mrs. Gardiner intends to wear at the event. There has been a rash of other robberies at Wood's previous social affairs and there is a concern that the valuable jewel may be stolen at the ball. Finally, there may be a mystery after all.

The Falcon agrees to attend and when he dances with Mrs. Gardiner, she inexplicably slips him the diamond, saying, "I suppose you want it now." Events move quickly after that (with the requisite comedy bits in between). Mrs. Gardiner is killed and Goldy is arrested for the crime. Laurence convinces the police to release Goldy so that the real killer can be captured. The Falcon, Goldy and Helen elude their police tail and when Laurence and Helen go to visit Maxine Wood, Goldy is captured by a tough guy, Noel Weber, who is after the diamond. There is then another murder, Goldy is arrested again, Laurence fights with his fiancée, and a man named Retana is determined to be the killer of Gardiner. It turns out that Mrs. Gardiner was supposed to slip the diamond to Retana at the charity ball as part of an insurance scam, but she mistook Laurence for Retana. At the end of the movie, the Falcon exposes Wood as the surprise head of the jewel theft ring.

Although Wood is the least likely (but most obvious to the experienced viewer) suspect, there is purportedly a clue to her guilt. When Goldy was captured by villain Noel Weber, after the Falcon, Goldy and Helen had eluded the police tail, the only person who could have tipped Weber off to Goldy's location was Maxine Wood. However, that clue is never revealed to the viewer during the course of the film; it is explained by the Falcon at the end of the movie. Thus, despite the implication at the end of the film, the viewer has no real clue to the head of the gang.

The Gay Falcon, in the relationship between Laurence and his fiancée, is a screwball comedy, something the Saint movies never were. Sanders seems to be enjoying himself in that format, particularly when there are unintentional misunderstandings and Laurence is caught by his fiancée in embarrassing moments with another woman. Sanders' reactions to each dilemma are quite amusing. Along with Sanders, the other members of the cast are excellent, including Wendy Barrie as Helen Reed, Turhan Bey as Retano and Gladys Cooper as Maxine Wood.

In the end, though Sanders is quite charming in the title role, this movie is sabotaged by the repetitive comedy scenes, particularly in Laurence's unfunny relationship with his fiancée. This is a screwball comedy, but unfortunately an unfunny screwball comedy. While Allen Jenkins is excellent in his comedy role as Goldy Locke, there is simply too much humor, or attempted humor, for the flimsy mystery plot. The movie only runs slightly over one hour, so if the plot had been sufficient, there would have been little need for comedy padding. All in all, this was not an auspicious beginning for a new mystery series.

Note on the Source Material: The credits state that the movie is "from the story by Michael Arlen." Since Michael Arlen wrote only one story about the Falcon, the reference must be to the short story, "Gay Falcon," first published in *Town and Country* magazine in May 1940. It was also published in the March 1945 issue of *Ellery Queen's Mystery Magazine* and then collected by Ellery Queen in his anthology, *To the Queen's Taste* (1946).

Despite the credit, the film is really an original work. It takes only two elements from the Arlen story. One is the scam involving the stealing of jewelry and the not-so-innocent victims making insurance claims for the missing items. The other is the surprise climax, with the suicide of the prime villain actually being a murder by an apparently innocent female character, who is in reality the true head of the gang. In both media, the murder weapon is a hypodermic needle filled with poison, and in both media the Falcon is not fooled by the ruse.

A DATE WITH THE FALCON (1942)

By only the second film in the series, the Falcon movies were perilously close to becoming very minor mystery movies, with little interest for the true mystery fan. There is nothing wrong with filming a very complex crime movie that is hard to follow, such as *The Big Sleep* (1946). There is everything wrong with filming a movie that is hard to follow because the plot makes no sense, and then to insert comedy interludes that disrupt any logical thread that the plot may have had. That is the problem with *A Date with the Falcon*.

At least this film opens with a crime, with Waldo Sampson, the inventor of a formula for creating synthetic diamonds, being kidnapped by some unknown parties. Inspector Mike O'Hara consults with Gay Lawrence (the new spelling of the name) and as a result of that one conversation, the villains focus on capturing or killing Lawrence throughout the film, seemingly forgetting that they have Sampson and the formula in their possession. If the villains had simply ignored Lawrence, who had no interest in the investigation of the crime in the first place, their scheme would have succeeded and they could have sold the formula for a large profit.

Gay Lawrence is kidnapped by one of the villains, Rita Mara, then escapes, is kidnapped by Rita again and then escapes again and is later knocked unconscious by Rita.

In *A Date with the Falcon* (1942), the lovely Rita Mara (Mona Maris) employs a handgun to persuade the Falcon (George Sanders) to take a trip with her. This will not be the only time Mara abducts Templar in the film.

Lawrence is suspected by the police of the murder of Waldo Sampson, and then is finally arrested by the police for a different murder. Often it seems that no headway is being made toward a resolution of the story line of the film. Is this any way to investigate a crime? Nevertheless, despite these frolics and detours, the Falcon somehow solves the crimes and saves the formula.

As the story progresses, it is hard to remember what the Falcon is investigating or to figure out why the villains are out to get the Falcon. In addition, throughout the story, Lawrence is trying to balance the demands of his fiancée, Helen Reed (from the prior film) against his crime detection activities. Once again, that creates screwball comedy moments, with misunderstandings between Lawrence and Helen, and stunts like Lawrence ending up on a high ledge of a hotel window and Helen believing he is going to commit suicide. Most viewers will be little amused by these many moments of purported comedy.

There is little to recommend in this film. Wendy Barrie reprises her role as Helen Reed from the first film in the series, and while Reed was an engaging character in *The Gay Falcon*, with her enthusiasm in becoming involved in a mystery investigation with a great detective, she is shrill and irritating in the sequel. While Barrie's performance was fine in the original, it is disappointing in this film. Even Allen Jenkins, reprising his role as Goldy Locke, is particularly unfunny in the sequel. He has become just another irritating interruption to the story.

There are a few interesting performers. George Sanders is suave and debonair as always. Argentinean-born Mona Maris is quite beautiful playing villainous Rita Mara, particularly in the clinging evening gown she wears throughout the second half of the film. James Gleason as Inspector O'Hara and Hans Conreid as a hotel clerk are always enjoyable to watch. They are not enough, however, to raise this film above the mundane and even the annoying. Perhaps that is why George Sanders was interested in exiting the film series as soon as possible.

THE FALCON TAKES OVER (1942)

It must have seemed like a good idea to base a Falcon movie on *Farewell, My Lovely*, one of the Raymond Chandler novels about detective Philip Marlowe. The previous Falcon movie, *A Date with the Falcon*, had a particularly weak plot and the Chandler novel did have a strong story line that should have been fairly easy to adapt into a compelling movie. However, good ideas alone do not make good movies, and once the plot of *Farewell, My Lovely* was recycled into a typical Falcon movie, there was not much left of the original Chandler tone and point of view. The result was an unsatisfactory film, at best.

In the opening, a tall hulk of a man, Moose Malloy, accosts Goldy Locke, who is in his car waiting to drive the Falcon home. Malloy asks Locke if he knows where Moose's girlfriend Velma is, and of course Goldy has no idea about whom Malloy is talking. Malloy then barrels his way into the exclusive Club 13, first by throwing the doorman to the ground and then by tossing the head waiter to the floor. A struggle then ensues in the manager's office, and when it is over, the manager is found lying on the floor, dead of a broken neck. Malloy rushes out of the nightclub and forces his way into Goldy's car, and Goldy, under duress, drives Malloy away.

This opening contains some of best moments in the film, with Ward Bond being a surprisingly effective Moose Malloy, menacing one and all as he towers over his victims, grabs them by the necks or knocks them to the floor. Malloy may well be the best villain in the entire Falcon series, particularly when his size and menace are emphasized. But, in sure Falcon style, some of the suspense and terror of Malloy is undercut by the comedy interplay between Goldie Locke and Malloy, with Allen Jenkins as Locke hamming it up about being scared to death of ever meeting the homicidal brute again.

Inspector O'Hara is called in to investigate the restaurant manager's murder and Gay Lawrence insinuates himself into the action. Lawrence investigates the house at which Goldy had dropped Malloy off, and there he meets Jessie Florian, who used to know Velma, but refuses to provide any information about her. Nevertheless, while there Lawrence discovers a clue about Malloy's whereabouts and sends Goldy to a spiritualist, just in time for Goldy to be present for two more murders by Malloy. There is also an apparently unrelated plot of the Falcon being hired to deliver ransom money on behalf of J. Quincy Marriot in order to recover a valuable stolen necklace. At the scene of the ransom turnover, Marriot shoots Lawrence in the back with Lawrence's gun, and then Marriot himself is killed by an unknown assailant. Eventually, Lawrence finds the real power behind a blackmail scheme and is also able to determine whether Velma is alive or dead.

Once again, the main problem with this feature is the insertion of intrusive comedy bits or supposedly humorous scenes into the film, instead of sticking with what could have been an excellent murder mystery. Allen Jenkins' mugging as Goldy becomes more irritating with each film. There is absolutely idiotic dialogue between Inspector O'Hara and his assistant Bates, none of which is even the slightest bit funny. There is also the cliché of a female reporter helping the Falcon, which helps to lighten the mood of the film, but that is just the opposite approach that this tale of blackmail and murder requires. The one strong point of the film is the direction of Irving Reis, who employs interesting camera angles and contrasting light and shadow to highlight the suspenseful scenes in the film. Unfortunately, it is just too difficult to find the suspenseful moments; they are hidden too well between the comedy vignettes.

The plot is unconvincing. Why did the Falcon get involved in the investigation of Moose Malloy at all? It had nothing to do with him. When Lawrence went out on the ransom-paying expedition with Marriot, why did Lawrence load his gun with blanks? Did he really expect Marriot to shoot him in the back, with the Falcon's own gun? Why did Moose Malloy ever take a manslaughter rap for Barnett, particularly since it would separate him from his true love Velma? That back story of the film is never explained or even addressed in the movie, leaving many unanswered questions.

The holes in the plot are caused, in part, by taking the storyline of a dark and complex mystery novel and then shoehorning that tale into the Falcon movie mold, with its light tone, use of extended comedy bits and short 60 minutes of running time. It simply does not work. *Farewell, My Lovely* deserved a better screen treatment, and it eventually received one in *Murder, My Sweet* (1944). There, Moose Malloy meets the real Philip Marlowe, played by Dick Powell, and Marlowe sets out on a search to find Velma, Moose's former girlfriend, in a film based more on the original Chandler novel than *The Falcon Takes Over*.

Note on the Source Material: It is surprising how much of this film is based on Raymond Chandler's *Farewell, My Lovely*. The opening scene with Moose tearing up the night club and killing the manager, Marlowe later questioning Jessie Florian about Velma, Marriot hiring Marlowe to assist in a ransom payoff at which time Marriot is killed, Jessie's later killing by Moose, and the blackmail racket in which Amthor is involved all come from the book. What is missing from the movie is the significance of the Amthor character, scenes involving Marlowe's incarceration and drugging at Dr. Sonderborg's sanitarium, the crookedness of the Bay City police, and any true development of the Diana Kenyon character (who is Helen Grayle in the book) and her relationships to the other characters. Helen Grayle is a key character in the novel. The plot of the film has been simplified and several items are left unexplained, such as the reason behind the stealing of the jade necklace, if there ever was a necklace.

Scenes that come from the book, however, are modified in the film. Thus, when Marlowe meets Jesse Florian for the first time in the book, he obtains information and a picture of Velma, while in the film version, the Falcon obtains information about Amthor, the psychic. In the book, when Marriott takes Marlowe to the ransom payoff site, Marriot expects Marlowe to be killed, but no attempt is actually made on Marlowe's life. In the film, Marriot attempts to kill the Falcon.

The strength of the plot from the book is a big plus for *The Falcon Takes Over*, providing the Falcon series with one of its most interesting storylines. However, that storyline, as noted above, is lost in the attempted humor and other diversions from the main plot. Nevertheless, screenwriters Lynn Root and Frank Fenton have done an admirable job of incorporating at least the highpoints of the Chandler novel into the script of a short second feature.

THE FALCON'S BROTHER (1942)

This is intrinsically the most interesting film in the Falcon series. George Sanders was no longer interested in playing the role of the Falcon, but rather than simply substituting actors without explanation, as was usually done in Hollywood mystery series (such as in the Saint series where Hugh Sinclair had substituted for George Sanders who had previously substituted for Louis Hayward) a transition movie was filmed. A new character, Tom Lawrence, the brother of Gay Lawrence, was introduced, and at the end of the film, the torch of carrying the Falcon movies was passed to the new actor. Adding spice to the transfer was that Tom Conway, cast as Tom Lawrence, was the real-life brother of George Sanders.

Two experienced mystery writers, Stuart Palmer (Hildegard Withers stories) and Craig Rice (John J. Malone stories), were employed by RKO to create the script that would explain the transition between the two Falcons. In addition to creating a new Falcon, other changes from prior films in the series were also made. A new director, Stanley Logan, was brought in, and Keye Luke substituted for prior actors in the role of Lawrence's valet. Also, the character of Goldy was eliminated, but he was replaced by a similar character, Lefty, played by Don Barclay. All but the last change were for the better. In particular, director Logan does spice up the filming somewhat with interesting shots and unusually lit scenes, a stylish approach to the direction that was missing from some of the prior films in the series.

Gay Lawrence and his new sidekick Lefty arrive at the docks to meet the Falcon's brother, Tom Lawrence, who is arriving that day on a Latin American cruise ship. Gay is immediately informed by the police that Tom just committed suicide on board the ship. The body was discovered by Diane Medford. Gay identifies the body but once he leaves the ship, he informs Lefty that the body was not that of his brother. Gay and Lefty tail Medford to Madame Arlett's fashion salon, where Gay meets fashion editor Paul Harrington and a newspaper reporter on the fashion beat, Marcia Brooks. As Gay attempts to interview Medford, she is shot and killed by an unknown assailant, with the murder weapon left lying near her body.

Gay is put out of the action when he is sideswiped by a car and Tom, who is very much alive, takes over the investigation. Other suspects for the crimes are a Latin American dance duo and the photographer for the fashion magazine. Eventually, Tom realizes that a gang of Nazi infiltrators are in the country, intending to kill a Latin-American diplomat at a New England Inn. Although Tom is captured by the spies, he manages to prevent the assassination with the help of the heroic Gay Lawrence, who arrives on the scene just in time to prevent one death while losing his life in the process.

Although the narrative does seem aimless at times and there are the usual light moments which are not all that amusing, this is an interesting film, with its plot truly reflecting the war year in which it was released, with references to Pearl Harbor and blackouts and a storyline related to Nazi sabotage and an attempted murder. There are surprise plot twists, such as the police ballistics expert unable to tie Harrington's gun into the bullets found in a victim, astonishing Tom Lawrence who is sure Harrington is the killer.

Obviously, it must have been a huge surprise to the audiences in 1943 that the lead character, Gay Falcon, died at the end of the movie. That had never happened before in a long-running mystery movie series. However, the filmmakers did miss an opportunity to exploit that death as it happens in long shot, is only later confirmed in a newspaper headline, and Gay never gets to give a dying declaration; but then a deathbed speech by the Falcon may have turned out too schmaltzy to be believed. All in all, this was a good film and gave hope to the viewer that the next set of Falcon films starring Tom Conway would be better than the previous ones starring George Sanders.

The Tom Conway Films

THE FALCON STRIKES BACK (1943)

This film proves that a little bit of style and a little bit of real humor can go a long way in raising a mystery movie above its second-feature status. *The Falcon Strikes Back* marks Tom Conway's first solo appearance as the Falcon and it is an auspicious debut.

The film opens with Tom Lawrence in bed, nursing a severe hangover, when a strange woman, Mia Bruger, enters his bedroom through the window and begs him for assistance in locating her missing brother. Never one to turn down an attractive woman, Lawrence agrees to accompany her to a cocktail bar where the brother was last seen. As Lawrence looks behind a curtain into a back room in the bar, he is slugged over the head. He wakes up in his car in the country, where he is promptly arrested for being involved in the theft of $250,000 of war bonds and the murder of a bank messenger. The several bullet holes in his car are important proof of the Falcon's involvement in the crimes.

The Falcon is therefore off to prove his innocence, against some terrific odds, since his best lead, the cocktail bar, has now turned into a women's knitting society. Nevertheless, a clue there leads to a resort in the country known as the Pinecrest Hotel, where the Falcon discovers the mysterious Mia Burger. When the Falcon tries to talk to her, she is suddenly murdered. With that lead gone, Lawrence is stuck with numerous potential suspects at the hotel, including Gwynne Gregory, the manager, Smiley Dugan, a man putting on a charity puppet show, Bruno Steffen, a supposedly invalid foreigner, and Bruno's nurse, Ricky Davis, a known criminal whom the Falcon once sent to jail. Eventually, Lawrence exposes the war bond profiteers and also identifies another individual who murdered Mia Bruger and was out to kill the rest of the gang.

This is a rare Falcon movie where there is complicated plot and thus some true detective work on the part of Lawrence. The Falcon follows clues from the knitting society to the hotel and there uses fingerprints to initially accuse the wrong person of the crimes but eventually find the correct villain. The overlay story of the puppeteer wanting revenge against the war bond criminals gives an added surprise at the end of the film, although his motives are not clearly explained and the ending is therefore somewhat murky. Nevertheless, these scenes add some depth to the mystery in which the Falcon has unwittingly become involved.

As to using a little bit of style, that is exemplified by the scene where Lawrence accosts Mia Bruger at the hotel. She denies knowing Lawrence, and so to escape from him she jumps into the swimming pool and swims away. In a very interesting tracking shot, Lawrence merely walks down the side of the pool, asking Bruger questions as she is swimming. He gets no response from her. At the end of the pool, Bruger gets out, walks up on the diving board and dives into the pool, intending to go off in the opposite direction from Lawrence. The Falcon therefore starts walking back along the pool side, intending to pepper Bruger with more questions. As the camera pans down the pool, it becomes apparent to Lawrence and the viewer at the same time that Bruger has not come out of the water. She is then found lying dead at the bottom of the pool, having been shot by an unknown person using a gun with a silencer.

The scenes at the swimming pool are beautifully composed and executed, adding to the surprise of the sudden murder of Mia Bruger. Other stylish scenes in the film are those shot in the dark in the puppet theater and the chase of the puppeteer over a rooftop at the end of the film.

As to real humor, when the Falcon wakes up in his car in the country, he is discovered by two tramps who make some acute comments about the wealthy and are able to tell the time by checking the shadow of a stick under the sun. It is a short but amusing scene, which does not deviate from the progression of the story in any way. Another of several examples in the film is Goldy pretending to be reporter Marcia Brooks' husband, forcing her to involuntarily spend more time at the knitting society instead of becoming involved in Lawrence's investigation.

This film, with more interesting shots and better written humor than prior films in the series, shows that a little attention to detail can go a long way toward increasing the entertainment value of a movie. With a plot that is a little more involved than usual, this is one of the best of the Falcon movies.

Note on the Production: While Tom Conway plays a character named Tom Lawrence in *The Falcon Strikes Back*, he is actually playing the original Falcon, Gay Lawrence. Tom lives in Gay's apartment, has the same houseboy Jerry, and Gay's sidekick, Goldy, is back and is completely loyal to Tom. Tom is now known as the Falcon, for no apparent reason, even to the general public, and he has a long history with the police department. In fact, there is never another reference made to Gay Lawrence in the entire Falcon series. It is as if the original Falcon never existed.

That suggests the question: why did the studio make a transition film, *The Falcon's Brother*, if in the end Tom Conway was simply being substituted as a new actor in the Falcon role? As noted in Jon Tuska's *The Detective in Hollywood*, RKO had no true interest in doing a transition film or keeping the franchise alive when Sanders wanted to leave the series. The creation of the plot for *The Falcon's Brother* and the use of Sanders' brother, Tom Conway, in the film was merely an attempt by the studio to get another Falcon movie out of Sanders.

The studio was surprised when Tom Conway caught on with the public in the role of the Falcon. It therefore continued making Falcon movies, essentially in the mold of the Sanders films with little variation, notwithstanding the fact that the Falcon's brother, a new character, had taken over the original Falcon's crimefighting career.

THE FALCON IN DANGER (1943)

This film possesses the best set-up of any movie in the Falcon series. The mystery is propelled by a stunning opening sequence, where an airplane from Washington is about to land at a small airport. As relatives and friends are waiting to meet the passengers, Inspector Timothy Donovan and his assistant Bates arrive. Suddenly, the plane appears but its landing lights are not on. The plane then hits the runway once, bounces back into the air and then crash lands slightly off the field. The police and airline personnel rush to the plane to help the passengers, but when the door to the plane is opened, there are no passengers inside. Even the cockpit is empty. This is surely a conundrum worthy of the attention of a great detective.

Since the Falcon is the only great detective in the general area of the plane crash, the police and Nancy Palmer, the daughter of industrialist Stanley Palmer, who was supposed to be on the airplane, ask the Falcon to assist in the investigation of the crime. The police quickly determine that the plane landed by automatic pilot. Most of the passengers had exited the plane at the prior stopover to stretch their legs, where they were stranded when the plane suddenly took off carrying only two passengers, Stanley Palmer and his assistant, Wally Fairchild. Fairchild was carrying a briefcase with $100,000 of securities in it. There are no clues as to what happened to the two passengers and the pilot between the plane's unexpected take-off at the prior stop and its crash landing at the airport with no one on board.

Tom Lawrence then meets Iris Fairchild, Wally Fairchild's niece, who, while she grew up with the Palmer family and was raised as if she were a member of the family, always sported a grudge against the Palmers for the way they treated her uncle in their business relations. Other potential suspects for the kidnapping include Nancy's fiancé, Ken Gibson, who seems to have a gambling problem, and Mr. Morley, an older fellow who runs an antique shop and clearly sent two ransom notes to the Palmer residence. However, when Stanley Palmer suddenly arrives back at his house, unhurt, with an explanation as to what happened to him on the plane, there is still the mystery as to what happened to Wally Fairchild, the pilot and the missing securities Fairchild was carrying.

This story is always absorbing, primarily because it constantly goes off in unexpected directions. For example, when Lawrence is talking to Morley about paying the ransom for the return of Palmer, news arrives that Palmer has just appeared back at his house. When the Falcon is just about convinced that Iris Fairchild is innocent, the missing securities turn up in her apartment. Toward the end of the film, the bodies of the pilot and Fairchild are unexpectedly found by the state police, but that discovery does not bring anyone closer to ascertaining what really happened on the airplane.

There are enough red herrings to make *The Falcon in Danger* a tantalizing mystery.

The actual solution to the kidnapping, the murders and the theft of the securities is quite clever and for once the culprit is not the least likely suspect, since there are some clues to the villain's involvement. The climax is fairly exciting, with the Falcon being forced to kill the actual murderer and the police arriving just in time to capture his co-conspirator.

As good as this feature is, it is after all a Falcon mystery, so not everything is executed to perfection. The comedy antics of Goldy Locke from the prior films are missing, but they are unfortunately replaced by the comedy antics of Tom Lawrence's fiancée, Bonnie Caldwell, who repeatedly advises everyone who will listen that she hails from Texas. Fiancée trouble must run in the Lawrence family, although this is the first film (and hopefully the last) in which Tom Lawrence has one on screen. Amelita Ward plays Bonnie Caldwell, and while she is quite good in the role and does engender a laugh or two, she is still an unwanted interruption to an engrossing mystery. During the last third of the film, the Caldwell character disappears from the story and it is amazing how much better the film becomes while she is gone.

The acting is some of the best in the series, particularly Clarence Kolb as Stanley Palmer and Felix Basch as Mr. Morley. It is always comfortable watching Ian Wolfe play a butler. As usual, Cliff Clark is excellent as Inspector Donovan and even though the part of his assistant, Bates, is seldom funny, Bates does participate in a fun scene at a roller skating rink, which while gratuitous does provide a good sense of how people entertained themselves in this country during World War II. This is a very good mystery, even better than *The Falcon Strikes Back*.

THE FALCON AND THE CO-EDS (1943)

This is a thin mystery, with little to recommend it. The script is particularly weak. The prior three Falcon movies had noted mystery writers Stuart Palmer, Craig Rice or both contributing to the scripts. Their inputs added to the cogency of the mystery elements of the movies. Once Palmer and Rice were gone and the storylines were handed over to lesser contributors, the quality of the films suffered. It is hard to tell from the final product in this case, but director William Clemens had substantial experience in directing mystery films, going back to the Perry Mason and Nancy Drew mysteries of the 1930s. However, the script for *The Falcon and the Co-Eds* gave him little opportunity to show his skills and the direction of the film is uninspired, at best.

The Falcon and the Co-Eds opens with Jane Harris, a student at the all-girls school Blue Cliff Seminary, seeking the Falcon's help in investigating the recent death of Professor Jamison. The official cause of death is natural causes, but Jane believes he was murdered. When Jane steals the Falcon's car, Tom Lawrence is off to the seminary to investigate the death, and, incidentally, to recover his vehicle.

Lawrence poses as an insurance investigator and quickly learns that most of the staff, such as Miss Keyes, the dean, Anatole Graelich, the psychology teacher, and Vicky Gaines, the drama teacher, believe that Jamison committed suicide by poisoning, probably as a result of his unrequited love for Vicky. The group then covered up the suicide to protect the reputation of the school. However, Miss Keyes is then killed and someone shoots at the Falcon, so it is then clear that Professor Jamison was also murdered. The Falcon finally determines that the music teacher, Mary Phoebus, is the culprit, although how he jumps to that conclusion is unclear and why she is supposed to have committed the crimes strains credulity.

There is simply not much mystery to the film. The Falcon is convinced to investigate a supposed murder by a high school student who steals his car, and Lawrence is silly enough to take the bait. Because the Falcon is not exactly a private detective and he is not an official representative from the police, it is often difficult for the screenwriters to devise a scheme to get him involved in a crime investigation, but this is clearly one of their weakest efforts.

It is almost 45 minutes into the film before Miss Keyes is killed, so prior to that event there is just a lot of talk back and forth concerning the "suicide" of Professor Jamison, along with frolics and detours by the Falcon, including a trip to a mortuary in town, which contribute little to the main story. The solutions to the crimes, as determined by Tom Lawrence, make no sense. Mary supposedly killed Jamison to frame Vicky and Graelich for murder, because she was jealous of the relationship between the two. If that were truly the case, she chose a strange way to kill him — by poison, permitting everyone to logically assume Jamison's death was a suicide, thwarting Mary's scheme. Mary then supposedly killed Keyes because Keyes covered up Jamison's death. How does that make any sense? How did that killing advance Mary's plot against Vicky and Graelich?

Even a rail-thin mystery should have some cohesion. While there is an attempt to create some mystery by focusing suspicion on the psychic student, Marguerita, who predicts both of the murders, there is no real motive given for her to commit the killings so she is never a realistic suspect. Indeed, Mary is not a particularly realistic suspect either. Perhaps that is why the filmmakers emphasized the music in this movie. There are several musical numbers performed at the girls' academy, to take the viewers' minds off the inadequacy of the plot. While that trick works for a few moments, it is not sufficient to cover up the sloppiness of the storyline of the film.

THE FALCON OUT WEST (1944)

Tom Lawrence is surely an unconventional detective. He is a witness to the murder of Tex Irwin in a New York night club and then immediately decides to investigate the crime at a ranch in Texas. Surprisingly, the Falcon is then followed to Texas by New York Police Inspector Timothy Donovan and his assistant, Bates, who are also investigating the New York murder. Of course, Donovan's and Bates' investigatory skills have been suspect for quite some time. Surprisingly (or perhaps not surprisingly), the Falcon's technique works and he is able to solve a New York murder by long distance detection conducted half-way across the country from the killing.

The film opens at a New York night club where the former wife of Tex Irwin asks the Falcon to act to prevent the marriage of Tex to Vanessa Drake, who Mrs. Irwin believes is a gold-digger. Lawrence is not interested in the situation at all until Tex stumbles off the dance floor, claiming he has been bitten by a rattlesnake. In fact there are two small pricks on Irwin's leg, which could have come from a rattlesnake, but it is hard to comprehend how a rattlesnake found entry into a New York City night club. Irwin dies from his wounds and Lawrence then discovers that Irwin's wallet is empty. When Vanessa grabs a train ticket from the table, the Falcon lifts another one, and the two are off to Texas.

Vanessa is obviously the prime suspect for the crime, except that she does not have a motive. In fact, since she was going to marry Tex, his death seems to leave her in the lurch. Previously Tex had deeded his ranch in Texas to her, but back in Texas, Tex's wall safe has been emptied and the deed is missing. Other potential suspects for the crime, if it was one, are Mrs. Irwin, who is arrested by the police, Mr. Colby, the business partner of Tex who

In *The Falcon Out West* (1944), the Falcon (Tom Conway, center, in the light suit) has just discovered the deed to Tex Irwin's ranch and a poison ring in the jewelry drawer of Dave Colby. Also pictured, from left to right, are Bates (Ed Gargan), the dumb policeman from New York City; Vanessa Drake (Carole Gallagher), the fiancée of Tex Irwin; the local sheriff (Wheaton Chambers); Dusty (Lee Trent), the cowhand who is infatuated with Vanessa; Dave Colby (Minor Watson); Timothy Donovan (Cliff Clark), a smarter policeman from New York City; and Dave Colby's daughter, Marion (Barbara Hale).

is also arrested, Stephen Hayden, Tex's attorney, and also some cowboys who are acting quite suspiciously.

Once again, there is not enough story material to fill an hour's worth of screen time. In this film, though, instead of filling the void with comedy bits only, the filmmakers have also added Western bits. Thus, there is a runaway stagecoach, a chase after a horse that supposedly has a killer on its back, cowboys preventing their boss being taken into custody by the police, and a vocal group singing Western songs. These scenes do not help. The film is still deadly dull.

The mystery itself has little interest, with few true suspects for the crime. The attorney is murdered, so he is not a suspect. Mr. Colby cannot be the killer, because the Falcon likes his daughter, Marion. Mrs. Irwin cannot be a true suspect because she is the first person arrested for the crime. That leaves Vanessa Drake as the killer, but while the audience can quickly guess that fact, no convincing explanation is given as to how the Falcon reached that conclusion.

As for the performances, sophisticated Tom Conway seems far out of place in the semi-wild West. It is interesting to see Barbara Hale, of Perry Mason television fame, playing Marion Colby, although at times she appears just a little bit chunky in the film. Also, the part of Marion Colby hardly stretched her acting talents. Ed Gargan as Bates finally has some humorous moments, as he says "How" to an Indian, who replies, "Very well. Thank you." This joke is repeated two more times, in clever variations.

There is some interest to the film. The murder of Tex by a supposed rattlesnake in New York is followed up by the death of attorney Hayden by another supposed rattlesnake attack in Texas. This method of murder is surely unique to a Hollywood murder mystery and when it eventually turns out that a poison ring was the more mundane murder weapon, that does not detract from the howdunit aspect of the story.

The ending is quite good, with the Falcon captured by Vanessa and her cowboy henchman after she admits her role in the murders to Lawrence and then tries to kill him with the ring of poison. This segues into a Western-style shootout, which is quite suspenseful. But in the end, an unconvincing mystery, deadly filler material and a humdrum pace sink any positives the film might have had.

THE FALCON IN MEXICO (1944)

This film is a surprise. Just when the Falcon movies were falling into a rut, with uninteresting plots being indifferently performed, produced and directed, *The Falcon in Mexico* breaks the pattern, resulting in perhaps the best film in the series.

The feature opens with Tom Lawrence, having just kissed his attractive date good-bye, walking down a New York street and being accosted by Dolores Ybarra, who asks his help in breaking into an art gallery to recover a stolen painting she says she has painted. Never one to turn down a damsel in distress (and because the movie has to start somewhere), the Falcon helps her break into the gallery. Once he sees the painting, though, Lawrence realizes that Dolores was not the painter but rather was the model. Before he can resolve the conflict, Lawrence discovers the dead body of the art dealer lying on the floor. When the security guards arrive, Lawrence realizes that Dolores has fled through an open window, leaving him holding the proverbial bag.

The Falcon is then puzzled to learn that the portrait was painted by Humphrey Wade, an artist who had been dead for 15 years. So, how could he have painted the portrait of the very lovely but very young Dolores? Lawrence escapes the security guards and proceeds to the home of Lucky Diamond Hughes, one of the greatest collectors of Humphrey Wade pictures. Hughes confirms that the painting is an original Wade, but he cannot explain the anomaly of the painting having been completed years after Wade's death. Hughes suggests that the Falcon visit Wade's daughter, Barbara. The Falcon does so and Barbara admits to Lawrence that she believes her father is still alive.

Lawrence and Barbara are then off to Mexico, with Lawrence looking for Dolores to help clear his name of the murder of the art dealer, and the two trying to determine if Humphrey Wade is still alive. Lawrence seems to bring a crime wave with him to Mexico, as there are two more killings of women who had some relationship to the dead artist, raising once again the question of whether Wade is still alive. Finally, Lawrence and the police set a trap for the real killer, who turns out to be Lucky Diamond Hughes. He was killing all of the people who knew that Wade was alive to protect the value of his collection of Wade paintings.

This film sometimes seems like a hardboiled thriller in the nature of a Ross MacDonald novel, with its motif of past events causing crimes in the present day. The overarching investigation in the movie is directed toward the question of whether Wade is alive or dead, and if alive, whether he is the murderer. Suspicious characters include Paula, the owner of the hotel where Wade died who was in love with Wade; Raquel, Wade's wife and mother of Barbara, who is now remarried to Anton, a mean-looking cabaret performer who has a bad attitude toward the Falcon; and Dolores, who is acting as suspiciously in Mexico as she did in the States. Everyone tries to convince the Falcon and Barbara that Wade is dead.

The hardboiled nature of the story is also conveyed by the innovative direction of William Berke, in his first film in the series. Berke is not afraid to take the time to use creative camera angles and lighting to enhance the sense of foreboding. This is not, however, a hardboiled film. The plot, while very interesting, is not that complicated, the streets of Mexico are not that mean and the Falcon is not much a man of the common people. Since the Falcon as portrayed by Conway is always a sophisticate and always has a light approach and attitude about him, this film could never create the milieu found in a Dashiell Hammet or Raymond Chandler story. Nevertheless, the plot is always challenging, the suspects always interesting and the setting always appealing. This film works substantially better than *The Falcon Takes Over*, which was in fact based upon a hardboiled mystery by Raymond Chandler.

In addition to using a new director for the series, the cast is very fresh for this film. In recent and later movies in the series, there seemed to be a stock cast of actors and actresses, such as Jean Brooks, Rita Corday and Ian Wolfe. In this case, Barbara Ward is portrayed by a young Martha Vickers (billed as Martha MacVicar), just a short time away from her memorable supporting performance in *The Big Sleep*. This is one of her first film roles and she is quite lovely in the part. Other unfamiliar faces are Mona Maris, as Wade's first wife, Raquel, Cecilia Callejo as Dolores, and Mary Currier as Paula, the owner of the local hotel. They all give excellent performances.

Acting honors go to Nestor Paiva as Manuel, the native Mexican who finagles his way into the Falcon's employ as a chauffeur, valet and assistant. One of the surprises toward the end of the film is the revelation that Manuel is actually a policeman. When Paiva is acting the part of a hired hand, he has a thick accent, pretending to be the stereotypical Mexican hireling. When Paiva is acting the part of the policeman, much of the accent disappears and Manuel seems competent and authoritative. It is a versatile and amusing performance by Paiva and actually makes fun of the audience's stereotypical belief concerning poorer Mexicans, which belief is undoubtedly driven by other screen portrayals of Hispanics in Hollywood films.

The true innovation in the film was to finally rid the series of Inspector Timothy Donovan and his assistant Bates. Cliff Clark usually played the role of the Inspector and while Clark was a likable enough performer, the role was written so that Donovan was always the foil of the Falcon, rather than being a competent policeman. Bates was one of the most irritating of the incompetent policemen of the 1940s mystery series so it is an incredible relief to see him finally gone. It is amazing how much better this movie is with those characters missing. *The Falcon in Mexico* illustrates that it is not necessary to have humorous policemen in a movie for a mystery film to be entertaining.

The film is hurt by overuse of process screen shots and unconvincing ones at that. The motivations of the characters are not always convincing and even the motive of the murderer strains credulity somewhat. But with a double mystery of whether Ward is alive and who the true murderer is, *The Falcon in Mexico* is always a challenging and interesting film. It is highly recommended.

The Falcon in Hollywood (1944)

This is another weak mystery in the Falcon series. As usual, the subject is murder but the tone is light throughout. Sometimes it can be hard to tell the Falcon movies apart, particularly because there is seldom an effort to create a compelling murder mystery with plausible suspects, believable motives and clever clues. In substitution for those attributes, each of the movies from around this time period simply had a new setting far from New York City. However, with the exception of *The Falcon in Mexico*, which had a dynamite plot, Tom Lawrence's trips out West added little to the effectiveness of the films.

There is some interest in *The Falcon in Hollywood* in the scenes shot in the Hollywood studio, as the viewer learns a bit of inside information about how Hollywood films are shot. RKO's studios doubled for the fictional studio in the film. There is also an interesting but gratuitous scene at the Los Angeles Coliseum — interesting for historical purposes, but since the facility is empty at the time, the value of the sequence is limited. There are also some long shots of the racing at the Hollywood Race Track, so this film does, at least, have a California feel to it, a mild plus for this movie, but not enough to compensate for its plot deficiencies.

The story starts out with the Falcon on vacation, playing the horses at the Hollywood Race Track. There he meets in turn: two detectives who are searching for Louie Buchanan, an escaped convict whom Lawrence had once helped send to jail; Louie himself, who is coincidentally standing in the row behind Lawrence; famous actress Lily D'Allio, who works at Sunset Studios; and Peggy Callahan, Louie's former girlfriend and an aspiring actress at Sunset Studios. When Peggy accidentally takes Lily's purse, Tom Lawrence is off to Sunset Studios to recover it, and presumably to become involved in a murder, since this is after all a Falcon mystery movie. It is not surprising that soon after entering the motion picture studio Lawrence discovers the body of Ted Miles, the husband of costume designer Roxanna and an investor in a movie currently being directed by Alex Hoffman, who may be in love with Roxanna or Lily.

The mystery concerns the murder of Ted Miles and the later killing of Louie Buchanan. While there are many suspects, there are no clues. The story moves from scene to scene, with not much being discovered about the murder of Miles. While many of the suspects may have had motives for the killing, each of their motives is quite thin. Since each person is suspected in turn by the Falcon and the police, that can only mean that someone else committed the murders, which is, of course, the case. The Falcon solves the crimes, not by detective work but by inspiration, making the denouement quite unconvincing. The conclusion, though, is not bad, as the Falcon chases the killer onto a studio sound stage and shoots him as his activities are being tracked by a powerful spotlight.

After six appearances in the series, Tom Conway seems bored playing the Falcon, and if he is not quite sleepwalking through the role, as others have observed, he clearly shows little enthusiasm for the part. Indeed, the only interesting performer in the film is Veda Ann Borg as Billie, the taxi driver who acts as a Goldy-like character to the Falcon. She is cute and perky and could easily have played Torchy Blane in the Warner Brothers mystery series featuring the vivacious female detective. Borg was a steady worker in Hollywood, appearing in about 100 films over 20 years, contributing other energetic performances in other mystery series such as the Kitty O'Day and Big Town series. It is a shame Borg did not reappear in later films in the Falcon series. She may have given the series the kick that it needed.

The Falcon in San Francisco (1945)

The Falcon left Hollywood and is now in San Francisco. That is known from the title, the name of the train on which the Falcon is riding as the film opens, some stock footage of the Golden Gate Bridge, other scenes of San Francisco projected on a screen behind the characters, and one gratuitous scene with the actors actually on location at Telegraph Hill. The new locale adds nothing to the film, as the story could have happened in any large city with a harbor. But, the return of Goldy Locke with some amusing lines, Tom Lawrence attempting to interact with a young child and some interesting direction raise this film above the average for the series.

The movie commences on a train, the *San Franciscan*, where the Falcon and Goldy meet young Annie Marshall, who tells them she is being held prisoner in her home by her nurse Carla Keyes and the butler, Loomis. Tom Lawrence is unsure as to the veracity of the story, but when the nurse is found murdered on the train, Lawrence's suspicions are aroused. At the conclusion of the train trip, Lawrence attempts to take Annie to her house in San Francisco but is interrupted when the police arrest him for kidnapping.

After some time in jail, the Falcon's bond is put up by an unknown woman, Doreen Temple, who promises to explain everything to him at dinner. In fact, Temple has her henchmen abduct the Falcon and bring him to her apartment. Temple quizzes Lawrence about the death of Nurse Keyes and about a man named Peter Vantine. After Lawrence is beaten up a little more, Temple warns him to stay away from a ship called the *Citadel*.

The rest of the film is very confusing, with the elements never coming together in a cohesive plot. The gravamen of the crimes is the smuggling of raw silk aboard the *Citadel* and the attempts of Temple and Vantine to collect the booty. Duke Monette, a racketeer from Prohibition days, is somehow also involved. In the end, of course, the Falcon solves the crimes, although he presumably does it by guesswork, since his explanation is unconvincing. All of the villains kill each other or die in a spectacular explosion on board the *Citadel*.

Much of the entertainment value in the film arises from the Falcon's interactions with little Annie Marshall. Tom Lawrence is clearly inexperienced with children, even forgetting to commence a bedtime story with those classic words, "Once upon a time." There is no plot reason for Goldy to reappear after several movie absences, and he is only in the story for comic relief. However, Goldy is not too intrusive to the story, and his lines about his prior life of crime are particularly amusing.

This was Joseph H. Lewis' only directorial effort in the Falcon series and he makes the most of it. Lewis was a B-movie director who attained cult status with some of his movies, such as the film noir classic *Gun Crazy* (1950). Just when *The Falcon in Hollywood* appears to be a run-of-the-mill series mystery, Lewis imbues the scenes at the Marshall mansion with a style that is far from run-of-the-mill. He uses creative shots, such as a tracking shot as Lawrence and the Marshalls walk up steps, a shot through a banister to avoid a cut, shots framed by a bed canopy, low angle shots of the characters, and shots with objects such as a lamp in the foreground to add interest to the view. The settings have ample contrasts of light and dark, with shadows on the walls and on the floors. This attention to detail by Lewis adds to the effectiveness of these scenes, creating the feel of a dark house mystery, which this film may be if the Marshalls are actually being held prisoner in their own home. Lewis' direction is an added plus throughout the film.

The Falcon in Hollywood is hardly a classic; there are better films in the Falcon series. However, if one can suspend disbelief with regard to most of the plot, there are just enough interesting elements to make this film worth an hour of the viewer's time.

THE FALCON'S ALIBI (1946)

Despite the fact that Rita Corday and Jean Brooks each make their fifth appearance in a Falcon movie, the best quality of The Falcon's Alibi is its fresh cast. Jane Greer makes her only appearance in the series, playing night club singer Lola Carpenter. Greer may be the most beautiful actress ever to appear in the series, with her attractiveness highlighted late in the movie when she wears a tight-fitting black gown. Greer is an icon of film noir for her performance as Kathie in Out of the Past (1947), one of the true femme fatales of the genre. While her part is not as challenging in The Falcon's Alibi, Greer brings a touch of class and beauty to the role that few other actresses could have provided.

Elisha Cook, Jr., is also an icon of film noir for his multiple appearances in the genre, such as playing Wilmer the gunsel in The Maltese Falcon (1941) and small-time hood Harry Jones in The Big Sleep (1946). His part in The Falcon's Alibi as lunatic killer Nick is closest to his performance as lunatic killer Harry in I Wake Up Screaming (1941). Cook had a very strange face, which could engender empathy, fear and even disdain, depending on the part he played. Cook is particularly excellent toward the end of this film, as the pressure of his crimes and the infidelity of his wife causes him to finally go off his rocker.

As the film opens, Joan Meredith, personal secretary to the flighty Mrs. Peabody, asks Tom Lawrence's help in locating a missing necklace. Previously Mrs. Peabody had reported one of her necklaces missing and made an insurance claim. Thereafter, Joan had been followed by an insurance investigator, Metcalfe, who believed Joan committed the theft. In order to protect herself from similar allegations, Joan then took another valuable pearl necklace of Mrs. Peabody's, worth $100,000, to a jeweler to have a copy made. Joan was then shocked when the jeweler told her the necklace was a fake.

In the hotel night club, beautiful singer, Lola Carpenter is secretly married to Nick, who runs an overnight request show on a radio station that broadcasts from the upper floor of the hotel. There have been a number of recent unsolved robberies at the hotel, which come to a head when a hotel employee is killed in Mrs. Peabody's suite, a crime that may be related to the stolen necklace and the other thefts. Are Nick and Lola somehow involved in the hotel thefts and now a murder?

This is a typical substandard movie in the Falcon series. The script is particularly weak. By the middle of the film, it is hard to remember what Tom Lawrence is investigating or how he got involved in the case in the first place. Less than halfway through the film, it is made quite clear that Nick took a shot at Lawrence and then returned to his radio studio,

Opposite top: In this publicity photo for *The Falcon in San Francisco* (1945), the Falcon (Tom Conway) is sitting on the staircase of the Marshall mansion, next to the little girl he befriends, Annie Marshall (Sharyn Moffett), and her older sister, Joan Marshall (Rita Corday). *Opposite bottom:* Two film noir icons appear in *The Falcon's Alibi* (1946). The lovely Jane Greer plays night club singer Lola Carpenter, and Elisha Cook, Jr., plays her unstable husband, Nick. At the end of the film, Nick, in a jealous rage, attacks Lola.

where a record was playing that concealed the fact Nick had left the studio. Thus, every viewer knows that Nick is the hotel thief and killer. There are no other potential suspects. Where is the mystery?

In fact, until the last ten minutes or so of the film, not much happens. In that last ten minutes, though, matters dramatically improve as Jane Greer and Elisha Cook come to the forefront of the story and the movie becomes both suspenseful and engaging. Yet these scenes almost seem to come from a different film; they seem unrelated to the jewel theft that the Falcon is apparently investigating.

Vince Barnett makes his only appearance as the Falcon's assistant, Goldy Locke, and he is clearly the least of the three actors who essayed the role. While the story does concern Nick's alibi while he is committing his thefts at the hotel, the Falcon uses no alibi during the film, so what is the sense of that title?

A mystery movie fan might want to take a look at this film just to see Jane Greer and Elisha Cook, Jr., at their best. That viewer will probably, however, want to fast forward through the slow parts of the movie. For others, there are many better ways to spend an hour of their lives.

THE FALCON'S ADVENTURE (1946)

This was the 13th Falcon film in the series and the 10th to star Tom Conway as the title character. It also marked the end of the RKO series about this other Robin Hood of Modern Crime. The Falcon series was up and down in quality over the years, but this last film is surprisingly quite engaging, showing that there was still some life left in the character even at this late date.

Tom Lawrence and Goldy are on their way to a fishing vacation when they spot an attractive young lady, Luisa Braganza, who is being kidnapped by a taxi driver, Mike Geary. Lawrence, always unable to ignore a damsel in distress, rescues Luisa from the hands of Geary. She then takes Lawrence back to her hotel to meet her uncle, Enrico. The uncle has developed a formula for manufacturing synthetic diamonds, which is being sought by a number of parties. When the Falcon and Luisa leave the hotel room for a few moments, Enrico is murdered by Geary, who has been searching in the hotel room for the formula. The Falcon, of course, is accused of the crime, and he is off to clear his own name as well as to deliver the formula to Professor Denison, Enrico's friend in Florida.

Up to this point, *The Falcon's Adventure* has been pretty standard fare for the Falcon series. A formula for synthetic diamonds was the MacGuffun in *A Date with the Falcon*, helping a damsel in distress fuelled the plots of *The Falcon in Mexico* and *The Falcon in Hollywood*, and there may have been one or two other movies in the series where the Falcon was falsely accused of a crime and had to clear his own name.

The quality of *The Falcon's Adventure*, after the mundane opening scenes, quickly turns to the better after the death of Enrico, with the film delivering surprise after surprise. In addition to the murderous Geary on the trail of the formula, Enrico's maid begins to act suspiciously, particularly when she turns up in Miami where the formula is to be delivered. On the train trip to Miami, a beautiful blond, Doris Blanding, seems to be accosted by another passenger named Benny. The Falcon rescues her and agrees to switch compartments with her for the night. It turns out that Doris and Benny also have designs on the formula and the switch of compartments was a ruse to drug Lawrence and Locke in order to steal the formula.

In Miami, the old gentleman who is supposed to be Professor Denison appears to act suspiciously, so maybe he is an imposter. Kenneth Sutton, Denison's wealthy friend, then wants to purchase the formula. What are his real motives? The plot is never predictable and the real intent of the characters as they appear from time to time in the movie is far from clear.

Director William Berke uses little style in shooting the film, a far cry from his work in *The Falcon in Mexico*, but his direction is surely adequate for the story. The acting is top-notch, as it always was in the series, even though most of the cast are relative unknowns. Goldy Locke delivers some funny lines or is involved in humorous situations, adding to the enjoyment of the film. The one clear drawback, other than the slow opening, is the ridiculous scene near the end where Lawrence uses a fake alligator to obtain a confession from one of the henchmen. It is an embarrassing scene.

It is not that *The Falcon's Adventure* is all that special. It is simply that the movie has many entertaining qualities. There is little filler material in the movie so the hour long film moves at a quick pace. The conclusion involves a surprisingly long fight on the deck of a yacht, which is quite enjoyable. The film demonstrates that a good plot can drive any mystery movie in a positive direction. *The Falcon's Adventure* is therefore recommended as an entertaining example of a 1940s second-feature mystery movie.

The John Calvert Films

DEVIL'S CARGO (1948)

After a hiatus of two years, the character of the Falcon returned to the big screen for three more movies before the series finally closed down. But, is this really the Falcon that viewers have come to know and love? Gone are Gay Lawrence and Tom Lawrence and in their places is a character named Michael Waring. Gone is trusty assistant Goldy Locke and in his place is a trusty and loyal canine named Brain Trust. Gone is the sophisticated soldier of fortune and in his place is a stage magician of great skill. Gone is the urbane and witty detective who tousled with the police, and in his place is the handsome but much quieter shamus who works with the police whenever possible. Nevertheless, whether this is truly a Falcon movie or simply a detective *sui generis*, *Devil's Cargo* is a clever mystery punctuated by some unexpected plot twists.

The film opens with several well-done sequences without dialogue, as the viewer, from the perspective of the street only, sees an apparent murder committed in silhouette through windows of a large house, two individuals talking, and then one individual exiting the house. Newspaper headlines announce that Lucky Conroy has been murdered. Next there are scenes of a man who will later be identified as Ramon Delgado being followed as he deposits a package in a locker at a bowling alley and then goes to a bank. These sequences are very mysterious and effective, except for the loud and inappropriate music playing in the background during the entire scenario.

Delgado goes to the Falcon's apartment and tells him that he has killed Conroy because Conroy had been involved with his wife, Margo. Delgado intends to give himself up and plead justifiable homicide, but before doing so, he gives the Falcon a key to hold for him. If Delgado gets out of jail immediately, he wants the key returned; if he does not, he wants the key given to whomever he employs as his attorney. The Falcon is suspicious but for a fee of $500, he takes the job.

Once Delgado is in jail, attorney Thomas Mallon arrives unexpectedly and agrees to represent Delgado for free. The Falcon is suspicious once again but Mallon claims he is doing it for publicity and prestige. Also included in the mix of characters and suspects are Delgado's wife Margo, who does not think much of Delgado and who may have been having an affair with Lucky Conway, and Conway's business partner, Johnny Morello, a character who seems less than honest.

The plot of this film is never trite, with the unexpected always happening. Naga, the hood who was trailing Delgado, is blown to bits when he tries to open the locker at the bowling alley, and Delgado is poisoned in prison, even though he only had one visitor. Both of these events truly come as shocks to the viewer. The solution to the crimes, and perhaps more importantly why all the characters do all the strange things that they do throughout the film, is surprising and quite intriguing.

In addition to being an actor, John Calvert was a successful stage magician who continued performing well into his later years after he was done with movies and television. Calvert displays many of his conjuring skills throughout the film. He is quite good as a magician but those skills are wholly irrelevant to the mystery being shown. Calvert's magic act is an irritating interruption to the fascinating plot and is the weakest aspect of the movie. Other than that, Calvert, although not well-known in comparison to George Sanders and Tom Conway, is fine in the part of the Falcon, albeit quieter and less witty than those who had the role before him.

Devil's Cargo suffers by comparison to its predecessors produced at RKO because of its low budget, but it is more than equal to the prior films in terms of its clever plot. If this first of the last three Falcon films is evaluated on its own and not in comparison to the more famous Sanders/Conway films, the feature is quite entertaining. Indeed, *Devil's Cargo* can be viewed as an auspicious beginning to a new mystery movie series.

APPOINTMENT WITH MURDER (1948)

John Calvert returns in his second film as the Falcon, but once again it seems that a new character has been created. Now the Falcon has a full-time job as an investigator for the International Surety Company, and he is so well-known throughout the world that a character in Milan, Italy, calls him "one of the foremost American detectives." Gone is the Falcon's sidekick, his loyal dog Brain Trust. Gone are the magic tricks to entertain and confuse the other characters. Gone is the character who lives the high life with no visible means of support.

Once again, there is an intriguing mystery afoot here, involving two paintings that may be real or may be fake, purportedly painted by the famous (but in fact fictional) artist Gabriel Montegna. The two were stolen from a Count Dalo during World War II, and in 1945 the International Surety Company paid Dalo $80,000 on his insurance claim. The Falcon is in Milan trying to recover one of the paintings, which is being held by an Italian artist, Giuseppe Donati. Donati is willing to sell it for $5000 to Waring, because he claims the painting is a fake. Donati is then killed and Waring disturbs an intruder in his hotel room, who is apparently attempting to steal the Montegna Waring is holding.

Back in Los Angeles, the sister painting to the Montegna that the Falcon brings to America is sitting in the Brinckley Art Galley. The Gallery has two partners, L.W. Brinckley, the attractive female face of the Gallery, and Norton Benedict, her heavy-set silent partner. Benedict brought the first Montegna to America and may have been the person who killed Donati in Italy in an attempt to obtain the companion piece. The Falcon's mission is to recover both paintings, find the killer of Donati, and hopefully clear Brinckley of any involvement in the crimes, as Waring has taken a shine to her.

There is a lot to like about the film. There are many competing forces at work, such as Donati's partner intending to steal the canvas back from the Falcon once he pays for it, Dalo not having the money to pay the insurance company back for the paintings that were stolen from him and therefore trying to bribe the Falcon, and even an art expert in Italy trying to buy the paintings from Waring. Instead of intrusive set-comedy pieces, which were usually the low points of the RKO series, *Appointment with Murder* is all business, with filler material being crime-related, such as a smuggler on an airplane trying to implicate Waring in his crimes, Donati's partner coming to America to steal the painting and getting into a fight with Waring, and two thugs trying to beat the location of the paintings out of Waring. While these scenes do not move the plot forward, they still add to the mystery element of the film.

All that said, the movie seems flat and is often quite boring. While John Calvert is quite good as the Falcon, and surely he is one of the most handsome of the 1940s detectives, the rest of the cast is generally disappointing. The actors in Italy, and even Count Dalo in America, seem to be overacting their Italian ethnicity, making the storyline seem somewhat unconvincing. The key villain in America is Norton Benedict, played by Jack Reitzen. Reitzen is neither menacing nor sophisticated in the role and his lack of true villainy undercuts the effectiveness of the film. Simply put, Reitzen is no Sidney Greenstreet.

The direction is never more than adequate and the low budget of the movie limits the action to just a few threadbare sets. There is a distinct lack of excitement to the ending of the film, and even though there is a shooting, it essentially takes place out of the view of the camera. The police simply capture the villain as he tries to walk past them. This soft ending is symptomatic of much of the film, which, while it has an interesting mystery, has no pace or excitement. It is still worth a view, so long as expectations are lowered for this late 1940s B-mystery production.

SEARCH FOR DANGER (1949)

This is the third John Calvert film in the Falcon series, and for the third time there is a new concept for the character. Michael Waring is apparently back to being a private detective, but this time he is from the Philip Marlowe school, narrating his own adventures at least for a part of the film. Actually, though, the initial narration sounds suspiciously like the opening of the *Dragnet* television program, with scenes of the City of Los Angeles being shown during the commentary, even though *Dragnet* did not come to television for several years after this movie was released.

Unlike the first two Calvert films, *Search for Danger* does not have a very interesting mystery premise. The Falcon has been hired by night club owners Kirk and Gregory to locate their missing partner, Larry Andrews, who unbeknownst to Waring has absconded with $100,000 of night club funds. Waring locates Andrews at a cheap hotel, and at the same time Waring realizes he has been followed by a private detective, Morris Jason. Waring scares Jason off and then collects his $500 for locating Andrews.

Shortly thereafter, Kirk and Gregory accuse Waring of taking the $100,000 from Andrews, causing Waring to go back to the hotel to confront Andrews, a task made impossible by the fatal bullethole in Andrews' body. Later, Waring discovers the body of Morris

Jason and the missing $100,000. There are four potential suspects for the murderer: Andrews' two former business partners and his two former lovers, or perhaps an unknown person committed the crimes. Waring then brings all of the suspects into the police station and reveals the surprise killer, Agatha Christie-style.

The one interesting aspect of the film is the identity of the killer of both Andrews and Jason. It is a true surprise, and yet if the audience has been listening carefully, there is a significant clue to the killer's identity. Nevertheless, much of the explanation given by Waring is pure guesswork and the killer would never have been discovered if he had not told a lie to Waring, which he had no need to tell. Thus, while the killer's identity is clever, the mystery does not hold together all that well. Also, Waring seems to have an awful lot of luck in solving the crimes.

Search for Danger has significant other problems. There is not enough story material to fill the 60 minute running time, but instead of using comedy bits for filler, the film inserts irrelevant plot ideas to soak up the minutes. Thus, Waring receives a visit from Elaine Carson, Andrews' girlfriend, who immediately leaves his apartment when the police arrive. Waring later traces her through Andrews' address book, and she is one of the suspects at the police station. But why is she even in the story? When Waring opens the door of his apartment to her knock, she is looking down the hallway to her right, for no apparent reason. (Perhaps the director was giving her acting tips.) This incident is symptomatic of the sloppy production values for *Search for Danger*, which, unfortunately, does include some continuity errors.

The direction by Jack Bernhard is incompetent at best, with very few close-ups, many scenes shot in long wide shots, scenes lingering on for too long, and irrelevant filler footage, such as long walks down hallways that only slow down the film. The most exciting scene in the film, a fight between Waring and an assailant in an alleyway, is shown almost entirely from a very long distance away, eliminating any excitement there may have been in the fisticuffs. That is almost the only scene shot outdoors in the feature, with most of the story being told on the same overused sets. The low budget of this film really shows through.

John Calvert was a fresh face for the series when he first appeared in *Devil's Cargo*, but his acting does not wear well over three films. The contrast with Tom Conway's performance as the Falcon is particularly apparent in this film, with Conway the sure winner in any head-to-head competition. By 1949, it was time for the Falcon series to end, and thankfully, with this film, it did.

Aftermath

Tom Conway appeared in minor films and horror movies after his participation in the Falcon series ended. He also continued to appear in mystery productions. Conway played another famous screen detective, Bulldog Drummond, in two films at Twentieth Century–Fox, *The Challenge* and *12 Lead Soldiers*, both from 1948. On the radio, Conway played Sherlock Holmes once Basil Rathbone left the radio series. Conway also appeared fairly regularly on television in the 1950s, including playing the lead in the television detective series, *Mark Saber*, from 1951 to 1955. Conway passed away in 1967. John Calvert's film career essentially ended with the Falcon series. He made only a few other appearances in films.

Although allegedly based on the Michael Arlen story, the Falcon films were essentially studio-created, and there was little incentive for the character to continue in films after the end of the movie series in 1949. However, after a short-lived series in 1943, there was a long-running radio program starring the Falcon which premiered on Mutual in 1945 and continued through the end of the decade. The Falcon's real name in the radio series was Michael Waring, just as in the last three films in the movie series. Also, film noir actor Charles McGraw starred in *The Adventures of the Falcon*, which was on television in syndication for one season during the mid–1950s for a total of 39 episodes in syndication. Once again, the Falcon's real name was Mike Waring.

Mr. District Attorney
Champion of the People

While attorneys have often been the lead detectives in crime and mystery novels (the most famous example, of course, being Perry Mason), those attorneys have usually been on the side of the defense. After all, the most famous district attorney in crime literature is Hamilton Burger, and he is known primarily for losing case after case to Perry Mason. There have been prosecutor-detectives in crime literature, however, including Doug Selby, whose stories were oddly enough written by Perry Mason's creator, Erle Stanley Gardner. Selby appeared in nine novels starting with *The D.A. Calls it Murder* (1937). However, the most famous prosecuting attorney in fictional crime from all media is a man who has no name but starred for many years in his own radio show.

Background

THE RADIO SHOW

For an extended period of time, *Mr. District Attorney* was one of the most popular crime shows on the radio. It debuted in April, 1939, as a 15-minute daily serialized drama, but that summer it was converted into a weekly half-hour program. In the new format, the show hit its stride. The stories were about a crusading district attorney who fought racketeers, con men, black marketers, killers and even Nazis. Through most of its long run, the title character remained unnamed, responding to the title "Mr. District Attorney" or from his employees, "Chief" or "Boss." The character was created by Ed Byron, former law student and a student of crime. Byron based his fictional prosecutor on the real-life exploits of Thomas Dewey, New York City's district attorney in the late 1930s who fought highly publicized battles against racketeers and corruption.

Phillips H. Lord, who was famous for other radio crime dramas such as *Gang Busters*, created the title *Mr. District Attorney* and worked with Byron on the early development of the series. Byron bought the title from Lord and agreed to credit Lord on the radio show and pay him royalties.

In addition to the lead character, other regulars were Harrington, the district attorney's investigator, Miss Miller, his secretary, and Miss Rand, the receptionist. The part of the district attorney was performed by several actors over the course of its run, but Jay Josten, who performed the role for about 12 years, is most associated with the part. Vicki Vola played Edith Miller during the entire run. The show was famous for its vivid opening, spoken by the "Voice of the Law," which began, "Mister District Attorney! Champion of the people! Guardian of our fundamental rights to life, liberty and the pursuit of happiness!"

THE FILM SERIES

Given the popularity of the radio show, it was natural for a film studio to create a series of Mr. District Attorney movies. But it was unusual for that series to be developed at Republic Pictures, which was not known for its mystery movies, although it released two Ellery Queen films in the 1930s. What is even more surprising is that Republic jettisoned the entire concept of the radio series, substituting a new viewpoint and set of characters. Indeed, if not for the title of the first film and the credit given to the radio drama in all of the films, it is unlikely that anyone would have associated the movies with the popular radio series.

The lead character in *Mr. District Attorney* (1941) is P. Cadwallader Jones, who is hired by the district attorney as a staff lawyer and only because of Jones' well-connected uncle. Jones bumbles through the movie and solves the crime with the assistance of newspaper reporter Terry Parker. The real district attorney in the film has only a small role. Dennis O'Keefe plays Jones and Florence Rice plays Terry Parker. Neither was a well-known performer in Hollywood at the time of this film, although both had been in films since the 1930s and Rice had been receiving some good supporting roles in movies such as *At the Circus* (1939) with the Marx Brothers. In the mystery field, Rice is best known for playing Garda Sloane in *Fast Company* (1938), the first film in a three-movie mystery series released by MGM.

The Carter Case (1941) involved the same cast of characters, although James Ellison now plays Jones and Virginia Gilmore plays Terry Parker. Although Ellison had been in Hollywood films for some time, he was not well-known in 1941, and Gilmore was just starting her career at the time of this film. Even the actor who played the district attorney changed, from Stanley Ridges in the first film to Paul Harvey in the second. Here, Jones and Parker investigate a crime on the day of their wedding.

The last film in the series produced at Republic was *Secrets of the Underground* (1942). Once again the entire cast changed, with John Hubbard playing Jones, Virginia Grey playing Parker and Pierre Watkin playing the district attorney, although part-way through the film, Jones is elevated to the top position. The two principals were not well-known in films, although Grey did have important roles in a few mysteries, such as *Another Thin Man* (1939) and *Whistling in the Dark* (1941). *Secrets of the Underground* involves the forging of governmental war tax stamps and the killing of the man who was forced against his will to assist the foreign agents.

In 1947, Columbia Pictures released a film entitled *Mr. District Attorney*, which was apparently intended to be the first film in a new series. It starred Adolphe Menjou in the title role, with Dennis O'Keefe playing his assistant. Menjou was the best-known performer ever to appear in this series of films, having been a star in Hollywood since the silent era. For mystery fans, Menjou played Police Commissioner Thatcher Colt in two mysteries released by Columbia in the early 1930s. The screenplay of *Mr. District Attorney* involved racketeers and a particularly murderous female villain. The film is unrelated to the three Republic programmers, being based more on the radio series than the Republic films were.

The Films

Mr. District Attorney (1941)

What a marvelous actor Peter Lorre was, particularly when he was thin, during the middle of his career, and playing a character of understated malevolence, such as in this film and in *Stranger on the Third Floor* (1940). Lorre's scenes in *Mr. District Attorney* truly provide a needed spark to an otherwise tepid story. Lorre first appears, playing the mysterious Mr. Hyde, when he confronts Mr. Winkle in the latter's apartment. Hyde arrives dressed in a black overcoat and dark hat. As he speaks, his face often turns in an instant from an insincere smile to a sudden visage of worry and hate. Hyde is fishing for information from Winkel, stringing him along until he needs him no more. As the scene fades to black, there is no mistaking Hyde's intent with regard to Winkle, just from Hyde's facial expressions and his dialogue.

The second time Lorre appears in the film, he has decided to dispose of Winkle's girlfriend, Betty Paradise, who also has some important information about Hyde that she may disclose to the district attorney. When Hyde arrives at Paradise's apartment, assistant district attorney P. Cadwallader Jones and newspaper reporter Terry Parker are with her. Therefore, it is time for the old movie cliché of Hyde killing Paradise just as she is about to blurt out the secret information. Here, though, the scene is handled in fabulous film noir style, with Hyde shown alternately in light and shadow from the blinking neon light outside, with the sudden shooting coming out of the dark; when the light blinks on, a cloud of smoke is coming from Hyde's right hand. It is a truly marvelous moment in the film.

Lorre is a rare actor whose mere presence adds to a scene, even before he begins to talk in that strange voice of his. When Peter Lorre is not onscreen, and unfortunately his part is quite small, the directorial style becomes mundane, the tone of the film becomes light, the music becomes playful and *Mr. District Attorney* becomes a minor mystery movie, at best, with very little to recommend it. Indeed, as often happens in 1940s mystery movies, the comedy overwhelms the mystery throughout most of the film.

Once the actual mystery plot of *Mr. District Attorney* gets going, which is many minutes into the movie, assistant district attorney Jones is given the task of reviewing the file on a Mr. Hyde, a public servant who disappeared with a substantial amount of public money. The bills Hyde purloined, however, were marked for identification and a few have recently turned up at a race track. That ties into the story of a meek bank clerk, Mr. Winkle, who has been lending large sums of money to his beautiful but inconsiderate girlfriend, Betty Paradise. It turns out that Winkle has been appropriating the funds from Hyde's safe deposit box at Winkle's bank, and Betty has been using the bills to make bets at the track. These events draw other characters into the story, such as the missing Mr. Hyde, his angry and murderous wife Mrs. Hyde, and a corrupt attorney, Barrett, who is trying to take the prosecutor's job away from the district attorney. Despite his apparent and overplayed incompetence, Jones, with the major assistance of Terry Parker, some how manages to solve the crimes and finally impress the district attorney.

The plot is actually quite good, but there is simply not enough of it. Most of the film involves the comic stylings of Jones and Parker, as they alternately knock into each other, mistakenly exchange hats, and let tear gas loose in their car during a high speed chase after the villains. Some of it is funny; some of it is charming. There is, however, just too much of it. *Mr. District Attorney* is a strange title for a screwball comedy.

Mr. District Attorney, Craig Warren (Adolphe Menjou, standing), berates his chief investigator, Harrington (Michael O'Shea) in *Mr. District Attorney* (1947).

The former assistant district attorney, Steve Bennett (Dennis O'Keefe, right) shoots James Randolph (George Coulouris), perhaps in self-defense, in *Mr. District Attorney* (1947).

Dennis O'Keefe and Florence Rice are quite good in the leads of Jones and Parker, respectively. They are truly an engaging couple. The other performances, even down to the smallest roles, are uniformly excellent. If not for all the silliness, this could have been an excellent movie. As it is, it is a disappointing mystery and not a fortuitous start to a new film series. Nevertheless, for fans of Peter Lorre and for those who can appreciate a film just for one striking performance, and also for the hint of film noir in the scenes in which Lorre appears, *Mr. District Attorney* is well worth a look.

THE CARTER CASE (1941)

[This is one of the two movies discussed in this book the author did not personally view.]

This mystery commences on the day of the wedding of Assistant District Attorney P. Cadwallader Jones and newspaper reporter Terry Parker when, not surprisingly, murder intrudes. In this case, it is three murders, starting with the stabbing of Elliot Carter, the publisher of a society gossip magazine. Terry believes in the innocence of the person arrested for the crime and off she goes to cover the trial and then to prove the suspect's innocence. In the meantime, the wedding plans have to be postponed. Film historian William K. Everson, in *The Detective in Film*, states that *The Carter Case* is less ambitious but superior in mystery content to the prior film, *Mr. District Attorney*, with the climax being a Mack Sennett-style slapstick chase.

This film has an entirely new set of actors, with James Ellison now playing Jones, Virginia Gilmore playing Terry, and Paul Harvey playing the district attorney. *The Carter Case* has a common background for a Hollywood mystery movie — the wedding or upcoming wedding of the detective. This can also be seen in *Dressed to Kill* (1941), from the Michael Shayne series, *Behind the Mask* (1946), from the Shadow series, and *The Case of the Velvet Claws* (1936), from the Perry Mason series.

Secrets of the Underground (1942)

This is one of those mystery movies that falls within a small group of films that might be dubbed the "screwball comedy mystery." Other examples include *Having Wonderful Crime* (1945) in the John J. Malone series, *Behind the Mask* (1946) in the Shadow series, and at least in part, *The Lone Wolf Spy Hunt* (1939). Most of *Secrets of the Underground* involves the antics of assistant district attorney Cadwallader Jones and his fiancée, Terry Parker, and their misunderstandings about who is being faithful to whom and whether they are truly in love. Along the way, there are also some serious crimes being investigated, but they are often well-hidden among the comedy elements.

As the film opens, French artist Paul Panois is being held captive by a group of Nazi sympathizers and being forced to prepare plates for counterfeiting United States war tax stamps. The villains have apparently told Panois that they are holding his daughter, Marianne, in France, and that if he does not cooperate, his daughter's life is at risk. Panois accidentally learns that his daughter is not being held by the Nazis, so he makes his escape. He also writes to the District Attorney's office, telling them that he has valuable information which he will provide to them, so long as they ensure his daughter's safety when she arrives in America by boat.

The district attorney sends Jones to the boat to greet and protect Marianne Dubois. Upon her arrival, there is a letter for her from her father which contains a baggage claim check. One of the gang grabs the ticket, but only gets away with half of the receipt. When Jones proceeds to the baggage claim desk with his partial claim check, he is advised that since no one claimed the trunk for over 30 days, the trunk is being offered for auction at a benefit for the Women's Defense Corp. At the auction, the body of Paul Panois is found in the trunk, and thereafter the district attorney must try to find the reason behind Panois' death and the subsequent murder of the baggage claim clerk.

The performances in *Secrets of the Underground*, particularly those of John Hubbard and Virginia Grey in the leads, are excellent. The two are very engaging and, indeed, the comedy moments involving them are often quite amusing. Much like the first film in the series, if *Secrets of the Underground* were only a comedy and not a mystery, it would play much better, not disappointing those who are looking to view a challenging mystery movie and who instead are presented with a screwball comedy.

The mystery encompasses very little of the running time of the film, and to make matters worse, it is very sloppily plotted. For example, when Paul Panois escapes from his captors, why did he not go to the District Attorney's office in person instead of creating his complex scheme about a checked bag, which results in Panois being captured again? Jones is later able to discover the location where Terry and Marianne are being held captive, when a secretary happens to mention to Jones, in passing, that someone has used a war tax stamp to mail him a letter. What a lucky break that is!

Coincidences abound. Terry arrives at Vaughn's dress shop just after Vaughn has captured Marianne, arousing Terry's suspicions. When she is standing outside the display window where Marianne's body has been temporarily placed as part of a war display, a roving photographer takes Jones' and Terry's picture, allowing Terry to discover the next day that it was Marianne's body in the window. With coincidences like these to aid in the investigation, who needs a quality detective?

There are two solid moments in the film. The first occurs when Panois' checked bag is opened at the auction and his body falls out. While perhaps not that unexpected, it is still the highlight of the movie. The other occurs when Terry and Marianne are trapped in a locked room in the basement of a farm silo, with grain falling on them from above, almost smothering them to death. It is a unique method of killing, even though it is ultimately not successful.

Unfortunately, much of the rest of the movie is silly. The scenes of the women from the Defense Corps trailing the villain's car are unconvincing, and when the women later become involved in the physical battle with the spies at the farm, well, that strains all credulity. The scenes may have worked better in the patriotic war year in which *Secrets of the Underground* was released, but by today's standards, the scenes look quite silly.

For comedy fans, *Secrets of the Underground* works very well. For those looking for a good mystery, there are better choices.

Mr. District Attorney (1947)

Marguerite Chapman may be the most beautiful actress to appear in a 1940s mystery movie series. With her long dark hair, piercing eyes and attractive figure displayed to great effect by the various provocative outfits that she wears in *Mr. District Attorney*, it is easy to understand why two of the principals in the feature fall desperately in love with her character. And that character, Marcia Manning, may be the most villainous of the femme fatales of the 1940s, brutally killing four men and just barely missing in her attempt to add a fifth murder to her resume.

The main story begins when District Attorney Craig Warren overhears attorney Steve Bennett resigning from his law firm because he refuses to present dishonest evidence in court on behalf of a man named Longfield. Warren decides to hire Bennett for his office and immediately sets him on track to prosecute his former client, Longfield, for criminal negligence. In the process of his investigation, Steve meets Marcia Manning, the secretary to crime boss James Randolph, who works at the same office where Longfield used to be employed. Steve immediately falls in love with Marcia, and perhaps she falls in love with him. What Steve does not know is that Marcia is as hard-hearted as Randolph when it comes to crime and personal relationships, and that she intends to marry Randoph not for love, but for money.

Mr. District Attorney is suspicious of Marcia and goes to her to convince her to give up Steve. That results in Marcia marrying Randolph and Steve being outraged at the district attorney's interference in his private affairs. Steve quits his job at the prosecutor's office and goes to work for Randolph. Steve later conceals evidence of Marcia's involvement in the killing of a lawyer, whom she pushed off a high ledge of an apartment building, and sullies his reputation by defending obvious criminals in court. By the end of the movie, Steve finally sees the light. All of the criminals are either caught or killed, and Steve is re-hired by the district attorney. Apparently Mr. District Attorney finds it easy to forgive Steve for his unethical and illegal activity throughout the film.

This 1947 version of *Mr. District Attorney* is much more closely related to the radio show than the films in the prior Republic series. Adolphe Menjou plays the district attorney (here, unlike in the radio show, given an actual name) and he does seem much like the aggressive and hard-hitting public servant of the radio programs. Menjou has the gravitas to carry the part and he is excellent in the role. Another character from the radio broadcasts, the district attorney's investigator Harrington, is engagingly played by Michael O'Shea. Even Miss Miller, the secretary from the original broadcasts, makes an appearance, although it is a very minor role.

Dennis O'Keefe, who was the star in the Republic film with the same title, coincidentally appears in this film also, once again playing an assistant district attorney. The role is not played for laughs, though, as it was in the prior incarnation. Unfortunately, the part is not particularly well-written, either. Ethics problems abound for Steve Bennett, as he attempts to prosecute a man he just defended, conceals crime scene evidence to protect his love, and goes to work for a man he knows to be a crook. The role is written in an unconvincing manner, making it difficult for O'Keefe to perform the part in a convincing manner.

As beautiful as Marguerite Chapman may be in the movie, Chapman's character of Marcia Manning is not that alluring. Indeed, she seems to have little sensuality, coming off more hard-hearted than sexy, seriously compromising the effectiveness of the part. There is more heat generated in the first meeting between Walter Neff and Phyllis Dietrichson in *Double Indemnity* (1944) than there is in all of *Mr. District Attorney*. There are no sparks between Marcia and Steve, and their relationship is far from scintillating. As a result, the two characters have to keep repeating to each other that they are in love, or otherwise no one would ever quite believe it. Perhaps for that reason, *Mr. District Attorney* seems less like a crime drama and more like a soap opera, with Steve in love with Marcia who marries Randolph for his wealth while the district attorney disapproves, interfering in the romance.

The film is longer than most mystery movies of this type, running about 80 minutes, when most crime stories of its ilk usually ran a little over 60 minutes. The extended running time causes the film to drag from time to time. Fortunately, there is no comic relief padding in the story, as the film is played straight, quite apropos for a movie with multiple murders.

Mr. District Attorney does have its interest, particularly in the lovely Marguerite Chapman, some excellent performances, and its unusual plot for this type of series feature. It is undercut by the lack of style in the direction and the soap-operatic feel to its story. Nevertheless, it is an interesting attempt at something different in a crime film series.

Afterwards

The radio show continued on the air on NBC in 30 minute episodes into 1951. Thereafter, it appeared on ABC and in syndication, ending its run in 1953. In all, the show was broadcast over the radio for 14 years.

Mr. District Attorney first made it to television in 1951, in a show broadcast on ABC for one season. Jay Jostyn played District Attorney Paul Garret, Len Doyle played his investigator Harrington, and Vicki Vola played his secretary, Miss Miller. Josten and Miller had played those roles on the radio show. The television program was done live and alternated weekly with *The Amazing Mr. Malone*, based on Craig Rice's attorney-detective who was the subject of a three-movie mystery series of the 1940s.

In 1954, there was a syndicated television version, with David Brian playing the district attorney and Jackie Loughery playing Miss Miller. The show lasted for one season.

Dennis O'Keefe, who played the lead in two of the four Mr. District Attorney movies, once in 1941 and once in 1947, worked steadily in films during the 1940s. His best-known crime films are probably *T-Men* (1947), where he plays a Treasury agent trying to break up a counterfeiting ring, and *Raw Deal* (1948), a film noir in which O'Keefe plays a prisoner who breaks out of jail. Most of his work in the 1950s was in television, culminating in *The Dennis O'Keefe Show*, which was a half-hour comedy that ran for one season on CBS starting in 1959. O'Keefe passed away in 1968.

11

Wally Benton
The "Whistling" Comedy Mysteries

One of the recurring themes of this book is the overuse of long comedy scenes in the mystery movies of the 1940s, detrimentally affecting the quality of those films. The Falcon, Boston Blackie and Ellery Queen mystery series contain prime examples of films that were substantially disadvantaged by their reliance on comedy as filler material, and not very funny comedy at that. Sometimes, those films seemed more like comedies with mystery interruptions instead of the other way around. Movies series that employed shorter, much cleverer and more subtle comedy, such as the Sherlock Holmes and Dick Tracy series, were far more successful and often substantially funnier.

The "Whistling" movies that MGM produced in the 1940s, with lead character Wally Benton, were also comedies with mystery interruptions, but in this case that was the intent from the beginning. Starring Red Skelton, the three Whistling movies successfully combined mystery with comedy, making the first two films quite entertaining, thus demonstrating that in just the right hands this type of entertainment could be very enjoyable.

Background

THE PLAY

The first movie in the series, *Whistling in the Dark*, was based on the stage play of the same name written by Laurence Gross and Edward Childs Carpenter. It opened on Broadway on January 19, 1932, at the Ethel Barrymore Theater. Later that year it moved to the Waldorf Theater. It ran for a total of 265 performances. The opening night cast included soon-to-be well-known cinema performers Edward Arnold and Claire Trevor.

In 1933, MGM released the first movie version of the play, also titled *Whistling in the Dark*. Ernest Truex as hero Wallace Porter and Edward Arnold as villain Jacob Dillon reprised their stage roles from the Broadway play. The plot of the 1933 movie had many similarities to the later Red Skelton version, although the hero in the earlier film was named Wallace Porter (just as in the play) and Porter was a mystery writer, not a radio star as he was in the later film. The first movie version was based more closely on the play than the 1941 movie remake would be.

THE FILM SERIES

Red Skelton was chosen to play the lead in MGM's 1941 remake of *Whistling in the Dark*. Skelton, who already had success in vaudeville, radio and personal appearances, would later become a success in movies and television, making him one of the most popular comedians of all time.

Richard Bernard Skelton was born in 1913 in Vincennes, Indiana. While just a youngster, he left home to perform with a traveling medicine show and then went on to perform in burlesque, vaudeville and circuses, among other venues. He came to Broadway and the radio in 1937 and first appeared in films the following year, with a role in *Having Wonderful Time* (1938). Thereafter, he appeared in shorts or small roles in feature films until he received his starring role in *Whistling in the Dark* (1941). The film was so successful that two sequels were produced.

In the trio of films, Skelton plays Wally Benton, the star of a popular weekly radio program in which he plays the Fox, a detective. The Fox is such a successful radio personality that, at least in the first two films, people seem to believe that Benton actually is an expert criminologist. In *Whistling in the Dark*, a gangster hires Benton to concoct a foolproof plan to dispose of a competing heir to a large fortune. In *Whistling in Dixie*, Benton's fiancée convinces Benton to travel to Georgia to help a sorority sister who has become involved in a murder. In the third and final feature, *Whistling in Brooklyn*, Benton captures a gang of killers while becoming involved in a baseball game with the Brooklyn Dodgers.

There are two other regulars in the series. One is Benton's girlfriend, Carol Lambert, who is played by Ann Rutherford in all three films. The Canadian actress was born in 1920 and first began appearing in films in 1935. She came to the public's attention playing the role of Polly Benedict in a number of Andy Hardy films, leading to the role of Scarlett O'Hara's younger sister in *Gone with the Wind* (1939), before appearing in the Whistling movies.

In *Whistling in the Dark*, Rags Ragland plays a semi-dumb criminal, Sylvester, and the role was so memorable, Ragland reprised the role in the next film along with the role of his twin brother, Chester, which part carried over into the third film. Ragland was born in 1905 in Louisville, Kentucky and performed in burlesque and on Broadway before entering the film business in 1941. For the next five years, he appeared in a number of comedies at MGM, in addition to the three Whistling movies.

The Films

WHISTLING IN THE DARK (1941)

In each episode of his popular radio program, Wally Benton, known as the Fox, creates the almost perfect crime, but then leaves one loophole in the story so that the villain can be caught by the end of the show. Because of Benton's intimate knowledge of crime and the criminal mind, it is natural for Johnny Jones, the leader of a fake spiritual cult known as Silver Haven, to kidnap Benton and force him to create the perfect real life murder of a man named Upshaw, who is the only person standing in the way of the cult receiving a million-dollar bequest.

Actually, Jones' idea of forcing Benton to create a perfect murder makes little sense, but this film is more comedy than mystery so the plot matters little. The villains kidnap Benton and in order to force him to do their bidding also kidnap Wally's fiancée, Carol Lambert and his sponsor's daughter, Fran Post, whom Benton had previously dated. Benton has no choice but to play along and devise a perfect scheme for the murder of Upshaw.

Benton proposes that a special poison be placed in Upshaw's tooth powder, and after he gargles all traces of the poison will disappear and the death will appear to be from heart failure. Jones likes the idea and decides to implement the plan. How Wally avoids killing Upshaw, escapes from confinement and catches the villains is at the core of the remainder of this film.

The success or lack of success of this movie was always going to turn on the performance of its star, Red Skelton, and luckily for the filmmakers, Skelton is a true wonder, especially for those people who only remember the older Red Skelton from his long-running television show. In the film, Skelton is young and energetic, as comfortable with taking a pratfall as he is with delivering Benton's clever lines and retorts. In some ways Skelton's face was his fortune. He seems to have an infinite number of expressions, ready at an instant with a new look when needed to react to events or statements from other characters.

The supporting cast is particularly fresh for a 1940s mystery series. Conrad Veidt (Major Strasser from *Casablanca* [1942]) plays Johnny Jones and he is quite good, as expected, as the villain, but he also adds some funny touches to the light moments in the movie. Ann Rutherford plays Carol Lambert as perky and witty, especially in her real and phony verbal jousts with Benton. Virginia Grey is lovely as Fran Post and she also gets off a number of excellent one-liners at the expense of Benton.

In *Whistling in the Dark* (1941), radio detective Wally Benton, also known as the Fox (Red Skelton), is pictured along with his girlfriend Carol Lambert (Ann Rutherford) and the owl that gave them a fright when they explored the dark mansion of the cult known as Silver Haven.

There are no laugh-out-loud moments in the feature, but there are surely many big-smile moments. The surprising element of this film, though, is how suspenseful the final third of the movie is. Although still in captivity, Benton rigs a radio set and converts it into a telephone to use in trying to contact the airplane where Upshaw is about to be poisoned. The villain on the plane, however, cuts the pilot's radio wires, eliminating that form of communication, and no one on the plane will allow the little boy who has a radio to turn it on to Benton's show, which is the only alternate means of communication. In the meantime, Johnny Jones is heading back to Silver Haven to finish off Benton, the New York police are on the way but are far away, and the local police refuse to respond to Benton's pleas over the radio because they were burned once before by the "War of the Worlds" radio broadcast by Orson Welles.

Some of the creators of the traditional mystery movies of the 1940s could have learned much from this movie about the creation of suspense at the end of a crime film. They definitely could have learned a lot about adding real humor to a mystery. This film is probably not for the fan of the conventional Hollywood mystery, but for those who want a change of pace, and a change in the right direction, this is the film to watch.

Note on the Source Material: As noted above, this film was based on the Gross and Carpenter play entitled *Whistling in the Dark,* which opened on Broadway in 1932. The play is more serious than the Skelton film, as mystery writer Wally Porter and his girlfriend Toby are trapped by some gangsters in an old house after Porter brags that, due to his infinite knowledge of crime, he can create the perfect murder. Villain Jacob Dillon decides to force Porter to create a real life scenario for the murder of McFarren, the head of the New York Crime Commission. Porter has no choice but to comply with Dillon's demand and he concocts a scheme about inserting a fast-working poison into McFarren's toothpaste, which will cause him to die on a train when he brushes his teeth in the morning.

The main change in the metamorphosis from play to Red Skelton film is the updating of the story to make the hero a radio writer and performer rather than a mystery writer. That allows the film to incorporate one-liners about the radio business and also capitalize on Red Skelton's broad comedy skills. Because the setting of the film is not confined to one set as the play was, the filmmakers are able to create significant suspense at the end of the film, cutting between the trapped Wally Benton at Silver Haven and the about-to-be-murdered Upshaw on the airplane. That opportunity was not available to the playwrights.

While only a few of the lines from the play make it into the movie, a significant number of moments from the play are incorporated into the film, such as the same murder scheme, the use of the poison on one of the gangsters who tries to double-cross the leader, the substitution by Wally of harmless sugar for the poison in an attempt to save McFarren's life, which attempt fails when the killer forgets to bring the original packet with him, and the rigging of a radio into a telephone to effectuate the release of Wally and his girlfriend.

The effectiveness of a theater work such as *Whistling in the Dark* is hard to determine just from reading the play, but the play does seem entertaining, if not as amusing as the 1940s film. Presumably the play is never performed any more, as it is somewhat dated. Indeed, it would be just about totally forgotten today if it were not for the two film versions and particularly the 1941 feature starring Red Skelton.

WHISTLING IN DIXIE (1942)

Whistling in the Dark was such a success for Red Skelton that not only was a sequel prepared, but in that sequel Skelton's name appeared above the title for the first time in his career. Having developed a successful approach to mystery and comedy in the first movie, the filmmakers decided to use the same formula for *Whistling in Dixie*. Although the sequel is not quite the success of the original entry, it is still entertaining enough in its own right.

As in the original film, *Dixie* has some opening scenes that emphasize both the mystery and the spooky settings that will be central in the development of the story. The film opens with a lone man, Martin Gordon, entering what appears to be a cemetery but turns out to be the grounds of a deserted Confederate fort in Georgia. He is being followed by a strange young woman, who will turn out to be Hattie Lee, who is in love with Gordon. Suddenly there is a shot and Gordon falls over, apparently dead. When Hattie returns with the sheriff, the body is missing.

Ellamae Downs, Hattie's cousin who is also in love with Martin Gordon, sends a message to her former sorority sister, Carol Lambert, that she needs help. Carol convinces her fiancé, the famous radio detective Wally Benton (The Fox), to go to Georgia for their wedding. In addition to getting married, Carol expects Wally to solve the crime of the apparently murdered Martin Gordon.

In the end, there is not much mystery to the story. Wally deduces that there is a valuable treasure buried in the ground inside the fort but is then surprised to learn that the

In ***Whistling in Dixie*** (1942), Wally Benton (Red Skelton) and Carol Lambert (Ann Rutherford, left) have just revived Ellamae Downs (Diana Lewis) after she fainted, when a strange voice startles them.

sheriff and the district attorney are involved in the crime, having kidnapped Martin Gordon to force him to disclose the location of the buried treasure. Gordon is still alive, so there is not even a real murder for the Fox to investigate.

An old nemesis of the Fox returns in this movie. Judge Lee, Hattie's father, has a chauffeur named Chester Conway, whose identical twin brother Sylvester Conway was one of the villains in *Whistling in the Dark*. This gives Rags Ragland the opportunity to recreate his original role from *Whistling in the Dark* and also to play two parts when Sylvester surprisingly re-appears.

The core scene in the film involves Benton and his entourage locked in a sealed room in the basement of the fort, left there to die by the district attorney. At that point, the film comes to life. It is a very suspenseful scene, as the captives try to figure out a way to escape while the room is being flooded with water. Skelton is quite amusing during this scene, as is Rags Ragland. After they escape from that trap, Benton is off to a barn to rescue Martin Gordon, fighting not only the district attorney but also one of the Conway brothers. Unfortunately, Benton can never quite figure out which one of the brothers he is fighting. This is another clever scene, mixing crime with humor, something these films did better than many other films of the 1940s mystery series.

In the earlier scenes, though, much of Skelton's humor falls flat, with substantial mugging by the comedian. Matters improve substantially in the last half of the film, as noted above. Just as in *Whistling in the Dark*, there is not much laugh-out-loud humor in the film but there are surely some amusing lines. In addition, the slapstick humor in the last scene in the barn is quite funny, if one appreciates that kind of thing.

The acting is generally quite good, although those thick Southern accents can become trying at times. Skelton and Ann Rutherford, both reprising their roles from the prior film, are quite engaging in their scenes together. While *Dixie* is not as good as *Whistling in the Dark*, it is surely the equal of, if not better than, most of the supposedly serious mysteries of the 1940s that relied very heavily on comedy filler material.

WHISTLING IN BROOKLYN (1943)

Whistling in Brooklyn is the third in the series of Wally Benton comedy-mysteries produced at MGM during the early 1940s. This time, however, while the comedy is there, the mystery is not, making this the weakest film in the series.

It seems there is a serial killer on the loose in New York who calls himself the "Constant Reader." After murdering a victim, seemingly at random, the Constant Reader hides the body and then writes a letter to the newspaper describing the location of the body, with the intent of humiliating the police. Because the most recent murder letter is surprisingly similar to the one that the Fox has just read on his mystery radio show, Inspector Holcomb jumps to the conclusion that Wally Benton is the Constant Reader. While it may not have been unreasonable for Inspector Farraday to suspect Boston Blackie of every theft in New York or Inspector Crane to suspect the Lone Wolf of every burglary in New York, can anyone really believe that Wally Benton is a serial killer?

Thereafter, the police are after Benton while Benton is after the real criminals. Benton is assisted by his bride-to-be Carol Lambert, his less-than-bright assistant Chester, and an aspiring cub reporter named Jean Pringle. Somehow, this quartet of bumblers eludes the police, solves the crimes, captures the real criminals, and clears Wally's name.

The first two films in the series, and particularly *Whistling in the Dark*, had a solid mystery story as the framework for the comedy antics of Red Skelton. The main problem with *Whistling in Brooklyn* is the lack of any true mystery story. Other than the first scene in the movie, where the police discover the body of a victim, the crimes seem far distant from the comic aspects of the story. The identity of the leader of the villains is apparent from the moment he enters the film as an apparently honest citizen, and if that were not enough, his identity is revealed to all about halfway through. Rather than trying to create a mystery with stunning surprises and unexpected plot twists, the writers simply chose to write a chase film, in the style of a comedy rather than a thriller.

Whistling in Brooklyn, therefore, has to be evaluated more on its comedy than its thrills, and even in that regard, the film is lacking. Of course comedy is a matter of taste, but in this film Red Skelton seems to be mugging more than usual, and most of the dialogue, while sometimes funny, is often artificial. As an example, there is a scene where Chester and Wally are trying to figure out a way to escape from the Creeper. This dialogue ensues:

CHESTER: "But I can tell him [The Creeper], I'll say, I ain't mad at you for hitting me, Creeper. I'll tell him, 'I'll give him the shirt right of your [Wally's] back.'"
WALLY: "Well, now that's mighty white of you."
CHESTER: "That's more than I can say for the shirt."

Wally Benton (Red Skelton, left) boards a freight elevator in order to escape the Constant Reader's gang in **Whistling in Brooklyn** (1943). Shown with Benton are, at the top, Jean Pringle (Jean Rogers), below her, Carol Lambert (Ann Rutherford), and on the right, Chester (Rags Raglund), who is employing an unusual technique to prevent Benton from sneezing.

While that dialogue is superficially funny, it sounds more like a comedy routine, with straight line and punch lines, rather than real movie dialogue. This is not an Abbott and Costello movie. *Whistling in Brooklyn* is supposed to be occurring in some type of reality. This artificial nature of the humor pervades much of the comedy elements throughout the movie, undercutting its effectiveness.

Despite all the problems, there are moments to appreciate in the film. Early in the movie, there is a very suspenseful scene in an elevator shaft, with the four members of the Whistling crew hanging for dear life from a cross bar. The fact that their escape defies all of the applicable laws of physics is of no moment. The best scene in the film, though, is near the end, when Skelton pitches one inning of baseball at Ebbets Field against the real Brooklyn Dodgers as he is trying to save Inspector Holcomb from becoming the next murder victim. A number of the real Brooklyn Dodgers, including manager Leo Durocher, appear in the scene. Also of interest are some historic shots of 1940s Brooklyn, as some of the film was shot on location in that borough.

There is also interest generated from some of the performers. Jean Rogers, of the Flash Gordon serials, appears as Jean Pringle, and it is interesting to see her perform in a feature film, although she is almost unrecognizable with her darker, curly hair. Sam Levene, who played a policeman in two Thin Man movies and most famously in the film noir classic *The Killers* (1946), plays the Creeper, which is a change of pace for him, although the part is played more for laughs than villainy. Film noir icon Mike Mazurki appears late in the film as one of the henchmen, but without the directorial style of a *Murder, My Sweet* (1944) or *Dick Tracy* (1945), Mazurki, for once, does not seem very menacing.

Despite a few positives, *Whistling in Brooklyn* is pretty dismal fare. The screenwriters had simply run out of ideas for the Wally Benton character by this third film in the Whistling series. It was time to retire the character and after this film was completed, MGM wisely chose to do so.

Afterwards

Wally "The Fox" Benton was essentially a Hollywood creation, and after the end of the three-movie series there were no more film or television productions featuring the character. Despite the fact that The Fox was supposedly a famous radio personality, he never received a radio show of his own.

Red Skelton's career flourished once his role as Wally Benton ended. He continued to appear in films at MGM throughout the 1940s and into the 1950s. His own radio show was on the air from 1941 to 1953. However, Skelton's greatest success came in television, where his show was on the air in various formats for over 20 years. He was famous for the characters he portrayed in sketches on the shows, such as Freddy the Freeloader, Clem Kaddi-dlehopper and Cauliflower McPugg. Skelton passed away in 1997.

Ann Rutherford continued working in films after the Whistling movies ended, appearing in several more films in the 1940s before receiving guest-star work in television in the 1950s. She also had a semi-recurring role as the mother of Suzanne Pleshette on *The Bob Newhart Show* in the 1970s.

Rags Raglund appeared in 18 MGM movies in the 1940s, including several other films with Red Skelton. Three years after *Whistling in Brooklyn* was released, Ragland died at the age of 46.

12

Crime Doctor
The Psychiatrist Detective

By the 1940s, it was hardly unusual for the detective in a mystery novel to be a doctor. There was Josephine Bell's David Wintringham, a junior assistant physician who worked at a hospital in London and solved crimes starting with *Murder in Hospital* (1937). There was also H.C. Bailey's Dr. Reginald Fortune, a practicing physician and surgeon who assisted Scotland Yard in solving crimes, beginning in 1920 in a collection of short stories titled *Call Mr. Fortune*. There was also R. Austin Freeman's Dr. Thorndyke, a lawyer and forensic scientist rather than a medical doctor, who was an expert in many subjects including anatomy and ophthalmology. Austin wrote the first Thorndyke novel (*The Red Thumb Mark*) in 1907 and continued writing Thorndyke mysteries into the early 1940s.

Psychiatrist/detectives were also not unknown in detective literature. One example is Helen McCoy's Dr. Basil Willing, who usually assisted Manhattan's district attorney with crimes involving medical matters, beginning with *Dance of Death* (1938) and continuing into the 1960s. However, the best known medical detective of them all, at least during the 1940s due to his success on the radio and in the movies, was Dr. Ordway, the Crime Doctor.

Background

THE RADIO SERIES

The Crime Doctor debuted on the CBS Radio Network on August 4, 1940, and continued on the air until October 19, 1947. It was created by Max Marcin, a German-American writer who was a successful playwright before creating the popular radio series. Marcin eventually received credit as part of the title of the radio program when the show was renamed *Max Marcin's Crime Doctor* in 1945. Marcin also received a significant billing in the credits of each of the movies in the Columbia film series.

The original concept of the show was that Benjamin Ordway, a criminal, had lost his memory from a blow to the head. With the help of a sympathetic doctor Ordway built a new life, studying medicine and eventually becoming a psychiatrist. Early in the series Ordway was appointed to the state parole board, listening to the pleas of inmates who came before him to tell their stories and to pray for an early release. The fate of the prisoner was then decided by a jury composed of members of the studio audience.

By the mid–1940s, the show changed into a more traditional detective story. In each show, the police called Ordway for help in solving a difficult crime. The first part of the show consisted of the story of the crime. In the second half, Ordway identified a mistake that the criminal had made, leading to his arrest. A number of well-known actors played Ordway on the radio over the years, including Ray Collins, John McIntire, Hugh Marlowe, Brian Donlevy and Everett Sloane.

THE FILM SERIES

Columbia produced ten Crime Doctor movies during the 1940s, each starring Warner Baxter as Dr. Robert Ordway, a name change from the original Benjamin Ordway of the radio show. In the first installment, *Crime Doctor* (1943), Ordway's past as a criminal, his amnesia, his study of medicine, his psychiatric practice, and his work on the parole board were all recounted, in a story-line similar to that of the early radio shows. Ray Collins played Dr. John Carey, the psychiatrist who helped Ordway turn his life around, and Margaret Lindsay played Grace Fielding, Ordway's love interest. By the end of the film, Ordway had regained his memory and received a suspended sentence for the crimes he had committed in his past life.

In the second film in the series, *The Crime Doctor's Strangest Case*, and then in all of the later movies, the trappings of the first film were eliminated. Ordway's partner, Dr. Carey, and his love interest, Grace Fielding, were gone with no explanation. Ordway had resigned from the parole board, again without explanation, eliminating a good source of potential plots for the film series. Constance Worth was back as Betty, Ordway's receptionist-nurse, for *The Crime Doctor's Strangest Case,* but that was her last appearance in the series. As to Ordway's nickname, "The Crime Doctor," a policeman in *Strangest Case* explains that Ordway got the name "because he likes to play at being a detective."

These films were modeled after the later radio shows, with the police often using Ordway as a consultant on a difficult case. Of course Ordway always solved the crime before the police were able to do so, even if there were no psychological aspects to the mystery.

The Crime Doctor was played by Warner Baxter in all of the films. Baxter, who was born in Columbus, Ohio, around 1889, began receiving credited appearances in silent films in the early 1920s. He won the Oscar for Best Actor for playing the Cisco Kid in the movie *In Old Arizona* (1929). Baxter went on to play the Cisco Kid in several other films. Baxter is best-remembered today for appearances in *42nd Street* (1933) as producer Julian Marsh and *The Prisoner of Shark Island* (1936) as Doctor Samuel Mudd, the physician who treated the injured John Wilkes Booth after the assassination of President Lincoln.

By the 1940s, Baxter was no longer receiving the best roles in Hollywood films and his health had deteriorated. Thus, the Crime Doctor series was a perfect fit for him, allowing him to continue working but on an easy schedule, with about two movies a year and with most scenes shot in the studio.

The Films

CRIME DOCTOR (1943)

In this always fascinating film, Dr. Robert J. Ordway, soon to become a psychiatrist-detective, must first solve the most important puzzle in his own life — who his true identity is. That theme makes this film unique among the Hollywood mystery series of the 1940s, for in the process of Ordway's discovery of his past, the origin of a movie detective is revealed. At the beginning of their film series, for example, Dick Tracy was already an important police detective, Boston Blackie was already out of jail and dueling with Inspector Farraday, and Sherlock Holmes was already the world's greatest detective. By contrast, at the beginning of *Crime Doctor*, the lead character eventually to be known as Dr. Ordway has been tossed out of a moving vehicle and is now in the hospital, an amnesia victim. His journey to move forward with his life while at the same time discovering his past is the central theme of this mystery movie.

Ordway comes under the care of Dr. John Carey, who, while he cures Ordway of his physical ailments, cannot solve the problem of his loss of memory. When the patient is well enough to leave the hospital, Carey asks the patient, now known as Robert Ordway (from the name of the ward in the hospital in which he was recuperating), to live with him so that together the two can solve Ordway's mental problems. When they meet with no success and Ordway becomes frustrated and depressed, Ordway decides to channel his energies into learning medicine and finding his own cure. Ten years later, Ordway has a degree in psychiatry and is in practice with Dr. Carey. Ordway has a specific interest and specialty in curing the problems of the incarcerated, and because of his success in those endeavors, Ordway is made the head of the state parole board.

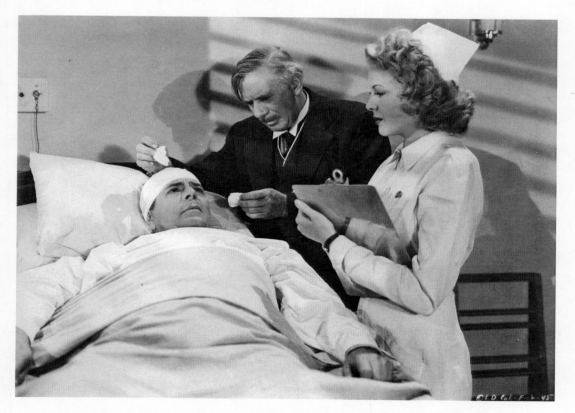

An amnesia patient (Warner Baxter), named "Ordway" by the nurses because of the room in which he is being treated, is examined by Dr. Carey (Ray Collins) and Nurse Betty (Constance Worth) in *Crime Doctor* (1943).

This is a mystery, though, and there is one worrisome moment when Ordway is first in the hospital. A man approaches him, calls Ordway "Phil," demands to know the location of a valise and then starts to strangle him when he is not satisfied with Ordway's answers. When Ordway buzzes for the nurse, the man, later identified as Emilio Caspari, runs away. Caspari is soon thereafter arrested by the police and sentenced to jail for ten years, conveniently putting him out of the story for the same period of time it takes Ordway to obtain his medical license.

When Caspari is released from prison, he meets up with two members of his old gang, who have spotted Ordway in a nightclub. The viewer comes to learn that many years before there was a payroll robbery of $200,000 and the money was never recovered. Ordway, as Phil Morgan, was the leader of the gang of thieves. Ordway's true identity is outed at a parole hearing of a female prisoner allied with the gang. Ordway finally regains his memory, captures the gang, retrieves the payroll and although he is then convicted of the crime, receives a suspended sentence because of his last ten years of good acts.

If there is a problem with the feature, it is that it ends quite abruptly. Once Ordway regains his memory, he grabs a gun in a struggle with the gang and then calls the police. The stolen payroll is discovered by Ordway off camera. The climax is rushed and is truly anticlimactic. The story, however, has been excellent up until then and there is a second climax, so to speak, in Ordway's subsequent trial and sentencing.

Veteran actor Warner Baxter is excellent in the film; he truly looks the part. In the later films in the series, where the scripts were often lacking, it is Baxter's performance that holds the stories together. Ray Collins as Dr. Carey is appropriately avuncular in his relationship with Ordway. Collins, best known to mystery fans as Lieutenant Tragg in the Perry Mason television programs, originated the role of Dr. Ordway on the radio, giving the movie an interesting back story. It is best to simply ignore Collins' strange hairstyle in the film.

Caspari is played by John Litel, who appeared in slightly less than 200 films in his career, usually in small parts such as a district attorney, police captain, prison chaplain or father of Nancy Drew. Caspari is one of Litel's best roles and Litel is excellent in the part, as he probes at Ordway to see if he really has amnesia, attempts to intimidate Ordway's girlfriend

The amnesia patient has become Dr. Robert Ordway, the Crime Doctor, played by Warner Baxter, immaculately dressed as always.

into staying out of his business, and stands or sits as close to Ordway as he can, intimidating him with his soft voice but imposingly tall body.

The direction moves the film at a quick clip, with interesting visuals telling the story. The time period of the first scene in the movie, in which Ordway's body is thrown out of the car, is established for the viewer by a passing billboard referring to the re-election of Herbert Hoover, with the slogan "Prosperity is just around the corner." There are two interesting montages, one of Carey and Ordway using name association to learn Ordway's true identity, and the other of Ordway's ten-year run through school and his entry into the medical profession. The story of Ordway's trial is told, in part, by the camera twice moving down a row of newspaper reporters, so that the viewer can hear bits of the reporters' conversations about the trial and its eventual outcome.

This style of writing and direction propels the story forward, with the effectiveness of the tale elevated by the clues or references to Ordway's past life sprinkled throughout the film. *Crime Doctor* is a mystery rather than a detective story and it succeeds quite well in that style. The challenge to the filmmakers in subsequent films in the series was to channel the concept of a psychiatrist interested in crime into a series of detective movies where Ordway was the detective only and not the story himself.

THE CRIME DOCTOR'S STRANGEST CASE (1943)

This film has an interesting mystery, told in an uninteresting manner. The plot contains two ingredients that usually result in an excellent whodunit, namely a locked-room murder and a murder that is heavily influenced by events from the past. Yet despite these positives, the film comes up short in terms of plot details and manner of execution. *The Crime Doctor's Strangest Case* is entertaining enough but the film is also disappointing in that it never reaches its full potential.

After a short opening, *The Crime Doctor's Strangest Case* moves to Dr. Ordway arriving at the Walter Burns' residence, only to be informed by the housekeeper, Patricia Cornwall, that Burns has just been murdered with poison. Ordway investigates and discovers that Burns did indeed die as a result of drinking poisoned coffee. Since the poison that was used causes instantaneous death and since the coffee cup was back on the nightstand and not lying on Burns' bed when the body was discovered, the death could not have been a suicide. The coffee was prepared by the cook, Mrs. Kepler, and carried to Burns' room by his wife of one year, Diana. When Diana left the coffee in the room, the only other person present with Burns was his secretary, Jimmy Trotter, whom Ordway had previously helped gain an acquittal in a similar murder charge. The window of the room was closed. Since Trotter was the last person seen alive with Burns in an otherwise locked room, he is arrested for the crime.

As the plot develops, it turns out that the cook, Mrs. Kepler, is a fake. She is actually the daughter of George Fenton, Burns' former business partner in the nightclub known as the Golden Nights Café, who disappeared many years ago after being accused of embezzlement by Burns. Fenton was never found, dead or alive. But why has Burns kept title to the Golden Nights Café property, when he has sold all of his other real estate holdings and the Club has been closed for many years?

Ordway discovers a method by which the poison could have been introduced into Burns' coffee cup, from outside the locked window of his room by way of a straw inserted through a hole in the window screen. Ordway also discovers Fenton's body at the Café and

Life can be very dangerous for a crime doctor, as exemplified from this moment in *The Crime Doctor's Strangest Case* (1943) where Paul Ashley (Reginald Denny, right) has a gun trained on Dr. Ordway (Warner Baxter) after Ordway has discovered a hidden safe in the basement of the deserted Golden Nights Café.

a secret safe with $100,000 in it, the latter being the motive for the crime. At the end of the story Ordway traps the real killer, establishing Jimmy Trotter's innocence.

With regard to the locked-room aspects of the tale, there is actually only a partially locked room, as several people other than the ultimate murderer were in and out of Burns' room on the night of the murder on a number of occasions. For that reason, the locked-room aspects of the crime are never completely established for the viewer and therefore Ordway's solution to the method of murder, which is not entirely convincing in any event, does not carry the surprise it would have if the locked-room aspect of the mystery were emphasized in the story. For better handling of locked-room murder mysteries, see the works of John Dickson Carr.

With regard to past events affecting present crimes, the story of the disappearance of George Fenton many years ago, Burns holding onto the nightclub property and Fenton's daughter now doing an investigation of her father's disappearance on her own, are all intriguing. Unfortunately, many of the facts that Ordway uncovers come from an unconvincing hypnosis scene between Ordway and the housekeeper, Patricia Cornwall. More information comes from a long segment wherein Ordway walks through the old café building, trying to discover anything of importance. Apparently he discovers a safe and Fenton's body in the deserted nightclub, but the viewer is not told about these discoveries until the film's conclusion, at which time it turns out that the past events were not even the cause of Burns' murder. For better handling of this type of mystery, see the works of Ross Mac-Donald.

At least the filmmakers were willing to devise a complex plot for this first detective story entry in the Crime Doctor series, one which clearly challenged Ordway's detective skills. Since Ordway's psychiatric advice to Jimmy Trotter at the beginning of the movie, where Ordway advised Jimmy not to get married immediately, is somewhat suspect, it is not surprising that Ordway continued to focus on crime detection rather than psychiatry in the later films of the series. An added point of interest for modern viewers is the appearance of a very young and very handsome Lloyd Bridges in the role of Jimmy Trotter.

Although *The Crime Doctor's Strangest Case* is interesting, it is ultimately disappointing. The film's emphasis on plot rather than comedy relief and Warner Baxter's excellent performance in the lead, however, gave hope for better entries in the upcoming films.

SHADOWS IN THE NIGHT (1944)

This is a good entry in the Crime Doctor series. It benefits from a change in setting, as the story moves out of the city and into an old dark house on cliffs overlooking a rocky beach. There are multiple suspects for the crime, always a decided plus for a mystery movie. There is the always welcome appearance of George Zucco as one of the suspects, playing a slightly mad scientist, surely a comfortable role for Zucco. Warner Baxter gives another solid performance as Dr. Ordway. Even though the plot itself makes little sense, there is more than enough mystery in *Shadows in the Night* to satisfy even the most devout crime aficionado.

The story opens, as many good mysteries do, on a dark and stormy night. Lois Collier, a textile designer, knocks on the door of Dr. Ordway's house at around 3:00 in the morning. Dr. Ordway, immaculately dressed as always, even in the middle of the night, has been reading a book by the fire. Lois asks for his immediate help, saying she is afraid she will not live through the night. A series of strange dreams have been haunting her for a number of successive nights, causing her several sleepwalking experiences. When Dr. Ordway discovers an open window in his house and some wet footprints on the floor, evidencing an intruder in his abode, he decides to move temporarily to Lois' mansion at Rocky Point to try to solve the strange goings-on.

The house itself is filled with an unusual menagerie of occupants. There are Mr. and Mrs. Riggs, the secretive husband and wife caretakers of the property; Nick Kallus, the cook, who lost his restaurant when he had to spend a year in jail for killing a man; Frank Swift, Lois' uncle who is a bit of a mad scientist as he once killed 15 people by selling defective medicine; Adele Carter, Lois' sister; and Stanley Carter, Adele's out-of-work but still conceited husband; Jess Hilton, who is in love with Lois; and Frederick Gordon, a lawyer, who is suspicious for that reason alone. So in addition to an old dark house mystery, there is an old-fashioned English-style whodunit, with multiple suspects in a large mansion.

On the first night of his stay, Ordway sleeps in Lois' room and he experiences the strange dream that Lois had previously experienced on many occasions. It seems to be the result of a gas that is being forced into the bedroom through a vent. Ordway also discovers the body of Raymond Shields, Lois' employer, although the corpse immediately disappears, causing many of the occupants of the house to believe that Ordway only dreamed about the body. Later, when the body is discovered for sure, just about everyone wants to believe that Shields' death was an accident and they all try to convince Ordway not to mention his previous discovery of the body at the upcoming inquest.

There are suspects galore in this whodunit. Everyone seems to have a motive and everyone also seems to act suspiciously in some regard. Unfortunately the solution is unconvincing, as it was Stanley Carter who attempted to drive Lois batty by a use of "hypnotic gas" so that she would not testify against Carter in a custody battle for a son from a previous marriage. This motive for the crimes seems particularly strained and farfetched. Carter then killed Shields and the caretaker, but it is not clear why he committed those murders other than to provide corpses for the plot. Also, how did this out-of-work actor obtain the hypnotic gas?

The film could have used more inventive direction to speed up the pace of the mystery. The story occasionally bogs down in incessant talk and sometimes grinds to a halt in slow walks through dark areas. Even though the story is quite good for the first 55 minutes or so, the explanation for the crimes is a severe letdown.

With all of its faults, the film does have has a unique setting and the plot is different than any other one in the series. *Shadows in the Night* is therefore recommended viewing for fans of the Crime Doctor.

THE CRIME DOCTOR'S COURAGE (1945)

This film starts out with one of the most interesting premises of any story in the Crime Doctor film series. High in the mountains of California, bride Evelyn Carson tries to convince her new husband, Gordon Carson, to extend their honeymoon. Evelyn steps out on a high rock and then gets into a small fight with her husband about his first wife, who died from drowning on her honeymoon. The cliff suddenly gives way, and Evelyn falls to her death. The brother of Carson's first wife, David Lee, tries to convince the sheriff that Carson is a homicidal maniac, but the coroner's jury concludes, just as one did at the time of the death of Carson's first wife, that Evelyn's death was accidental.

The story moves to the present, when Carson's third wife and new bride, Kathleen Carson, learns about the prior deaths of Carson's former wives and asks Dr. Ordway to come to dinner that night at her house to meet her husband, and determine if he is a demented killer. Ordway is on vacation and Kathleen meets him at the swimming pool of his hotel. Nevertheless, Ordway is immaculately dressed as always.

Ordway comes to dinner and meets all of the Carsons' friends. David Lee is also in the house acting as a waiter, and this leads to a loud confrontation with Gordon Carson. Carson retreats to his room, a gun goes off, Carson's body is found and Ordway suspects murder, even though the killing took place in a locked room. Eventually, Ordway discovers the true murderer and also solves the mystery of a Spanish dance duo, Miguel and Dolores Bragga, who seem to incorporate the power of invisibility into their dance act.

After the engrossing opening with the mystery surrounding the deaths of Gordon's first two wives and whether or not murder was involved, that story is simply forgotten once the death of Gordon Carson occurs. At that point, the mystery focuses on the dance duo and the potential that they are actually vampires. The locked-room aspect of the crime is solved when Ordway discovers that the bars on the window can be dropped by use of a switch, allowing the murderer to enter or leave the room with ease, even though there appears to be no exit. But how did the murderer know about that device and why was everyone else unaware of it? For that matter, why was the device installed in the first place?

Sometimes this film seems to be one of the Inner Sanctum mystery movies produced by Universal in the 1940s. Do the Braggas have the ability to become invisible, as they appear to do each night in their dance performance? Since there is a portrait of the Braggas hanging in their residence which purports to come from the 1840s, have the Braggas also discovered the secret of prolonging life, as they claim? Are the Braggas actually vampires who sleep in the two coffins lying in their cellar? Sometimes it all seems a bit much for the viewer, and for Dr. Ordway, who is hardly the type to be fooled by fake supernatural stories. In addition to solving the murder, Ordway discovers the truth about the Braggs, which is not unexpectedly based in reality and not in horror.

The main plot of the story has its interest, particularly in the method by which the female dancer disappears and re-appears in the dance act. A locked-room murder always has a little more spice than a regular murder. The suspects are played by familiar 1940s mystery movie regulars, such as Hillary Brooke, Jerome Cowan and Lloyd Corrigan (Arthur Manleder in the Boston Blackie movies), and it is always nice to see those performers from time to time. *The Crime Doctor's Courage* is a pleasant enough tale; it simply does not fulfill the promise of the early scenes. Also, what courage did Dr. Ordway display in the film?

CRIME DOCTOR'S WARNING (1945)

With a plot that is convoluted and makes little sense, *Crime Doctor's Warning* is the weakest entry in the series to date. The movie starts out with Dr. Ordway having his silhouette cut by an artist at a carnival. The artist is a suspect in a murder that has just occurred, because at the scene of the crime a newspaper was found with the silhouette of the victim cut out. While the cutout silhouette is supposed to be an important clue in the case, note that this plot point is forgotten once the real murderer is discovered.

The police have called Dr. Ordway in to assist in the murder investigation. The victim was a model, Helene Stewart, who had just arrived in town. The ostensible reason for calling in Ordway is that Inspector Dawes believes there is a psychological aspect to the crime. What he is thinking about is particularly hard to discern, but it is the only excuse the writers had for bringing Ordway into the case.

While walking home after investigating the murder scene, Ordway is followed very closely by a young man dressed in a dark hat and raincoat. When Ordway turns around to look at him, the man disappears. The next day, however, he shows up at Ordway's office, asking for help. His name is Clive Lake and he is a painter who has bouts of amnesia, in which he blanks out for about 15 minutes and cannot remember what he has done.

Dr. Ordway decides to help Lake with his confidence, so he proceeds to an art gallery owned by Frederick Malone and convinces Malone to display a work of Lake's in the gallery. Malone is then to tell Lake that the painting has sold, but in reality it is Ordway who will have purchased the painting, for the $200 that Ordway gives Malone.

The story cuts to a scene where Lake is painting model Connie Mace and has one of his attacks. Lake calls Ordway and then proceeds to the roof of his building, to get some fresh air. A dark figure then enters the studio and kills Mace. When the body is discovered later that evening at a party, Lake is arrested for the crime. What a coincidence — the person who came to Ordway for psychiatric help is also involved in the crime that Ordway is investigating.

The story then rambles from scene to scene, including those illustrating the difficult relationship between Lake and his mother, which, while interesting, have nothing to do with the mystery. Ordway is convinced the murders relate to an old painting of three models titled "The Ring." Two of the three models have just been killed. Eventually Malone, the art gallery owner, is determined to be the killer, for a motive quite difficult to explain.

Malone is not just the least likely suspect; he is no suspect at all. Ordway would never have met Malone in the film without Ordway concocting his ridiculous scheme of trying to trick Lake into believing he had sold a painting. Thus, the whole idea of the sale of a Lake painting was merely an excuse to introduce the eventual murderer into the film. Ordway solves the crime by luck. He happens to see an empty frame that could have contained "The Ring" when he meets Malone at his gallery. On this occasion, unlike the other times they meet in the film, Ordway meets Malone in his studio rather than his office, simply so that Ordway can find the picture frame.

The climax of the film, where Ordway breaks into the art gallery on his own (surely not the best activity for Ordway, a convicted criminal serving a suspended sentence) and then is rescued by the police (who arrive just in time for no apparent reason), is particularly weak. Scenes follow scenes in the film for purposes of introducing characters, suspects and clues, as noted above, and not for any logical reason. There are some good performances in the smaller parts (although Coulter Irwin as Clive Lake is unconvincing), but even William Castle, a director who showed some inventiveness in other mystery movies of the 1940s, directs this movie as if it were just a second-feature programmer unworthy of his talents. If Castle shows no interest in the story, why should the viewer?

CRIME DOCTOR'S MAN HUNT (1946)

Much like *Crime Doctor's Warning* just before it, *Crime Doctor's Man Hunt* begins at a carnival, but in the latter case, the scene is the prelude to an interesting tale of psychosis, dual identity and murder. The plot takes unpredictable twists and turns and while the surprise ending may not seem like much of a surprise to viewers of today, having been reared on *Psycho* and the like, it was surely inventive in its day and still packs a bit of a wallop for the modern viewer.

As noted in the discussion of *Crime Doctor's Warning*, the plot of this film, just like many other entries in the Crime Doctor series, suffers from scenes being inserted for purposes of introducing characters to the story or clues to the crimes, and not for purposes of developing a cogent storyline. At that opening scene in the carnival, for example, a strange young man, later identified as Philip Armstrong, considers trying his luck at a shooting gallery but decides against it, acting as if he is not sure exactly where he is. The main purpose of the scene is not to introduce the man, but rather to introduce the air gun that will be an important element in the first murder.

Armstrong then consults with Dr. Ordway concerning his periodic amnesia problems, probably caused by bomb shock suffered during the war. However, those amnesia problems are unrelated to the main plot, so Armstrong's medical problem is simply a writer's device to introduce Ordway to that young man. About a week later, when Ordway is in the neighborhood of the carnival investigating the young man's story, he spots two men dragging a body. Coincidentally, it turns out that the body is that of Ordway's patient, Armstrong, who is the fiancé of a woman named Irene Cotter.

At that point the story becomes quite complicated, as a woman with long blonde hair and glasses appears to have hired the two thugs to kill Armstrong; the two thugs are then killed by the woman. Irene Cotter has a sister named Natalie who is estranged from her

Dr. Ordway (Warner Baxter) is shown here with Ruby Farrell (Claire Carleton) who runs the shooting concession at the local carnival in *Crime Doctor's Man Hunt* (1946).

father and has disappeared, an astrologer had previously predicted the premature death of Armstrong, and there are strange goings-on in an old house still owned by the Cotter family. Finally, it is determined that Irene is slightly batty and has been dressing up as Natalie in the blonde wig and glasses, leading to the string of murders as she tried to keep her psychiatric problems a secret.

While the story may not always be plausible, it is also never predictable, making it an interesting view for the mystery fan. It is peopled with interesting character actors, such as William Frawley of *I Love Lucy* fame, playing a policeman; Frank Sully, from Boston Blackie fame (Sergeant Matthews) playing one of the thugs; and familiar face Olin Howland as one of the suspects. Howland gets off the best line in the movie. After asking Frawley if he has a search warrant and Frawley asking Howland if he wants to be technical, Holloway replies, somewhat wistfully, "No. It's only I dream of some day finding a policeman that has one." There are other funny lines sprinkled throughout the film.

Ellen Drew is attractive and quite good as the psychotic Irene Cotter. Director William Castle gives *Crime Doctor's Man Hunt* an interesting feel, making the opening at the carnival seem spooky even though there is really nothing spooky in the scene, never permitting a clear shot of the blonde woman when she is talking to her hired thugs (adding to the mysteriousness of that character) and staging the film's conclusion in the old house lit only by candles, which are carried from room to room. The score is also quite effective, particularly near the end of the film when Irene, now dressed as Natalie, walks up steps carrying the candles, obviously intent on killing Dr. Ordway.

The psychiatry is probably not accurate, with Ordway making quick diagnoses without adequate interaction with the characters. The police work is suspect, with the detectives seeming to rely more on Ordway's skills than their own abilities to solve the crimes. The plot itself seems better suited for the Whistler or I Love a Mystery crime series. Nevertheless, the film is always entertaining, often surprising and seldom boring, making it a worthwhile entry in the Crime Doctor series.

JUST BEFORE DAWN (1946)

Finally there is a Crime Doctor film that should have been called *The Crime Doctor's Strangest Case*, but since the film makers had negligently and inappropriately used that title for the second film in the series, they were forced to use a more mundane title. In *Just Before Dawn*, Ordway is shot at close range causing temporary blindness, knowingly takes a drink containing poison, and masquerades as a criminal, wearing a suit that is far below Ordway's usual style of immaculate menswear. If this is not the Crime Doctor's strangest case, then nothing is.

The story develops in two separate arcs. At the opening, there is a scene in a funeral home and mortuary where the owner, Karl Ganns, provides a criminal type known as Casper with a case containing a needle and a bottle marked as insulin. Ganns makes it clear that the bottle does not in fact contain insulin. As Casper sets off, it is unclear whether this will be a mystery, a horror film or a spy story.

Toward the end of the movie, Ordway learns that the funeral home is being used by a doctor to perform plastic surgery on convicts, who are in immediate need of a face change and fingerprint removal. Ordway goes undercover as Pete Hastings, a wanted criminal, in order to smoke out the evildoings at the Ganns establishment. Ordway is almost killed in the process, when Casper learns on the radio that the real Pete Hastings has just been captured.

The scenes that relate to the funeral home and mortuary are the best parts of the movie. The setting obviously provides its own sense of eeriness, and Martin Kosleck as Ganns and Marvin Miller as Casper are excellent villains. This is also one of Warner Baxter's best performances in the series. He is totally convincing when he is masquerading as Hastings. Indeed, it is hard to believe that Baxter is the performer under the makeup.

In the main plot to the serial, Dr. Ordway, immaculately dressed as always, is home one evening reading a book when a neighbor comes to the door, telling Ordway that a guest at her party has suddenly collapsed. Ordway rushes over and learns that the victim, Walter Foster, is a diabetic who has not taken his daily injection of insulin. Ordway directs the house boy to get the insulin from Foster's coat, and Ordway gives Foster an injection. A few minutes later, Foster dies. Ordway is actually the killer.

The police quickly determine that Foster's death was murder because Foster died from poison, but when they check the insulin bottle in Foster's coat, the bottle contains only insulin. Someone at the party had substituted the poison bottle for the insulin bottle, and after Foster's death substituted the real insulin bottle back into the case.

In a moment that can only happen in a Hollywood mystery, the police then ask Ordway to investigate the murder because, well, Ordway lives close to the murder scene, and, well, for no other good reason, not that the first reason was any good. At that point in the story, the police actually do nothing. Instead, they let the amateur Crime Doctor investigate the case.

Here the film turns into a true whodunit, with Ordway interviewing all of the witnesses, and much like Sergeant Friday some years later, meeting some strange people along the way. This is an interesting segment of the story, although Ordway finds few clues that are helpful to his investigation. In the end, Ordway tricks one of the guests at the party, who is an unlicensed surgeon who was doing the surgeries at the funeral home, to confess. He killed Foster because Foster had learned the truth and was blackmailing him. Of course if the police had been doing their job and not handed the work over to an amateur they would have checked all of the suspects' backgrounds, discovered the killer's shady past as a doctor, solved the case and probably prevented two other murders. But, then, this is a Hollywood mystery.

The separate stories are interesting on their own, but they do not fit together that well. The scenes at the mortuary, which are written as a suspense thriller, are shot with some inventiveness, with a use of shadows and interesting close-ups. The whodunit segment contains more talk than action. Also, the scene where Ordway pretends to be blind and the scene where the murderer is tricked into confessing his guilt are not very convincing. Nevertheless, the film has a different feel than most entries in the series and indeed of other mystery movies of the 1940s. It is worth a look.

THE MILLERSON CASE (1947)

This film starts with the most shocking moment in the entire series. Dr. Ordway walks into his office wearing a hat, slacks, a plaid hunting shirt and hunting boots. Gone are the immaculate suit, nifty tie and handkerchief in the pocket. Also gone is the smoking jacket he often wears late into the night at home. It seems that Ordway has decided to go on his first vacation in five years, and as a result he has loosened up his very strict dress code.

Ordway arrives in the rural town of Brook Falls, where he has rented a room from Sam Millerson, the local doctor. Millerson is unfamiliar with modern medical techniques and usually treats the townspeople with old-fashioned remedies. His technique is particularly perilous for his patients this time, as several people have fallen ill with what the doctor calls the "summer complaint," but which is actually a typhoid epidemic. The county quarantines the town and Dr. Ordway is asked to help with inoculating the townspeople from the disease.

In analyzing the blood work of three of the victims, Ordway discovers that one, Ward Beechy, the town barber, did not have the typhoid bacilli in his blood. Another doctor who examines Beechy's body finds a similar problem with Beechy's death, in that the body exhibited signs of corrosive poisoning throughout. As a result of these observations, it is clear that Beechy's death is now a case of murder by poisoning. Luckily the Crime Doctor is in town, just when a sophisticated detective from the big city is needed.

At the behest of the county prosecutor, Ordway starts to interview all of the suspects in the community. There are many for Ordway to meet, since Beechy was quite a womanizer. At this point, the case becomes somewhat of a police procedural, or perhaps a psychiatrist procedural. However, even though suspicion moves from suspect to suspect, there are no true clues to the real murderer. When the killer is finally discovered by Ordway, it seems more like guesswork than detective work. Indeed, if a different character had been fingered as the murderer by the Crime Doctor, the solution would have been just as convincing to the viewer.

There is a strange incident late in the film when it appears that Ordway has decided to trap the killer by offering a prize for the best sharpshooter at the local picnic, since someone had taken a shot at the county doctor during the crime investigation. It is not clear what Ordway's idea is, but the concept is forgotten almost immediately, particularly since the person who turns out to be the killer did not even participate in the sharpshooting contest. Indeed, there is never an explanation given for why someone took a shot at the county doctor.

More importantly, there is no real explanation for the subsequent killing of the local doctor, Sam Millerson. Ordway explains that the killer committed that act because he had once asked the doctor about poison and the killer was afraid the doctor might incriminate him. Yet the poisoning of Beechy took place at least a week before the doctor's killing, and the doctor told no one of the conversation. For that matter, how did Ordway know about that conversation between the killer and the doctor? If Ordway learned of the conversation, he should have caught the killer much earlier, sparing Dr. Millerson's life. The murder of Dr. Millerson was inserted into the end of the movie in a weak attempt to inject some suspense into the film. It makes little sense.

Many of the early scenes in the film are insulting to locals, making most of them seem to be ignorant hillbillies. Indeed, Ordway's questioning of two of the female suspects provokes a catfight between the two on the main street of the town, to the excitement of all of the males in Brook Falls. It is an embarrassing moment in the film, once again slurring the rural population without moving the plot forward.

The real problem with the story, though, is its lack of pacing. It is about 20 minutes into the film before the murder is discovered, and thereafter there is just a lot of talk, with little action as the slow investigation proceeds. Since the solution to the murders is far from clever, the whole affair seems quite dull. It is true that the concept of a murder among real typhoid deaths is quite compelling. It was also a good notion to vary the series by moving Ordway into a country setting, but in the end the idea did not work. One hopes Ordway's next criminal investigation will occur in the big city, where Ordway can dress once again in an immaculate suit and take on the sophisticated criminals of the asphalt jungle.

THE CRIME DOCTOR'S GAMBLE (1947)

After his rural adventure in *The Millerson Case*, Dr. Ordway did not immediately return to his practice in New York City but instead was off to the mean streets of Paris for another murder investigation. The several changes of setting for the Crime Doctor films were surely a positive for the mystery series. In addition to the viewers of *The Crime Doctor's Gamble* being able to witness some stock footage of post-war Paris, those viewers learn that in France everyone speaks English, although with a thick French accent. However, even though no one speaks the French language in France, all of the signs in the country are written in French.

Even with the welcome change of setting, *The Crime Doctor's Gamble* is still a boring murder mystery with little pacing. It opens with Dr. Ordway in France giving a series of lectures on crime and psychiatry. After one of those lectures he meets his old friend Jacques Morrell, who is now the Chief of Police. Morrell takes Ordway clubbing around the hot spots in Paris, ending in a small nightclub that features a dance duo performing a Parisian specialty known as an Apache dance and Maurice Duval and his daughter Mignon performing an exciting knife-throwing act. Unfortunately, the two shows at the nightclub constitute the highlight of the film, not much of a compliment for a murder mystery. There is actually more action and suspense inherent in those stage acts than there is in the entire remainder of the feature.

Despite professing no interest in investigating a crime in France, Dr. Ordway is drawn into the story of Henri Jardin, who has been arrested for the murder of his father. After learning of Henri's marriage to Mignon Duval, the woman in the knife-throwing act, Henri's father disowns him. When the father's body is found the next day with a knife in the back, Henri is the obvious suspect. Ordway is not so sure and begins to investigate the case on his own, much as he was apt to do in his own country. Apparently, much like in America, the police in France do not mind if a psychiatrist does most of their work for them. There are several suspects for the crime other than Henri, with motives generally arising out of the unpopular marriage between Henri and Mignon. Unfortunately, as soon as someone other than Henri appears to be the chief suspect, that person dies.

The scenes in which Ordway investigates the crimes tend to be talk-fests and are therefore quite boring, although the film does pick up at the end when the true motive for the murders turns out to be a substitution of a clever forgery for a genuine and valuable painting. Thus, the unpopular marriage of Henri and Mignon has been a clever red herring throughout the film. Even the ruse Ordway devises to catch the real killer has some interest and there is finally a little bit of action when Ordway confronts the real killer.

The film employs the usual trappings of a 1940s mystery: the villain being the least likely suspect (or, in this case, not a suspect at all), no evidence to convict the villain of the crime, a trap to trick the villain into confessing and then a confession by the villain at just the appropriate time. As there is no gamble made by Dr. Ordway in the film, the title makes no sense (which was often the case of titles in mystery movie series from the 1940s). Without any clever direction, surprising plot twists or startling deductions, this is a minor Crime Doctor film that is easily forgettable, except for the unforgettable piece of information that everyone in France speaks English, even to each other.

The Crime Doctor's Diary (1949)

The last film in the series marks a return to the original concept, with Dr. Ordway apparently back on the parole board, having just authorized the release of Steve Carter, who was in prison for the arson fire at the Bellem Music Company where Steve had worked as the sales manager. Dr. Ordway had testified at Carter's trial, opining that Carter was sane, resulting in his incarceration in prison rather than in an asylum. Carter always maintained his innocence and perhaps Ordway believed him, as Carter was released from the penitentiary after serving only three years of his original ten-year term.

Carter believes he was framed by either Anson, his replacement who was in love with his girlfriend Jane Darrin, or "Goldie" Harrigan, who operates a jukebox business in competition with Bellum's service, where songs are piped into bars and similar establishments over the phone lines. Right before the fire, Carter had dumped Jane Darrin for Inez Grey, who now works for Harrigan. Since the viewer must assume, in accordance with the mystery conventions of the day, that Carter is innocent of the arson (or why make this film in the first place), the viewer also has to consider two other suspects for the arson. One is Philip Bellum, the owner of the music company who received a substantial insurance payment at the time of the fire, and the other is his slow-witted brother Pete Bellum, who only seems interested in the music he writes.

This is an appealing mystery movie, with the early scenes at the prison having an intrinsic interest all of their own. As the story moves outside the prison walls and into the lives, motives and loves of each of the characters, an intriguing mystery develops. Anson is murdered under circumstances that lead the police to suspect Carter, resulting in an exciting chase as Carter exits Jane's apartment. There are enough good suspects for the crime that the solution is truly unexpected, even though the true villain falls into the least likely suspect category.

The only weak part of the feature is its ending, as events seem rushed and not all of the characters' motivations seem consistent with prior events depicted in the film. Also, the solution to the crime involves a recording of the voice of the killer accidentally made during the commission of the crime. Thus there is no true detective work done by Ordway, who always seemed to have psychiatrist's luck in solving crimes that baffle the police. In addition and keeping with a tradition of this series, the title has no relation to the plot, as Ordway never keeps a diary.

The heart of the series was always Warner Baxter in the role of The Crime Doctor. Even when the scripts were weak, he could infuse believability into the plots that could convince the viewer to gloss over the unconvincing parts. Baxter is excellent in this film as he always was in the series. He is supported by a number of familiar character actors, such as Don Beddoe (Philip Bellum), Whit Bissell (Pete Bellum), Robert Armstrong (Goldie Harrigan) and Selmer Jackson (the warden). Adele Jurgens is beautiful as Inez Grey, particularly in one scene where she wears a sexy negligee. Lois Maxwell, later to become famous as Miss Moneypenney in the James Bond series, is fine as Jane Darrin.

The return to a story about Ordway on the parole board was clearly a good idea, showing what a mistake it was for this aspect of Ordway's career to be deleted from the prior Crime Doctor films after the first one. *The Crime Doctor's Diary* is a fitting end to a series which, while it had its ups and downs, tried to be innovative in plots and settings, and perhaps most importantly, always took its mysteries seriously.

After the Crime Doctor

The Crime Doctor film series actually outlasted the radio series, with the latter ending its broadcasts in 1947. There have been no other movies or television shows involving the Crime Doctor.

While Warner Baxter was appearing in the Crime Doctor series, he made only a handful of other appearances in the movies. Once the series ended, he appeared in just a few other films. He passed away in 1951.

The Whistler

The Man Who Knew Many Things

A man in a hat and raincoat walks slowly down the road, with just his shadow visible on the wall for anyone to see. The only sound is a haunting 13-note melody, whistled by the dark figure. Two notes are struck on a tympani and then the strange words come:

> I am the Whistler, and I know many things, for I walk by night. I know many strange tales, hidden in the hearts of men and women who have stepped into the shadows. Yes, I know the nameless terrors of which they dare not speak.

That was the opening for an eight-movie series produced by Columbia Pictures from 1944 to 1948. Unlike the other Hollywood mystery series of the 1940s, with the exception of the Inner Sanctum films produced by Universal, the Whistler movies did not have a private detective who appeared in each movie. There was no continuing cast of lead and supporting characters. Instead, the Whistler series was an anthology of unrelated movies, tied together only by the opening narration of the Whistler character, his reappearance from time to time during the film to comment on aspects of the story, the theme of crime and mystery, and in seven of the eight films, a starring role for Richard Dix.

Without an ongoing detective and without the movies being based on a character from the literature of detective fiction, the Whistler movies are often forgotten today. That is an unfortunate oversight as they are some of the best examples of crime in Hollywood in the 1940s.

Background

THE RADIO SHOW

By the 1940s, it was not unusual for a mystery series to be based on a popular radio program. Obvious examples include the Crime Doctor, Mr. District Attorney and Whistler movie series. While the first two shows were based on national radio broadcasts, *The Whistler* was primarily a regional radio show only, appearing on the West Coast regional network of CBS from 1942 to 1954. Its main sponsor, Signal Oil, only operated in the West and there was little incentive to make the show a national broadcast. *The Whistler* was broadcast nationally for two short periods, once in the summer of 1946 and then once again for about 18 months starting in March 1947. Throughout its run, the show was broadcast in individual 30-minute shows. A total of 692 episodes were produced.

Much like the movie series to come, the show opened with echoing footsteps, a haunting whistled melody and then the opening speech set forth above. In the earliest days of the show, the Whistler sometimes talked or argued with the characters, playing the conscience of the murderer or another protagonist of the story. The final act was not dramatized, but rather was summarized by the Whistler in an epilogue. By 1944, the show turned to the format with which it is most associated. The Whistler became the narrator only and the entire story was dramatized. The program would often end with a final twist related by the Whistler, his voice dripping with grim irony, often mocking the characters. Most stories were about a person who decided to commit an act of villainy, usually murder, but sometimes the stories were about innocent people unwittingly caught up in a crime.

The identity of the actor who portrayed the Whistler for most of the series was a well-kept secret. In 1951, it was finally disclosed that the Whistler was played by Bill Forman. Forman apparently was also the voice of the Whistler on the short-lived television program in the 1950s. Dorothy Roberts supplied the actual whistling for the character, providing those services once a week for thirteen years. Wilbur Hatch composed the music for the show, including the Whistler's signature 13-note tune. If that name seems familiar, Hatch was credited on the *I Love Lucy* television series as the conductor of the Desi Arnaz Orchestra.

THE FILM SERIES

The first movie in the series, *The Whistler*, was released in 1944. As with all of the subsequent films, the Whistler introduced the story, appeared from time to time during the film to explain the action or provide segues between scenes, and then in all but one movie to provide a concluding narration, often explaining what happened after the main film ended. Originally, there was no intent to produce a series of movies, but when this first one became profitable, Columbia decided to turn the concept into a mystery series. In all, there were eight films released by Columbia from 1944 to 1948.

Richard Dix starred in seven of the eight films, most often playing the villain but sometimes playing the hero, or at least an ambiguous character. Dix was born in the mid–1890s in St. Paul, Minnesota. After working in local theater and on the New York stage, Dix moved to California in the late 1920s, where he began appearing in silent films. In 1929 he was signed by RKO, where he had most of his screen success. He was nominated for the Academy Award for Best Actor for his performance in *Cimarron* in 1931. The film won the Oscar for Best Picture that year. Throughout the 1930s, Dix appeared in many popular pictures for RKO before finishing his career with the Whistler movies at Columbia.

The other acting role associated with the series is the voice of the Whistler. While the voice sometimes sounds like that of Vincent Price, it is not. The role is usually credited to actor Otto Forrest, about whom not much is known.

Another constant in the films was the tune whistled by the Whistler at the opening of each film. It was the same tune composed by Wilbur Hatch for the radio series.

William Castle was the director of four of the eight Whistler movies, including the first in the series, *The Whistler*, which was only the second movie Castle directed. Castle is better known today as the producer and/or director and promoter of B-horror movies such as *The Tingler* (1959), *House on Haunted Hill* (1959) and *13 Ghosts* (1960). He often appeared in the trailers for those types of movies and even made cameo appearances in his films.

As a result of those activities and the types of films with which he was associated, Castle does not have the best reputation in Hollywood. That is a shame because Castle could be an excellent director, as is evident in his work in the Whistler series. Castle was a major contributor to the success of the films, providing quality mystery movies on a sparse budget.

The Films

THE WHISTLER (1944)

The man sitting alone is a stranger here. He has means and a responsible position in society. He is a man who is more at home in a fashionable club than in a waterfront bar. But tonight he has turned from the comfort and security of his own world to meet a man whose business is death.

For the first film in the series, the writers (one of whom was J. Donald Wilson, the creator of the radio show), chose this interesting tale of a man, Earl Conrad, despondent over the death of his wife in an ocean tragedy, who hires a hit man to kill himself. When he later learns that his wife has been in a Japanese internment camp for the last three years and is alive, Conrad changes his mind, but by then it is too late. The killer is already stalking him and is determined to fulfill the contract.

The story is powered by its first scene, set in a bar, where Conrad pays Lefty Vigran to hire a hit man to kill one Earl Conrad. At that point the viewer does not know that Conrad is the one doing the hiring. Lefty gives a deaf mute in the bar an envelope with the name of the intended victim, along with a payment of $5,000. Suddenly, Lefty is killed by the police as he tries to leave the bar. After Lefty's death, the deaf mute delivers the envelope and money to the hit man. Thus Conrad has set the machinery in motion for his own killing, and there will be no way for him to prevent it later.

Early on there are some good suspense scenes, as Conrad returns to his home, sees a window broken, and then is surprised by a man in the house claiming to be a telephone repairman. Conrad believes the man claiming to be the repairman is the killer, but in fact the phone is truly dead and the man is a legitimate, although very scary, telephone repairman. At the same time, the killer is lurking in the house ready to kill Conrad until his secretary, Alice Walker, shows up. The hit man decides to kill Conrad by shooting him through a window, but then he hears some whistling and decides to forgo the attempt.

This is a strange moment for the film. The shadow of the Whistler appears and the audience can hear the whistling, but so can the characters. Two of them even comment on the whistling. This interaction between the Whistler and the characters, however slight, is reminiscent of the early days of the radio show. In the other movies in the series, whenever the Whistler appears or is heard whistling, the Whistler is solely the narrator, the characters never see or hear the Whistler, and there is no interaction with any of the characters.

At this point, the story starts to fall apart. Rather than simply killing Conrad as he had many chances to do, the killer decides to scare Conrad to death. He does this by openly trailing Conrad and hoping, at some point, that just by showing Conrad a gun, Conrad will be so scared that he will have a heart attack. This change in the killer's approach is very hard to believe, and would not appear to be standard operating procedure for a hit man. Surely this strategy was not worth the $5,000 payment the killer received.

The story also goes off on several tangents. Mrs. Vigran, believing that Conrad set up her husband, Lefty, to be killed by the police, kidnaps Conrad, an event that ends in a car crash over a steep hill. As a result of that action, Conrad flees from the police and therefore must spend the night in a flophouse, leading to more events having nothing to do with the main story. Indeed, at one point, as a vagrant is about to hit Conrad over the head with a pipe, probably killing him, the hit man saves Conrad's life by shooting the drifter. Why did he do that? The vagrant would have fulfilled the hit man's contract for him.

Near the end of the movie, the killer finally tries to dispatch Conrad with a gunshot, a more traditional approach for the professional that he is. Unfortunately for him, he chooses to do it with the police around, who then shoot and kill the hit man.

Richard Dix is only okay as the protagonist, Earl Conrad. Early on, Dix does not speak his lines with much conviction. He does get better, however, as the movie goes along, particularly in the scenes in which he is attempting to elude the hit man. J. Carrol Naish is fine as the killer but it is a relatively small role. The movie is well-directed, particularly in the last ten minutes or so when the film gets back into focus and the hit man is finally stalking Conrad with a real intent to kill him. Good suspense is created in a scene where there is cross-cutting of shots of only the legs of a man following Conrad and the legs of Conrad walking fast. The scene ends in a surprise when another man, not the hit man, discovers the fallen body of Conrad, relieving the audience who believe that Conrad was surely going to be killed immediately.

While always interesting, the film also seems flat in spots, with short scenes of good suspense alternating with unusual frolics and detours from the main story. While the film improves at the end, with the killer close to completing his assignment, the story then ends suddenly and without much of a surprise.

The concept of the story was good, but there was not enough meat in the script to fill an hour-long movie. This would have worked much better as a half-hour radio show or as an entry on the half-hour television program, *Alfred Hitchcock Presents.*

> It was this man's destiny to die tonight. Earl Conrad lives because Man cannot change his destiny. And after this dark night he will recover from his mental illness and there will come a new chapter in his life which will bring happiness to him. I know because I am the Whistler.

Note on the Supporting Players: In this film, Richard Dix was supported by two well-known veterans of film: Gloria Stuart as Alice Walker, Conrad's secretary and the woman who is in love with him, and J. Carrol Naish as the killer. As the series progressed, however, Columbia used the series to showcase its young and hopefully up-and-coming performers, to the exclusion of known faces. Thus most of the leads (other than Dix), and most of the supporting cast were unknown at the time of the making of a *Whistler* film; unfortunately, because of the quality of their performances or whatever else they may have been lacking, they remained unknown for the remainder of their careers. Since television was just on the horizon, with an almost insatiable need for new performers, the fact that none of the Whistler players could make the mark in the new medium tells much about the quality of the casts in these films.

That is not to say that there were not any good performances by these young actors, but the fact remains that a number of the performances were disappointing, detracting from the success of the films. As John McElwee has noted at his website *Greenbriar Picture Shows*, many of the leads were played by "callow youngsters auditioning before Columbia cameras [and] Dix really carries a lot of dead weight among so-called supporting casts."

THE MARK OF THE WHISTLER (1944)

> This man is a human derelict, broke, discouraged, unable to hold a job because of ill health. His name is Lee Selfridge Nugent. I knew him in better days when he possessed money, power,

influence, but Fate decreed that those material things should slip away, and that I, the Whistler, should find him tonight alone in a strange city on this park bench. What can the future hold for a man like this?

This might be called an "anticipation mystery," as most perfect crime stories are. The viewer knows that something is going to go wrong with the best laid plans of Lee Selfridge Nugent as he tries to steal a dormant bank account in the name of a different Lee Nugent. However, the viewer is not exactly sure what will go wrong and when. Thus, the interest in the film is not just in the twists and turns of the plot but also in the anticipation of the impending doom for Nugent, which Nugent has no idea is on the way.

Lee Selfridge Nugent, a derelict who is down on his luck because of ill health, spots a newspaper advertisement concerning a number of dormant bank accounts, i.e., accounts that have money in them but have been inactive for some time. Unless the proper person claims the money, the accounts will have to be escheated by the banks to the state. One account is in the name of "Lee Nugent" and although Nugent knows it is not his account, he decides to go after it anyway. He investigates all of the information he can obtain about the history of Lee Nugent and his family and then, discarding all qualms he may have, sets off to make his claim.

This is an interesting part of the film, first in Nugent's investigation and then in his approach to the bank. Nugent is nervous, with the bank guard seeming to have a peculiar interest in him. Once the bank decides to give Nugent the money, it seems as if everyone in the bank is looking at Nugent. Also during this section of the film, Porter Hall plays the owner of a clothing store who loans Nugent a suit and some money, and continually walks with Nugent to the bank to protect his interest in the suit. Some of the dialogue here is particularly amusing.

Nugent gets his money; the bank is not suspicious. What could possibly go wrong? Of course, the answer to that question is "everything." As Nugent exits the bank, he knocks over a peddler, Limpy Smith. A reporter for the local newspaper, Patricia Henley, peppers him with questions and then his picture is taken, which ends up on the front page of a newspaper. Eddie Donnelly, who has a grudge against the real Lee Nugent, spots the photograph and sets out to kill the fake Lee Nugent, believing he is the son of the man who caused his father to be sent to jail for a crime the father did not commit.

The rest of the film involves the fake Lee Nugent's attempts to evade Donnelly, with the help of Limpy and Patricia. In the end, the police kill Donnelly after he starts shooting at Nugent, Limpy turns out to be the real Lee Nugent, and as the film ends the fake Lee Nugent is going off to prison for his fraud on the bank while the real Lee Nugent gets the money in the dormant account.

This is a film of coincidences. There is Lee Selfridge Nugent having the same name as the name on the dormant bank account, the bell captain at the hotel recognizing Nugent and knowing to call Donnelly about him, Nugent escaping from Donnelly right near Limpy's apartment (the address of which Limpy has just told Nugent), and the police killing Donnelly just in time to relieve both of the Nugents of their anxieties about being killed by him. All of the coincidences in the film work except for one. The surprise that Limpy is the real Lee Nugent and happened to get bowled over by the fake Lee Nugent at the bank does strain credulity.

On the other hand, maybe it does make sense. Limpy may have deliberately knocked into Nugent outside the bank to make his acquaintance and to protect his interest in the dormant account. That would explain Limpy warning Nugent that Donnelly was waiting for him at the hotel. Limpy knew all about Donnelly and perhaps he wanted to make sure the fake Nugent remained alive long enough for Limpy to obtain the money from the fake Nugent. Indeed, unbeknownst to Nugent, Limpy does steal the money back from him. So Limpy, while he appears to be friendly, is not all he seems to be, even though the two Nugents end up as friends at the end of the film.

The feature might have been better with a bit more innovative direction by William Castle. He brings little style to the film. Janis Carter is unconvincing as Patricia Henley, in a part that is not well-written in any event. The interruptions to the story by the Whistler seem particularly irritating in this film. However, these are minor criticisms. Despite the coincidences in the plot, the feature is always interesting, and perhaps more importantly always surprising. This is a mystery movie for mystery fans who love a mystery movie.

> Yes, the amazing story of how Fate dealt with Lee Selfridge Nugent, who learned the hard way that there is no compromise with conscience. Now he will pay his debt to society and after he has paid that debt, Fate will be kinder to him. I know, because I am the Whistler.

Note on the Source Material: *The Mark of the Whistler* was based on Cornell Woolrich's short story "Dormant Account" (sometimes called "Chance") which was first published in *Black Mask* magazine in its May 1942 issue. It was reprinted in the May 1953 issue of *Ellery Queen's Mystery Magazine*. The plot of the movie is based substantially on the short story, although the film plot was embellished with some new ideas to stretch the length of the film to one hour. Thus the clothing store owner who lends the fake Nugent a suit and the female newspaper reporter who becomes involved in the action are all new to the film.

There are also subtle differences between the two works, such as the fake Nugent in the story picking the dormant account of Lee Nugent out of the newspaper by chance, sticking a pin in the paper. The fake Nugent's real name in the story is George Palmer. But in essence, the two works are the same. Neither of them explains the incredible coincidence that Limpy is actually the real Lee Nugent.

The Power of the Whistler (1945)

> Here is a strange man, formed in God's image according to the Bible. But how far is image from mirage? The two words sound alike. This man looks like all others. But what separates him from his fellows? It cannot be seen by the naked eye.

This is an intriguing story of amnesia and mental illness punctuated by an excellent performance by Richard Dix. As was often the case with movies in the Whistler series, the story starts off slowly but then rushes to a suspenseful climax in the second half.

A man steps off a curb on a busy city street, is struck by a car and knocked to the ground where he hits his head on a lamppost. The Whistler identifies the man as William Everest, but the accident has caused him to lose his memory. He walks into a café and sits at the bar, where he is spotted by three people playing cards. One is blonde-haired Jean Lang, continuing a tradition of blonde females in important roles in the Whistler series. Jean is with her sister, Francine, and Francine's fiancé, Charlie Kent. Jean decides to use the playing cards to tell the fortune of Everest from a distance. The cards tell Jean that Everest will die within 24 hours.

Even though Everest is a stranger to her, Jean tells him about the dire prediction. At

Opposite: In this poster from *The Power of the Whistler* (1945), Richard Dix is shown as William Everest, an amnesiac who has escaped from a mental institution, and Janis Carter is shown as Jean Lang, a woman who innocently accompanies Everest on his journey to recover his memory.

that point, Jean first becomes aware that Everest has amnesia. She then works with him to attempt to determine his identity from the documents in his pockets. Despite Jean's strong efforts, they are unsuccessful. In this section of the film, Dix plays Everest as an amiable fellow and the audience is on his side in the interesting quest to determine his identity.

There are some foreboding signs however. A cat that Everest has been watching for a little girl turns up dead. The audience learns that fact through a shot out the back window of the car, and the evidence seems inconclusive but foreboding, both to the audience and Jean. However, with the death of a bird, Francine's pet, and the later death of a squirrel, it is clear that Everest may not be what he seems to be. There is also a foreshadowing shot of Everest on a bed, with the slats of the blinds making the shadow of prison bars across his body, again raising questions about his motives.

In the second half of the film, Everest regains his memory but does not tell Jean. Dix's performance as Everest starts to change subtly at this time, as he becomes slightly less likable, but only to the audience as Everest conceals his real personality from Jean. Everest convinces Jean to go north to chase after an Edward Nesbitt, a name he pretends he has just remembered. Meanwhile, Francine, a better detective than Jean, has concluded that Everest is an escaped mental patient and he has sent a poisoned cake to kill Dr. John Crawford, the head of the mental institution from which Everest has escaped.

On the trip north, Dix's performance changes again, now embodying the mental illness of Everest. Jean finally realizes the true situation, and to protect herself from an attack by Everest, kills Everest with a pitchfork in a barn. The original prophecy of Everest's death within 24 hours has been fulfilled.

This mystery works because the investigation to determine Everest's true identity is naturally interesting. Also, the little hints that there may be something wrong with Everest's character add some intrigue to the first part of the film. The second half is suspenseful and then exciting, with a last-minute save of Dr. Crawford and Jean finally saving her own life by killing Everest. The death scene is particularly well-shot, with Everest climbing a ladder in the barn, talking crazily and shown in and out of shadows. The surprise thrust of the pitchfork and the long shot of Dix falling with the pitchfork in him provides a strong climax to the scene. The bookend theme of the prediction of Everest's death within 24 hours adds some spice to the plot.

It is the performance of Richard Dix, however, that makes the film work. This story stretched his acting abilities as no other film in the series would, and Dix, the veteran actor, met the challenge. This is probably his best performance of the series.

> In a city full of strange adventures, this, which happened to Jean Lang, has been one of the most amazing. Protected by the resilience of youth, Jean Lang will carry no scars on her soul from her encounter with William Everest. And as time passes, even the nightmare memory will not disturb her innocent sleep. She will marry in time the man destined for her and live long and happily in the fullness of her years. I know, because I am the Whistler.

VOICE OF THE WHISTLER (1945)

> And one of the greatest of these terrors is loneliness. In my wanderings, I have seen the lonely people of the Earth. I have seen their drawn and haunted faces in the city of teeming millions. And I have seen them too in places that have been long deserted and forgotten.

The Whistler starts this tale by presenting a haunted scene in a deserted lighthouse, with a woman who lives there all alone, accompanied only by her cat. It is an evocative opening to the film, perhaps presaging an old dark house mystery. It is an effective book-end to the actual movie, which immediately turns to generally bright and happy scenes, only to suddenly end in mystery and death.

The first scene in the movie is a short film about the career of wealthy John Sinclair, played by Richard Dix. It is not clear why the short movie was shown as no one will confuse this Whistler movie with *Citizen Kane*. As wealthy as Sinclair may be, he is in poor health and he has no friends. His doctor orders him to take a long vacation, away from business. However, in Chicago he collapses in a taxi driven by Ernie Sparrow, who takes Sinclair to his apartment to recuperate. Sinclair does not tell Sparrow his real name or anything about his wealth.

This first section of the film is somewhat bland, almost like a grade-school lesson in life. Sparrow convinces Sinclair, by example, that having friends is the most important thing in life. Sinclair meets two of Sparrow's friends, Joan Martin, a nurse at the local clinic, and Fred Graham, her fiancé and struggling intern. The doctor at the clinic recommends a trip to the coast of Maine for the healthy sea air. Sparrow, believing Sinclair is poor, offers to pay for the ticket. Sinclair is grateful, finally discloses that he has money and invites Sparrow on the trip.

In *Voice of the Whistler* (1945), John Sinclair (Richard Dix, left) is talking to the two people he will invite with him to travel to the coast of Maine, where a murder is in the offing. They are cab driver Ernie Sparrow (Rhys Williams) and nurse Joan Martin (Lynn Merrick).

The story then makes a quick turn. Sinclair asks Joan to marry him and come to the coast with him. Since Sinclair has only a few months to live, Joan is being given a chance at wealth for very little effort. As Sinclair puts it, "My entire fortune for a few months of your life." Surprisingly, Joan accepts the indecent proposal. Her boyfriend Fred, not surprisingly, is quite upset. At this point, the story is unconvincing as Joan's acceptance of the offer and Sparrow's acquiescence in it are out of character from the story (and the life lesson) that has preceded it. On the other hand, this is a *Whistler* movie and the opening of the film did tease some mystery ahead, so perhaps the plot twist is not so unexpected.

The story turns more interesting when it moves to the Maine coast. Six months have gone by. Sinclair has recovered his health and is not going to die. Also he has fallen in love with Joan, which unsurprisingly does not make Joan very happy. Joan has been lonely and depressed lately, particularly since Sinclair has not kept his end of the bargain by dying. When Fred shows up for a visit, Sinclair, who is jealous of him, decides to kill Fred by pushing him out a high lighthouse window. His method is to try to trick Fred into attempting to kill him, and then turning the tables. Once again, Fred's change of character in attempting to kill Sinclair is totally out of keeping with his prior actions in the film. Sinclair does manage to kill Fred, but unfortunately for Sinclair, there are witnesses. Sinclair is arrested, and as the Whistler advises, pays the ultimate price. Tormented by what happened, Joan becomes the lonely woman in the lighthouse shown at the beginning of the film. Even though Joan is wealthy, she has no friends.

The story has a surprise ending, because Sinclair's murder plot requires throwing Fred out the lighthouse window. However, Fred has set up his murder of Sinclair by telling Sparrow that Sinclair has been walking in his sleep. Unknown to anyone, Sparrow nailed the lighthouse windows shut, thus ruining Sinclair's perfect crime.

This plot twist is not enough to save the film, which waits far too long for any true mystery to begin. Given the inconsistent character development throughout the film, the crime, when it finally occurs, is unconvincing. This is one of the weakest Whistler movies, mainly because of its unfocused and unpersuasive plot.

> But constantly haunting her was the tragedy that cost the lives of the man she loved and the man she married. She travelled from city to city seeking forgetfulness but there was no escape from the past. She came back at last to live out a life of torment in the solitude and desolation of the lighthouse. I know, because I am the Whistler.

MYSTERIOUS INTRUDER (1946)

> It is Edward Stillwell who walks alone. He is a kindly, unimportant little man, the type you pass on the street without noticing. Tonight, however, something will happen to him that changes everything, something to make his life important and exciting and dangerous.

Most of the Whistler films have noir elements, but *Mysterious Intruder* is a true film noir. It has several plot elements that are typical of film noir, including a private detective of questionable honesty and a woman with blonde hair who may be honest or may be a true femme fatale. The story is shot in shadows, with characters moving in and out of the dark, and indeed, much of the story is shot at night or in unlit parts of buildings. These elements, plus a plot that always keeps the viewer guessing, makes this one of the best of the Whistler movies.

Edward Stillwell hires private detective Don Gale (Richard Dix) to locate Elora Lund, whom he has not seen for seven years. Elora left Stillwell's neighborhood at the time of her mother's death, when she was only 14 years old. Stillwell is unable to give Gale a good description of Elora other than that she was thin, had long blonde curls and big blue eyes. When Stillwell and Gale haggle over price, Stillwell tells the detective that if he finds Elora Lund, she will make the detective a wealthy man.

Stillwell owns a music store in the neighborhood. A few days later Elora arrives at Stillwell's shop, having seen an ad that Stillwell had previously placed in a newspaper personal column. The two are overheard by Harry Pontos, a hulking brute of a man, played by 1940s heavy Mike Mazurki. Stillwell tells Elora that some of the items her mother once left him to sell for her account turned out to have great value. When Stillwell leaves the shop, Pontos enters and takes a box of items marked with Lund's name. Pontos then kills Stillwell and kidnaps Lund.

Later, it turns out that Elora Lund was an impostor, Freda Hanson, hired by Gale to impersonate Lund and find out Stillwell's valuable secret. It turns out that while Gale was double-crossing Stillwell with Hanson, Hanson was double crossing Gale with Pontos. There are more plot surprises, as Pontos is killed by the police and Hanson is killed by her other accomplices. The real Elora Lund also shows up and Gale tries to cheat her out of her inheritance, which turns out to be wax disks of Jenny Lind recordings which are now quite valuable. (Jenny Lind was a famous Swedish opera singer, dubbed the "Swedish Nightingale," who died in 1887.) At the end of the story, Gale recovers the disks and calls the police so that the disks can be given to the real Elora Lund. However, before that can occur, Gale is accidentally shot and killed by two policemen, and in the battle the valuable cylinders are broken.

This has one of the better casts for a Whistler movie. Barton MacLane and Charles Lane are familiar faces playing police detectives Taggart and Burns, displaying some competence in their investigation, as contrasted with the usual policemen in 1940s mysteries. The part of Freda Hanson is played by Helen Mowery in her first film in her very short screen career. Mowery is beautiful and dangerous as Freda Hanson, with an excellent performance as the lovely blonde-haired femme fatale. If this film were not part of a series and if her character had not been killed so early in the movie, Mowery would be remembered as one of the best of the dangerous females from the 1940s noir films.

The mystery is enhanced considerably by the skill of director William Castle and the use of shadow and light, particularly the clever use of artificial light such as a blinking sign, shadows created by streetlights and contrasts created by restaurant radiance. The close-ups of Mazurki are particularly frightening because in addition to his size, Mazurki's face is quite horrifying. Gale and Hanson are contradictory characters, sometimes appearing to be honest and sometimes appearing to be villains of the highest degree, thus adding to the mystery. The final plot twist of the killing of Gale and the destruction of the cylinders is clever, and given what has gone before, the viewer is more upset with the loss of the discs than the loss of Gale's life. *Mysterious Intruder* may be the least recognized and most under-appreciated film noir of the 1940s.

> And so, after long years of balancing precariously on the borderline of the law, Don Gale was trying at the end to do the right thing. But he made one fatal mistake. Thinking that one of the killers had come back to attack him, he fired blindly. Taggart and Burns will never know that Gales' shots were not meant for them.

THE SECRET OF THE WHISTLER (1946)

And tonight, in this obscure section of a large city, we find a woman shopping for an unusual item.

This tale of marital infidelity, murder and attempted murder is the weakest film in the entire series. It suffers from a lack of mystery, an even greater lack of suspense, and a weak performance by one of the leads.

The story opens with an intriguing scene, where a woman orders an expensive marble gravestone for one Edith Harrison. The woman knows the date of birth but not the date of death. When asked her name, the strange woman says, "Edith Harrison."

The story shifts to a party being held in his art studio by Edith's husband, Ralph Harrison, played by Richard Dix. There he meets the lovely Kay Morrell and immediately becomes infatuated with her. However, the party is interrupted when Harrison is called home because Edith has suffered another heart attack. Harrison, who is not much of an artist, has been essentially living on his wife's income throughout the marriage. Once home, the doctor informs Harrison that Edith has only a short time to live.

Over the next weeks, while Edith is bedridden, Harrison starts an affair with Kay, who at the same time confides in a friend that she is interested in Harrison only for his money. After a new treatment, Edith suddenly gets better and decides to surprise Ralph at his studio. There she learns about the affair by overhearing Ralph and Kay talking. That night, Edith throws Ralph out of the house after advising him that she intends to cut him out of her will. Harrison, who is now desperate, sneaks back into the house later that night and puts poison in his wife's medicine bottle while she is apparently sleeping. Edith is actually awake at the time and notices what Ralph is doing, but the next day, Edith is found dead anyway.

Believing he has killed Edith, Ralph has Edith's body cremated. He then marries Kay and they move back to the family house. There, with the aid of the housekeeper Laura, who overheard the conversation between Ralph and Edith on the night of Edith's death, Kay finds evidence incriminating Ralph, including the medicine bottle with traces of the poison still in it. However, Kay removes a page from Edith's diary, in which Edith wrote that she saw Ralph place poison in her medicine bottle and she would have it analyzed the next day.

Events then move quickly. Kay has the medicine analyzed and poison is found. The police are on their way. Ralph has overheard Kay's conversation on the phone and strangles her. Ralph is shot by the police and when they discover the diary page on Kay's body, one comments that the page would have cleared Harrison of murder.

The problems with the film are many. The intriguing opening, with Edith's purchase of the tombstone, really has nothing to do with the rest of the story. There is no explanation of why Edith never tells Ralph about the purchase or why Edith thought she was about to die. It is as if the writers wanted to start the movie with something mysterious but then they could never connect the idea to a reasonable story.

The film moves very slowly, with the attempted murder of Edith not occurring until the second half of the tale. Even then, it takes some time for Kay to suspect the truth about Edith's death. Then, as is common in a Whistler movie, events seem to rush together in the last five minutes. Unfortunately, the only surprise there is the death of Kay, which is not all that surprising.

Kay, of course, is the beautiful blonde femme fatale of film noir movies, as she is only in it for the money and is just waiting for a chance to get out of her marriage with Ralph. But Leslie Brooks is no Barbara Stanwyck or Lana Turner. She is attractive but bland and does not have the screen persona to pull off the part. The movie would have been substantially better with an actress of greater stature in the role.

While the film has noir elements, it is not shot in the noir style and there are strange directorial touches, such as a two-shot of the actors with one face hidden behind a lamp, or on another occasion, one face hidden behind an easel. There is no apparent reason for these confusing shots. Even the strangling of Kay at the end is strangely filmed, as it is shot from behind, with Kay appearing not to struggle and seeming to smile throughout.

The Whistler movies were about plot and mystery and when those are missing, not much is left. Indeed, even the Whistler himself had nothing to say at the end of the film, as his shadow sneaks out the door in the fadeout.

THE THIRTEENTH HOUR (1947)

> And tonight, at this lonely spot on a highway near a small town, we find an unusual birthday celebration in full swing.

This was the seventh and last Whistler film in which Richard Dix appeared. He was not in good health at the time, and he retired from acting once this film was completed. Unfortunately, the film was not the best ending for his celebrated career. He seems tired in the movie, only giving a half-hearted and unconvincing performance. That is one of the reasons that *The Thirteenth Hour* never rises above the average. It is not, however, the only reason.

The film opens at the birthday party of Eileen Blair, who runs a diner along the highway. Present are many of her regular customers, including her fiancé, Steve Reynolds, who has just given her an engagement ring. After one drink, Reynolds goes out on the road in his large truck to make a delivery. There, a strange twist of events puts him in a tight spot. He picks up a hitchhiker, delaying his journey for about one minute. That puts him on the highway just in time to be almost hit by a drunk driver, causing Steve to crash his truck into a gas station building, right near a motorcycle police officer, Don Parker, who also had an interest in Eileen. The hitchhiker then mysteriously disappears. Reynolds is arrested and convicted for drunk driving and loses his driver's license for six months.

Later, Reynolds is forced to drive his truck without a license. A mysterious masked figure drops out of the truck, knocks Reynolds out, and then backs the truck over Don Parker, killing the policeman. Reynolds flees the scene, and then much like Richard Kimble must prove his innocence before the police capture him. It appears that the crime may have been caused by a less than reputable competing trucking company, or by a search for missing diamonds, but it turns out that the crime was unrelated to either. There is a surprise villain, but the surprise seems forced, as if the writers knew that the only way the film could be interesting to anyone was if a plot twist could be thrown into the story at the end.

In addition to the tepid performance of Richard Dix, the other performances in the film are average at best. Karen Morley seems uninvolved in her role as Eileen Blair, Reynolds' girlfriend. John Kellogg is inadequate as Charlie Cook, Reynolds' business partner and perhaps villain of the piece. Other fine character actors, such as Regis Toomey, Cliff Clark, Anthony Warde and Ernie Adams appear, but they are given little to do.

The direction of William Clemens is pedestrian at best. The film moves at a languid pace, even in scenes that take place in moving vehicles along the highway. There are few quick cuts or unusual camera angles, depressing any excitement there may have been to the story. Some of the last scenes in the film, supposedly occurring on a street outside an apartment building, are so obviously shot on a "city street" of a studio back lot that they seem particularly unconvincing. Much of the rest of the film is shot on small indoor sets.

If one steps back from the events as they are happening in the film and starts to analyze the plot once the entire film has been viewed, the story makes little sense. Why did the hitchhiker disappear from Reynolds' truck after the crash into the gas station? For that matter, how did he disappear? Why did Reynolds' truck stall on the road, giving the hooded figure the chance to attack him? If the purpose of the whole incident was to kill the policeman, Parker, how did the villain know where Parker was and that he would chase the speeding truck? Why did the killer take the diamonds along with him on the job?

Of course, it may not be fair to over-analyze the plots of these mystery movies, as they often cannot withstand close scrutiny. However, the storyline of *The Thirteenth Hour* is particularly unpersuasive. Nevertheless, it has a different type of story than most of the movies in the Hollywood mystery movie series of the 1940s. For that, it deserves at least a little credit.

> Yes, Steve. You were lucky. Stopping just 60 seconds to give a stranger a lift did change the whole pattern of your life. It might have ended in disgrace or even death, but Fate was kind to you.

The Return of the Whistler (1948)

> And here tonight, driving through this rain-swept countryside, are two young people about to embark on the greatest venture of their lives. Whether for better or for worse, only time will tell.

Of all the Whistler mysteries, this one is the most mysterious. Indeed, the first 10 minutes or so of the film seem more like a *Twilight Zone* television episode than a movie.

The plot of the film develops in three story arcs. In the first one, Ted Nichols has brought his fiancée, Alice Dupres Barkley, to a small town to be married. Unfortunately, the justice of the peace is away and an unknown figure sabotages Nichols' car. The local hotel does not have any regular rooms available, so Nichols has to leave Alice at a hotel by herself. When he returns the next day, Alice is missing.

This is the strongest section of the film, with solid writing and directing, creating a sense of foreboding throughout. The early scenes near the home of the justice of the peace are enhanced by shooting with shadows and in the rain. The first sequences in the car are eerie, as they are shot through the front window with the wiper blades moving and then shot through a side window with the reflection of the blades and the rain visible. As Ted and Alice approach the door of the justice's home, their bodies are hidden from view by the shadows of the trees. If the viewer did not know better, he might assume that this is the start of an old dark house horror film.

In the second section, a private detective, Gaylord Traynor, offers to help Ted find Alice. They decide to return to Ted's apartment to locate pictures of Alice. On the ride, the story of Ted and Alice's relationship is told in flashback. Alice is a French war widow of an American who was killed on their wedding night. She came to America to meet her husband's family. There were some problems there and when she tried to escape from the family, Ted found her and took her in. After only two weeks together, Ted and Alice decided to get married.

As Ted relates this story to Traynor, both Traynor and the audience reach the conclusion that Alice was probably scamming Ted in some way. Ted knows very little about Alice and the decision to get married was reached rather quickly by the two. However, when Ted and Traynor return to the apartment and locate pictures and Alice's marriage license, Traynor knocks Ted out and takes the documents.

There is an odd moment in one of the flashbacks where a strange visitor sneaks into

In *The Return of the Whistler* (1948), Ted Nichols (Michael Duane, left), whose fiancée, Alice, has gone missing, is discussing the situation with a private detective, Gaylord Traynor (Richard Lane). Lane, of course, played Inspector Farraday in the Boston Blackie series.

Alice's room to search for something. The figure is generally shown only in shadows, including one that moves along the wall. It is as if the Whistler himself has become involved in the plot.

In the final story arc, Ted learns that Alice's story has been true and that it was relatives of her husband who had kidnapped her so that she would not receive the family inheritance. At the same time, Traynor also discovers the truth and calls the police. Ted then makes an exciting rescue of Alice from sanatorium. As the film ends, Alice and Ted are about to be married and this time it is assumed that the ceremony will take place.

Although the second half of the film does not match the quality of the first half and the ending seems somewhat anti-climatic, this is an excellent film for the series. It is the only Whistler film in which Richard Dix did not appear. Dix had a heart attack in 1948, ending his film career. In any event, although Dix was a major plus for this series of films, there was really no part for him in this story. Dix was too old to play the newlywed Ted, and if he had been cast as the detective Traynor, Dix would have overshadowed the rest of the actors and inflated the significance of the part. Indeed, Richard Lane from the Boston Blackie series (Inspector Farraday) is quite good as Traynor and it is nice to see him playing a competent detective for once.

The rest of the cast, as was usual for the Whistler movies, is basically unknown, but in this case they are quite effective. This is one of the best of the Whistler movies and if the series had to end, this was a good way to go out.

> You certainly were lucky, Ted. It might have ended differently, with you and Alice worlds apart. But fate this time was on your side.

Notes on the Source Material: This film has elements similar to other films in which a woman or other character goes missing and all of the other characters deny the missing person ever existed, except for one person who will not be dissuaded from finding the missing person. This plot can be seen in Hitchcock's *The Lady Vanishes* (1938), where an old lady, Miss Froy, goes missing on a train and Iris Henderson fights to prove her existence, and in *So Long at the Fair* (1950), where Vicky Barton's brother goes missing from his hotel room on a trip to the Paris Exposition and everyone else in the film denies ever seeing him.

However, *The Return of the Whistler* was not based on other movies, but rather was based on a short story by Cornell Woolrich entitled "All at Once, No Alice," first published in *Argosy* magazine on March 2, 1940. It was reprinted in the November 1951 issue of *Ellery Queen's Mystery Magazine*, and in the collection of stories, *Eyes That Watch You* (1952) by William Irish, a pseudonym of Woolrich's. What is interesting is that the first story arc of the film is based almost entirely on the Woolrich story.

As the short story begins, Alice Brown and James Cannon are married by a justice of the peace on the highway between their homes in Lake City and the small city of Michianopolis. When they arrive in Michianopolis, they cannot find a hotel room for the two of them, so Cannon decides to leave Alice in a very small room with a cot at one hotel while he spends the night at the local Y. When he returns to the hotel the next morning, however, he cannot find Alice and everyone denies her existence.

Cannon enlists the aid of the police but they doubt his story because Detective Ainslee cannot find proof of the existence of Alice. Even the justice of the peace and the people at the home in Lake City where Alice supposedly worked as a maid deny knowing anything about her. Just when everything seems hopeless, Cannon finds a handkerchief in his pockets with the initials A.B., and that is enough to convince Ainslee to return to Lake City with Cannon to look for Alice Brown. There they find her and when they do so, they find that Alice is about to be murdered by unscrupulous relatives, who were trying to kill her because she was not a maid but rather, was Alma Beresford, the sole heir to a fortune. There is a last-minute rescue of Alma/Alice and the story ends happily.

The best part of the movie is the part based on the Woolrich story, as Alice disappears and Ted is frustrated by everyone denying she ever existed. The film, though, is an improvement on the story, both because of the excellent writing and directing in the first story arc, but also because in the remainder of the film the writers give a more interesting and detailed explanation for Alice's disappearance than in the story. Also, the film ends with an exciting rescue of Alice. Although the film is hardly of the quality of Hitchcock's *Rear Window* (1954), the two are both examples of excellent mystery films based upon a short story by Cornell Woolrich. And isn't the title "All at Once, No Alice" much more intriguing than the generic title of the movie, *The Return of the Whistler*?

Afterwards

After appearing in almost 100 movies, Richard Dix retired from acting after his starring role in *The Thirteenth Hour* (1947). Dix died of a heart attack less than two years later in 1949 at the age of 56.

The radio series, *The Whistler*, continued on the air until 1955. There was a short-lived television series based on *The Whistler* radio program, which was broadcast during the 1954–1955 television season. There were no subsequent Whistler movies.

The actual influence of the Whistler movies in television can be seen in two well-known television programs. The first is *Alfred Hitchcock Presents* (and its one-hour successor, *The Alfred Hitchcock Hour*), which ran for a total of seven seasons on CBS from 1955 to 1962. The shows were mysteries hosted by director Alfred Hitchcock, who introduced and closed the shows, much like the Whistler did in the movies. Indeed, several of the television programs were based on stories by Cornell Woolrich, much like the movie series.

The other show is *The Twilight Zone*, which ran for five seasons on CBS starting in 1959. The shows were hosted by creator Rod Serling, who spoke about the episodes at the beginning and the end. While *The Twilight Zone* was a mixture of science fiction, horror and fantasy, and the Whistler movies always remained crime stories rooted in reality, there is a tie between the anthology nature of each series, the mystery that surrounded all of the plots and the use of an on- and off-screen narrator.

Unfortunately, the crime and mystery anthology series has disappeared from the small screen, probably never to return. All that remains of this genre are the repeats of television shows from the 1950s and 1960s and their heritage in the Whistler movies of the 1940s.

Inner Sanctum

The Mystery of the Mind

This is the Inner Sanctum, a strange, fantastic world, controlled by a mass of living, pulsating flesh — the mind. It destroys, distorts, creates monsters, commits murder. Yes, even you without knowing can commit murder.

In the opening scene in most of the Inner Sanctum mystery films, a disembodied head inside a crystal ball on a boardroom table speaks those strange words directly to the audience. The scene was eliminated in the last film in the series, perhaps because the words make little sense or maybe because the statement is unrelated to the plot of any of the movies. One critic believed that this opening was the best part of the Inner Sanctum movies, a not-too-subtle jab at the quality of the films. However, the Inner Sanctum movies are not as bad as their reputation might indicate, and much like the Whistler films bring a variety of plot and theme to the 1940s mystery movie series.

Background

THE BOOKS AND THE RADIO SERIES

Each of the films in the Universal Inner Sanctum series starts with the following acknowledgment: "Universal presents an Inner Sanctum mystery by arrangement with Simon and Schuster, Inc. Publishers." Starting in the 1930s, Simon and Schuster published a set of mystery novels in paperback under the generic title "Inner Sanctum." This was a common practice of mystery publishers of the era. Other well-known mystery imprints are the Crime Club (Doubleday), Red Badge Mysteries (Dodd Mead), Cock Robin Mysteries (Macmillan), and Rinehart Suspense Novels (Holt).

NBC bought the radio rights to the name "Inner Sanctum" from Simon and Schuster, and beginning in January 1941, the NBC Blue Network broadcast a weekly, half-hour radio show entitled *Inner Sanctum Mysteries*. The shows eventually moved to other networks during the course of its run. The series was a weekly anthology of mystery and suspense stories. Its signature element in the early years was its host, Raymond, and his sarcastic comments on the stories and his closing tag line, which was an elongated, "Pleasant dreeeeaaaammss." In the later years, Raymond was replaced by a man known only as "Your Host" or "Mr. Host." The voice was supplied by Paul McGrath. Another show trademark was the sound of a creaking door which opened and closed the show.

There were a number of famous guest stars on the radio show over the years, including Boris Karloff, Laird Cregar, Claude Rains and Peter Lorre. In fact, Karloff appeared 15 times in the first year of the show and then sporadically thereafter.

THE FILM SERIES

According to *Hollywood Reporter*, as quoted at the Turner Classic Movies website, Universal purchased the screen rights to the "Inner Sanctum" name from Simon and Schuster, Inc. in June 1943. Under its agreement with Simon and Schuster, Universal did not obtain any story rights to the novels released under its mystery imprint or to the radio programs. The movies are therefore original works, except for *Weird Woman*, which is based on the novel *Conjure Wife* by Fritz Lieber, and *Strange Confession*, which was based on a play.

In all, there were six films in the Universal film series, commencing with *Calling Dr. Death* in 1943. Much like the Whistler film series, there were no continuing characters or continuing storylines from film to film. What the features had in common was a mystery or suspense tale, often with a hint of the supernatural or some other unexplained phenomenon, and Lon Chaney, Jr., as the star.

Chaney, who had the given name of Creighton Chaney, was the son of Lon Chaney, the famous silent film horror star. After his father's death in 1930, Creighton Chaney moved into films, usually in small roles such as playing henchmen in serials, until a breakout opportunity on stage in the role of Lenny in John Steinbeck's *Of Mice and Men*. Chaney received good reviews for his stage performance and he was chosen to reprise the role of Lenny in the film version, which was released in 1939. Chaney received good reviews for his performance in the film, but his career still stalled.

Chaney therefore moved to Universal for the second Hollywood horror film cycle, which began around 1940. While at Universal, he played the Wolf Man, Dracula, Frankenstein and the Mummy, among other horror figures. By the mid–1940s, Chaney had become a very recognizable star, at least in horror films, and it was natural for Universal to choose Chaney to star in a low-budget series of mysteries with some elements of horror.

The only other continuing character in the film series is David Hoffman, portraying the disembodied figure in the crystal ball at the beginning of most of the films. Hoffman had an otherwise forgettable film and television career.

The Films

CALLING DR. DEATH (1943)

This first entry in the Inner Sanctum series is surprisingly interesting, with some unusual plot twists and creative storytelling techniques. While the film can hardly withstand intense scrutiny of its plot (with for example the police missing an obvious physical clue at the scene of the crime and convicting one man of murder while suspecting another), there are few Hollywood mystery films that do not have some plot holes in them. With several potential suspects for the crime, innovative direction and a particularly good performance in one of the supporting roles, this is an excellent first entry for this Universal Pictures mystery series.

The movie starts out in the office of neurologist Mark Steele, who is treating a young woman who has lost her voice after her parents broke up her relationship with a young man they believed was no good. In an instant diagnosis worthy of Dr. Ordway, the Crime Doctor himself, Steele advises the parents to allow the youngsters to get back together again for the sake of the daughter's health.

The point of the opening is to demonstrate that Steele is a success in his professional life as a neurologist. The viewer then quickly learns that Steele's personal life is a mess. His wife Maria is seeing other men but refuses Steele a divorce because she likes the wealth and stature of being married to a successful doctor. After they fight one night, Maria takes off for the weekend without telling Steele. The doctor then goes off on a long drive on his own and he is next discovered Monday morning by his nurse, Sheila Madden. Steele has blacked out and cannot remember what happened over the weekend,

Unfortunately, what did happen over the weekend was that Maria was bludgeoned to death and the perpetrator then destroyed her face with acid. Maria's lover, Robert Duval, is arrested for the murder, but the lead detective, Inspector Gregg, still suspects Steele. Other suspects for the crime are Nurse Sheila Madden, Duval's invalid wife, and even Dr. Steele himself, since Steele believes he may have committed the crime during his blackout period. In the end, it is the nurse who committed the crime, since she was in love with Steele and hoped to marry him, but also because she was involved with Duval in embezzling money from his wife.

Mark Steele (Lon Chaney, Jr.) accosts his wife, Maria (Ramsay Ames) on the night of her murder, in a flashback sequence near the end of *Calling Dr. Death* (1943).

Much of the success of the film must be credited to director Reginald LeBorg, who was not just going through the motions as many directors of 1940s mystery films were. LeBorg employs interesting shot compositions and unusual camera angles so that the viewer never becomes bored with the presentation. For example, an early scene at Steele's house where Maria is not home for dinner is shot with Steele seated at the end of a long dining room table, his upper body framed by four candles, emphasizing his loneliness. When Steele first gets to see Duval, the man accused of his wife's murder, the camera remains stationary, behind Steele's shoulder, as Duval walks down a long hallway toward the camera, his face slowly coming into view. This shot highlights the upper hand that Steele has at that point in the story, as Duval is about to beg Steele to help prove his innocence.

Duval's trial, guilty verdict and death sentence are cleverly conveyed in under 20 seconds of footage, with Steele thinking about the trial as a few silent scenes from the courtroom are shown, followed by four quick newspaper headlines that call the play-by-play. Indeed, much of the story is told from Steele's inner thoughts as narrated by Chaney, and while few films would lend themselves to that storytelling technique, it works here because so much of the story is about the psychological. Indeed, when Steele or other characters relate events from the past, the narrative is conveyed solely by speech and without any flashbacks. Again, while not necessarily a preferred technique, it works in this film because it makes the surprise ending to the movie more effective. When Nurse Madden, under hypnosis, relates the events of the killing of Maria, the flashbacks used truly stand out, since they are the first flashbacks employed in the film. This enhances the interest and suspense of those scenes. Indeed, the scene just before Madden confesses is shot from below the actors, with the room somewhat tilted, a foreshadowing of the somewhat bizarre story Madden is about to tell, also adding to the power of the finish.

J. Carrol Naish portrays Inspector Gregg and it is the performance of the film. He is a character of quiet dangerousness, apparently suspecting Steele of the crime from the beginning and not afraid to remind Steele of his suspicions. Naish was an underrated actor during his career (although he received two Academy Award nominations for Best Supporting Actor). Even though he is playing a policeman and is small in stature standing next to Lon Chaney, there is always an air of commanding malevolence about him. Chaney is merely okay in the role of Dr. Steele and the lovely Ramsay Ames is wasted as Maria, as Ames often was in her few film appearances. *Calling Dr. Death*, though, belongs to the director and LeBorg comes through, elevating the picture above later entries in this series and other entries in more prestigious mystery movie series of the decade.

WEIRD WOMAN (1944)

Many of the Inner Sanctum movies involve an unusual series of events which appear to implicate the supernatural or some other unexplained phenomenon, but turn out to involve a relatively simple crime with a rational explanation. Of all the movies in the series, *Weird Woman* fits that pattern best, with more than a hint of witchcraft in the first half of the film turning into a more mundane story of a jealous woman's quest to punish her former lover in the second half.

The early scenes in the film involve a series of flashbacks from the memories of Norman Reed, a professor at Monroe College. While doing research on a South Seas island, Reed met Paula, a white woman, who was raised by a high voodoo princess after her parents died. Reed fell in love with Paula and brought her back to America as his bride. How-

Anne Gwynne plays Paula, who was raised on a South Seas island by a high voodoo priestess in *Weird Woman* (1944). Gwynne never appears in this garb in the film and she is never as menacing as she appears to be in this publicity photo.

ever, Paula did not easily give up her native superstitions, bringing many of her native implements with her, including the pendant she always wears around her neck to protect herself.

When Reed first arrived back at Monroe College, he attended a party celebrating his return. At the event, it came as a great shock to Reed's former girlfriend, Ilona Carr, that Reed was married, as Ilona had been making other plans with regard to Reed. Despite Ilona's antipathy toward Paula, things went very well for Reed at first. His book was published to great reviews and awards and he was the odds-on favorite to become the new head of the sociology department at the college.

The early scenes from the South Seas island are the highlight of the film, creating the atmosphere of a horror film, more like the Val Lewton films of the era than the traditional Universal horror film. There is a strange native dance, a falling star, and a line of stones that cannot be crossed without the person becoming a sacrifice to the god Kauna-Ana-Ana. When the flashbacks move to America, the introduction of Ilona as the evil protagonist begins to move the story forward. Is it only Paula's magic that is making Reed a success despite Ilona's evil plotting against him?

The answer to that question may be "Yes," because once Reed realizes that Paula still uses her voodoo tools at night in a graveyard, Reed orders them all destroyed, including the pendant around Paula's neck. As soon as that item is destroyed in the fire with a pop, Reed's troubles start. He is accused of contributing to the suicide of one colleague, making improper advances to one student and killing another. Finally Reed realizes that Ilona is causing the problems, and by tricking her into believing that there is real voodoo involved, he convinces Ilona to confess.

The first half of the movie is quite intriguing. One fun part of reading murder mysteries is to guess in advance which character is likely to be the murder victim. In this case, so many characters hate Reed that Reed is likely to be the victim, if not for the fact that Reed is played by the star, Lon Chaney, Jr. Instead, it turns out that there are no murders in the film. In fact, there are probably no crimes committed throughout the entire feature. That is probably the reason the second half of the film seems flat. The last half of the movie is quite predictable, with Reed tricking Ilona into a confession because, as is usual in many of these 1940s mysteries, there is no real evidence against her for her immoral if not illegal acts. Since the viewer knows from the beginning that Ilona is the perpetrator of all of the havoc, there is no real surprise at the end of the film. For those reasons, the last half of the film is a letdown from the strong start of the movie.

The acting is very good, particularly Anne Gwynne as Paula and Evelyn Ankers, in a rare evil role, as Ilona. Of particular interest in this film is Elizabeth Russell as Evelyn Sawtelle, the ambitious wife of a college professor who commits suicide at the instigation of Ilona Carr. Russell, who was used to great effect in minor roles in several of the Val Lewton horror films, is always frightening to look at. Perhaps it is her gaunt face with the piercing eyes, but whatever it is, she surely adds a sense of eeriness into any film in which she appears.

The direction by Reginald LeBorg is above average for this type of film, if not as good as it was in *Calling Dr. Death*. Nevertheless, in the end, the plot is weak in the second half of the feature, making this an interesting but not wholly successful mystery movie.

Note on the Source Material: *Weird Woman* was based on *Conjure Wife*, a 1943 work by Fritz Lieber. In the novel, Norman Saylor, a professor of sociology at Hempnell College, discovers that his wife Tansy has been secretly involved for many years in the practice of witchcraft in order to protect Norman and further his academic career. Norman insists that Tansy destroy all the instruments and paraphernalia of the practice, which had been hidden all over the house, in the garage and even in the car, and so into the fire go her charms, Although Tansy tells Norman that all her items of witchcraft have been discovered and destroyed, Norman later finds one more charm in a locket that Tansy had once given him. Into the fire it also goes.

Almost immediately the phone rings, and a student threatens Norman about the grades Norman had given him. The next day, the student menaces Norman with a gun, another female student accuses him of improper advances, Norman is accused of stealing the ideas from a former student's thesis, and there are allegations against Norman about a wild Christmas party he had attended in New York City. It appears that Norman may now lose the chairmanship of his department to the far less qualified Professor Sawtelle.

The similarities between the above plot synopsis and the film *Weird Woman* are obvious. But at that point, the two stories diverge. *Weird Woman* is a true mystery movie, with most of Professor Reed's problems being traceable to the very rational conduct of Ilona Carr. *Conjure Wife* is a tale of the supernatural and witchcraft, with Norman and Tansy in a titanic struggle against three real witches who are the wives of other professors at Hempnell College. In the process, Norman has to overcome his logical analyses and professorial habits and embrace the practice of witchcraft to save Tansy's life.

Conjure Wife is quite good, although it is surely the only non-mystery novel that will be discussed in this book. The Inner Sanctum series was always intended to be a mystery series, not an extension of the Universal horror product, and perhaps for that reason *Conjure Wife* was not faithfully adapted in the movie. In 1962, a film version of *Conjure Wife* that did embrace its supernatural elements was released. It was titled *Burn, Witch, Burn* (in America) and starred Peter Wyngarde and Janet Blair. That version was much more faithful to the original Lieber novel.

DEAD MAN'S EYES (1944)

This is a strange tale with some unusual plot twists, but in the end, the film never rises above the average, despite some good performances in the supporting roles. Lon Chaney, Jr., stars as Dave Stuart, a professional painter who is engaged to Heather Hayden, the daughter of wealthy "Dad" Hayden. After painting his model Tanya one day, Stuart performs his usual routine of washing his eyes with a benign Boric acid solution, but on this day Tanya has accidentally switched the bottles on the shelves and Stuart uses real acid on his eyes. The painful accident causes Stuart to go blind. This scene, foreshadowed by the proximity of the two bottles on the shelf, is an excruciating moment in the film for the viewer but is still probably the highlight of the film.

Stuart's only hope of restoring his sight is a corneal transplant, but it is difficult to find a donor. Dad Hayden, an elderly fellow, advises Stuart that when he dies, he has willed his eyes to Stuart for use in the operation, in the hope that Stuart's eyesight will return. While that is a noble gesture on Hayden's part, this is, after all, an Inner Sanctum mystery, and surely Hayden has set himself up to be murdered. Soon thereafter, Heather finds the blind Stuart standing over her murdered father's body. Stuart is arrested for the crime but the authorities still allow the transplant operation to be performed. However, even with the use of the dead man's eyes, the operation does not appear to be a success.

There are several suspects for the crime other than Stuart. Tanya, who is in love with Stuart, is angry at Hayden for his comments about her. So is Nick Phillips, a potential suitor for Hayden's daughter. In addition to motive, each appeared to be on the way to Hayden's house at the time of the murder and each acts suspiciously throughout the film. Of course, that means that neither of them can be the true murderer, who turns out to be a least likely suspect, trapped into the usual confession by Stuart, whose eyesight has secretly returned.

This film has a wonderful set of actors in supporting roles, which was typical of the Inner Sanctum films. Jonathan Hale (Inspector Fernack from the Saint series) portrays Stuart's eye doctor, Paul Kelly plays one of the suspects, a doctor and psychiatrist who is in love with Tanya, and Thomas Gomez plays the lead detective, a role similar to the one J. Carrol Naish had in *Calling Dr. Death* (although Naish seemed more menacing than Gomez, even though both torture Lon Chaney over his presumed guilt). Lovely Jean Parker plays Heather Hayden and she is surely a welcome addition to the movie, being a fresh face for this type of film.

It is hard to pinpoint exactly where this film is lacking. Lon Chaney only gives a fair performance in the lead role. He is miscast in this film, as he was in many entries in the series. Chaney could give a good performance in non-mystery and non-horror films (see *Of Mice and Men* [1939] or *High Noon* [1952]) but he is unconvincing here in his role as the blind artist. Acquanetta, as the model Tanya, is quite attractive but she has difficulty in even speaking her lines, much less delivering them with any sense of meaning.

Dave Stuart (Lon Chaney, Jr., center), after the accident to his eyes, is surrounded by his girlfriend, Heather Hayden (Jean Parker), and his doctor (Jonathan Hale), who is explaining that Stuart's eyesight could be restored with the donation of an eye from a newly deceased, in *Dead Man's Eyes* (1944).

The direction is mundane at best, with Reginald LeBorg never taking the time, as he did in *Calling Dr. Death*, to set up interesting shots to keep the picture from becoming boring in its visuals. Indeed, there is more talk than action in the film, contributing to the viewers' sense of ennui. The plot with one person loving another who does not love him or her and that being the motive for the killing of Hayden starts to become ridiculous at times.

This is not a bad film; it is surely better than its reputation. At a running time of just over one hour, it is well worth a look, if only to see the very unusual motives that many of the characters have for killing Hayden. However, as this series was progressing, the quality of the films seemed to be dropping and that did not bode well for the remaining three movies in the Inner Sanctum series.

THE FROZEN GHOST (1945)

In *The Frozen Ghost*, three attractive young women have the hots for the character played by Lon Chaney, Jr., just as three pretty young women were in love with Chaney's character in *Weird Woman*. In *Calling Dr. Death* and *Dead Man's Eyes*, two lovely women were vying for Chaney's affections. Lon Chaney, Jr., always seemed slightly or significantly miscast in the Inner Sanctum movies, and perhaps his supposed sex appeal was one of the reasons. Chaney was no Clark Gable and his attractiveness to women in these films is often unconvincing, thereby undercutting the effectiveness of the plot of several of the features.

In this film, Chaney plays Gregor the Great, a stage hypnotist whose act involves entrancing his assistant Maura, which somehow permits her to read minds or to see what happened in the past. When a drunken member of his studio radio audience challenges him, Gregor tries to hypnotize the cynic to prove that the act is real. The man then slumps to the floor, and even though he died of a heart attack, Gregor believes that he actually killed him with his malevolent thoughts and his piercing eyes.

As Chaney's character always did in the prior films in the series, Gregor, when things are bothering him, thinks out loud (and in a very loud voice), probably disturbing the neighbors but surely irritating all those women who are interested in him. What woman would be willing to spend a lifetime suffering through all of Chaney's constant outpourings of self-doubt and his loud expressions of his innermost thoughts? Indeed, as this storytelling device was repeated from film to film in the Inner Sanctum series, it became harder and harder for the viewer to be always forced to listen to Chaney's inner musings, hoping beyond hope that Chaney would finally take some action on his problems instead of just thinking about them all of the time.

After walking around and thinking aloud about the death of the audience member for some time, Gregor decides to give up the act and his fiancée, Maura. For peace and quiet, he moves into a wax museum run by Valerie Monet, who is infatuated with him, as is

Gregor the Great (Lon Chaney, Jr.) discusses the strange goings on at the wax museum with his former assistant, Maura (Evelyn Ankers), in *The Frozen Ghost* (1945).

Valerie's niece, Nina. There is a mysterious character at the museum named Rudi, who creates all of the wax figures on display. Rudi is a former plastic surgeon who was run out of the profession when one of his operations went awry. After some disputes with Rudi about his attitude toward Nina, Gregor gets into an argument with Valerie and Valerie collapses, leading Gregor to believe that he has killed another person with his eyes. Other people tend to agree with Gregor, particularly since Valerie has disappeared and Gregor has her scarf in his possession.

Eventually, it is determined that Rudi and Gregor's agent, George Keene, are in a scheme to drive Gregor insane so that they can control Gregor's huge estate. After Valerie fainted in the presence of Gregor and Gregor ran away to think out loud, Rudi took Valerie's body, put it into suspended animation and then placed it on display in the museum. This brings back memories of the famous early mystery and horror film, *The Mystery of the Wax Museum* (1933) starring Lionel Atwill and Fay Wray. The comparison between the two films, though, is not flattering to *The Frozen Ghost*.

While *The Frozen Ghost* has some interest from time to time, particularly in the scenes in the wax museum shot in the semi-dark, it is very difficult to get past the ridiculous plot. Surely the death of the audience member, as well as Valerie's collapse when fighting with Gregor, were unexpected, so how could those events have been a part of a scheme to drive Gregor insane? Why would anyone place Valerie's body on display in the wax museum, which was sure to disclose the criminal enterprise to anyone familiar with Valerie's face (which is exactly what happens in this film when Nina first sees the body)? When did Gregor suddenly become rich? Indeed, that latter point illustrates the sloppy writing in the screenplay, with no foundation laid earlier in the film for the sudden concoction later in the film of the scheme to steal Gregor's supposed vast wealth.

The story of *The Frozen Ghost* is ill-conceived and makes little sense, even though the movie's production values and acting performances are generally good. Although the Inner Sanctum films always had supernatural or science fiction overtones to them, *The Frozen Ghost* is different from the other movies, since the plot turns on several unscientific elements, such as putting people into suspended animation and Maura having true mind-reading skills. While those story lines might have worked for a Universal horror film of the era, mysteries are supposed to be exercises in the rational, and in the end *The Frozen Ghost* becomes an exercise in the irrational, and indeed, the ridiculous.

STRANGE CONFESSION (1945)

It is not that *Strange Confession* is a bad film. It is just that it is not a true mystery, even though it is included in a Hollywood mystery series. The filmmakers probably recognized that problem and therefore, to create an aura of mystery about the story, included a tantalizing opening segment to the film.

As the feature opens, a policeman is walking down the street from the left to the right of the screen, as the chimes of midnight start to toll. The policeman pauses in front of a large house to check his watch, and as he starts walking again, chemist Jeff Carter exits the house and starts walking down the street from right to left. Carter is carrying a large black valise. The scene is shot without a cut, in stark blacks and whites.

Carter continues to walk down the street, at one point avoiding a policeman, until he reaches the home of a childhood acquaintance, Brandon, who is now a successful criminal defense attorney. To convince Brandon to listen to his story, Carter shows him the contents of the valise. Whatever is in there, it shocks Brandon. He then listens to Carter's story, which becomes almost the entire remainder of the film, told in flashback.

This opening is the strongest section of the film, with beautifully composed shots and unconventional camera angles, designed to create an aura of mystery and foreboding for the story that Carter is about to tell. Unfortunately, the rest of the film does not match the quality of this opening segment.

Carter is a brilliant chemist whose ruthless employer, Roger Graham, a drug manufacturer, profits from the ideas that Carter generates but pays him little for his services. Carter lives on a tight budget in a boarding house with his wife, Mary, and his son, Tommy. Carter expresses little interest in becoming wealthy as his goal in life is to develop medicines for the good of mankind. When Graham insists on rushing a drug to market without adequate testing, Carter quits his job. Later, when Graham asks him to come back to work for a much higher compensation and on his own terms, Carter is suspicious, but his wife is tired of living just on the edge of poverty and convinces him to take the job.

After substantial research, Carter creates a new drug he calls Zymurgine. Graham decides to market it to the public, even though Carter needs one more ingredient to safely release the drug on the market. Graham ships Carter off to South America so that he can market the defective drug without Carter's knowledge, and incidentally so that Graham can go after Mary. However, when Carter's son Tommy dies during a flu epidemic after receiving the defective drug, Carter returns from South America, and in a fit of rage beheads Graham with a large bayonet which was hanging above his fireplace. It was Graham's head which was in the valise Carter carried to Attorney Brandon's house at the beginning of the film.

The first half of the flashback is an only mildly interesting tale of the life of Carter and his family, as his home and job situation evolves without a hint of mystery. In the last 15 minutes or so of the feature, the story picks up as the viewer reacts with horror when he learns that Tommy will be treated with the defective drug. At that point in the film, though, the rest of the story becomes obvious, and even the beheading of Graham is not that shocking. While the introductory scene is interesting, it raises more questions than it answers, such as Carter recalling events he had no knowledge of since he was in South America, such as the courting of Mary by Graham, or the fact that after beheading Graham at Graham's house, Carter must have just left Mary there all alone, without discussing the matter with her.

Strange Confession is a well-directed movie. The acting is first rate, particularly the ever reliable J. Carrol Naish as Graham. Some of the repetitive conventions of the prior films in the series, such as multiple women chasing after Chaney and Chaney's thoughts spoken aloud in a voiceover, are thankfully eliminated in this film. Even with all of those positive attributes, the film is not a success because it is not a true mystery, and in particular does not have any of the supernatural overtones expected in an Inner Sanctum mystery. With a slow-moving and unexciting story, it can be difficult to get all the way through the feature to its conclusion. If the viewer can do so, the end of the movie has some interest.

Note on the Source Material: This film has a very strange writing credit. It states that it is "based on a Composition by Jean Bart," almost as if the film were based on an orchestral score rather than on a novel. In fact, the screenplay was based on a play written by Jean Bart, titled *The Man Who Reclaimed His Head*. The play opened on Broadway at the Broadhurst Theatre on September 8, 1932, and closed shortly thereafter in October 1932. Claude Rains played the lead in the show and Jean Arthur played his wife.

Since the production ran for only 28 performances, it is nearly impossible to obtain a copy of the script, and of course the play is no longer performed. Secondary sources indicate that the play is about a French man named Paul Verin who marries the very pretty Adele. Paul is a newspaper writer and when he realizes that Adele is unhappy with their economic situation, he goes to work for Henri Berthaud, a politician. At the outbreak of World War I, before Verin is called to fight for his country, Verin advises Berthaud to desert his pacifist party and vote for war. As a result, Berthaud wins the premiership and takes Adele as his mistress. When Verin learns about these developments, he rushes back from the front and beheads Berthaud.

From that description, the play was not a mystery but a melodrama, representative of the plays of its time period. The story was first filmed by Universal in 1934 under its original title, *The Man Who Reclaimed His Head*. The movie starred Claude Rains, repeating his stage role, along with Joan Bennett and Lionel Atwill. In the film, which is also set in France around the time of World War I, Paul Verin agrees to write pacifist articles under the name of his publisher, Henri Dumont, which brings the publisher great fame. However, as World War I begins, Dumont sells out his pacifist positions for a profit, and when Paul, who is away at the front, learns about that and Dumont's possible affair with his wife, he returns to France and beheads Dumont with a bayonet.

Once again, the first movie version was more melodrama than mystery, with the important difference between the first two versions and *Strange Confession* being the MacGuffins. The first two works involved the publication or promotion of pacifist positions while *Strange Confession* involves the dissemination of unperfected drugs. The use of the latter plot element is an attempt to transform the plot from a simple drama into a mystery story. However, that change does not entirely work and the origin of the story in a drama rather than in a mystery highlights the unwise decision of trying to remake the plot into a mystery movie. That is why *Strange Confession* seems boring and out of place in the Inner Sanctum series. The film may not have been so disappointing if the movie had been promoted individually and not as part of the series.

Note on the Production: There was a dispute between Jean Bart and Universal as to whether Universal had the right to produce a second version of the play or whether Universal's rights to the play were limited to one screen version. As a result of the rights dispute, when the Inner Sanctum films were first released to television, *Strange Confession* was not included in the package.

Pillow of Death (1945)

In the last movie of the series, Universal finally got it right, with a whodunit that cleverly throws suspicion on multiple characters, with the ultimate villain being a true but realistic surprise. Even if the story does not make complete sense, the last half hour of the film is one of the most engrossing mysteries of the 1940s mystery series.

Most of the action takes place at the old Kincaid mansion, where wealthy spinster Belle Kincaid lives with Samuel, her brother, Amelia, her indigent cousin from England, and Donna Kincaid, her young niece. Belle is particularly upset that Donna spends substantial time with her employer, Wayne Fletcher, a prominent local lawyer. Although Fletcher is married, Donna and Fletcher are in love. As Fletcher drops Donna off at the foreboding Kincaid mansion one night, he tells Donna he is finally going to have it out with his wife, Vivian, and ask for a divorce.

When Fletcher returns to his house, he discovers the police there. Vivian has been murdered by suffocation and Fletcher is the most likely suspect. The police later discover that he lied about being at the office with Donna at 7:00 P.M. Fletcher did not arrive at the office until around 7:15 P.M, and therefore he has no alibi for the time of the murder. Fletcher is arrested for the murder but is soon released for lack of evidence.

The early part of the movie is slow-moving, with very little action. There is also a strange character, Bruce Malone, who is smitten with Donna, who appears at windows and sneaks through hidden passages in the Kincaid mansion. A supernatural element is added as Belle and Amelia believe in communication with the dead, and therefore after Vivian's death they have medium Julian Julian conduct a séance to contact Vivian, who was also a believer. At the séance, the voice of Vivian is heard, and she accuses Fletcher of being her murderer. Adding to the supernatural element is a walk through the old rooms of the house to locate the "ghosts" that seem to be haunting the old dark mansion. While these scenes are not all that convincing, they are relieved by the sarcastic and funny comments of Samuel Kincaid, beautifully portrayed by George Cleveland.

Donna Kincaid (Brenda Joyce) is surrounded, from left to right, by Captain McCracken (Wilton Graff), who is investigating the murder of Vivian Fletcher, Donna's uncle Samuel Kincaid (George Cleveland), psychic Julian Julian (J. Edward Bromberg), and Bruce Malone (Bernard B. Thomas), Donna's unrequited suitor in *Pillow of Death* (1945). The setting is the "haunted" attic of the Kincaid mansion.

The second half of the film picks up substantially, as Samuel Kincaid and then Belle Kincaid are found murdered on successive mornings. Suspicion travels from Amelia to Bruce to Donna, until the surprise conclusion that Fletcher is, indeed, the multiple murderer. For once, the most likely suspect turns out to be the killer.

The last half of the film is all plot, with a beautifully conceived mystery wherein any of a number of suspects could be the killer. The supernatural aspects of the story add some freshness to the plot, although it is not clear at the end whether Fletcher, who was surely crazy, simply imagined his wife was talking to him, or whether it was a trick by the police, aided by ventriloquist Julian Julian, to obtain a confession from Fletcher. It does not matter. The ending is a surprise and a clever one at that.

The acting burden in the film is on Brenda Joyce as Donna Kincaid, and the pretty young actress gives a convincing performance as a young woman who is attempting to strike out from the suffocating atmosphere of the Kincaid house. Unlike prior films in the series, Lon Chaney is not in that many scenes, which makes his performance all the more effective when he does appear. The title, however, is somewhat perplexing, as there are no "pillows of death" in the film.

With the interesting setting of the Kincaid mansion and a side trip to a graveyard, the typical wonderful acting of the Inner Sanctum series, and the clever plot, this is probably the best movie in this six-film series. Since even the weaker films in the series have some interesting mystery elements, the Inner Sanctum series is far better than its reputation might indicate. In particular, *Pillow of Death* and *Calling Dr. Death* are highly recommended.

Afterwards

The radio show continued on the air after the film series ended. The last episode of the radio show aired in October 1952, on CBS. In 1954, NBC Films syndicated 39 episodes of a television series titled *Inner Sanctum*. It featured Paul McGrath as the off-camera host and narrator, a role he had performed for the radio series.

In 1948, independent studio M.R.S. Pictures released a film titled *Inner Sanctum*, starring Charles Russell and Mary Beth Hughes and directed by Lew Landers. It was a B-movie mystery about a man who kills a woman and then is trapped in a small town when the bridge out of town is washed away. The killer is forced to stay at a small boarding house where a young boy, the one person who saw him commit a part of the crime, is also staying. The killer's efforts to stay out of trouble until he can leave the town constitute the bulk of the story.

Although *Inner Sanctum* did not star Lon Chaney, Jr., the film could have fit into the Universal Inner Sanctum series, particularly since there is a framing story that gives the movie the feel of a *Twilight Zone* television episode. Another interesting connection with the Universal series is that Dr. Valonius, the psychic on the train, is played by Fritz Lieber, the father of Fritz Lieber, Jr., the author of *Conjure Wife*, the book which was the basis for the 1943 film, *Weird Woman*.

The end of the Inner Sanctum series at Universal coincided with the end of the Universal horror cycle. Lon Chaney, Jr., made only one other horror film for Universal and that was *Abbott and Costello Meet Frankenstein* (1948). Thereafter, Chaney generally worked in bottom-basement horror films and television, although he would occasionally receive a good character part in a major film, such as *High Noon* (1952). Chaney died in 1973.

Dick Tracy
The Police Detective

Dick Tracy has been called the second-most famous fictional detective in the world, behind only Sherlock Holmes. Tracy's fame, of course, comes from his comic strip, first published in 1931 and continuing in the papers to this day. Tracy's fame has been enhanced by his long-running radio show, four movie serials, feature film appearances and a television show.

In the mid–1940s, RKO decided to produce a mystery series starring the famous detective. Even though it lasted for only four films, those films are very well done and are better remembered today than the more recent movie starring Warren Beatty.

Background

THE COMICS

The comic strip *Dick Tracy* was first published in 1931, in both Sunday and daily versions, by the Chicago Tribune-New York Times Syndicate. It told the story of a police detective from a city resembling Chicago who pursued a set of vicious but colorful characters, such as Pruneface (reflecting the distortion of his sun-damaged face), Flattop (reflecting the shape of his head), the Blank (a killer made faceless after being shot in the face with a gun), the Brow (who had scars across his forehead), Mumbles (who was very hard to understand from the way he talked) and the Mole (who lived underground).

Other early regulars in the comic strip included Tess Trueheart (Tracy's girlfriend and eventual wife), Pat Patton (Tracy's sidekick), and Junior (an orphan adopted by Tracy, who eventually became a police artist). The comic strips were famous for some of the gadgets invented by Diet Smith, a millionaire industrialist who was a friend of Tracy's. Those inventions included the two-way wrist radio which was eventually upgraded to a two-way wrist television in later adventures.

THE SERIALS AND THE FILM SERIES

Dick Tracy's first appearance on film was via four movie serials released by Republic starting in the late 1930s, namely *Dick Tracy* (1937), *Dick Tracy Returns* (1938), *Dick Tracy's G-Men* (1939) and *Dick Tracy vs. Crime, Inc.* (1941). The serials brought almost nothing from the comic strip, even though each had a credit for the cartoon strip by Chester Gould. In the serials, Dick Tracy was turned into an FBI agent. Junior was introduced in the first serial and the character was carried over into the second serial. However, none of the other regulars appeared in the serials and none of the memorable villains were used, although the serials had their own interesting villains, namely the Lame One, Pa Stark, Zarnoff and the Ghost.

The Dick Tracy serial series was the longest in serial history, with each of the four serials being fifteen chapters in length. The sixty chapters ran a total of approximately eighteen hours. Ralph Byrd played Dick Tracy in all of the serials.

When RKO decided to produce a Dick Tracy movie, it turned to actor Morgan Conway for the lead role rather than Ralph Byrd. At least one source states that Byrd had been involved in an auto accident and was not healthy enough to star in the film series at that time. Unlike the Republic serials, the RKO movie series took much from the comic strips. Tracy was the head of the homicide department on a big city police force, just as in the comic strips. His assistant was Pat Patton, his girlfriend was Tess Trueheart and other regulars from the comic pages also appeared, such as Junior and Vitamin Flintheart. Characters and places had strange names, and each film had a larger-than-life villain as a foe for Tracy.

These films are true police procedurals, several years before that form of detective story became popular in mystery fiction and then on television (i.e., *Dragnet*). From the

Dick Tracy first made it to the silver screen in four serials released by Republic, with the third one being *Dick Tracy's G-Men* (1939). Here, the evil Zarnoff (Irving Pichel, by the door) has his henchman tie Dick Tracy (Ralph Byrd) to a chair, as part of a gun trap to kill the FBI agents who will come to rescue Tracy.

opening moments of each movie, the audience knows who the criminal is. The mystery arises from following Tracy's detective skills to see how he will discover the villain and then capture him. Thus, these films are unlike any of the other films in the Hollywood mystery movie series of the 1940s.

The first actor to play Dick Tracy in the series, Morgan Conway, was born in 1903 in Newark, New Jersey and started appearing in films in 1934. He was a contract player and character actor throughout his film career, having small roles in several Hollywood mystery movies. He is best known today for his two appearances as Dick Tracy. The most famous Dick Tracy of them all, Ralph Byrd, was born in 1909 in Dayton, Ohio. He began his career in show business as a singer and dancer on the Broadway stage. That background came in handy as he did his own singing in his last serial, *The Vigilante*. While Byrd appeared in a number of features over the years, he is best-remembered for playing Dick Tracy in the four movie serials, two of the feature films in this series and a television series. Square-jawed himself, Byrd somewhat resembled the drawing of Dick Tracy and was remarkably well-suited to the role.

The role of Pat Patton, Tracy's policeman assistant, was played by Lyle Lattel in all four films. Lattel was a character actor throughout his entire film career. For mystery fans, he played Sgt. Matthews in one Boston Blackie movie, *One Mysterious Night* (1944). Matthews was a similar character to Pat Patton, both providing comic relief, although Matthews was far more of a bumbler than Patton.

The Films

DICK TRACY (1945)

This is a beautifully directed film, making use of shadows, sounds and unusual camera angles to create an atmosphere of evil and suspense. It starts with an excellent scene in which schoolteacher Dorothy Stafford exits a bus and walks down a quiet street, when she hears the sound of footsteps behind her. The footsteps stop when she stops; they start again when she starts. There is a shadow of a man and then the sound of his shoes alternating with the sound of Stafford's heels, as the camera takes a long view of the quiet street, before cutting between closer rear and front shots of Stafford. Suddenly Stafford is attacked from behind and then the assailant runs off, with another view of the street in partial shadows, lit by the spherical streetlight in the top left of the screen. Another woman walks by and when she discovers Stafford's body, the quiet street is pierced by her loud scream.

While the rest of the movie does not match the quality of this opening, it comes quite close as director William Berke continues to use shadows, interesting camera angles and sounds to increase the anxiety of the viewer. Characters are sometimes shot from below and above rather than straight on, with the film never degenerating into boring filmmaking. This movie was made at RKO and evidences some of the qualities of the Val Lewton horror movies made at the studio around the same time. Indeed, the opening scene described above evokes memories of a similar scene in *Cat People* (1942), in which a young woman also walks down a lonely street, fearful she is being pursued by an unknown horror.

Dick Tracy, along with policeman Pat Patton, is assigned to the case of the slashing murder of Dorothy Stafford. Tracy finds a note in Stafford's purse, demanding $500 in extortion money and signed by "Splitface." The Mayor receives a similar note, although the demand from him is for $10,000 in cash. Following a lead, the policemen find a man slashed to death at his home in the same manner as Stafford. Tracy then follows additional leads and eventually discovers that an ex-convict, who had his face slashed in prison, is behind the killings. However, Splitface is on to Tracy and in order to encourage Tracy to give up the case, he kidnaps Tess Truehart and then Junior. In an exciting conclusion, Tracy is able to rescue the two, capturing Splitface in the process.

Although the character of Splitface is an original concoction for the film, he does fit the classic mold of the villains from the Dick Tracy comic strip, who were often named for their physical attributes or deformities. Mike Mazurki plays Splitface and the hulking former professional wrestler is menacing in the role, even though he does not have any dialogue until the last third of the movie. Mazurki was used to great effect in several 1940s mysteries, most notably in *Murder, My Sweet* (1944), playing Moose Malloy.

Ralph Byrd is the quintessential Dick Tracy in films and Morgan Conway could accurately be described as the forgotten Tracy. Yet, with his deep voice, serious manner and erect posture, Conway gives an excellent performance as the great policeman, at least in this film. The supporting roles in the film are well-performed although Jane Greer, soon to be famous for appearances in two film noirs, is wasted in her role as the club owner's daughter.

The story does go off into the improbable at times, as Tracy figures out that Splitface is killing members of the jury that sent Splitface to prison, as a result of an occult professor obtaining the information from a crystal ball. Tracy meets and spends some time with the owner of the Paradise Club and his daughter, and while it seems that they have some involvement in the crimes, they apparently do not and are soon forgotten.

Those are minor matters, as the plot is always interesting, enhanced by several violent deaths in addition to the opening murder of Dorothy Stafford. With real humor that comes from the interplay between the characters rather than through slapstick or outright silliness, this is an excellent opening film for this short-lived series.

DICK TRACY VS. CUEBALL (1946)

This film contains a menagerie of wonderful characters, played by wonderful character actors whose faces, if not their names, are familiar to B-movie fans. There is Byron Foulger playing an amateur and very nervous thief named Simon Little, Skelton Knaggs with his thick glasses and craggy face playing a diamond cutter named Rudolph, Esther Howard playing Filthy Flora, dishonest owner of The Dripping Dagger, Douglas Walton as larcenous antique shop owner Percival Priceless, strange-faced and bald-headed Milton Parsons playing Higby, an employee at the antique shop, and Ian Keith playing Vitamin Flintheart as if he were a famous Shakespearean actor. All of the sets are busy, with the antique store full of many objects and sculptures, and the basement in Little's house filled with benches, books and equipment. Both of these elements add to the effectiveness of *Dick Tracy vs. Cueball*, one of the most violent movies of the 1940s mystery series.

As the story opens, baldheaded thug Cueball steals a valuable shipment of diamonds from a courier on board a ship, and in the process strangles the courier to death with a leather strap. Tracy is called in and traces the dead man back to his employer, gem dealer Jules Sparkle. Tracy is curious about one of the assistants in the office, Mona, and follows her to the antiques shop of Percival Priceless. While Tracy has suspicions, he has no facts, and he is unable to tie Mona or Percival into the crime at that time.

Cueball expects to be paid for the diamonds by Simon Little, an employee of Sparkle, but Little is frightened by the killing of the courier. Cueball demands more money, further arousing Little's anxieties. Cueball is then hidden in a secret basement of The Dripping Dagger, a strangely named bar, by its owner Filthy Flora. As Cueball becomes more frustrated from his inability to receive fair payment for the diamonds, he strangles Priceless and then Flora. Tracy finally learns about Cueball's involvement by tracing the leather strap that he uses back to the prison from which Cueball was just released. After using Tess Trueheart as a decoy, Tracy finally smokes out Cueball. That leads to an exciting climax with a car chase through city streets and then a foot race through a railroad yard, where Cueball gets his foot stuck in a switch track and is run over by a train.

The leads in the serial are somewhat disappointing. Morgan Conway is one-dimensional as Dick Tracy in this film. He never seems to become excited about anything that happens, whether it is another killing or another clue. Anne Jeffreys is wasted in the role of Tess Trueheart, only receiving some good scenes in the final minutes of the film. It is not surprising that she left the series after this movie.

It is the other actors in the film, however, who carry the mystery forward to its exciting conclusion. In addition to the wonderful actors in the small roles in the film, as noted above, a major asset to the story is Dick Wessel who plays Cueball. Many people have criticized Wessel for his limited acting range in this film, but that only adds to the danger embodied in the character. Cueball himself is a character of limited range of thought and all he can do is strike out and kill those he believes have double-crossed him. Wessel is a hulking brute of a man, just as large and foreboding as Mike Mazurki was in the first film in the series. The director uses tight close-ups of Wessel's face to enhance the horror, not just of his killings, but also of his touch of insanity when things go slightly wrong. Wessel is a strong plus for the film.

Dick Tracy vs. Cueball has a plot that constantly moves forward, from clue to clue and from killing to killing. Tracy does some concrete police work in the film, being consistent with the police procedural that a Dick Tracy movie is supposed to be. Comedy bits are held to a minimum, befitting the seriousness of the crimes involved. This is another good entry in the Dick Tracy series.

Note on the Production: Each of the four Dick Tracy movies has drawings of the characters from the comics on each page of the credits. For *Dick Tracy vs. Cueball*, the drawings include Dick Tracy, the great detective himself, B.O. Plenty, a small time whiskered crook with a farmer's hat, Vitamin Flintheart, an eccentric friend of Tracy's, Flattop Jones, a villain, Tess Trueheart, Tracy's love interest, and Gravel Gertie, who eventually married B.O. Plenty in the comic strips. The last drawing in each of the credits of the films, starting with this one, is that of the upcoming main villain. In this film of course the drawing is Cueball, played by Dick Wessell.

DICK TRACY'S DILEMMA (1947)

This is another excellent entry in the Dick Tracy series, energized by the return of Ralph Byrd to the role with which he is most associated. Director John Rawlins, also new to the series, adds to the mystery and horror of the story with the contrasting use of shadow and light in many shots and by focusing on the reflected shadows of the action on a wall when some of the more violent scenes occur. While showing violent scenes in shadows was a com-

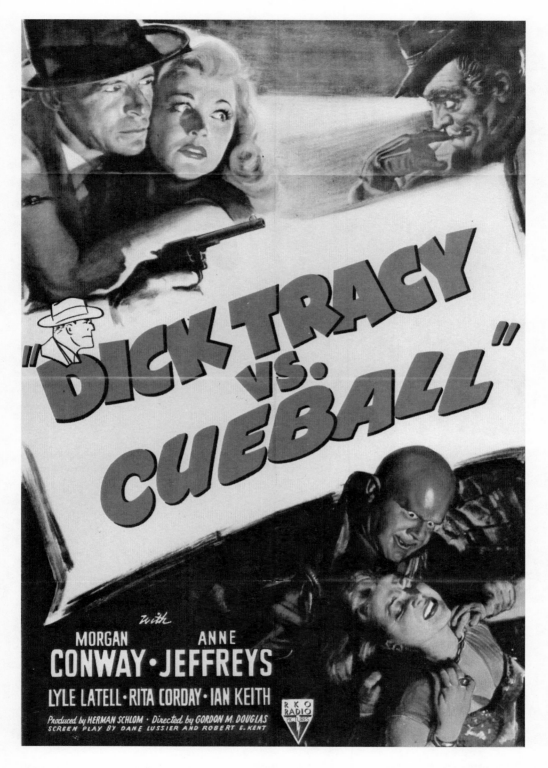

The focus in this poster for *Dick Tracy vs. Cueball* (1946) is the crazed killer, Cueball (Dick Wessel), shown strangling another victim. Pictured at the top left are Dick Tracy (Morgan Conway) and his girlfriend, Tess Trueheart (Anne Jeffreys), and at the top right, Vitamin Flintheart (Ian Keith).

Dick Tracy (Morgan Conway, on the right) has trailed the mysterious Mona Clyde to the antiques store of Percival Priceless (Douglas Walton) where Tracy demands to see the note Mona left under the shop's outside door, in *Dick Tracy vs. Cueball* (1946).

mon film convention of the era to avoid the showing of graphic violence, the technique works particularly well in *Dick Tracy's Dilemma*, since much of the film is set amidst darkness and shadows.

The film starts with an eerie scene in which a frightening man, dragging his foot, walks toward a fur storage facility. He enters a room where a man is washing his face at a sink. The man turns around, there is fright on his face, then the shot of an arm with a metal hook on the end coming down, and then the shadow and sound of the man being hit over the head. There is no dialogue in this stunning opening scene to the film.

The man with the metal hook, later to be known as the Claw, and two other men are stealing furs from the Flawless Furs warehouse. When the man who was attacked, who turns out to be the night watchman, wakes up and tries to prevent the theft, the Claw dispatches him, permanently this time, with a belt to the head.

Dick Tracy is called in to investigate the murder and the theft. There are several potential suspects for the Claw's boss, including Humphreys, the owner of the fur company who

Dick Tracy's Dilemma (1947) brought two new stars to the series — Ralph Byrd as Dick Tracy and Kay Christopher as Tess Trueheart, pictured in the center. The villain is the Claw, played by Jack Lambert. Some of the colorful characters in the film are Longshot Lillie (Bernadene Hayes), Vitamin Flintheart (Ian Keith) and Sightless (Jimmy Conlin).

FAMOUS MAN-HUNTER STALKED BY "THE CLAW"!
"DICK TRACY'S Dilemma"
LONGSHOT LILLIE
VITAMIN
SIGHTLESS
RKO RADIO
with
RALPH BYRD
KAY CHRISTOPHER
Produced by HERMAN SCHLOM · Directed by JOHN RAWLINS · Screen Play by ROBERT STEPHEN BRODE

could be making an insurance claim, Peter Premium, the owner of the Honesty Insurance Company which has just insured the furs, and Cudd, the insurance company's investigator. Tracy is able to solve the crimes through old-fashioned police work, including using fingerprints to identify the Claw and a phone number that the Claw dialed while using his hooked hand, leading to the phone number of the head villain scratched on the phone dial.

The movie is filled with wonderful moments. One involves the Claw out to kill Sightless, a not-so-blind beggar who has been spying on the Claw for Dick Tracy. The Claw chases Sightless down dark city streets, the suspense heightened by the shadows through which pursuer and pursued run, with the sound of the Claw's dragging foot emphasizing how close he is to Sightless. The Claw then traps Sightless in a blind alley and contrasting shots of the Claw advancing and Sightless begging for his life are intercut.

Sightless runs to the end of the alley and then bangs on a door marked "No Trespassing," in the faint hope someone will open it. Just when all hope is lost, the door opens and Sightless is saved. But no, the guard will not let him in the door. He shoos Sightless back down the alley, toward the upraised hooked arm of the Claw. When all seems lost for Sightless once again, the guard opens the door just to make sure Sightless has left. Sightless flees down the alley and hails a taxi cab, temporarily saving his life. It is a suspenseful chase scene, with the unexpected happening several times along the way, acted and directed flawlessly.

Ian Keith is quite amusing once again as Vitamin Flintheart, with his incredible vocabulary and disdain for those who cannot meet his intellectual refinement. Lyle Lattel is not too irritating as Pat Patton. Kay Christopher takes over the role of Tess Truehart in this film but her part is negligible.

Dick Tracy's Dilemma ends with a great chase scene through a junkyard and into an electrical substation, ending in an ironic death for the Claw. The film, much like the prior ones in the series, is particularly violent for a 1940s mystery, although that use of violence is reflective of the tone of the Dick Tracy comic strip on which it is based. This has been an excellent series so far and this may be the best film in the series.

Dick Tracy Meets Gruesome (1947)

Many people believe that this is the best film in the series, probably because of the marquee name of Boris Karloff playing the title villain with the apropos moniker of "Gruesome." By 1947, the second Hollywood horror film cycle was about over and Karloff was astute enough to realize that if he desired to remain working in films, he would have to branch out into areas other than horror movies (which he had been doing, to some degree, during his entire career). In this case, though, Gruesome is close to a figure of horror, so Karloff did not stray far from his horror film background in taking the part. Actually, Gruesome's manners and homicidal tendencies bring back memories of Karloff's role as Bateman in *The Raven* (1935), at least before Bela Lugosi disfigured Bateman's face in that film.

The story starts out with Gruesome, having just been released from prison, finding his old accomplice Melody (a piano player) and then going to see "The Doctor," a crime boss, about a new caper. While waiting for the boss to appear, Gruesome noses around, opens a test tube vial and inhales gas, which makes him sick. He stumbles out of the hideout and collapses in the street in front of The Hangman's Knot bar and appears to have died. Even at the mortuary, the doctor declares him dead. Since Karloff is the star of the film, that cannot be true and soon Gruesome wakes up and makes his escape from the morgue.

Gruesome had inhaled an early version of a gas that paralyzes the victim for a short period of time but has no permanent effects. Soon thereafter, Gruesome and Melody use an improved version of the gas at a bank, paralyzing all of the patrons and staff so that they can walk out unseen with all the money. They have bad luck, however, as Dick Tracy's girlfriend, Tess Trueheart, is in the bank at the time of the robbery; because she is in a telephone booth, she is unaffected by the gas. She calls Tracy from the bank but by the time the police arrive Gruesome and Melody have left. In the escape, Melody kills a uniformed policeman.

By luck and trickery, Tracy finally locates Gruesome, but not before Gruesome has killed several members of the criminal enterprise. The film ends with an exciting chase, a trademark of the Dick Tracy films, with Tracy actually saving Gruesome from a particularly gruesome ending as the villain's prone body almost lands in an incinerator.

Karloff is excellent as expected in the role of Gruesome. He gives a subdued performance, seldom raising his voice or speaking quickly but always conveying the evil incarnate in the soul of Gruesome. But for all of that, Gruesome is the weakest of the four villains in this RKO series. Splitface, in the person of Mike Mazurki, and Cueball, in the person of Dick Wessel, were huge and intimidating. The Claw, as portrayed by Jack Lambert, had that metal hook for a hand which made him particularly terrifying. Gruesome is no walk in the park but he is also not the larger-than-life villain expected in a Dick Tracy adventure.

As usual, the other acting in the film is excellent, particularly June Clayworth as I.M. Learned, the assistant to the main villain who becomes trapped in a web of crime from which she sees no release. She is particularly good in the scenes where her character spars with Dick Tracy, never giving an inch no matter how intense the questioning. Lyle Lattel as policeman Pat Patton has a scene in the morgue where a body disappears and one in a taxidermy shop chasing Gruesome that are played somewhat for comedy. In those scenes, Lattel reminds viewers of Lou Costello; they have the same shape for their bodies and Costello was known for playing horror and suspense scenes for laughs.

John Rawlins made his second directorial effort for the series in this film and while he employs some unusual camera angles and interesting compositions for his shots, this film does not have the distinctive style of *Dick Tracy's Dilemma*. The special effects, when the people are frozen in the bank, are embarrassing as they consist of simply freezing the frame of film. Also, unlike the prior films, Tracy does little true detective work, using a trick to ensnare the villain rather than good old-fashioned "pounding the pavement" police work to identify the criminals. It is not that this is a bad film; it is simply the weakest film in an excellent mystery series. It is a shame that RKO discontinued the Dick Tracy series after this film.

Aftermath

Ralph Byrd, who played Dick Tracy in all of the serials and two of the movies, starred in the television show, *Dick Tracy*, which ran on ABC starting in 1950. Although Tracy did battle with some of the famous comic strip villains such as The Mole and Pruneface, this was apparently a low-budget show with more talk than action. The show only lasted for one season on the network, for 26 episodes. Byrd made another 13 shows for syndication until his sudden death at the age of 43 in 1952.

The *Dick Tracy* radio show was on the air in different formats from 1934 to 1948, sometimes in a 15-minute daily serial format and sometimes in single weekly 30-minute episodes. At different times it was on all four of the major radio networks, ending its run on ABC.

Another movie version of the character titled *Dick Tracy* was released in 1990. It starred Warren Beatty as the famous detective. In the movie he met a number of the comic strip villains, such as the Rodent, the Brow and Flattop. It is the only Tracy movie shot in color, and those colors are quite dazzling, creating the effect of a comic strip from the Sunday papers.

The comic strip itself continues in the newspapers to this day. However, it no longer has the huge circulation that it once had in the 1930s and 1940s.

Philip Marlowe
The Hardboiled Detective

In his essay "The Simple Art of Murder," Raymond Chandler describes the detective in realistic mystery fiction as a special type of man. Chandler writes that he must be a hero, a man of honor, and a man fit for adventure. He must be a common man who can go among the common people and yet he must be a lonely man. He must talk as a man of his age talks, with a rude wit and a disgust for sham or pettiness. "He must be the best man in his world and a good enough man for any world."

In the Hollywood of the 1940s, there were four films about Philip Marlowe based upon the Chandler novels of the era, with a detective much like the one Chandler describes in his essay. Each film had a gritty realism, with a setting on the mean streets of a hardboiled city. The murders were committed, as Chandler wrote, by people who commit them for reasons and not just to provide a corpse. Because the films were made at different studios with different stars and production values, the films varied in quality but each made a good faith attempt to recreate the milieu in which Chandler's Philip Marlowe operated.

Background

RAYMOND CHANDLER

Raymond Chandler was born in 1888 in Chicago, Illinois. He was taken by his mother to England at a young age, where he spent most of his formative years. Chandler attended college in London, where he then became a teacher and a newspaper reporter before returning to the United States in 1912. He then moved to California where he became at various times a reporter, a bookkeeper (with a detour into the Canadian Army during World War I), and then an executive with California oil companies, until the Depression caused a collapse in that industry.

At the age of 45 Chandler began writing fiction, authoring 20 novelettes for the *Black Mask* and other mystery magazines of the era. However, his fame and reputation in the mystery field did not come until he turned to writing mystery novels, the first one being *The Big Sleep* (1939). In all, he wrote seven mystery novels. Twelve of his pulp magazine stories were collected in *The Simple Art of Murder* (1950), and his other novelettes were published after his death in *Killer in the Rain* (1964).

All of Chandler's novels feature detective Philip Marlowe, and even in the re-printed short stories the detective's name was changed to Marlowe. Marlowe is the quintessential hardboiled detective. He is a loner, with no secretary or friends. He is a man of honor in a world of corruption, blackmail and murder. Marlowe has a sense of character, as he remains loyal to his clients despite bribes and threats of violence. Marlowe is not himself mean, nor is he tarnished or afraid. Marlowe is the detective Chandler wrote about in "The Simple Art of Murder."

THE FILM SERIES

There is actually no film series about Chandler's hardboiled detective, Philip Marlowe. The first film based on a Chandler work was *The Falcon Takes Over* (1942), a version of the novel *Farewell, My Lovely*, which was published in 1940. The detective is Gay Lawrence, a.k.a. the Falcon, and the setting is moved from Chandler's California to the semi-mean streets of New York.

The next Chandler mystery novel that reached the screen was *The High Window*, published in 1942. It was filmed under the name *Time to Kill* and was one of the Michael Shayne mystery movies. Each of those films is addressed in this book within the mystery movie series in which it was made.

The first real Marlowe to reach the screen was in the second movie version of *Farewell, My Lovely*, which was filmed in 1944 under the name *Murder, My Sweet*. Dick Powell played the hardboiled detective in a film directed by Edward Dmytryk and released by RKO. By 1944, Dick Powell was best known for his appearances in musicals, usually playing the juvenile lead in the Busby Berkley backstage musicals such as *42nd Street* and *Gold Diggers of 1933*, both from 1933. With his well-received performance in *Murder, My Sweet*, Powell was able to break out of his musical stereotype and star in several additional film noirs, such as *Cornered* (1945) and *Cry Danger* (1951).

The next Chandler novel to be filmed was *The Big Sleep* (1946) based on the 1939 novel of the same name. It was released by Warner Brothers, directed by Howard Hawks and starred Humphrey Bogart as Philip Marlowe. Bogart was, of course, one of the greatest of the Hollywood stars, originally famous for playing supporting roles as gangsters. After becoming a star, he was also well-known for playing two hardboiled detectives, i.e., Philip Marlowe and, of course, Sam Spade in *The Maltese Falcon* (1941).

The next Marlowe movie mystery was *Lady in the Lake*, released in 1946 by MGM. The book on which the film was based was published in 1943. The film starred Robert Montgomery as Philip Marlowe. Montgomery also directed the film, which is famous for its subjective camera technique wherein the camera becomes the eyes of Marlowe. Robert Montgomery was in films since the beginning of the sound era, mainly at MGM. Although he is not known for appearing in detective movies, Montgomery had previously appeared as detective Joel Sloane in *Fast and Loose* (1939), the third film in an MGM mystery series, and as Dorothy Sayers' famous detective Lord Peter Wimsey in *Busman's Honeymoon* (1940).

The last 1940s release of a Marlowe mystery was *The Brasher Doubloon* (1947). This was the second filming of Chandler's novel *The High Window*. It starred George Montgomery, was directed by John Brahm, and was released by Twentieth Century–Fox. George Montgomery Letz was a contract player at Republic at the start of his career, where he did bit parts and supporting roles in about thirty films, most of which were B-Westerns. In 1938, Letz moved to Twentieth Century–Fox and shortened his name to George Montgomery. There he starred in several major Hollywood productions such as *Orchestra Wives*

(1942) with Glenn Miller, *Roxie Hart* (1942) with Ginger Rogers, and *Coney Island* (1943) with Betty Grable. *The Brasher Doubloon* was his only major mystery role.

The Films

MURDER, MY SWEET (1944)

Moose Malloy is an iconic figure of film noir and detective movies. Played by Mike Mazurki, a former professional wrestler, Malloy is tall, strong, overbearing and intimidating. He has the strength to throw a large man across the room; he has the ability to twist a man's neck until it snaps in two. In *Murder, My Sweet*, because of the stylistic manner in which his appearances are presented, Malloy seems to materialize from out of nowhere, making him a character of mythic proportions.

Malloy's first appearance occurs when Marlowe is sitting in his darkened office, with the only light provided by a blinking neon sign outside the window. As the light goes on and off, Malloy's reflection flashes in and out on the upper window pane. When Marlowe spins around in his chair, he sees the towering figure of Malloy in front of him. This is a terrific introduction to the character that provides the catalyst for the plot. Later in the film, Malloy suddenly appears in a shot when Marlowe is resting against a pillar on a public street, and thereafter suddenly appears in a shot when Marlowe is in his desk chair looking at a picture of a person who may be Velma. These stylistic introductions of the Moose Malloy character add to the ominous nature of his being.

All Moose Malloy wants is for Marlowe to locate his girlfriend, Velma. Malloy has not seen her for eight years, which makes sense since Malloy has been in prison for that entire time. Marlowe and Malloy first go to Florian's, the nightclub where Velma used to work. Florian's is now just a bar and no one knows Velma there after eight long years. Marlowe then goes to the house of Jessie Florian, the drunken wife of the former owner of the nightclub. She denies ever knowing Velma but Marlowe spots a photo of Velma, which Jessie tries to hide from him. Jessie then tells Marlowe that Velma is dead. When Marlowe leaves the house, he looks back through the window and sees the suddenly sober Jessie placing a call to an unknown person.

When Marlowe returns to his office he encounters a new client, Lindsay Marriot, who hires Marlowe to accompany him to a secluded canyon to pay the ransom money for a jade necklace that was stolen from a friend of his. Marlowe is suspicious but the lure of a large fee is enticing, so he reluctantly accompanies Marriot on the mission. While Marlow is waiting, he is knocked unconscious and when he awakes he discovers Marriot's murdered body.

The trail leads to the Grayle residence, and to Helen Grayle, the pretty young wife of a wealthy and much older gentleman who is a collector of jade. Helen's jade necklace was stolen from her at gunpoint and Marriot, a friend, was trying to get it back. The remainder of the film involves the search for the stolen jade, the involvement of a mysterious psychic named Jules Amthor, and the final determination of whether Velma is alive or dead.

Murder, My Sweet opens with a direct shot of a bright light under the credits, and then voices are heard of the police interrogating a reticent Philip Marlowe. When Lieutenant Randall finally arrives, Marlowe is willing to tell his story. At that point there is a shot of Marlowe revealing that Marlowe has bandages around his eyes. It will take until the end of the movie before the viewer learns why Marlowe's eyes are bandaged.

Claire Trevor plays Helen Grayle, a classic blonde femme fatale, in the film noir classic *Murder, My Sweet* (1944). Grayle is shown in the outfit she wears when she first meets Philip Marlowe.

The story of the film is then told in flashback by Marlowe, creating the feel of the original novels, which were written in the first person. The approach to the film gives Marlowe the ability to comment on the plot or the characters with his usual cynical attitude. Thus, as he reflects on the original owner of Florian's, Marlowe states, "He died in 1940 in the middle of a glass of beer. His wife, Jessie, finished it for him." When Marlowe arrives at the Grayle home and has to wait in the large marble hall, he says, "It was like waiting by a crypt in a mausoleum." These types of comments by Marlowe evoke some of the tone of the novel.

While the first half of the film creates a complex but intriguing mystery, the film does come to a dead stop about partway through when Marlowe is knocked unconscious by Jules Amthor and taken to a hospital, where he is locked in a room and drugged over a several-day period. This leads to a dream sequence that looks like it comes from *The Twilight Zone*, with lots of doors floating in space and different characters from the movie chasing or talking to him. This is then followed by several moments where the film seems to be shot through gauze, symbolizing the fog and smoke of Marlowe's drugged mind as he tries to get his faculties together. The whole episode seems out of place in the gritty film noir that has preceded it and the scenes do little to move the plot forward. Fortunately, once these scenes are resolved, the movie moves back to its noir sentiments, although it does take a little time for the story to get going again.

Dick Powell was best known for the musicals in which he appeared in the 1930s, usually playing the juvenile. By the 1940s, that aspect of his career was quickly coming to an end and he knew that unless he made a career move quickly, he was likely to be out of the motion picture business in just a few years. That is why he lobbied for the role of Philip Marlowe in *Murder, My Sweet*. Some people prefer Humphrey Bogart (*The Big Sleep* [1946]) or Robert Mitchum (*Farewell, My Lovely* [1975]) in the role. Powell, however, is the right age for the part (30 years old) and displays more energy than the other older performers. Powell's Philip Marlowe is sometimes unshaven, is knocked unconscious several times and gets roughed up by Moose Malloy on occasion, but he is still the tough, cynical, hardboiled detective of film noir, quick with a witty comment and always willing, when necessary, to dispatch a beautiful but villainous woman. Powell is fine in the role.

Claire Trevor is striking in her portrayal of Helen Grayle. In the first shot of her in the film, which is essentially in profile, she is sitting in a high-back chair with one beautiful leg sticking out from her short dress. It is an eye-catching introduction to the character. When Helen is alone with Marlowe for the first time, she immediately tries to seduce him. Indeed, her seething sexuality is one of the most important assets she has, even though her demeanor is paradoxically like ice. Helen's motives are always unclear. She is the epitome of the blond femme fatale of film noir, and is a worthy successor to Phyllis Dietrichson of *Double Indemnity*, also from 1944.

Esther Howard does a short but convincing turn as Jesse Florian, with her strange laugh, apparent inebriation and bits like sneezing on her bathrobe or screaming when she hears the name of Moose Malloy. Otto Kruger plays Jules Amthor, with a carnation in his lapel, as a sophisticated but devious criminal. It is a somewhat typical role for Kruger, as he had, for example, a similar part in Alfred Hitchcock's *Saboteur* (1942). Other good performances come from Mike Mazurki as Moose Malloy and Anne Shirley as Ann Grayle.

The use of the narration to allow Marlowe to comment on the film, some point-of-view shots such as a black pool closing over Marlowe when he is knocked unconscious, the sudden insertion of the large frame of Moose Malloy in a shot, the low-key lighting and the use of shadows and light make this an essential film noir. With a strong plot and excellent performances, this is one of the premier detective movies of the 1940s.

Note on the Source Material: *Murder, My Sweet* was based upon Raymond Chandler's 1940 novel, *Farewell, My Lovely*. Indeed, that was the title of the film when it was initially released in New England and Minneapolis. Audiences apparently mistook the film for another Dick Powell musical and the movie was not successful. RKO changed the name for its national release, and as *Murder, My Sweet* the film was more successful. In fact, neither title makes much sense.

The film generally follows the plot of the book but only through the first two-thirds of the film. The ending events of the two works are generally different although the guilty party and the resolution of the Velma issue are the same.

The movie version makes two key changes in the story, which are a plus for the film. First, there is a greater focus on Moose Malloy, who reappears several times in the film, which also results in a greater focus on the search for Velma. In the book, Malloy appears at the beginning and then his only other significant appearance is at the end. Also, having Malloy employ Marlowe to locate Velma, which occurs in the movie, is more logical than the approach in the novel, where Malloy drags Marlowe, a stranger, into Florian's to see if Velma is there and then abandons him. Second, there is more emphasis in the film on Helen Grayle, her sexuality, and the femme fatale nature of her character. There is also much about Grayle in the book, but she appears so seldom in the novel that her impact there is diluted.

A less effective change is the movie's attempt to create a love interest for Marlowe in the person of Ann Grayle, the stepdaughter of Helen Grayle. (A similar character in the book is named Anne Riordan; she is unrelated to the Grayles.) While the relationship between Marlowe and Ann Grayle is not without some interest, the addition of a love story is the standard (and in this case, somewhat trite) Hollywood approach to adapting a written work without a love interest for the screen. This is also done to a less obvious degree in the film versions of *The Big Sleep* and *The Lady in the Lake*.

The movie discards events from the book related to the marihuana cigarettes with Amthor's card rolled up in each, the dishonesty of the Bay City police and a trip to a gambling boat anchored beyond the three-mile limit. In each version there are lapses in the logic of the investigation. For example, in the book an interloper, Anne Riordan, gives Marlowe his first clues to the involvement of the Grayles in the killing of Marriot. In the film Marlowe becomes suspicious of Amthor, only because the police gratuitously warn the detective to stay away from him. Neither event makes much sense and is only employed in the respective medium to keep Marlowe's investigation moving along.

Generally, the cinematic revisions to the story from the novel allow the movie to concentrate on more dramatic and sensual matters than the book, adding to the effectiveness of the film. A strong argument can be made that *Murder, My Sweet* is a more effective work than *Farewell, My Lovely*.

THE BIG SLEEP (1946)

The Big Sleep and *The Maltese Falcon* (1941) are probably the two most famous detective movies of the 1940s. Each is based on a work by a famous pioneer of the hardboiled detective novel, Raymond Chandler and Dashiell Hammet respectively. Each film stars Humphrey Bogart as the lead detective. Each is directed by one of the most respected directors in Hollywood history, although John Huston was just starting out in his directorial career when he helmed *The Maltese Falcon* while Howard Hawks was well-established in Hollywood when he directed *The Big Sleep*.

The Big Sleep is famous for its complex plot. As Hollywood legend has it, during the course of shooting, Howard Hawks was so confused as to who committed one of the murders that he telegrammed Raymond Chandler for his input, and Chandler was unable to help. Also, the original cut of the film was finished in 1945 but parts were re-shot in 1946 to bring out more of the sexual tension between Humphrey Bogart and Lauren Bacall. In the process, several explanatory scenes from the first cut were eliminated, making the story slightly different in each version. For these reasons, a detailed summary of the plot has scant benefit.

Suffice it to say, Philip Marlowe is called out to the Sternwood Estate to meet wealthy invalid, General Sternwood, who wants Marlowe to end the blackmailing of his daughter Carmen by book dealer Arthur Geiger. At the estate, Marlowe meets the childish but sensuous Carmen and the more mature but still sensuous other daughter of Sternwood, Vivian Rutledge. General Sternwood also mentions that his employee, Sean Regan, who had handled a previous blackmail attempt on the family, has since disappeared.

There are then three murders in quick succession. The story becomes particularly complicated here, as each murder is committed by a different person (although it is not 100 percent clear who killed the Sternwoods' chauffeur, Owen Taylor). Once Marlowe solves those crimes the story seems to come to an end, but then Marlowe starts to push his investigation into the disappearance of Sean Regan, leading to more dealings with Eddie Mars, a casino owner whose wife disappeared at the same time as Regan. In the end, it turns out that Carmen killed Regan when she was high on drugs, although Marlowe tells the police that it was Mars, now dead, who committed the murder. That means that the four murders in the movie were committed by four different people. No wonder the plot seems so confusing; it is.

However, it is not the plot that brings people back to this film time and time again. In part, the draw is Bogart in the lead, essentially reprising his role as Sam Spade in *The Maltese Falcon*. For whatever the reason, Bogart always seemed perfect in the role of a hardboiled detective. In addition, his scenes with Bacall are dynamite, just as they were in their first film, *To Have and Have Not*, with sexual tension always at the forefront when the insolent Bacall verbally jousts with the sarcastic Bogart.

The acting is excellent in the lead roles but it also superb in the many interesting supporting parts. Martha Vickers is incredible as the luscious and sultry Carmen, particularly in the opening scene of the movie where she first meets Marlowe. Charles Waldron as General Sternwood conveys the ailing and eccentric family patriarch with just the right combination of bite and wistfulness. Bob Steele as the vicious killer Canino raises the standard for this type of movie role, making him one of the nastiest screen hit men of all time. Elisha Cook, Jr., always a welcome addition to any Hollywood mystery, provides a spark to the second half of the film in his small role as Harry Jones, always trying to be tough when dealing with Marlowe and Canino but having little to back up his false bravado. Even though it is a brief appearance, Cook is so engaging in the role that the audience is as upset as Marlowe is when Jones is brutally poisoned by Canino.

This film has the best dialogue in any mystery movie since *Double Indemnity* (1944), coincidentally a film for which Raymond Chandler contributed to the screenplay. At one point, as Canino brandishes a gun to convince Jones to talk, Canino says, "You want me to count to three or something, like a movie?" Later Marlowe, in describing what Canino will do to him once he learns that Marlowe witnessed Jones' murder, states that Canino "will beat my teeth out and then kick me in the stomach for mumbling." (That line comes from the Chandler novel.) There are other wonderful lines of dialogue, many taken directly from the novel, evoking the unique flavor of Chandler's style of writing in the hardboiled genre.

As to which version is better, the one from 1945 or the revised one from 1946, for those who have only seen the second version, which was the one traditionally shown on television, the 1945 cut is somewhat less complicated and explains more of the plot. However, the film's long-standing reputation comes from the later version, which has just a little more spice to it in the relationship between Bogie and Bacall than the first cut does. Both versions are highly recommended.

Note on the Source Material: *The Big Sleep*, published in 1939, was Raymond Chandler's first novel. Just about every major scene from the movie comes from the book. Thus, at the beginning of the novel Philip Marlowe comes to the Sternwood mansion to receive his assignment from General Sternwood concerning the attempted blackmail by Arthur Geiger. There Marlowe meets the General's two unusual daughters and learns about the disappearance of Rusty Regan (note the slight change in character name), who in this version was married to Vivian. Three murders quickly ensue and then Marlowe decides to try to locate Regan. In the process, Harry Jones is murdered and Marlowe barely escapes with his life from the hideaway where Eddie Mars' wife has been hiding.

One of the changes between the Chandler version and the film version is that the film eliminates or hides the more prurient aspects of the novel. Thus, in the novel Geiger clearly runs a pornographic book store and is a homosexual. Carmen appears naked twice, once in Marlowe's bed. These topics or scenes were too hot to handle for a film made in 1946. In their place, the film puts an emphasis on the potential romance between Marlowe and Vivian, making Vivian a more important character in the film than in the book. Thus, Vivian is a key figure in the scene near the end of the film where Marlowe escapes from Canino; Vivian is not present when that incident occurs in the novel. Also, Vivian's singing at Eddie Mars' casino is a Hollywood innovation, inserted solely to highlight Lauren Bacall's musical talents.

The main difference between the two versions is in the ending. The scene in the film where Eddie Mars accosts Marlowe at Geiger's house and is killed by his own gunmen is a Hollywood concoction. It is more spectacular, although not necessarily more interesting, than the ending in the book where Carmen attempts to shoot Marlowe, just as she had previously killed Regan in a fit. Also, in the novel Vivian was involved in trying to dispose of Regan's body after he was killed by Carmen. In the movie that element is eliminated, probably in order to make Vivian more likable and to permit the romance between Marlowe and Vivian to possibly continue after the film ends.

The Big Sleep is a rare example of a Hollywood mystery movie of the late 1930s and 1940s whose script is truly based upon the source material. Indeed, much of the dialogue in the film comes directly from the book. Other examples of films truly based on their source material are *The Saint in New York*, *The Maltese Falcon* and *The Hound of the Baskervilles*. It is interesting that those four films are some of the best mystery movies of the era. It is a shame that more filmmakers did not accord more respect to the written source from which their mystery movies supposedly originated. They might have made better films.

Lady in the Lake (1947)

This film is well-known for its subjective camera technique. All of the action is shown from the point of view of Philip Marlowe, with the camera literally becoming the eyes of the private detective. As Marlowe's investigation continues, the camera and the viewer see only what Marlowe sees and nothing else. Marlowe's face is not even shown in the film, except when he is narrating the story and speaks directly to the audience, or during the story when he looks in a mirror.

A Philip Marlowe novel was an appropriate selection for an experiment with this unusual camera technique. Unlike the traditional whodunit where the story was often narrated by a Dr. Watson-like character, the Marlowe novels were written in the first person from the point of view of the detective. Thus, the reader never had any more information about the mystery and the characters than Marlowe did, and the reader learned the story contemporaneously with Marlowe. By using the point-of-view camera technique in the film, everything is filtered through Marlowe's eyes and viewpoint, just as in the novel.

The subjective camera technique thus recreates some of the feel and attitude of the original Chandler novel. For that reason, it was a good idea. The open question, though, was whether in practice the technique would overwhelm the story to its detriment or whether the technique would add to the effectiveness of the story, creating a compelling mystery movie.

Hoping to sell a detective story to Kingsby Publications, Marlowe is instead hired by the company's editor, Adrienne Fromsett, to locate Chrystal Kingsby, the missing wife of the publisher, Derace Kingsby. Although he suspects that Adrienne is trying to break up the Kingsby marriage and take Derace for herself, Marlowe takes the case. He starts his investigation by interviewing lothario Chris Lavery, with whom Chrystal may have gone away. That leads to Lavery knocking Marlowe cold and a few hours later, Marlowe waking up in the Bay City jail. There he meets Lt. DeGarmot for the first time.

Marlowe's investigation then leads to Little Fawn Lake, where Chrystal was supposedly last seen about a month ago. There Marlowe learns that the body of Muriel Chess, the wife of the caretaker, has been found in the lake. With further investigation, Marlowe learns that Chess was really Mildred Havelend, who was being pursued by an unknown man. Adrienne suspects that Chrystal killed Muriel but Marlowe is not so sure, believing that policeman DeGarmot may be involved. The death of Lavery and the apparent re-appearance of Chrystal lead to a surprising conclusion as to the identity of the lady in the lake and the killer of three people.

The subjective camera technique does, in fact, add to the effectiveness of the mystery story. Because the story is told from Marlowe's point of view, there are generally long scenes in the film, with almost no cuts in the movie except for transitions between scenes. This technique has the effect of emphasizing dialogue and character development, and since there are few intrinsically exciting moments in the film, the technique does not dampen the pace of the story but rather adds to its suspense. Because the subjective technique is unusual, with the viewer never quite knowing what to expect next in terms of visuals, it always keeps the viewer on edge, increasing the tension of the film. It is particularly effective in the scene where Marlowe leaves the Elmore house, spots a car across the street, is tailed by the car and then eventually becomes involved in an automobile accident. The audience almost experiences Marlowe's anxiety as his suspicions about the tailing car increase and the danger of his situation becomes apparent.

The technique also emphasizes the faces of the actors, particularly the face of Audrey Totter, who as Adrienne Fromsett has the most screen time in the movie. She gives an excellent performance in the role, particularly with her very expressive face which is high-

Robert Montgomery plays Philip Marlowe and Audrey Totter plays Adrienne Fromsett in *Lady in the Lake* (1947). This is an obvious publicity photo, as the film is shot from the point of view of Philip Marlowe and his face and body are never shown in this manner in the film. Note the misspelling of Marlowe's first name.

lighted throughout the film. The enigma that is her character is conveyed by the changing expressions of her face, and the audience has the opportunity to closely examine her appearance and the way she talks; but just like Marlowe, the viewer finds it difficult to determine if she is really an honest person or a true femme fatale.

The other acting is superb in the film, down to the smallest parts, such as Lloyd Nolan as dishonest cop Lt. DeGarmot and Tom Tully as tough but honest policeman Captain Kane. A particularly impressive performance is given by Jayne Meadows, first when she masquerades as landlady Mrs. Fallbrook, playing her as a true eccentric, and later in her actual identity as killer Mildred Havelend, with her emotions and character seeming to change every thirty seconds. This is a crucial role in the film and it needed an actress of Meadows' caliber to pull it off.

The story is always intriguing and is never hard to follow, despite the clever plot twists. The one significant storytelling omission is that the important scenes that occur at Little Fawn Lake, which Marlowe visits in person to investigate the lady in the lake, are never shown to the viewer but are only related to the audience after the fact in one of the story interruptions where Marlowe speaks directly to the audience. The film does not quite seem whole without those missing scenes. It is as if the viewer is watching the movie on late-night television and the local channel has cut those scenes from the movie to fit a 90-minute time spot with commercials. This is a serious flaw in the movie, particularly since important facts are learned by Marlowe at the lake.

The subjective camera technique was seldom used again in mystery films, with the first half of *Dark Passage* (1947) being a significant exception. It does start to wear thin on the viewer after a while and could hardly be used over and over again in many other films. Few other mystery movies were shot in long takes with limited cuts, a notable exception being Alfred Hitchcock's *Rope* (1948). But with an already strong plot, clever dialogue and excellent acting, the subjective camera technique complements those attributes and makes *Lady in the Lake* another excellent mystery movie based upon a Raymond Chandler novel.

Note on the Source Material: *The Lady in the Lake* by Raymond Chandler was first published in 1943. As Marlowe says at the beginning of the movie, "It's a good title. It fits." Unfortunately, the title fits the novel much better than the movie, since the events at Little Fawn Lake are related in detail in real time by Marlowe in the book, including the discovery of the body in the lake. As noted above, those scenes are missing from the film. A reading of the novel highlights the detrimental effect on the film of the omission of the Little Fawn Lake scenes from the screenplay.

In the novel, Marlowe is hired by Derace Kingsley, here the owner of a perfume company, to find his missing wife Crystal. (This is a more logical beginning to the story than Adrienne Fromsett hiring Marlowe to locate Derace's wife, which is the premise of the movie.) Marlowe's first stop is at the home of the womanizer Chris Lavery, and then Marlowe is off to Little Fawn Lake, where Crystal was last seen alive. There he meets the caretaker, Bill Chess, whose wife Muriel has been missing for about a month, the same amount of time that Crystal has been gone. Shortly thereafter, Marlowe and Chess find the bloated and unrecognizable body of Muriel Chess in the lake.

Marlowe quickly learns that Muriel Chess is really Mildred Haviland, who was involved in a suspicious death at the home of Dr. Almore, who lives across the street from Lavery. In the course of the book, Marlowe meets Lavery's supposed landlord Mrs. Fallbrook, and then Marlowe discovers the body of Lavery in the shower of Lavery's house. Marlowe then has several run-ins with bad cop Lt. Degarmot of the Bay City police, who was previously married to Haviland. While the killers are the same in each version, in the novel Marlowe exposes Degarmot as the killer of Haviland only after another trip back to Little Fawn Lake where Degarmot meets a violent death.

The movie is based substantially on the Chandler novel. One significant change between novel and film is that in the novel Adrienne Fromsett is a minor character who only appears a few times. In the movie she becomes a significant character, in part to create a love interest for Marlowe. The movie is set around Christmas while the novel takes place in the summer. This gives the movie an interesting flavor, with its tale of murder and illicit love contrasting with the religious season that surrounds it.

In an interesting moment near the end of the book, when Haviland captures Marlowe, the detective tells Haviland that he never liked this scene from the movies where the detective is captured, the murderer explains the whole story to the detective before shooting him, but then the murderer never kills the detective. "Something always happens to prevent it." Of course, that is exactly what happens in the film version so Chandler was somewhat prescient in predicting how Hollywood would handle the filming of his novel.

The Brasher Doubloon (1947)

The Brasher Doubloon is usually considered inferior to the other 1940s Philip Marlowe movies, except by those who dislike the subjective camera technique of *Lady in the Lake*. The obvious problem with the film is the performance of George Montgomery in the lead role. The less obvious problem is the lack of pace in the storytelling. However, *The Brasher Doubloon* does have a strong mystery plot and excellent performances in the supporting roles, and therefore, although it may be the least of the Marlowes, it is still a pretty good film.

As the feature opens, Philip Marlowe arrives at the estate of wealthy widow Elizabeth Murdock, who is considering hiring him for some detective work. The door is opened by Murdock's pretty secretary, Merle Davis, and before Marlowe can meet Mrs. Murdock her son Leslie tries to convince him to leave the mansion. Marlowe persists and is called in to meet Mrs. Murdock, who wants him to locate a valuable coin known as the Brasher Doubloon, which has been stolen from her. Marlowe is inclined to turn down the case because Mrs. Murdock refuses to tell him all she knows about the theft, but Merle's entreaties convince him to continue.

Thereafter, Marlowe meets a number of unusual individuals who are interested in the Brasher Doubloon. They include Eddie Prue, a small-time hood who works for gambler Vince Blair, and coin dealer Elisha Morningstar, who was recently asked to authenticate the coin by a person he will not identify to Marlowe. Death follows upon death, with almost everyone who is after the doubloon being permanently dispatched by person or persons unknown. Marlowe finally realizes that the current set of events and the search for the doubloon are related to the fall out of a high office window five years before by Mrs. Murdock's late husband while he was watching the Tournament of Roses Parade. With that knowledge, Marlowe is able to identify the real killer and clear Merle Davis of all criminal suspicion.

The Brasher Doubloon is filled with wonderful performances in the supporting roles. Florence Bates is terrific as the aging dowager Mrs. Murdock, mean-spirited and villainous, cantankerous and evil. She is well-known to mystery fans for her performance as Mrs. Van Hopper in the early scenes in *Rebecca* (1940), a role somewhat similar to Mrs. Murdock in *The Brasher Doubloon*. Conrad Janis plays Murdock's son Leslie as a diminutive yet flashy character, easy to dislike but not necessarily capable of any of the murders that have been committed. Alfred Linder has a good bit as Eddie Prue, with his scarred face and stitched-closed eye, playing a role similar to that of Wilmer the gunsel in *The Maltese Falcon* (1941), even drawing a gun on Philip Marlowe in Marlowe's office, just as Wilmer once did to Sam Spade. Houseley Stevenson as Elisha Morningstar and Marvin Miller as Vince Blair also stand out in the cast, even though they only have bit parts. All of these actors add a seedy authenticity to of Marlowe's world.

The mystery of the doubloon is always interesting and never trite. The bodies pile up at a rapid rate and just as one character is murdered, a new one appears in a quest for the valuable coin, always keeping the viewer slightly behind the curve in trying to solve the puzzle. The melding of the contemporaneous story of the search for the doubloon with the death of Mr. Murdock in the past is well-handled, also adding a layer of complexity to the narrative. Since this is a hardboiled detective story, the beautiful but seemingly innocent female character whom the detective likes is always a prime suspect. Here Nancy Guild as Merle Davis gives an excellent performance, alternating between flighty and evil, innocent and devious, making it difficult to determine her true character.

Philip Marlowe (George Montgomery) confronts Merle Davis (Nancy Guild), the neurotic secretary to the domineering Mrs. Murdock, in *The Brasher Doubloon* (1947).

The most significant problem with the film is obvious. George Montgomery is a poor choice for the lead role of detective Philip Marlowe. Montgomery seems too young and is probably too handsome for the part. He does not have the gravitas for such an important and serious role, and is never able to convey the weariness of the detective in the hard, cruel world in which he must work. Other movie Marlowes spit out sarcastic dialogue just like Montgomery does in this film, but there was always a hard edge to their sense of humor. Montgomery tends to play the role in a light manner, just the inapposite approach in performing the part of the tough-minded detective.

Director John Brahm's directorial style is inconsistent. Sometimes he employs interesting camera angles, extreme close-ups and long shots to add variety to the film. Other times he employs a mundane directorial technique. As a result, the pace of the movie is very slow, with surprisingly large amounts of down time in a film with multiple murders. A few scenes in the movie are shot in a film noir style. Most scenes, though, are simply staged and shot in a typical Hollywood fashion, unrelated to the substance of the material being presented. Better direction and a more convincing actor in the lead role could have raised this movie to the upper rungs of the 1940s Hollywood mystery movies.

Nevertheless, *The Brasher Doubloon* is an entertaining mystery; it simply suffers in comparison to *Murder, My Sweet* and *The Big Sleep*. If the film had been made in any other mystery series, it would engender substantially more respect. As it is, *The Brasher Doubloon* is the forgotten film of the four 1940s Philip Marlowe mystery movies.

Note on the Source Material: *The Brasher Doubloon* was based on Raymond Chandler's third novel, *The High Window*, published in 1942. The book was previously filmed as *Time to Kill* (1943) in the Michael Shayne series.

In keeping with the practice of the other Philip Marlowe movies from the 1940s, *The Brasher Doubloon* relies heavily on the Chandler novel for its plot, with most of the scenes in the movie coming from the book. Thus, in the novel Elizabeth Murdock hires Marlowe to recover a valuable and rare coin, although unlike the movie, she believes it was stolen by the wife of her son. Along the way, Marlowe meets a number of strange characters who are familiar from the movie, such as Murdock's flighty secretary Merle Davis, her unlike-able son Leslie, and also blackmailer Vannier, coin dealer Elisha Morningstar and hench-man Eddie Prue. The death many years before of Mrs. Murdock's first husband from a fall out of a high window also plays an important part in the story.

There are significant differences between the two works. The plot of the movie has been streamlined from the novel, which contains a number of characters who did not appear in the movie, such as Leslie Murdock's wife Linda Conquest, her former roommate Lois Magic who is married to gambler Alex Morney (Vince Blair in the film), private detective George Phillips (who has just been murdered when Marlowe discovers his body in the film) and the couple who live across the hall from Phillips and who may have been involved in his murder. Also, although the victims are the same in the novel and the film, the identities of the murderers are different. Even though *The High Window* contains one of Raymond Chan-dler's best plots, the movie denouement actually makes more sense, with the Brasher Dou-bloon being better connected to the fall of Mrs. Murdock's husband out of the high window than it was in the novel.

The Brasher Doubloon continues two practices from the other 1940s Marlowe movies. The part of Merle Davis is expanded in the film to give Marlowe somewhat of a love inter-est, with implications of a relationship after the end of the movie. By contrast, at the end of the novel Marlowe takes Merle back to her family in Wichita where she will hopefully be safe from Mrs. Murdock and be able to recover from her emotional problems. In the other Marlowe films, and particularly *The Big Sleep* and *Lady in the Lake*, the parts of female characters in the books are built up in the movies to give Marlowe a love interest. Also, in each of the four Marlowe movies there is more than one killing and they are committed by more than one person. None of the other films, however, exceeded the standard of *The Big Sleep*, with four killings and (apparently) four different killers. In *The Brasher Doubloon*, there are a total of four killings although by only two murderers.

Aftermath

Raymond Chandler continued writing Marlowe novels into the 1950s. His output was not prodigious, as he spent much of his time caring for his invalid wife, and after her death he did little writing as his own health deteriorated. His most famous novel from this time period is *The Long Goodbye* (1953). Chandler died in 1959.

The Marlowe novels have often been adapted to the screen, with James Garner star-ring in *Marlowe* in 1959 (an adaptation of *The Little Sister*), Elliot Gould playing Marlowe in *The Long Goodbye* (1973) and Robert Mitchum playing the detective in two remakes of Chandler novels, *Farewell, My Lovely* (1975) and *The Big Sleep* (1978). The first of the two Mitchum films received good reviews.

Philip Marlowe was also on the radio. Dick Powell reprised his role as Marlowe in "Murder, My Sweet" for Lux Radio Theatre in 1945. (Claire Trevor also reprised her role from the 1944 film.) Powell repeated that performance in a shorter version of the story in 1948 on *Hollywood Star Time*. That same year, Robert Montgomery repeated his screen role as Marlowe in *Lady in the Lake*, also for Lux Radio Theatre. *The Adventures of Philip Marlowe*, starring Van Heflin, was on the air in 1947 on NBC radio. The program only lasted for a few months. The show returned in 1948 to CBS radio, also titled *The Adventures of Philip Marlowe*, with Gerald Mohr in the lead. This version of the show was very popular. It ran for 119 episodes until 1951.

Dick Powell was not only the first person to play Philip Marlowe in the movies and on the radio, he was also the first actor to act the part of Marlowe on television. Powell played Marlowe in "The Long Goodbye," an episode of the live television dramatic anthology series, *Climax*, which ran on CBS in the mid–1950s. The Marlowe episode aired on October 7, 1954. Philip Carey was the first actor to appear as Marlowe on a television series, in a 26-episode program that ran on ABC in 1959 and 1960. Two decades later, in 1983 and 1984, Powers Booth played Marlowe in a series of one-hour adaptations of the Chandler short stories about Marlowe, titled *Philip Marlowe, Private Eye*. There were only 11 episodes of the series, which was shown on HBO.

Jack Packard and Doc Long
I Love a Mystery

With the success of the Crime Doctor and the Whistler movies, each based on a well-known radio show, Columbia decided to create a mystery series based upon one of the most famous radio titles of them all, *I Love a Mystery*. However, rather than employing a star of the stature of a Warner Baxter or a Richard Dix, Columbia went with a relatively unknown actor, Jim Bannon, as the lead detective. That turned out to be a poor decision, and perhaps because there was no star of any renown playing the lead, the series lasted for only three films.

Background

THE RADIO SERIES

I Love a Mystery premiered on the NBC West Coast network on January 16, 1939, and moved to the full network later that year. The broadcasts, produced in Hollywood, were originally daily shows of 15 minutes each in a serial format, although at other times *I Love a Mystery* was a weekly or bi-weekly 30-minute program. The show told the story of three young adventurers who fought on the side of China in its war with Japan. After that war was over, the trio returned to California to set up the A-1 Detective Agency. Although their office was just off Hollywood Boulevard (and one flight up), the detectives could seldom be found in their offices as their cases took them to exotic places all over the world. Unlike other radio detectives of the era, their assignments often seemingly involved the supernatural, such as headless killers, werewolves and vampires.

Jack Packard, who was thrown out of medical school after getting a girl in trouble, was the head of the group. The role was originally performed by Michael Raffetto. Packard was assisted by Doc Long, his Texas-born sidekick who loved women and fights, a role originally played by Barton Yarborough. The third member of the group was Reggie York, a cool Englishman. That role was originally played by Walter Paterson. The shows were created and written by Carleton E. Morse, who was also the creator of a well-known radio family drama, *One Man's Family*.

THE FILM SERIES

The film series was true to the radio series, with each film having a beginning narration and parts of the plot told by sound and dialogue rather than visuals. (Some of these instances will be highlighted in the discussion of the individual movies.) The films also had supernatural themes, such as ancient secret societies, prophecies of death, old dark houses and shrunken heads. Jack Packard and Doc Long were the detectives in the films; the character of Reggie York was eliminated.

Each of the films employed the same production team, including Harry Levin as director. Jack Packard was played by Jim Bannon, a contract player at Columbia who had an undistinguished career in films. He is known today mainly for this series and some B-Westerns in which he played Red Ryder. Bannon did not even receive top billing in the second and third films of the series. Doc Long was played by Barton Yarborough, who originated the role on the radio. Yarborough also had an undistinguished film career and he is better known for his radio work, including a long-running role on Carleton E. Morse's other radio hit, *One Man's Family*.

The Films

I LOVE A MYSTERY (1945)

I Love a Mystery is an excellent start to an unfortunately short-lived film series. The first half of this story seems like an Inner Sanctum mystery, with its tale of a secret cult and a body preserved for hundreds of years. The second half feels more like a Whistler story with twists and turns in the plot and then an ironic conclusion.

The movie commences with a framing story, with the body of Jefferson Monk being whisked in an ambulance to the morgue. His body was decapitated in a traffic accident. In these scenes, the story is carried by the dialogue, with the viewer cleverly learning that the victim is Jefferson Monk and that his head is missing, the latter fact learned when the attendant at the morgue asks how to spell the word "decapitated." (These scenes emulate radio's effective use of dialogue to convey the facts of a story.) The viewer quickly learns that Monk's death fulfilled a prophecy and that Monk died on the exact day predicted.

The rest of the movie is a flashback related by detectives Jack Packard and Doc Long. The history of Monk is told in an internal flashback narrated by Monk (George Macready). Monk and his wife Ellen are traveling in the Orient where he is stalked by a native playing a strange melody on an ancient instrument. Upon returning to San Francisco, his wife is kidnapped and Monk is brought to a hidden temple of an ancient Eastern secret cult where the leader, Dr. G, makes him a strange proposition. The cult will pay Monk $10,000 for his head, to replace the deteriorating head on the body of their cult leader, which has been preserved for hundreds of years. The leader's head looks surprisingly like the head of Jefferson Monk. Dr. G predicts that Monk will die one year from that date and the cult is willing to wait that long to complete the transaction. Monk reluctantly agrees.

As the year anniversary approaches, Monk receives a message from the cult that his wife will become an invalid, and that prediction immediately comes true. Ellen is wheelchair-bound. Monk is also being stalked by a strange peg-legged figure carrying a black valise, which is just the right size for Monk's head. In a restaurant, Monk is approached by a beautiful young lady whose mission appears to be to further agitate the already severely agitated Monk.

This first half of the story plays much like a mild horror film, augmented by the strange melody that stalks Monk, the fantastic meeting with Dr. G and the suspenseful trailing of

This poster illustrates some of the key moments in *I Love a Mystery* (1945) — Jefferson Monk (George Macready) meeting the cult leader who wants his head, the car crash in which Monk is decapitated, and the strange figure stalking Monk. Also shown is Monk's wife, Ellen, played by Nina Foch.

Monk by the peg-legged man. There is also a frightening close up of the severely deformed face of the peg-legged man, adding to the horror.

In the second half of the film, Packard quickly learns that the entire episode was a clever concoction of Monk's wife, Ellen, and five co-conspirators, to cause Monk to commit suicide so that Ellen can receive his inheritance. Indeed, Ellen has no trouble walking. Around that same time, Monk also figures out the plot against him and starts to kill the conspirators one by one. This leads to Monk attempting to kill Packard. In Monk's desperate attempt at escape, his fast-moving car crashes, Monk is killed and the body is beheaded. However, no one is able to find the head.

This is a very entertaining story, with just the right balance of horror and mystery. It is aided considerably by the performance of George Macready as Monk, particularly when he is narrating a long flashback in his cultured voice. Barton Yarborough as Doc is always interesting, particularly when he speaks in his long Texas drawl. Harry Levin does a competent job directing the story, particularly in one of the later scenes where Monk is about to kill Packard, who is sitting at a piano. There are interesting framing shots of Packard in the triangular space between the piano and the lid and Monk's gun in the foreground, all presaging how Packard will effectuate his escape.

Jefferson Monk (George Macready, left) introduces his perhaps invalid wife, Ellen Monk (Nina Foch, seated), to Jack Packard (Jim Bannon, near right) and Doc Long (Barton Yarborough, far right) in *I Love a Mystery* (1945) as Nurse Osgood (Isabel Withers) looks on.

The weak spot in the film is Jim Bannon's performance as Jack Packard. He is unable to convey the depth of experience and knowledge that Packard must have had to solve the case. It is hard to believe that this lug would recognize a strange Oriental melody as actually coming from a Tchaikovsky symphony, be able to speak Russian to trick a suspect, or know how the ancient Orientals created their portraits. Where is Philo Vance when you need him? Other mystery series of the 1940s, even though they were usually B-movies, generally used actors of some stature, such as Basil Rathbone, Warren William, Richard Dix or Warner Baxter. Jim Bannon does not fit the bill.

Nevertheless, this story is always fascinating, with enough surprises to keep the viewer interested. It is highly recommended.

Note on the Source Material: "The Decapitation of Jefferson Monk" (also known as "The Head of Jefferson Monk") was a multi-episode continuity that originally ran on the radio in the *I Love a Mystery* series from August 30, 1943, through October 1, 1943. In all, there were 25 episodes in the story, each of which was 15 minutes in length. That means that the entire story, including openings, closings and commercials, ran for well over six hours. Since the movie was about 70 minutes in length, obviously much of the plot of the radio drama had to be condensed for the film.

Nevertheless, the two stories were substantially similar. One change is that on the radio show, Doc did much of the investigation himself. There were four killings in the radio broadcasts as contrasted with only three in the movie. Also, Ellen Monk, played by Mercedes McCambridge, has a stroke at the end of the radio show when she hears about her husband's decapitation. Thus, in an ironic ending, she will remain an invalid for the rest of her life. That incident, which is a very clever twist, was not shown in the film.

When the second run of the serial began in 1949, "The Decapitation of Jefferson Monk" was one of the stories that was re-done. Once again, it ran for 25 15-minute episodes, this time from March 10, 1952, to April 1, 1952.

The Devil's Mask (1946)

For the second film in the series, the writers developed another story based on decapitation, which in this case is a shrunken head discovered in the wreckage of a plane crash. That brings Captain Quinn of the San Francisco police to a local museum for advice. There, Captain Quinn coincidentally runs into Jack Packard and Doc Long, who are waiting to meet a new client, Louise Mitchell, the wife of the museum director, Quentin Mitchell, who recently disappeared on a South American expedition. Louise's stepdaughter Janet believes that Louise and another colleague, Dr. Logan, were having an affair and that the two killed Quentin Mitchell on the safari. Janet has enlisted her boyfriend, Rex Kennedy, to follow her stepmother, apparently to harass her.

The opening highlights the problem with this mystery — its lack of cohesion or logic. The only reason the screenplay has Louise meet Packard and Long at the museum is so the detectives can learn about the shrunken head, which will later become integral to the whereabouts of Quentin Mitchell. Indeed, right after that encounter, Louise invites the detectives to her house, so why not do that in the first place? Another strange plot point is that Packard and Long are hired by Louise to protect her, but instead they spend most of the movie protecting Janet. Events follow events for no reason, other than to allow Packard and Long to get closer to the truth concerning Mitchell's disappearance.

During the course of the movie, the viewers meet Arthur Logan, who shows slides of the expedition, including one of Quentin Mitchell with a blowgun; Dr. Karger, a neurologist with a shady and unethical past; and taxidermist Leon Hartman, who is like an uncle to Janet, even though he keeps a large panther caged in his offices. Rex Kennedy's bona fides are questioned by all involved. There is a suspenseful moment in the middle of the film when a blowgun dart is shot at Logan at the Mitchell house, and subsequently, the butler is killed with another arrow from the blowgun. Janet believes her father may be alive (and also be a killer) because the family dog, in a homage to Sherlock Holmes, did not bark when the blowgun killer arrived.

In the end the least likely suspect, Leon Hartman, an animal rights enthusiast, turns out to be the killer. His twisted motive is that when Quentin Mitchell went on expeditions, he killed innocent animals and then had Hartman stuff them, which apparently greatly irritated Hartman over the years. The explanation as to why Hartman shrunk Mitchell's head and was sending it out of the country at the beginning of the film is unconvincing. There is no explanation as to why Hartman tried to kill Logan at the Mitchell house, other than to create an exciting moment in a film that desperately needed one.

The film is shot in a noir style, with shadows from artificial light or with faces of the actors in the dark even when they are speaking. But this is not a noir film, because it is missing noir characters. This is just a straightforward mystery, with a heroic detective, mul-

In ***The Devil's Mask*** (1946), the investigations of Jack Packard (Jim Bannon, center) and Doc Long (Barton Yarborough, right) lead to the strange taxidermy office of Leon Hartman (Paul E. Burns).

tiple suspects and several red herrings. The noir style actually conflicts with the whodunit nature of the piece and may even detract from the effectiveness of the mystery elements.

The best part of the movie is when Hartman releases his panther to kill Packard. Packard escapes behind a closed door and it is Hartman who is mauled by the panther. Packard narrates the events from behind the door, trying to frighten Hartman, and the effect is that Packard becomes the narrator of the movie, as if the story were still being done on radio. This is an effective scene and once again illustrates how suspense could be created on the radio by clever use of dialogue.

Anita Louise as Janet is quite awful in the role. She has no ability to convey differing emotions, and when toward the middle of the film she is trying to explain her doubts about Kennedy, her father and her stepmother, the performance creates a cringe in the audience. Packard solves the case because he is familiar with the poem "The Rime of the Ancient Mariner." Luckily, this was not a Sam Spade or Boston Blackie movie, or the crime would never have been solved. Packard is surely one of the best-educated detectives of all time.

THE UNKNOWN (1946)

This is the strangest movie in this very strange three-movie mystery series. The long opening segment is narrated by Phoebe Martin (once again acknowledging its radio origins) as the camera comes through the gate and pans around the Southern mansion of the Martin family, which seems to have fallen on hard times. This evokes memories of the beginning of *Rebecca* (1940) — "Last night I dreamt I went to Manderley again." With a mad woman lurking around the old house, it is hard not to recall *Jane Eyre*, and with an old mansion, strange passageways and lurking figures, the silent, old dark house mystery film *Cat and the Canary* (1927) quickly comes to mind.

The story starts in the past, at the engagement party of young Rachel Martin, who is set to marry the aristocratic and wealthy James Wetherford. Unfortunately, Rachel is already married to a much more common fellow, Richard Arnold. When Rachel's father Captain Selby Martin finds out, he pulls a gun on young Arnold. In the ensuing struggle, Captain Martin is shot and killed. Rachel's tyrannical mother, Phoebe Martin, orders Arnold from the house at the threat of prosecution for murder, and then has Captain Selby's body walled up behind the fireplace in his study.

This is a good opening sequence for the film, giving *The Unknown* a different flavor from most mysteries of the era, almost as if the film were an adaptation of a classic gothic novel. What is also unusual about this opening is that the film shows actual scenes in the past rather than having the characters merely talk about them. It was rare for 1940s series mystery movie to spend the time and effort to do that.

The main story begins many years later at the time of Phoebe's death. Rachel is grown up and gone mad, first at the loss of her husband and second at the loss of a baby girl she had with Martin, the baby having been taken from her at any early age. Rachel has two brothers who also do not seem to have everything together, as there appears to be a touch of insanity throughout the entire household. The grown child, Nina Arnold, comes to the house for the reading of Phoebe's will. Nina is accompanied by Jack Packard and Doc Long, who have been hired to protect her. Along the way, the viewer meets the young attorney who has been called to the house to read the will, and the faithful family servant Joshua who has been with the family throughout its troubles. Then partway through the movie,

Mr. Arnold returns. Thus there are a number of potential suspects for whatever crime might be committed.

The will disappears, brother Edward is killed, Nina is pushed down some stairs, and in a major surprise, Phoebe Martin turns up alive. She has arranged her fake death to right the wrongs of many years before, in an attempt to reunite Rachael, Nina and Arnold. However, Phoebe's plans go astray, she is killed, and the murderer turns out to be brother Ralph, who was indeed insane, just like most of the rest of the family.

This mystery is always interesting, punctuated by excellent performances by Karen Morley as Rachel Martin Arnold and Helen Freeman as Phoebe Martin. Also, J. Louis Johnson as Joshua is stately and cultured as the family servant. It is an excellent role for an African American, as he is treated with respect by all and he has a pivotal role in the story. The writing puts to shame the other mystery movies of the era that used African American characters for comic relief and not much more.

Packard and Long have relatively small roles in the movie, and probably for that reason Jim Bannon gives his best performance in the series as Packard. With secret passages, walks through crypts in the dark, hooded figures and ghostly children's cries in the night, this is an excellent example of an old dark house mystery. It is a shame that there were not more films in this short-lived mystery series.

Afterwards

After the I Love a Mystery series ended, Jim Bannon appeared in some B-Westerns and then made numerous guest appearances on television. He died in 1984. Barton Yarborough eventually appeared on the radio as Jack Webb's partner in *Dragnet* and continued with the show when it moved to television in 1951. However, after filming just two episodes, Yarborough became ill and died four days later.

The radio show *I Love a Mystery* ended its initial run in California in 1944. The show then moved to New York in 1949 and stayed on the air into 1952, reusing the scripts from the Hollywood run. Tony Randall played Reggie Yorke in this new series of adventures. A made-for-television movie titled *I Love a Mystery* aired in 1973 with Les Crane as Jack Packard, David Hartman as Doc and Hagen Beggs as Reggie. It was supposed to be a pilot for a television series but the quality was so poor that the movie was not broadcast until several years after it was made. Thus no television series was produced.

Steve Wilson
and Lorelei Kilbourne
The Big Town Reporters

With a few exceptions, such as Geoffrey Homes' Robin Bishop, a Los Angeles news-paperman who investigated crimes in books published in the 1930s, newspaper reporters did not often double as detectives in early crime fiction. In fact, the most famous reporter-detective of them all is probably Lois Lane of *The Daily Planet,* and she had her origin in the Superman comic books beginning in the late 1930s and not in any mystery novels or short stories.

In movies, however, it was not unusual for reporters to become the lead investigators in a crime film. A prime example was Torchy Blane, a female newspaper reporter who always seemed to become involved in the investigation of a murder, in a mystery series from Warner Brothers which began in the 1930s. There were also the Roving Reporters who investigated crime in a three-movie series from Twentieth Century–Fox in the late 1930s. Other non-series examples occurred in *Mystery of the Wax Museum* (1933) and *Call North-side 777* (1948).

In 1947, independent studio Pine-Thomas Productions began a series of films about a big city newspaper whose managing editor and reporters often became involved in crime investigations in order to obtain a good story. While the four films in the series are not well-known today, as a group they provide an interesting if unrealistic look at the lives and challenges of reporters on the crime beat for a great metropolitan newspaper.

Background

THE RADIO SERIES

The *Big Town* radio series debuted on CBS on October 19, 1937. It told the stories of Steve Wilson, the crusading managing editor of *The Illustrated Press,* and Lorelei Kilbourne, society editor and sometimes crime reporter for the newspaper, in their racket-busting adventures in a great United States city known only as Big Town. The first cast of the show was particularly illustrious, with Edward G. Robinson playing Steve Wilson and Claire Trevor playing Lorelei Kilbourne. The two would later appear together in *The Amazing Dr. Clitterhouse* (1938) and then in *Key Largo* (1948), for which Trevor would win an Oscar for Best Supporting Actress. Ona Munson replaced Trevor in some of the later Robinson episodes. During the Robinson years, the shows were broadcast from Hollywood.

Beginning in 1943, the production moved to New York City. Broadway actor Edward Pawley was cast as Steve Wilson and Fran Carlton played Lorelei Kilbourne. At this time the show became hugely popular, and at one point was rated the top crime show on the radio.

The radio series was written by Jerry McGill, an ex-newspaperman. Each episode started with a newsboy shouting some variation of "Extra, extra, extra, get your *Illustrated Press*," and then tying the headline of the newspaper into the story of that week's episode. The stories promoted freedom of the press, in the process creating a memorable catch phrase: "The power and the freedom of the press is a flaming sword. Use it justly. Hold it high. Guard it well."

THE FILM SERIES

Given the popularity of the radio series, it was natural that a film series be made about Big Town. However, none of the major studios came up with the idea and the film series was finally developed at an independent studio, Pine-Thomas Productions. The Big Town film series is as much about newspapers as it is about crime, but there is enough mystery or emphasis on criminal activities in each film that the series is clearly a mystery movie series.

The films relate the adventures of Steve Wilson, the managing editor of *The Illustrated Press*, and his favorite reporter, Lorelei Kilbourne, as they investigate crime and other newsworthy stories in the big city. Although none of the catch phrases of the radio show are incorporated into the films, the film series generally follows the format of the radio show.In the first film in the series, *Big Town*, the viewer learns how Steve becomes the managing editor of the newspaper, how he first meets Lorelei, and the changes the two make to the stories that *The Illustrated Press* covers. Later movies in the series involve murders, extortion, gambling syndicates and the like.

Philip Reed plays Steve Wilson in all four films in the series. Reed was an unfamiliar face to movie fans in the late 1940s, even though he had been appearing in films since the early 1930s. Born in 1908 in New York City, Reed appeared in a few other mystery films during his career, such as *The Case of the Curious Bride* (1935) and *Song of the Thin Man* (1947), but he is best known today for his appearances in the Big Town series.

On the other hand, Hillary Brooke, who plays Lorelei Kilbourne in all four films, is very familiar to movie mystery fans. Born in Astoria, New York, in 1914, the usually blonde actress affected a British accent in many of her films. Brooke was a regular performer in 1940s mystery series, had small or uncredited parts in several major films, and had an occasional featured part in a major production such as *Road to Utopia* (1946) with Bob Hope and Bing Crosby.

There are a few other regulars in the series. Robert Lowery plays reporter Pete Ryan in two of the films. While Lowery appeared in over a hundred films in his career, he is probably best known today for playing Batman in the 1949 serial *Batman and Robin*. Charles Arndt plays newspaper publisher Amos Peabody in three of the films. Arndt also appeared in over a hundred films in his career, usually in small character parts, many times in films from a mystery movie series. Character actor Vince Barnett plays Louis Sneed, a bail bondsman who provides needed information to Lorelei in three of the films. Barnett appeared in a number of mystery movies over the years, even playing Goldy Locke in *The Falcon's Alibi* (1946). He is perhaps best remembered today for playing small-time hood Charleston in the film noir classic *The Killers* (1946).

The Films

BIG TOWN (1947)

This is a mildly interesting tale of the metamorphosis of a big city (or big town) newspaper from a stodgy daily with no pictures on the front page and boring stories throughout, to a vibrant rag with big headlines, stylish front pages and investigative features, to a tabloid that practices a form of yellow journalism, to a paper that promises to become a crusader against evil in the city. The catalyst for these transformations is Steve Wilson, who is brought on board as managing editor of *The Illustrated Press*, one of Big Town's two newspapers, to increase its circulation. He does so and in the process his paper solves some crimes and Wilson gets a life lesson in the ethics of journalism.

The movie develops in several story arcs, as the newspaper's reporters investigate various potential news items. The first arc involves a young girl found dead of a heart attack

In *Big Town* (1947), Editor Steve Wilson (Philip Reed) gives Lorelei Kilbourne (Hillary Brooke) an assignment concerning a woman found dead in a state senator's hotel room.

in a senator's office. Wilson publicizes the story over the objections of Lorelei Kilbourne, a friend of the family. Next the newspaper solves the crime of a female sharpshooter who robbed a movie theatre. Then the newspaper prepares an exposé of dishonesty and negligence at the local amusement park. Finally, *The Illustrated Press* talks up a series of murders of young women, dubs them the "vampire murders" and harasses a suspect about the crimes. The suspect turns out to be innocent, and his death causes Steve Wilson to reconsider his managerial approach for the paper.

The most interesting story arc involves the female sharpshooter. The police and the competing newspaper, *The Chronicle*, believe the criminal is male. *The Illustrated Press* sticks by its story that the villain is a woman, because Lorelei found a lipstick case at the scene of a gun battle between the suspect and the police. The byplay between the two newspapers and the police on this topic is quite interesting and the vignette is topped off by an excellent performance by Veda Ann Borg as Vivian LeRoy, a professional sharpshooter who decided to use her shooting skills in a life of crime.

It is interesting to see Hillary Brooke in a starring role in a 1940s mystery movie. She played a number of supporting roles in films in other mystery series of the 1940s, such as a prime villain in *The Woman in Green* (1945) from the Sherlock Holmes series, and a small part as the female lead in *Counter-Espionage* (1942) from the Lone Wolf series. Brooke is

Vance Crane (Byron Barr, center) has been arrested for the murder of a young girl and is now being questioned by Chief Masters (Harry Cheshire) in *Big Town* (1947). Reporters Lorelei Kilbourne (Hillary Brooke) and Pete Ryan (Robert Lowery), on the left, believe Crane is innocent.

fine in the movie, although the part hardly taxed her acting skills. The rest of the cast is also good, if not outstanding, with Philip Reed competent enough in the lead role of Steve Wilson.

The problem with the film is in the writing. If the purpose of the film was to be a denunciation of yellow journalism, the movie takes a long time getting there. For the first several story arcs, while the paper may be overplaying the manner in which it presents some of the stories in print, its actions do not seem all that bad and are usually quite justified. Surely the paper went overboard on its coverage of the "vampire murders," but the connection between that story and the concept of yellow journalism seems to come out of nowhere. There are legitimate issues raised by the film about the manner in which the press covers stories and its effects on individuals caught up in the news, but those issues are not addressed in a sophisticated manner. None of the nuances of what aggressive journalism is versus what yellow journalism is are discussed and debated.

On the other hand, this is just a B-movie about the inner workings of a metropolitan newspaper. Perhaps it is not proper to overanalyze a low-budget film that is nothing more than an attempt to recreate some aspects of big town journalism, with a few crime stories thrown into the mix. If that is all the film was striving for, then on that basis *Big Town* is a mildly enjoyable film and provides an interesting look at life on a big town newspaper.

I Cover Big Town (1947)

[This is one of the two movies discussed in this book the author did not personally view.]

This second film in the series brought back the three main performers from the first film. Philip Reed plays managing editor Steve Wilson, Hillary Brooke plays newspaper reporter Lorelei Kilbourne and Robert Lowery returns as reporter Pete Ryan, although in this film Ryan is working for a competing newspaper. *I Cover Big Town* seems to be more crime-oriented than the prior movie, with *The Illustrated Press* helping the police solve the murder of a body found in a trunk, among other incidents.

Big Town After Dark (1947)

Big Town after Dark is a great title for a mystery movie. It promises a noir tale of crime and corruption, impure motives and devious actions, set (as Raymond Chandler once wrote) on streets that are dark with something more than night. What a disappointing film *Big Town after Dark* actually is. With a flimsy plot, pedestrian direction and indifferent acting, the film never delivers anything that the title promises. If you cannot tell a book by its cover, you surely cannot tell a mystery movie by its title.

After receiving news that her first novel is about to be published and after a small disagreement with managing editor Steve Wilson, Lorelei Kilbourne decides to leave *The Illustrated Press*. In order to make Lorelei jealous so that she will not actually leave when her two-weeks' notice is up, Steve hires Susan Peabody, the niece of the owner, to take her place as the paper's crime reporter. Susan convinces Steve to investigate the Winners' Club, a gambling hall located just out of town, and perhaps write a series of exposés so that all the gambling halls in the area are closed down. At the club, Steve gets into an altercation during a poker match and is beaten up. He wakes up the next day in the hospital, only to find Susan missing, possibly having been kidnapped.

Indeed, Chuck LaRue, the owner of the Winner's Club, is blackmailing Peabody for the return of his niece by a clever scheme that appears to be legal. He forces Amos Peabody to buy stock in the club for $50,000, without explicitly stating that the payment is for the release of Susan. Once LaRue deposits the check he is immediately arrested, but he is then quickly released when Susan shows up and denies that she was kidnapped. Steve and Lorelei are both suspicious, and separately each start to investigate Susan, leading to the final capture of LaRue, the recovery of the $50,000 and the death of two of the villains.

The plot of the film meanders from topic to topic, without any significant development of any of the story elements and with several questions left unanswered. Was the Winners' Club an honest gambling hall or did it cheat its customers? Was Susan really having an affair with Jake Sebastian, her college boyfriend? How did Susan and LaRue expect to get away with the extortion, when it was obvious to everyone that Susan was involved in the scheme once she turned up unharmed?

If this were the first film in the series, the whole extortion story would have been one of three or four stories covered in the film, each perhaps involving 15 minutes of screen time. Here, the story of Susan's kidnapping stretches out to 70 minutes, making for very dull going. Even the final scene, involving the killing of two of the characters and a last minute save of Steve Wilson's life, lacks any suspense.

The direction is particularly poor. There are very few close-ups in the film. Most people are shot in medium two-shots or from even longer distances, and the lack of shot variety adds to the tedium of the movie. Scenes often linger on for a few seconds too long, such as Loreliei and Susan leaving the press room but then being shown in the hallway walking to the elevator. Most films would have cut directly to the elevator to keep the pace of the film moving. This failure to quickly cut from scene to scene, which occurs several other times in the film, drags an otherwise boring movie down even further.

Big Town after Dark has a great 1940s femme fatale in Susan Peabody, surely as duplicatus and conniving as other female icons of 1940s film noir. Unfortunately, Susan is played by Anne Gillis, a 20-year-old actress of limited range and just about no allure. She is clearly too young for the role and she is wholly inadequate for the part of a woman who has supposedly turned the heads of three men while at the same time working to stick a knife in their respective backs. While *Big Town after Dark* is merely a second feature, this part still required an actress of some stature, or at least some ability. Where are Claire Trevor, Barbara Stanwyck or Ava Gardner when you need them?

While the plot is weak, a little bit of innovation in the direction could have gone a long way into improving the effectiveness of this feature, and a better actress in the role of Susan Peabody could have turned the film around. Without those attributes, *Big Town after Dark* is a second-feature programmer of little merit.

BIG TOWN SCANDAL (1948)

The star of this film, Stanley Clements, started his career playing Stash, one of the East Side Kids, a gang of juvenile delinquents who were an offshoot of the original Dead End Kids. The East Side Kids tended to get involved in low-grade melodramas with some criminal aspects to them and usually with a life lesson to be learned at the end of the film. Since that is a fairly succinct summary of the plot of *Big Town Scandal*, Clements was a natural to cast in this film as juvenile delinquent Tommy Malone. Indeed, Clements is the true star of *Big Town Scandal*, as he has substantially more screen time than the purported stars, Philip Reed and Hillary Brooke, who are shunted off to the side of the story.

The film opens with a gang of juvenile delinquents attempting to rob a sporting goods store but being caught by the police. One of the youths is the nephew of bail bondsman Louie Sneed, who convinces Lorelei Kilbourne to come with him and attend the group's hearing in a judge's chambers. There, in order to avoid having all the youngsters sent to reform school, Lorelei volunteers Steve Wilson as a substantial public citizen who will take custody of the kids. Steve is tricked into agreeing to this implausible situation (given that he is single and probably lives in a small apartment), but later becomes enthusiastic about the arrangement when he realizes it could be the basis for an interesting series of newspaper articles. Frankly, it is all pretty silly stuff.

One of the youths, Tommy Malone, gets involved with two low-grade hoods who are using the garage of the recreation building of *The Illustrated Press* to store stolen goods. Tommy is assisting them with the contraband, leading others to wonder where he gets all the dough he seems to have. Tommy gets involved deeper and deeper in the racket, requiring him to throw the basketball game of the newspaper's amateur team, known as the Big Town Big Shots. That leads to a semi-exciting conclusion, when Tommy must decide whether to throw another basketball game or risk getting literally shot on the court.

This story really did belong in one of the East Side Kids or Little Tough Guy Kids movies that were made in the 1940s, although their popularity was waning by the time *Big Town Scandal* was made. Interest had moved to the Bowery Boys style of film, and indeed Clements made some appearances in those films, replacing Leo Gorcey near the end of that series, in the middle 1950s. Clements is fine in *Big Town Scandal*, but at the age of 22 he was just about ending his run in this type of movie.

This is just an average film, inappropriate for the Big Town series, which was popular on radio for adults. Indeed, the first three films in the series were geared to adults. It is simply not clear why this movie, which is geared to children, was made. Were there not some better stories from the radio show that could have been adapted into the fourth film in the series?

There is some interest to the film, but it is unrelated to the quality of the movie. Some of the youths are played by Darryl Hickman (a child performer in a number of A-productions in the 1940s, such as *The Grapes of Wrath* [1940]), and Carl "Alfalfa" Switzer and Tommy Bond (from the *Our Gang* comedies). It is interesting to see them in films when they are a little bit older than in their most famous screen performances. There is a lot of basketball shown, and it is interesting to see the difference in the game then and now, with the jump shot apparently not being invented by the time of *Big Town Scandal* and free throws attempted with underhand shots. One of the Big Town Big Shot's opponents is named the Big Town Scrubs, so maybe the word "scrubs" had a different meaning then than it does now; but would anyone really want to play on a team called The Scrubs?

This is a true low-budget film, with the sporting goods store the boys burglarize early on looking substantially like the fur store they attempt to enter at the end of the film. Most of the action in the film is confined to the basketball court, and even there the games are low-scoring and slow-moving. In fact, that is an accurate and concise description of this film: low-scoring and slow-moving.

Afterwards

The *Big Town* radio series stayed on the air until 1952, long after the movie series ended. In the last few episodes of the show, Walter Greaza took over the role of Steve Wilson.

While the radio show was still on the air, *Big Town* came to television. The show first aired on CBS from 1950 to 1954, with the first two seasons done live from New York City. It ended its television run on NBC, from 1955 to 1956. Reruns of the shows were broadcast under different names: *City Assignment, Heart of the City, Headline* and *Byline Steve Wilson.*

Much like the movies, the television show was about Big Town's big newspaper, *The Illustrated Press,* and the reporters that worked there. The managing editor of the paper was Steve Wilson, played by Patrick McVey during the first four years of the series and then by Mark Stevens from 1954 to 1956. Five actresses played the part of Lorelei Kilbourne over the show's long run.

While there were no more movies made about Big Town, there was a comic book issued by DC Comics. It ran for 50 issues, beginning in January 1951. The stories were similar in tone to the radio show and movie series.

Philip Reed appeared in a few movies after the Big Town series ended, but most of his subsequent work was in television. He died in 1996. Hillary Brooke also appeared in a few films after the series ended, such as essaying a small part in Alfred Hitchcock's *The Man Who Knew Too Much* (1956), but most of Brooke's subsequent work was also in television. She will never be forgotten for the year she spent on *The Abbott and Costello Show* (1952–1953) playing the comedian's attractive neighbor, named, oddly enough, "Hillary Brooke." The actress died in 1999.

19

John J. Malone
The Attorney Detective

As the radio show *Murder and Mr. Malone* opens, the narrator of the program refers to John J. Malone as "fiction's most famous criminal lawyer." That is a difficult claim to uphold, given the success of Erle Stanley Gardner's criminal defense attorney Perry Mason, but for a time John J. Malone was quite a popular star of crime fiction. At one time, author Craig Rice's sales purportedly rivaled those of Agatha Christie, leading to Rice appearing on the cover of the June 28, 1946 issue of *Time Magazine*, which featured an article on the mystery genre. Rice is the only mystery writer ever to receive that honor. So while Perry Mason is still a readily recognized figure today, and John J. Malone is essentially forgotten, Malone was popular enough in the 1940s to spawn three movies about the character.

Background

THE NOVELS AND SHORT STORIES

Female mystery writer Craig Rice (Georgiana Ann Randolph) was born in 1908 in Chicago, Illinois. She had a difficult childhood, usually living in the care of her aunt, Mrs. Elton Rice, from whom she took her pseudonym. Rice turned to writing mysteries after attempting unsuccessfully to write straight novels, poetry and music. She published her first John J. Malone mystery in 1939, eventually producing a total of twelve Malone novels and some short stories. She also became a publicity agent and a screenwriter, contributing two screenplays to The Falcon series.

Although Rice wrote about other detectives, her most famous creation is John J. Malone, a Chicago attorney who has a predilection for both women and the bottle. Despite those weaknesses, Malone is still one of the best trial lawyers in the city. As Malone puts it, he never lost a client. Malone is friends with Helene Brand, an attractive socialite, and Jake Justus, a press agent. In the early novels, Helene and Jake are trying to get married but murder intervenes, dragging Malone into another crime investigation. Indeed, the early stories were just as much about Helene and Jake as they were about Malone. Other regulars in the series include Maggie Cassidy, Malone's loyal secretary, and Daniel von Flanagan, the head of the homicide squad. Eventually, Helene and Jake got married.

Stuart Palmer was a good friend of Craig Rice's and fellow mystery writer. They worked together on the screenplay for *The Falcon's Brother* (1942), the famous film in which the original Falcon played by George Sanders was killed, and his brother played by Tom Conway replaced him in the series. Palmer is most famous as the author of fourteen detective novels involving Miss Hildegard Withers, a schoolteacher and amateur detective, who along with her friend and foil Inspector Oscar Piper of the New York City Police Department solved a number of puzzling murder mysteries. Withers and Piper were the subjects of a six-film mystery series in the 1930s released by RKO.

Starting in the late 1940s, Rice and Palmer collaborated on six short stories for *Ellery Queen's Mystery Magazine* that teamed Withers and Malone in the investigation of a crime. The stories were later collected in *People vs. Withers and Malone* (1963). One of those stories, "Once upon a Train," was the basis for the third film in the Malone series, *Mrs. O'Malley and Mr. Malone*.

THE FILM SERIES

The first film to feature attorney-detective John J. Malone was *Having Wonderful Crime*, a 1945 film released by RKO. In addition to Malone solving the death of a disappearing magician, Helene and Jake Justus appear, just married and trying to celebrate their honeymoon. Pat O'Brien essayed the role of John J. Malone. O'Brien was a star for many years at Warner Brothers, appearing in a number of gangster films such as *Angels with Dirty Faces* (1938), almost always playing a priest, a warden or other person on the right side of the law. However, O'Brien's best remembered film role is that of the most famous college football coach of all time in *Knute Rockne, All American* (1940).

The second Malone film was *The Lucky Stiff*, a 1949 production from United Artists. Here, Malone solves the death of a nightclub owner who was involved in the rackets. The Justuses are not in this movie but two other characters from the novels, Malone's secretary Maggie Cassidy and Inspector Von Flanagan, have significant roles. John J. Malone is played by Brian Donlevy, a familiar face to moviegoers who had been in films since the silent era. While Donlevy had appeared in a number of crime films over the years, such as *The Glass Key* (1942) and *Kiss of Death* (1947), he is best remembered today for his starring role in a Preston Sturges comedy, *The Great McGinty* (1940), playing the title character, a role he would reprise in *The Miracle of Morgan's Creek* (1944).

As noted above, MGM decided to produce a film series on the collaboration between schoolteacher Hildegard Withers and attorney John J. Malone as set forth in the six stories jointly written by Stuart Palmer and Craig Rice. The studio purchased two of the stories, and in 1950 released *Mrs. O'Malley and Mr. Malone*, which was based on the 1950 short story "Once Upon a Train." While the character of John Malone was consistent with the manner in which the attorney was portrayed in the short stories, the character of schoolteacher Hildegard Withers was replaced with Mrs. O'Malley, a hillbilly character from Montana.

Mrs. O'Malley is played by Marjorie Main, well known at the time for playing Ma Kettle in the *Ma and Pa Kettle* films, starting with *The Egg and I* (1947), for which Main was nominated for an Academy Award as best supporting actress. The Mrs. O'Malley character was written in the style of Ma Kettle, seemingly a country hick, so perhaps that is why Marjorie Main was chosen for the role. Main could, however, be an actress of some depth. She is particularly well-remembered for playing Humphrey Bogart's mother in *Dead End* (1937), a small but significant role in the film.

The third John J. Malone of the screen was James Whitmore, the youngest actor to portray the part in films. Whitmore began appearing in films in 1949, receiving an Oscar nomination for best supporting actor for *Battleground* (1949), his second screen appearance. He also played one of the villains in the famous crime film *The Asphalt Jungle* (1950), before appearing in *Mrs. O'Malley and Mr. Malone.*

Despite the expectation of producing a mystery series based on the characters of O'Malley and Malone, no sequel was ever made. By 1950, the Hollywood mystery movie series had substantially come to an end. Interestingly, the three films about Malone have completely different versions of the Craig Rice stories, with Helene and Jake Justus playing prominent roles in *Having Wonderful Crime* (1945), Malone then becoming the central character in the story in *The Lucky Stiff* (1949) and Malone teaming with a Hildegard Withers-type character in *Mrs. O'Malley and Mr. Malone* (1950).

The Films

HAVING WONDERFUL CRIME (1945)

If a mystery movie is employed as the framework for something else, it is important that the mystery elements themselves be intriguing, perhaps suspenseful, but surely mysterious. For example, a murder mystery was used to explore anti–Semitism in the 1947 film *Crossfire*, and racism in the 1967 film *In the Heat of the Night*. Those films were successful, not only for the important subject matters addressed therein, but also because they never forgot to tell a good mystery story. Mystery and detective plots can also be the framework for a good comedy film. In that regard, the gold standard is the Red Skelton comedy *Whistling in the Dark* (1941), which had an interesting mystery and a suspenseful conclusion, even though it was primarily a comedy. The same principle works for comedy-horror films. *Abbott and Costello Meet Frankenstein* (1948) and *Young Frankenstein* (1974) are excellent comedies, partially because the horror scenes are handled so honestly and effectively.

Having Wonderful Crime never purports to be more than a screwball comedy with mystery interruptions, similar to the "Whistling" movies starring Red Skelton; but the filmmakers never understood that it was important to start with a solid mystery on which the comedy would be based. As a result *Having Wonderful Crime* can be slightly funny at times and therefore has some interest for those who like silly movies with engaging stars. However, for those mystery fans who are open to watching a comedy so long as it has engrossing mystery elements, *Having Wonderful Crime* is not the film to view.

The mystery in *Having Wonderful Crime* is flimsy at best. A magician has disappeared for real while performing a disappearing act on stage. Attorney James J. Malone and his two friends, newlyweds Jake and Helene Justus, flee the theater so as not to become involved in the investigation. They drive to the Lenhart Lodge, where the Justuses intend to celebrate their honeymoon. On the way, they coincidentally become involved in a car accident with Gilda Mayfair, the magician's assistant, and offer her a lift to the lodge, since she is coincidentally going to the same place they are. Malone and the Justuses believe, for no apparent reason, that the magician's body may be in Gilda's trunk, but when they finally open the trunk, it only contains the magician's props. Inside one of the props they also find a check for $50,000 made out to the magician, written by Elizabeth Lenhart, coincidentally one of the owners of the Lodge. Belying the whole crime element, the magician then appears in person, so where is the mystery?

In *Having Wonderful Crime* (1945), Helene Justus (Carole Landis) opens the trunk of Movel the Magician, expecting to find a dead body therein, as Jake Justus (George Murphy, left) and John J. Malone (Pat O'Brien) look on.

Of course the magician does end up dead later, and of course his body is found in the trunk, so Malone and his friends set out to solve the crime. That they do, but without making any serious investigation and in the process, jumping to wild conclusions which, surprisingly, turn out to be accurate. The motive for the crime and the identity of the murderer make little sense and there is absolutely no suspense at the end of the film, even though the trio of investigators is almost killed. The number of coincidences in the story is also quite depressing.

There are some funny moments in the film, such as when Malone uses a magician's prop to predict that a beautiful woman will soon appear and then the less-than-attractive hotel maid walks in. There is comedy of the absurd, such as when the Malone and the newlyweds each force medicine down the throat of Gilda Mayfair, each believing they are following her doctor's orders. There is much slapstick comedy, such as when Malone and Jake fall from a ladder they are using to sneak into the Lenhart mansion. There is surely lots of comedy in the film, but what there is not very much of, unfortunately, is a good mystery.

Having Wonderful Crime has a more renowned starring cast than most B-mysteries of the 1940s. Pat O'Brien, who previously had a very successful career at Warner Brothers, stars as John J. Malone. O'Brien is a good actor, but he is slightly miscast in the semi-comedic role of the detective-attorney. George Murphy plays Jake Justus, the fast-talking newlywed. It is a typical role for Murphy and he does a nice job in the part. The revelation is Carole Landis, playing new bride Helene Justus. The beautiful Landis wears some interesting modern outfits, plus a bathing suit and a negligee, all of which show off her magnificence to the greatest degree possible in a film from the 1940s. In addition to her beauty, Landis is quite good in the role, playing a dumb but lovable blonde, but perhaps with a little more on the ball than expected. It is a shame that Landis did not get the chance to do more screwball comedies in her short career. More distressing is the fact that Landis committed suicide at the age of 29, just three years after this film was released.

George Zucco plays the magician Movel, and when a filmmaker cannot gain any purchase from a great character actor such as Zucco, the film is in serious trouble. The only exciting moment in the film is when a flag pole crashes down, almost killing several players who are watching a water show. Unfortunately, that accident/attempted murder makes no sense within the flimsy plot of the movie and no one even tries to explain the event at the end of the film. When a comedy-mystery lacks the mystery, the comedy portion of the film also suffers. *Having Wonderful Crime* is running on no cylinders, neither successful as a mystery nor as a comedy, and is not worth a view, except for seeing the lovely Carole Landis in one of her best film roles.

Note on the Source Material: The source credit in the film claims an "Original Story by Craig Rice," without identifying the story. Most people cite Rice's 1943 book, *Having Wonderful Crime*, as the source for the movie of the same name. In fact, other than the title and the main characters, the book has nothing in common with the movie.

In the novel, Malone, Jake and Helene are in New York, investigating a murder in a hotel room of wealthy Bertha Morrison, which occurs on the night of Bertha's marriage to former escort Dennis Morrison, who went off on a binge on the wedding night. When he returns to Bertha's room, the police advise him that his new wife has been murdered by decapitation. When Morrison views the head, he realizes it is not the head of his new wife, and later it becomes unclear whether the head belongs to the body found in the hotel room.

There are many quite funny comedy incidents built onto the fascinating mystery of the body parts found in Bertha's room, such as Malone being unable to find a taxi to follow Helene when she tries to go off secretly, Jake hiding from the police in a bathroom shower which starts to leak water on him, and Helene pretending to be drunk when she goes out on the town with an escort. The whole story works, mystery and comedy all, because Craig Rice never forgot what the makers of the film *Having Wonderful Crime* did, which was that the mystery element in a comedy-mystery is just as important as, if not more important than, the comedy element.

THE LUCKY STIFF (1949)

For those interested in watching a good detective movie, it is disconcerting to discover in the opening credits that the producer of *The Lucky Stiff* is the famous comedian Jack Benny. That could not bode well for the seriousness of this feature. Yet, while there are a number of comedy bits in the film, those scenes never overwhelm the mystery story as they often did in the other two Malone movies, thus making *The Lucky Stiff* the best of the John J. Malone features.

The story develops in two separate plots, which eventually become intertwined. First, Malone's best client, elderly dowager Hattie Hatfield, requests that Malone investigate the protection racket that is hurting the owner of her local delicatessen. Later, Joe "Angel" DiAngelo, a friend of Malone's, also seeks his assistance to defeat the racketeers who are demanding protection money from him for his bar and funeral parlor. Malone takes on both tasks.

In the meantime, Malone has become infatuated with singer Anna Marie St. Clair, who performs nightly at the Casino Club, which is owned by gangster Big Jim Childers. Malone has been at the club for five straight nights to watch Anna Marie, and on this night, Malone is willing to pay $1000 for one personal performance of her stage show. Before that deal can be finalized, Jim Childers is shot to death on some stairs in the middle of the club floor and Anna Marie is standing over him, holding the murder gun. Malone offers to defend her but she uses Jessie Conway instead, resulting in her conviction for first-degree murder. Fortunately for Anna Marie, Malloy, the man who shot Childers, gives a deathbed confession, although he dies before he can tell the police who hired him to do the killing. Anna Marie is exonerated, although her "execution" goes forward in a crazy scheme to trap the real killer.

At this point the story goes off in a silly direction, with Anna Marie's "ghost" appearing in an attempt to frighten the real killer into a confession. Since Malone has no idea who the real killer is, he simply has the ghost harass all of the potential suspects, hoping one will crack. Then, out of the blue, he determines that Childers' wife and Eddie Britt, the manager of the Casino Club, hired Malloy to kill Childers and frame Anna Marie. Malone then traps Britt at the club with the "ghost" of Anna Marie, resulting in the arrest of Britt and his accomplice.

In addition to Malone having no clues to make his clever deductions about the murderers, there is never an explanation as to how Malloy killed Childers in front of the patrons of the nightclub without being discovered, and how the murder weapon ended up in Anna Marie's hand. Without any details or clues about the crime itself, it is hard for the viewer to care much about who committed the deed.

In what is also a common denouement in these types of films and books, Anna Marie, although she was not involved in the murder, was the head of the protection racket, and despite Malone's serious interest in her, he decides to turn her over to the police. A similar ending can be seen in Dashiell Hammett's novel *The Maltese Falcon* and several Mickey Spillane books, including *I, the Jury*. It is also quite obvious to the viewer that Anna Marie is involved, since she excuses herself from a scene where two henchmen are about to identify the head of the protection racket and a few minutes later a bomb is introduced into the room, allowing the henchmen to escape. Where Anna Marie got the bomb without much prior notice is difficult to determine.

Despite those criticisms, *The Lucky Stiff* is always an entertaining film. Part of the reason is the sterling cast. Wearing his hat tilted back on his head, Brian Donlevy is the best of the screen Malones, convincingly infatuated with Anna Marie and wearied by having to turn her into the police at the end. Dorothy Lamour is spectacularly alluring as Anna Marie, whether in her low-cut stage gown, showing some leg to Malone in his office, or even when wearing a cape and a hood. Claire Trevor as Malone's secretary can hold her own against Lamour in the beauty department, and convincingly plays Maggie as an infatuated if sometimes exasperated assistant to the famous attorney. Performances in the smaller roles are also fine, such as Billy Vine, who is quite funny as Joe the Angel, and Marjorie Rambeau, looking a little like Ethel Barrymore, as the eccentric Hattie Hatfield.

While the plot cannot withstand much scrutiny, it does move quickly and there are

John J. Malone (Brian Donlevy) and the ghostly Anna Marie St. Clair (Dorothy Lamour) discover the body of Jesse Conway, Anna's attorney, in Big Jim Childers' apartment in *The Lucky Stiff* (1949).

many interesting scenes, such as the apparent execution of Anna Marie, the hoods harassing Joe the Angel at his bar, the several appearances of the "ghost," and the last scene shot from above out of Malone's window, showing the police arresting Anna Marie. There are also interesting non-plot moments in the movie, such as Anna Marie singing the song "Loneliness" during her stage show, two garbage men talking about proper disposal technique as Malone chases a potential murderer down an alley, and the strange little electric car that Hattie drives. Also, Claire Trevor contributes some funny lines to the proceedings.

As a mystery, *The Lucky Stiff* may come up a little short. Considered as a total package, the feature is quite entertaining, sparked by some excellent performances. A John J. Malone series starring Brian Donlevy and Claire Trevor would seem to have had a lot of potential (although apparently this film was not a financial success). By 1949, however, the Hollywood movie mystery series had just about come to an end, so there was no direct sequel to *The Lucky Stiff*.

Note on the Source Material: *The Lucky Stiff* was based on Craig Rice's 1945 novel of the same name. The book opens with Anna Marie St. Clair about to be executed for the murder of her lover, Big Joe Childers, when she is reprieved by the confession of the man who did the actual shooting. Anna Marie decides that her "execution" should go forward so that no one will know she is still alive. She then meets up with attorney John J. Malone, who has fallen in love with her simply from reading newspaper stories about her. The two decide to use the "ghost" of Anna Marie to find Childers' murderer, who also attempted to pin the murder on Anna Marie.

Although that scenario is similar to the way the story develops in the film, there are obvious differences. Indeed, the film is a clever re-working of the novel, with most of the major incidents in the film coming from the novel, although often modified in some way. Jake and Helene Justus are important characters in the book; they were eliminated in the film and replaced by a new character, Hattie Hatfield. The protection racket angle is better developed in the movie, while Malone's infatuation with Anna Marie is better developed in the written work.

There are two significant changes in the metamorphosis from novel to film. The murderer of Childers is different in each medium and so is the motive, and frankly it all makes more sense in the film, although the clues are not well developed. At the end of the book, when Malone outs Anna Marie as the leader of the protection racket, he does not turn her in as he does in the film. Of course, based on the Hollywood standards of the day, there was no way that Anna Marie could go free in the movie.

MRS. O'MALLEY AND MR. MALONE (1950)

Even though it supposedly received good reviews at the time of its release, this film is a failure as a detective movie. Indeed, the only way to discern that the movie is indeed a murder mystery is from the fact that there are two bodies and two detectives in the tale. At times the film seems more like a comedy, as James Whitmore mugs his way through his starring role as attorney John J. Malone, apparently believing he is Harpo Marx (as he eyes the girls) or Lou Costello (as he keeps discovering dead bodies in unexpected locations). At other times, the movie seems to be a musical, with its insipid theme song over the opening and closing credits and then Marjorie Main giving an unusual singing performance of the hit song "Possum Up a Gum Stump." What the movie is not is a cogent or even interesting detective film, all the more sad because it is based on a story by two of the leading mystery authors of the day, Craig Rice and Stuart Palmer.

It seems that Steve Kepplar, one of attorney John J. Malone's clients, has just been paroled from prison due to the efforts of Malone. Kepplar was incarcerated for stealing $100,000, and the money was never found. With Kepplar's release from jail, Malone hopes to be paid his promised $10,000 fee out of the stolen money. Other people who want all or a part of the money are Kepplar's ex-wife Connie, who is seeking alimony payments, Myron Brynk, Kepplar's former business partner and accomplice in the crime, and Lola Gillway, who may have a romantic interest in Kepplar. Kepplar decides to escape from all of the people who are after his money by way of the overnight train from Chicago to New York. Unfortunately for Kepplar, a number of his "creditors" and a policeman board the train with the hope of locating him and obtaining their "rightful" share of the money. Also on board is Mrs. Malone (Marjorie Main), who is heading to New York to collect the prize in a radio contest she won.

Along the way, Kepplar's body is discovered, and Mr. Malone and Mrs. O'Malley decide to dispose of it so they are not implicated in the crime. However, the body has a nasty habit of reappearing at inconvenient times and in such locations as to incriminate Malone in the homicide. After another murder and the arrest of O'Malley and Malone, Malone finds the real killer and the money is recovered.

There are a few amusing lines in the film, usually said as an aside by Mrs. O'Malley.

There are even some amusing scenes in the film, such as Malone's accidental harassment of a fellow passenger or the appearance of some of the missing money just when Malone asks what his possible motive for the murder could be.

Most of the comedy, however, is uninspired and falls flat. O'Malley and Malone try to hide one of the bodies by carrying it through the train, supposedly disguised as O'Malley's drunken mother. Another body is hidden in the flip-up bed of a train compartment, falling down right in front of the policeman. This wacky type of mystery, which was really the specialty of Abbott and Costello, was going out of style by 1950, and Malone's habit of lusting after pretty women, chasing them around desks and leering at them as they walk by has surely gone out of style today. The hokey theme song seems to be a true anachronism, more appropriate for television than the movies. The supposedly funny written introduction and conclusion, which suggests that the American Bar Association should disbar Malone, seems juvenile. If the filmmakers had researched the issue properly, they would have found that disbarment of attorneys is a state function and not that of the bar association,

The movie never takes advantage of the cinematic benefits of a mystery on a train, as *Terror by Night* (1946) and *The Lady Vanishes* (1938) were able to do. There are few shots from the outside of the train and little of the sound of the train, thereby downplaying both the interesting location of the story and the tension that is usually generated from that setting by a director attuned to its possibilities. With a poor plot, silly antics and uninspired direction, the film is truly disappointing. MGM was prescient in not preparing a sequel to what was supposed to be the first film in a new movie series.

Note on the Source Material: The film was based upon the short story "Once upon a Train" by Stuart Palmer and Craig Rice, first published in the October 1950 issue of *Ellery Queen's Mystery Magazine*. The story is sometimes titled "The Loco Motive." It was later collected with five other stories about Hildegarde Withers and John J. Malone in *People vs. Withers and Malone* (1963).

Given the lack of quality of the film, it is surprising how much of the screenplay is based on the short story. In the story, John J. Malone and others board the *Super-Century* train, which is en route overnight from Chicago to New York, in order to chase after the recently acquitted Stephen Larsen, who was accused of stealing money from the municipal till. Everyone thinks he has the money with him on board the train and each wants to collect his "rightful" share.

Once on the train, Malone meets Hildegarde Withers, the famous schoolteacher-detective. Just as in the movie, Malone convinces a railroad porter to change his compartment so that he can be next to Withers' compartment, believing that a beautiful young girl is traveling therein. However, when Larsen's naked body shows up in Withers' compartment and the knife that did the deadly deed shows up in Malone's compartment, the matter turns serious.

In the story, the killer turns out to be a slightly different character than in the movie. However, just as in the movie, the killer murdered Larsen and stole the sailor's suit in which Larsen was disguised so that he could exit the train safely with the money, and just as in the movie, Withers and Malone catch the killer at the train station in New York, with the decisive clue being the slit in the back of the sailor's suit where the knife had gone through as it killed Larsen.

The story has a light tone and is a pleasant if not particularly special tale. Unfortunately, the screenwriters changed the light tone of the story into the broad comedic antics of the movie, underplaying the mystery elements, yet adding little to the humor. The replacement of the always appealing Hildegarde Withers with the much less interesting Mrs. O'Malley is also a negative for the film.

"Once upon a Train" is quite short in length so some scenes had to be added to the movie script for *Mrs. O'Malley and Mr. Malone* to extend the film to feature length. Unfortunately, the filmmakers chose comedy over mystery for those new scenes, to the detriment of the story.

Afterwards

Craig Rice continued writing John J. Malone novels and shorts stories throughout the 1950s, with a final book published in 1957. She died of an apparent accidental combination of alcohol and barbiturates in 1957 at the age of 49.

The Chicago attorney appeared on the radio in *The Amazing Mr. Malone*, which was also known as *Murder and Mr. Malone*. The program was originally broadcast on the ABC network in 1947, continuing on the air until 1951 and ending its run on NBC. Frank Lovejoy originated the role of Chicago's hardest drinking attorney. Gene Raymond and George Petrie later played the part. For most of its run, each episode started with a man or a woman being beat up, grabbing a telephone and saying, "Operator. Operator. Get me the office of John J. Malone." The narrator then described Malone as "the lawyer whose practice before every type of bar has become a legend."

John J. Malone came to television in 1951 in *The Amazing Mr. Malone*, which aired for one season on ABC. Lee Tracy played the title role. The show was broadcast live and alternated on a weekly basis with *Mr. District Attorney*, which was based on a radio show that became a four movie mystery series of the 1940s. There have been no other movie versions of the character.

Bibliography

Aaker, Everett. *Encyclopedia of Early Television Crime Fighters: All Regular Cast Members in American Crime and Mystery Series, 1948–1959.* Jefferson, NC: McFarland, 2006.

Barer, Burl. *The Saint: A Complete History in Print, Radio, Film and Televison of Leslie Charteris' Robin Hood of Modern Crime, Simon Templar, 1928–1992.* Jefferson, NC: McFarland, 1993.

Baring-Gould, William S. *The Annotated Sherlock Holmes.* New York: Clarkson N. Potter, 1967.

Brooks, Tim, and Marsh Earle. *The Complete Directory to Prime Time Network TV Shows 1946–Present.* New York: Ballantine Books, 1981.

Chandler, Raymond. "The Simple Art of Murder." In Frank McShayne, ed., *Chandler: Later Novels and Other Writings.* New York: Library of America, 1995.

Conquest, John. *Trouble Is Their Business: Private Eyes in Fiction, Film, and Television, 1927–1988.* New York: Garland, 1990.

Cox, Randolph J. "The Nick Carter Stories." In Robin W. Winks, ed., *The Scribner Writer Series: Mystery and Suspense Writers.* New York: Scribner, 1998.

DeAndrea, William. *Encyclopedia Mysteriosa.* New York: Macmillan, 1994.

Dunning, John. *On the Air: The Encyclopedia of Old Time Radio.* New York: Oxford University Press, 1998.

Everson, William K. *The Detective in Film.* Secaucus, NJ: Citadel Press, 1972.

Grost, Michael E. "Scientific Detectives." http://mikegrost.com/moffett.htm#Stagg.

Halliwell, Leslie. *Halliwell's Filmgoer's Companion.* 8th ed. New York: Scribner's, 1985.

Herman, James. "I Love a Mystery." http://i_love_a_mystery.tripod.com/ILoveAMystery.html.

Hoch, Edward D. "Introduction." *Boston Blackie* by Jack Boyle. Boston: Gregg Press, 1979.

Jewell, Richard B. *The RKO Story.* New York: Arlington House, 1982.

Kelley, Gordon E. *Sherlock Holmes Screen and Sound Guide.* Metuchen, NJ: Scarecrow Press, 1994.

Lackman, Ron. *The Encyclopedia of American Radio.* New York: Checkmark Books, 2000.

Mantle, Burns, ed. *The Best Plays of 1932-33 and the Year Book of Drama in America.* New York: Dodd, Mead, 1933.

McElwee, John. *Greenbriar Picture Shows.* http://greenbriarpictureshows.blogspot.com/.

Muller, Marcia, and Pronzini, Bill, eds. *Detective Duos: The Best Adventures of Twenty-Five Crime-Solving Twosomes.* New York: Oxford University Press, 1997.

Nevins, Francis M. *Royal Bloodline: Ellery Queen, Author and Detective.* Bowling Green, OH: Bowling Green State University Popular Press, 1974.

Olse, John. "The Shadow in Review." http://www.spaceports.com/~deshadow/.

Pitts, Michael R. *Famous Movie Detectives.* Metuchen, NJ: Scarecrow Press, 1979.

_____. *Famous Movie Detectives II.* Metuchen, NJ: Scarecrow Press, 1991.

Queen, Ellery, ed. *To the Queen's Taste.* Boston: Little, Brown, 1946.

Steinbrenner, Chris, and Otto Penzler. *Encyclopedia of Mystery and Detection.* New York: McGraw-Hill, 1976.

Turner Classic Movies Movie Database. http://www.tcm.com/index.jsp.

Tuska, Jon. *The Detective in Hollywood.* Garden City, NY: Doubleday, 1978.

Index

Numbers in ***bold italics*** indicate pages with photographs.

315